THE GENTLEMAN'S GUIDE TO

Passages South

by Bruce Van Sant

Sailing directions for easier windward passage making
in the islands from Florida to Venezuela
and a handbook for Caribbean cruising.

Distributed by:

CRUISING GUIDE PUBLICATIONS

P.O. Box 1017
Dunedin, FL 34697-1017
Phone: (813) 733-5322 • Fax: (813) 734-8179

THE GENTLEMAN'S GUIDE TO

Passages South

IMPORTANT NOTICE:

The chartlets in this guide are intended to assist the reader in following the sailing tactics described, not for taking meaningful measurements for navigation. The prudent mariner will avail himself of official charts and publications, some of which are recommended in this guide, as well as any navigational methods and tools required to ensure the safety of the vessel and the accuracy of navigation. There are no warranties, either expressed or implied, as to the usability of the information contained herein for any purpose whatever.

PUBLISHED BY:
Bruce Van Sant & Cruising Guide Publications, Inc.
P.O. Box 1017, Dunedin, FL 34697-1017
Phone: (813) 733-5322

BY BRUCE VAN SANT

Front Cover Photo
ANTHONY BLAKE

Art Direction & Cover Design
IDEAS TO IMAGES, INC.

SIXTH EDITION

ISBN 0-944428-44-4

Library of Congress 90-102996

Printed in the U.S.A.

How to Use This Guide

It was many trips south before I dared give the least advice to anyone. Invited to cockpit games and beach seminars with cruisers headed south, I often felt I learned more than I contributed. Steadily, the compendium of notes and sketches increased. Evidence grew that my notes were saving cruisers from repeating my own, and other's, misadventures. Now this book. Even after all the years gunk-holing the path described in this book, I still quail at giving unhedged counsel. Nonetheless, I bit the bullet and wrote down unequivocal sailing directions, spurning all but the most durable land-based tips.

I've assumed the subject is a small boat jamming 1200 miles to *windward* with sexagenarians at the helm. That's what I see down here. These folks are sufficiently in harm's way without a guide that gives ten ways to do everything. This is a *windward* guide. It shows you the safe, comfortable way, against the normal trades, using *prevailing conditions* (see Glossary) when you don't get the weather you want. I've pruned the hedges and peeled back the quibbles to make it useful to my mythical couple. A book of plain-spoken, straightforward skinny unsoftened by perhapses and maybes has resulted. If you think it dogmatic or opinionated, you shall miss the systematic solutions proposed.

Special shore side attention is given to Puerto Rico and the Dominican Republic because no guides exist, yet one must spend significant time in them. I based from both islands for many years and know them well. I have only included harbors necessary to give the reader details for making the shortest passage in comfort and safety.

Regardless of how much geography you find in these pages, this book's advice for *thornless* cruising against the trades is about *HOW* and *WHEN* to go, not about *WHERE*..

Bold face phrases appear in the INDEX in the back of this guide. Most bold face phrases, which are not geographical names, are defined in the GLOSSARY.

All degree readings on chartlets have T or M indicators for True or Magnetic. True degrees are used to assist the reader with chart work and course plotting. Magnetic degrees are used to provide bearings for deck work.

Why a *Gentleman's* Guide?

When yachting began in England in the mid 1800's the young ladies and gentlemen of the privileged classes would take the train down to the south coast where paid crews had delivered their yachts, often made-over workboats. They lounged on the white, canvas covered decks in their white duck trousers and their white linen dresses. They rolled home under a billow of running white sail. Deck stewards served gin and tonic to the gents and cooled Advocaat to the ladies. *"A gentleman never sails to windward,"* they said. A note to the ladies: when the title of this book came about I was unaware of the American sensitivity to gender references. The historical reference is to convey the book's message and not to slight my favorite people. Apologies, though not required, are abjectly rendered when solicited.

This guide, for Ladies as well as Gentlemen, gives the lie to that oldest of yachting's traditional sayings. *The Gentleman's Guide to Passages South* connects the major cruising grounds with 18 windward passages between Florida and Venezuela. Each passage is divided into an average of four safe and easy sails for a total of over 100 anchorages enroute. You may dawdle in each cruising area until your heart is content, but you must return to these tried and true passages when you are prepared to go on to the next. If you want to avoid a shellacking on your windward cruise, you need to have this guide aboard, and you need to have read it cover to cover before setting out.

WHY *THORNLESS*?

The windward way south through the islands is referred to as the ***Thorny Path*** to the Caribbean for good reason. As an often single-handed senior, living aboard a sailboat in the Caribbean, I always sought to take the thorns out of my travels by taking the most comfortable and safest passages. I have researched a *thornless path* south since sailing into these waters from Europe in 1979. It is the alternative to beating one's brains out in the ocean, bypassing all the island cruising grounds that should be enjoyed. Why not *bay-sail* and *daysail* to Venezuela?

In the tropics, each season brings it's own surprises in the weather. No year is just like another. No day is like another. My *thornless strategies* count on and use this constant variation in wind and wave. With a 6.5 foot draft, long-keeled ketch, and now my small trawler, I have hoofed up and down my ***Thornless Path*** and found that, with careful study of the weather and patience in applying my methods, it's *thornless* in any season.

WHO NEEDS THIS GUIDE?

The Gentleman's Guide to Passages South is aimed at the live-aboard, long-term cruiser who can take the time necessary to have a safe and leisurely cruise south. Cruisers like: Mom and Pop who are on their dream retirement cruise, the neophyte cruiser who just bought his first boat, the single-hander who must reduce risk, and the sailors like me, who don't want to get their boats (or themselves) broken, who seek comfort before challenges, and who, like me, are sensibly scared of the sea.

If you are not among the above, you probably don't want this guide. It's purpose is to deliver these cruisers to their various paradises with themselves, their boats and their relationships still intact and healthy. I illustrate each passage with *real* examples. Either I was there when it happened, or it happened to me directly. I also have tried to keep the cruising mates in mind, debunking some of the bar story bugbears that can intimidate, while involving them in what should, and can be, the cruise of a lifetime.

ARE OTHER GUIDES NEEDED?

You bet! This guide is for your *passage making* between major cruising grounds, not a guide for cruising each one. You will need other guides to properly do each. It assumes you already have aboard appropriate charts and navigation equipment, that you have read this entire guide, and that, for details of each cruising area, you have a suitable guide from this list:

Field's *Yachtsman's Guide to the **Bahamas*** (formerly Kline's)

Nancy & Simon Scott's *Cruising Guide to the **Virgin Islands***

Doyle's *Cruising Guide to the **Leeward Islands***

Doyle's *Sailor's Guide to the **Windward Islands***

Doyle's *Cruising Guide to **Trinidad & Tobago, Venezuela and Bonaire***

Bruce Van Sant, aboard Tidak Apa

Contents

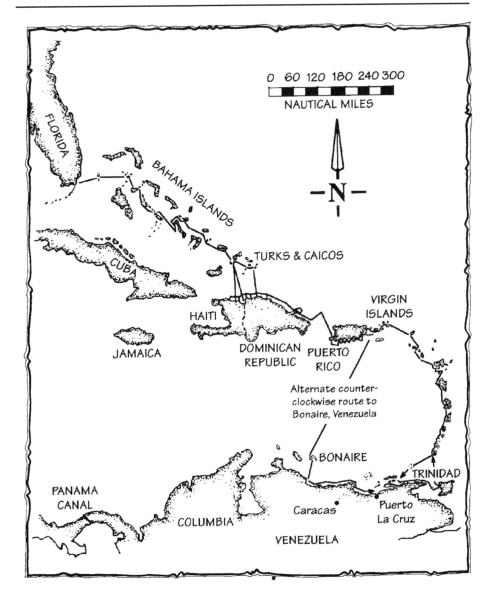

BAYSAILING AND DAYSAILING TO VENEZUELA

I have divided the path into short and easy passages between way stations where you can wait for weather. Each passage is divided into short and easy daysails and baysails. Every small step has the objective of being in a snug harbor in time to fish up dinner and relax with a sundowner. *Jalan Jalan* and I have learned the hard way to not skip a step of the path, no matter how small, especially on the south coast of Puerto Rico.

THE BASIC PATH

Thornless cruising is less *where* to cruise than *how*, yet the principle of threading the island lees dictates a basic path which links the major cruising areas: The Bahamas, Hispaniola, Puerto Rico, The Virgins, Leewards, Windwards and South America.

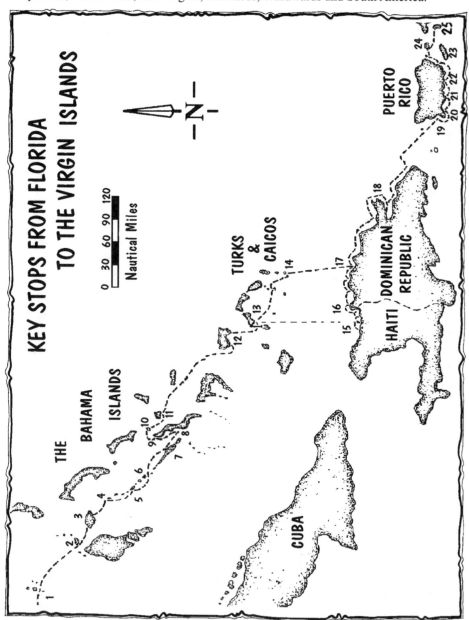

Here are some typical stations on the **Thornless Path** from Florida to the Virgin Islands. These are the key anchorages between which the **Leisure Sailor** can make **Leisure Sails** in short legs and at which boat and crew shall be snug in a safe haven during the next wait on a weather window.

Wait for Weather

Some stops, such as **Ambergris, Sosua** or **Escondido**, are not on the below list because they are not long term anchorages. Yet, without a west wind, those stops are dead necessary for a displacement sailboat or single screw trawler laboring to windward in search of a Thornless Passage. Conversely, not every station shown is necessary, depending on conditions and the cruiser's inclination.

For instance, **Georgetown** to **Conception Island** can be a fun seven hour sail in a good southeaster, missing Long Island entirely, although missing Long Island is a shame, and seven hours of sailing is twice too much when you don't have to. Finally, other stations are possible (e.g., **San Salvador**) which are slightly off the path but useful in the right conditions. (See *Keep North to Go South*). **Haiti** and the western half of the north coast of the **Dominican Republic** are included as an alternate path for the cruiser who wants to tour **Hispaniola** properly. For older cruisers and single-handers I recommend **West Caicos** to **Manzanillo** (13-16) as an easier route with smaller, less windward steps. Haiti may be toured by land while the boat stays at Manzanillo, if you don't want to sail to Haiti's ports of entry at **Cap Haïtien** or **Fort Liberté**.

1. Gun Cay		14. Big Sand Cay	
2. Chubb Cay		15. (alternate) Cap Haitien	3
3. Nassau	2,3	15. (alternate) Fort Liberté	1
4. Allen's Cay		16. (alternate) Manzanillo	1
5. Sampson Cay	2	17. Luperón	1,3
6. Cave Cay		18. Samaná	1,2
7. Georgetown	1,2,3	19. Boquerón	1,3
8. Salt Pond		20. Gu·nica	1
9. Calabash Bay		21. Ponce	2,3
10. Conception Island		22. Salinas	1,2,3
11. Rum Cay		23. Palmas del Mar	1,2,3
12. Mayaguana		24. Culebra	1,3
13. Sapodilla Bay	3	25. Crown Bay, St. Thomas	2,3

Note 1: Stops at which you can safely leave the boat in hurricane season.

Note 2: Fuel can be pumped from barrels almost everywhere, but these stops have <u>dockside</u> fuel accommodating a <u>draft of up to seven feet</u>.

Note 3: Access to airline connections for the embarking and receiving of guests.

GETTING STARTED

A journey of a thousand miles may start with a single step, but it continues with a gazillion more. It is those steps at which stumbles occur, not the expedition itself. Ensure each task on your provision and to-do list targets daily existence. Don't gladden the chandlery cash registers preparing for the ultimate wave to cast you upon the shores of disconsolate wilderness. Some become enamored of cruise preparation itself, and only leave starting mode when they return. If you haven't cruised foreign before, get a reality check by a winter's cruise through the Bahamas **Far Out Islands**, then return to Florida for a summer's realistic refit. The second time out you'll be an old hand.

GREAT EXPECTATIONS

Do your friends and family ever ask, "What on earth do you do with all that time on your hands?" You can't make them understand, can you? Once I imagined myself languidly cruising the Mediterranean in endless summers. Boy! Did I learn fast! My work list grew three lines for every one I struck through. I found the Caribbean's no different.

The gap between expectations and the daily unveiling of reality accounts for why cruisers start south with lots of man overboard equipment and little or nothing with which to receive original source weather data; with full game shelves and book shelves but few or no engine spares and supplies; yoghurt and sourdough starter but no resin catalyst; colored cloth to make courtesy flags but no fiberglass or sheet rubber; shot records and pet pedigrees and no engine shop manual.

Invest in equipment and skill to read the weather, and enable yourself to hop *between* ultimate waves. The last time anyone asked me for shot records I didn't have any, so they pulled me aside and gave me a free smallpox vaccination. That was in Hong Kong in 1974. It's never been mentioned since, nor has my sloppy flag etiquette. My interest in local language and culture often attract attention, however.

I've always had pets aboard. Officials have only petted them, not that exceptions don't exist, or one's behavior can't provoke inquiry. Target your preparations more effectively with some Spanish lessons. Replace thrillers and romances with readings about the islands. The more remote from your experience, the more you shall need to study. The differences between what you expect and what you shall find should liven your day, enthuse and invigorate, not frustrate, enervate or cause strokes. Most of your first year shall be spent in Haiti, the Dominican Republic, Puerto Rico, the Papiamento and French islands. Make that several years if you cruise *leisurely*.

Don't expect to evade the recessive ills of society. They often dominate in the Caribbean. Ineluctable authorities, unfair taxes, irreversible poverty, rampant greed, welfare amuck, little opportunity, low wages and you name it! Everywhere in the Caribbean one or all of these flourish in the tropic sun, dwarfing more temperate varieties to the north.

FINDING A CRUISING STYLE

An itinerant myself for half a century I can certify to the old refrains "You can't run away from yourself", "The grass always looks greener...", etc. The newcomer to Caribbean life aboard, recently unchained from responsibility's chafe, often careers along blinded by childhood's "new puppy" malady, or the adolescent "new car" syndrome. Eventually that wears thin and everyone finds their own style of cruising or they give up the game. I have drifted through several styles myself and feel another coming on.

I was a **globetrotter** for years in Europe, but I metamorphosed. Globetrotters charge about the sea testing self and boat in persistent replays of sailing magazine articles. They become instant experts and write articles as the Old Caribbean Hand who has done it all, spawning new generations of the same ilk. If that's you, go for it, but drop this book now.

While rearing children I could only cruise for long weekends, vacations and summers relocating between jobs. Even though living aboard, I was a **camper** when out cruising. Long term cruising cannot be sustained as a series of camping adventures. When not adventuring at sea, I was repairing ashore. I was awfully alive but not living a life.

Cruising **tourists** rarely leave the comfort of their nautical nests. They cruise the Caribbean like passengers in a safari park, noses pressed against the glass, marveling at the dangers around them. The Virgin Islands is a rest stop for these cruisers from which they can fly home for respite. But the Leeward and Windward Islands, Trinidad and Tobago and South America are excellent opportunities to get back on track.

Potluckers and **raftuppers** see cruising as a continuous 4th of July. If this is your style, you must get to the Virgin Islands or Grenada before the egg salad sandwiches run out, the keg dries up and the stories grow stale. I return to Georgetown each year for mine.

Some of my favorite couples are **airstreamers**. They poke around marinas and sea parks scattered along the seaways, not unlike Mom and Pop who settle into RV parks between highway excursions in their Air Stream trailers. If this road gypsy life becomes you, as it still does me, the whole crescent from Georgetown to Morrocoy is your I-75.

LEISURE SAILOR

A chance encounter brought me to this cruising style. I met a toad named Thornton in Georgetown one year, Thornton Throckmorton Thorndike the Third, actually. My charter guests had left and I was morosely considering the return trip south over the last of the ship's supply of Bermudez *añejo*. Thornton hopped over to cheer me up. He was a gentleman sailor. While participating in the Thornypath Semifinals of 1933, Thornton told me he discovered an entirely new method for heading south against the **prevailing winds**.

Skilled in the art of steering with his big toe, while jigging for grouper over the stern, he and his long-keeled beamy yawl were totally unprepared for the cutthroat competition in the Thornypath Semifinals. The high-tech go-to-windward carbon filament keel-less burgee bearers backing and filling at the starting line awed him. Was his pokey little boat, *Rose*, up to it? Thornton thrilled at the threat and was ever more determined.

As the only member of the leisure class to compete, Thornton had a unique advantage: leisure. He laid on capers from Exuma Market to gormandize his usually superb Nassau Grouper *Au Vin Blanc* (see appendix). He researched his Rolodex file of anchorages, fishing holes and recipes. He prepared his lists of dinner guests for each anchorage, being careful to invite each of the competing skippers on exactly three occasions, never hosting the same three twice. He underestimated his competition.

Four of the other yachts were crewed by professional delivery crews, only one of whose boats survived, but in such condition it was subsequently scrapped for spare parts for the Tortola charter fleet. Two contestants were on one year sabbaticals to sail around the world. Two were on two week vacations. One had to meet a seaplane in St. Thomas. From this field of ten tough competitors there were five DNF's, three divorces and one case of road hypnosis who eventually ran ashore on the Cape Verdes.

And there was Thornton. Thornton won. This guide spells out Thornton's winning strategy: how to take the thorns out of the Thorny Path. After a few tries at the Thorny Path, I've spent many happy years on his ***Thornless Path***.

Thornton aboard his yawl Rose

CULTURE SHOCK

Ever look forward to October's bracing chill and the smell of burning leaves? Bottle it. The closest the tropics have to offer is mosquito mugginess of the autumnal troughs and the black rain from burning sugar fields. You may have already girded yourself for nature's changes. How about the accommodations you must make to differences in mores, tact, dignity, decency, body language and much more, among the different peoples you shall encounter in those new environments?

INTRUDERS

On two occasions I have been roused from my bunk by nighttime intruders while in a remote anchorage. The first time it happened I had not slept in two days.

When I finally made harbor, I doused the adrenaline level with a couple of **SG&T**s, then dropped like an anchor into my bunk. At four in the morning I was shaken semiconscious by an unshaven, red-eyed, dirty and, except for old and holed jockey shorts, naked man. The hand not rousing me held what appeared to be an AR15 automatic.

In my befuddlement, I suspected that anyone, even naked, with a weapon like that had to be a Huk guerrilla, a dope smuggler or an official of a banana republic. Smugglers can afford clothes. I hadn't heard about any revolution and I wasn't in the Philippines.

Fortunately for me, I sleepily guessed that he had a permit for the gun and that he represented some authority who had bought it for him, he not appearing to have the resources to buy one for himself. I mumbled, *"Buenos dias"*. And so my day began.

The intruder was the local part-time representative of the Navy whose responsibility it was to inquire at the boat which had surreptitiously slid into the bay that night. He was out fishing all night with buddies in his little log canoe. Upon returning to port with the dawn they had knocked on the hull to no avail. Being a serious man, he went the next step and stepped aboard. Still with no sign from me, he stepped inside.

Good thing I didn't grab my gun, a hand-sized automatic on the shelf over my pillow. Had I done so we would both have drowned from water pouring through the holes he could make in my hull with his machine gun.

Instead, we had an amiable beer together the next day and he warned me again not to go sneaking up on his beach like a Cuban fifth columnist. He suggested that if I really wanted a special reception, I might try night anchoring unannounced in Cuba under Fidel. Talk about stress!

Stress at any level has its price.

A TIP

In a "going south" meeting on the beach at Georgetown a lady expressed concern with the entrance charges in the Dominican Republic. I told her they were about half the charges in Nassau where I had to negotiate "transportation charges". She appeared annoyed with that answer. She wanted to know what was *official* and what wasn't. She wanted a tale of corruption, and I wasn't biting. I addressed the group instead.

Is there corruption in the islands? You bet there is; the same kind as everywhere, but to a much lesser degree. By definition a small country has only petty officials, therefore the corruption, by large country standards, is quite petty, and abuse of power in smaller countries is more likely to touch the individual. In the yachties' countries billions are wasted (stolen) daily, but they're not overly annoyed. If an island official makes a sly suggestion that one buy him a beer, however, some yachties become outraged.

The lady of the "unofficial charges" now asked about tipping. I told her Latin Americans generally tip only when something superlative merits it. They also enjoy doing favors for each other to express their appreciation more than do Europeans or Americans. Taxi drivers aren't tipped as a fast rule. Waiters' tips are sometimes on the bill, and one leaves the change. A driver might not understand a tip, but he might understand "Keep the change". If not tipping a waiter makes you uncomfortable, then use 10 percent, plus or minus, as the Americans use 20 percent. Overtipping wins disrespect and larger charges next time.

She was incredulous. Not tip? Then followed a long harangue about her daughter making it through college from tips as a waitress. I worked my way through high school as a hotel bell hop. I think I know about tips: no begrudging someone who forgets, and rules be damned, you only get what you *earn*. She really lay into me, railing my selfishness. Trying not to respond to personal attack, I gave the point but warned the group that tipping too much, or when not expected to, could cause embarrassment. The waiter of a small *tipico* might be both cook and owner, proud to be independent after a lifetime's struggle. Attempts to tip could be insulting. Watch what others do, and when in Rome ...

The officials in Nassau, by the way, threatened to impound my cat, because I wanted to pay only one $10 transportation charge, since they had come in the same car. I dangled the cat overboard, preferring to dispose of it myself than to let the state mess up the job. The officers agreed immediately to a single charge. They were as afraid for the cat as they were that I might insist they take it, and we all had a $10 laugh.

THE PRICE OF STRESS

Signs of normalcy in one culture may be alarm signals in another. For example, Latinos like to carry guns as a sign of authority. Why not?

Sometimes, the smaller the authority, the larger the guns. Larger guns are usually cheaper. Guns from the former eastern block are very cheap in quantity, and because you haven't seen them before, they look all the more sinister. Unless you are well traveled you are likely to suppose a revolution is in progress when you see poorly clad citizens roaming the streets with Russian machine guns and rifles.

Culturally transmitted visual stimuli and their culturally correct responses do not map easily from one culture to another. They can, in fact, be in direct opposition. The receiving organism — that's you — will undergo stress depending on the extent to which responses expected by the two cultures to the same stimulus differ. If the conflict is mild and occasional, you giggle. If strong and continuous you will undergo a stress reaction called **Culture Shock**.

You may have a repertoire of cocktail stories of what happened to you on your tour of Thailand. In that case, you understand the phenomenon being discussed, but you may never have experienced it in shock dimensions. If you have lived on the local economy of another nation for extended periods, and you have been forced to use their language exclusively as, say, a member of the Peace Corps, you know well the phenomenon at shock levels.

Roaming around the Caribbean on a small boat provides greater exposure to local people and their customs than does jetting in and out of well protected resort complexes. If you haven't had the opportunity of experiencing Culture Shock before, you are about to learn on your own slow moving sailboat. When it gets unpleasant you can't simply take a cab to the airport.

There are many symptoms of Culture Shock with which you should be familiar before leaving home. Your ability to communicate with or without language, your capacity to get what you want, say, an engine part, are dependent on your skill in cutting through the background noise of your culturally learned responses and creating a totally new set of responses which achieve your goal.

The better your skills in creating useful new responses to confusing stimuli, however, the higher stress levels you may suffer due to the number of unsatisfied natural responses you have accumulated.

You may be successful handling the customs guys, finding clean fuel, provisioning at fair prices, replacing a motor part, and so forth, but you shall build a head of steam that's got to be blown off. It's the price you pay for coping successfully.

I've been known to blow my safety valve right in customs and get charged entrance fees others don't have to pay. I've seen others air ship expensive parts from home with all the attendant hassles of telephoning, wiring funds, misdirections and delays, when they could have cut through the static of their learned responses and bought an equivalent (sometimes even superior) part locally in two days for less money.

In other words, it is possible to buy off **Culture Shock** with money or to mute it with anger: take it in the purse or in the gut. It is your decision how you pay the price of Culture Shock but pay it you shall. Unfortunately, some people get others to pay it for them.

For example, the Albert Schweitzer in you might want to enfold the entire disadvantaged population of the Third World in his compassionate embrace. You settle for inviting a couple of homeless street urchins aboard for peanut butter and jelly sandwiches. Your finer instincts may be stroked by your behavior, but watch the kids don't walk in uninvited with their friends later on. Your behavior may appear bizarre to them, remember, and they might expect you're going to adopt them and take them off to New York to pick gold up off the streets. Why otherwise would you usher them aboard what is as foreign to them as a spaceship would be to your kids? Obviously you're going to take them to Mars if not New York, right?

Some years ago, I witnessed an incident that illustrates the point.

SPACESHIP YACHT

Two American couples in a motor yacht moored next to me brought some kids aboard their boat with results that were tragic for the children. The kids were given a tour of the yacht, an old classic motorboat, once belonging to a famous man. They were then fed peanut butter and jelly sandwiches on deck. A few days later the couples discovered the kids had come back aboard and some costume jewelry was missing.

Seeing themselves as having participated directly, and with great humanity, in the work of *Save The Children* by their charitable invitation to peanut butter and jelly, the cruisers were justifiably outraged that the children had come back to *steal*. They complained to the police. Because offenses against tourists were a quite serious thing in their fragile tourist sector, the state security police, the dreaded *Ton Ton Macoute*, took direct charge of the situation.

As a result of their investigation one child was crippled and two were badly and bloodily injured. When asked if all her plastic bracelets had been returned, one of the women from the yacht, panicked by the beatings going on in the next room, cried, "No, but they don't matter, just, for God's sake, please stop beating them!" The beatings, of course,

9

went on, since she said the property hadn't been fully recovered.

The child probably didn't want to give up his bit of brightly colored plastic because it was a link to the goddess-mother from the spaceship. She who had him experience motherly warmth, perhaps for the first time in his life, along with peanut butter and jelly. She who seemed to promise to carry him off to another and better star.

So they broke his arm. He and the other children paid the price of the yachties' inappropriate responses. The yachties, blaming it all on the police, rushed to their boat and vroomed out of the harbor for home. I got one of the dock lines they left behind.

THE REMEDY

Culture Shock is responsible for the flocking syndrome of expatriates in any country. Latin Americans, for instance, or Americans in Latin America. While living in Paris I always noticed Americans *klatsch*ing with other Americans to whom they wouldn't speak while on their native soil. Matrons from Old Greenwich would eagerly trade recipes with the wives of North Sea oil roustabouts from Louisiana. They clutched together for the sole purpose of hearing their native tongue and bad-mouthing the Parisians.

Grumbling about the environment producing your stress is normal and even necessary. Frenchmen do it in America, Germans do it in Spain and Englishmen do it everywhere. But watch where you do your grouching. You are not in the private *salons* of Paris while on a cruising sailboat or sitting in a cheap restaurant. You are on display. Bitching about the local environment while under the gaze of petty port officials, dock boys and small time secret police, isn't too *suave*. Doing it in a restaurant where the couple at the next table run the local grocery shall get you higher prices on your veggies tomorrow.

It is best to find your own general remedy to the stress of Culture Shock, and apply it at appropriate times and places. Whether yoga, expatriate *kaffee klatches*, or self flagellation, a personalized remedy should permit daily satisfaction of personal and boat oriented goals while increasing your enjoyment of the different scenes.

Some boaters crawl into a VCR-induced haze, not leaving their boats for days at a time. Others meet every evening for a happy hour where they massage each other's spirits with spirits. The **SG&T**. While a dandy motivation to be at anchor early and safely, the G&T is a poor remedy to the stress of Culture Shock. The ports of Asia and Latin America teem with besotted ex-pats who have taken this false remedy to their destructions.

Whether you go into frenzies of varnishing, practice meditation, write long letters to the kids or *klatch* on the SSB, your remedy should be a task you recognize as working off the stress of learning new responses. You will reduce the costs of making inappropriate responses in the future and increase your enjoyment of cruising life.

Beware, though, that *klatsch*ing on the **SSB** has far-ranging effects, as did a story going around in **Georgetown** for years. Read on . . .

PIRATES!

Returning to **Georgetown** from **Puerto Plata** one year, a friend grabbed me and said, "God, it's good to see you. I heard you had gone into **Abraham Bay** at **Mayaguana**." After massaging the blood back into my arm I learned that the **SSB** nets were full of tales of piracy in Mayaguana.

It was said that three boats were in the anchorage there. One boat was boarded by pirates in blue jump suits masquerading as Bahamas customs officials. A fight ensued in which one of the boats was *lost*.

Over the Regatta period the essentials of the story changed little but the details, for no one actually knew for sure, ranged from gory to grisly. After Regatta I returned home to Puerto Plata, stopping, of course, at Mayaguana. This time I bypassed my usual **Start Bay** and set anchor in Abraham Bay so I could visit the settlement and get the dirt first hand.

The two constables on the island, one twenty-two years old, the other twenty and just out of the academy in Nassau, were wearing blue jump suits. Being the Bahamas, they of course had no guns. I chatted various sea stories with them, including their recent un-armed arrest of eight Colombians with Uzzis. They were the crew of a freighter which grounded in **Horse Pond Bay**. The *unarmed* constables went to make the arrest in a little borrowed rowboat. The prisoners were put up in islanders' houses until Nassau could send a plane down for them. That's how life is in the **Far Out Islands**.

With a little conversational nudging on my part a story gradually emerged about a power boat that had come in one evening while two sailboats were already in the anchor-age. The boat didn't answer the constables' hails so they borrowed a rowboat and stroked out to say "hi". The owner/skipper looked tired, perhaps even intoxicated.

Their queries as to where and where bound were met with growls of "I don't want any" and "get away" from the owner, a big florid faced man.

Being good constables the two young men smelled something awry. They asked if there were any arms aboard, the next question in the rote. When this was met with a surly shout they decided this boat definitely didn't pass the smell test.

Instead of bidding the yachtsman a warm welcome to **Mayaguana** and paddling home, they started to tie their painter to the big gin palace and requested permission to come aboard. Not ever anticipating a negative response to this rote question, the younger of the two climbed aboard whereupon the owner skittered into the saloon and emerged waving a shotgun. With a foaming roar of curses he shoved the young constable into the bay, where, given the sudden appearance of this maniac with a gun, he was glad to be.

The yachtsman immediately upped his anchor and blasted out through the cut in the reef even though the sun was nearly setting. He was soon lost to sight. The next morning's cruiser nets were ablaze with the story.

"Pirates masquerading as customs officials" probably was reported by the guy in the gin palace. The "fight" would naturally come from the sailboats observing from some distance away and hearing nothing but dim shouts, seeing the brandishing of guns and a body going overboard. The "three boats in the anchorage" was quite true. That one boat was "lost" might come from a mike switch being released too soon, untimely radio inter-ference or simple embellishment.

The whole pirate story came about through the klatsching of the cruising community on their radios, sopping up their alienation and **Culture Shock** at the expense of two fine young Bahamian officers and the reputation of an island badly in need of visitors. Three years later I was still being approached at the Two Turtles barbecue with anxious queries as to piracy in Mayaguana.

Lately, at the barbecue, I heard a fellow at the next table authoritatively replaying one of the scarier versions of the old story, but, like all good stories, the essentials hadn't changed. Two guys in blue, a fight, a lost boat.

But I learned myself, long ago, the price of correcting a know-it-all in public is too high for me to pay. Instead of bringing them all down on my head, I ordered another Gin and Tonic. After all, no one likes a spoil sport and everyone likes a good story. Especially me!

OTHER SHOCKS

A NOTE TO TYPE A SAILORS

Failure to wait patiently for a good **weather window** is, in my experience, the over-whelming contributing factor to unhappy cruises. Yet patience is hardly the hallmark of many cruisers. Most cruisers are independent types. Many skippers are strong willed and self confident, and tend to take charge easily. Those are the very traits that lead some to seek the challenge and independence of life on the sea. These so-called "Type A" people come in both gender flavors, and I commiserate with them for their jumpiness, because I am one too. I'm still a time stuffer. I listen to the news while reading the paper while carrying on a conversation (poorly). Getting all set to go, then having to sit at home day after day, unable to go out, unable to schedule anything — and boy! do Type A's like to schedule — just waiting on a bus that never comes; that's enough to try a saint. When a window does open, most Type A's jump at it immediately. They take the first hours of a three day window. The swells are still up, the winds aren't yet down, and they sit in the next anchorage for the best part of the window. I don't wish to play psychologist, but a bit of my own experience might help.

In my first few tough trips on the **thorny path**, I recognized behavior in myself and others which I had seen many years ago as a full time air traveler. The first-in first-out queues of taxis, ticketing, and baggage checking drove me bananas. Waiting in line infu-riates me. Being herded like cattle does likewise. It wasn't long before I learned to be a contrarian. I became the last on the plane, strolling through an empty waiting room. I sat in the plane doing some work when it was time to deplane, while most people crammed the aisles for 20 minutes. Then they rode busses crammed to overflowing, then they waited at the empty baggage carousel for 20 minutes more, while I lolled around in a half filled bus and strolled up to the carousel just in time to lift off my bag. There were a hundred other tricks to air travel then, and I'm sure there are more and different ones today, but does that translate to cruising on a sailboat? You bet it does: Type A's can always find a useful way to pass time without *waiting*.

Sir Francis Bacon, father of the Age of Reason, patriarch of all modern science and mathematics, says, "Nature, to be commanded, must be obeyed." You can make Nature serve you only by knowing Nature's elements and arranging them *and* your purpose in accordance. To the cruiser with a hard science education, engineering, physics and what not, this is not news. To everyone else, it is not only news, it is a *revelation*. I have good news to these unfortunates: there exists a way out short of an epiphany in monstrous seas.

You don't have to deny your Type A nature. *Use* it to outflank the forces frustrating it. Get busy! Study the weather. Become a weather maven. Get a computer fax. Gather data. Sharpen your own deck level observations. If one has to stay put, there is nothing quite as fine for a Type A as being *in control* of the situation through knowledge, unless it's the payoff of the smooth passage that results.

Think weather watching takes time? During my waits I spend a good <u>4 hours a day</u> on the weather. How so much? I listen to Herb and David, or whatever weather nets are extant, while doing some fixit project. I get the Offshore Reports, then Satellite views, then the Tropical Weather Discussion. Midday are the Prognosis Blends (regular weather charts) and Surface Pressure Charts. Late afternoons repeat the morning routine. Add to those 4 hours a couple for meals, a couple of hours for swimming and diving, a couple reading and varnishing, and a nap — where did the day go? After some years at it I find my **Wait for Weather** is full of accomplishment, while, as I grow older, the rounds of provisioning, potlucks and happy hours demand more patience.

SIMPLE THINGS

AIR

If you have been in the Bahamas several months, as far as your allergic reactions are concerned, you have been *at sea* several months. While at Hispaniola you will be bathed for twelve hours a day by air sliding down from the middle of the 250 kilometer wide, high island. This air brings with it all the pollens and allergens of practically every type of flora known and then some. You haven't seen a deciduous tree or grasses in several months. Keep your antihistamines handy and double your vitamin intake.

WATER

Most maladies reported by yachties arriving directly on Hispaniola from an extended stay in the Bahamas are due to these effects of climatic and allergen change. But like the New Yorker visiting New Jersey in the summer, they blame everything on the water.

On the other hand, all developing countries are notorious for poor public sanitation coupled with poor or intermittent pressure in their town water lines. The H_2O from the mountains in the DR is delicious. Like in New Jersey, however, wait a couple of days after an outage before tanking up on the water. And, as in Florida, *always* treat it.

Jerry jugging can become a way of life. If you count on catching water, you can be sure it won't rain for weeks, so load up when you can. I have found it convenient to have several 6 gallon jerry jugs for water and diesel. Larger sizes become unmanageable and smaller sizes make for too many trips. You should equip for it. We take 1 or 2 showers a day (albeit Navy showers) and wash dishes in fresh water. That means a little more than 2 gallons a day per person, or one jug run every 3 days when 2 are aboard. If you can afford it, here's a real back saver: use a large flexible tank with a 12 volt in-line pump with which to pump water aboard via the dinghy. Look, Ma, no hands!

WASHING FRUITS AND VEGETABLES

You shall be using markets most places you cruise which are no different from the kind of markets your grandparents used, and perhaps your grandchildren shall again. Fresh lettuce, cabbage and tomatoes may have the dirt in which they were raised still clinging to them. Eggs can have residue of that end of the chicken from which they exit. Rural communities in the Caribbean have no major sanitary infrastructure. All farm products must be washed thoroughly in good water. Fruits are not a problem if you peel them.

DOING WITHOUT MR. CLEAN

American products are clever and useful and well packaged. When they are for the marine environment they're clever, useful, well packaged and expensive, and, in the Caribbean, generally unavailable. You can port 50 bottles of each product and displace 10 cases of rum, or you can carry the following generic chemicals, refilling the product bottle with a substitute solution which is sometimes better and always cheaper. Remember the first two principles of provisioning:

The Highest Utility for the Least Space, and *The Greatest Savings First*.

In other words, a boat full of small bottles of cheap, but high quality rum, and a year's supply of cleaning agents packed in a few chemical flasks is both a happy and clean boat.

Remember also to store and handle all chemicals with the care they deserve. I use sturdy, well sealed plastic containers. I snugly wedge them into plastic milk cartons so they cannot move around and chafe. Never place plastic bottles against fiberglass mat or other rough surfaces. Stowage techniques which worked great while fattening the kitty from a mooring or a marina, suddenly can cause ghastly accidents on a passage. Think of a container of muriatic acid leaking into the bilge together with a bottle of ammonia. You'll have a clean and bug free bilge if you survive the gas.

Dish Soap

I carry Joy by the gallon. Others swear by other products, but Joy is the only one I've found to foam abundantly in salt water. Cheaper still and as effective are the non petroleum based industrial degreasers. The jug usually says *biodegradable* and it smells like soap, not oil. We used to make it even cheaper in chemistry class, but too long ago for me to remember how. I can't bring myself to use degreasers for the dishes, though.

Non petroleum, biodegradable degreasers will:

— Clean the bilge.

— Degrease the engine and engine room.

— Prepare the deck around the deckfill for diesel spills.

— Emulsify any spills when squirted on the surface and spread with a hose.

— Keep dirt and grease from under your nails if rubbed there before starting a dirty job.

Ammonia

Foaming ammonia strips the wax off woodwork with a soft scratch pad. I keep a squirt bottle on deck of 10 % ammonia, 5% Joy and 85% water. It's good for any cleanup.

Alcohol

I used Aramis aftershave since the 1960's. When I cruised back to America and found it expensive, I changed to a mixture of alcohol and witch hazel. Eventually I settled on only alcohol. Stove alcohol, or waterless alcohol (99% pure), thins epoxy beautifully, making thick roofing epoxy do jobs not worthy of more expensive stuff, and making the expensive stuff penetrate better. You may find it in refrigeration or hardware stores.

Alcohol acts as a great astringent for skin problems, and it stuns fish for boarding and slaughter (see *Trolling*). Have gallons aboard.

Hydrogen Peroxide

Pour over abrasions, cuts and wounds of all kinds to disinfect before applying topical antibiotics. Have gallons aboard if you ding yourself as much as I do.

Boric Acid Powder

Sprinkled or "puffed" lightly in all unseen areas, (under drawers, beneath cabinets, or the lazarette), Boric Acid will keep the boat roach free as long as it stays dry. Eggs that hatch after 6 to 8 weeks are also taken care of since the little fellows take it back to their nests on the hair of their legs. Then they explode when they groom each other!

Mixed with honey, boric acid also takes care of ants who carry it as a present to the Queen.

See *Mauny's Cookies* in the recipe section.

Muriatic Acid

This is ordinary **HCl**, or the stuff that's in your stomach. Don't add any down there, though, it's powerful and dangerous stuff. You get it at hardware and swimming pool stores, and it's usually 20%. Don't dare breathe its acrid fumes when its opened to the air, even at 20%. Always mix it with lots of water, pouring the acid into the water. It will:

1. eliminate rust stains and gelcoat chalking when mixed 1:10 in a spray bottle, costing a hundred times less than some products which are the same;

2. make your corroded 12 Volt deck sockets work instantly if sprayed into them (or your brass boat horn as I once had to demonstrate to the USCG boarders);

3. keep your coolers and heat exchangers bright and new inside when mixed 1:8 (stainless and copper only, not aluminum);

4. keep your head clean and unclogged by calcium buildups when mixed 1:6 (rubber and neoprene seals only — no leathers);

5. become Part B of two part teak cleaners when mixed 1:5 with water. Plain old lye crystals and water become Part A (NaOH). Lye can be found in some toilet bowl or drain cleaners. Be sure you have <u>pure lye</u> and not some explosive mixture! In developing countries lye is readily available.

Of course, acid should not be allowed to react too long without being flushed away.

Swimming pool shock treatment which comes in rapidly dissolving granules and has *only chlorine* as the active ingredient will provide you with a year or more supply of chlorine bleach for:

> — treating the head
>
> — pouring in the bilge
>
> — doing your laundry
>
> — killing black pin mold when sprayed on teak
>
> — purifying your water

To get normal strength bleach put one to two tablespoons into a gallon of water and mix thoroughly.

Good quality **mineral spirits** will:

> — burn more cleanly in your oil lamps than specially concocted products,
>
> — thin your paints and varnishes,
>
> — clean and oil your interior woods,
>
> — start your fires and
>
> — run in your diesel when you're out of fuel.

Besides all of that, mineral spirits is cheaper than most of the products whose use it can supplant. In Georgetown, Bahamas, Marshall's has white Kerosene at one of their gas pumps which makes a reasonable substitute, though it may have a slight odor in lamps that the purest of mineral spirits does not have. It is readily available at hardware stores and general stores in the Dominican Republic.

COMMUNICATIONS

Mail

It is usually best to use **General Delivery**, the **Virgin Islands** notably excepted. Cafés, bars and marinas go out of business, change owners and policies. Unless you use couriers like **Federal Express**, it is best to let the official postal system hold your mail for pickup, with the possible exception of the US Virgins. Postal services are generally incorruptible, and provide sorting and secure warehousing services, which are their business. They are reasonably conscious of an obligation to you with respect to your mail. These things can not be said about a bar, restaurant or hotel where your mail will be pawed over by hundreds of cruisers, each one dripping wet and anxious to get to the bottom of the pile.

Your mail will be more conscientiously looked for by postal officials around the world if you follow this simple routine the first and every time you ask for it. Face the clerk squarely and look directly into his or her eyes. Smile brightly. Say "Good morning. How are you?" Pause and look like you're about to say good-bye, that you had only come there to make them happy. Then, with a shrug, remember you had minor business and, regretfully, wonder if they couldn't help you find your mail. Give them a card with your name written in large block letters. This gambit works miracles everywhere. Even in the US Virgins. If your name is Van Somethingorother, tell them sometimes it's filed under *Ess*.

In **Puerto Rico** use "General Delivery". In the **Dominican Republic** and **Venezuela** it's *Lista de Correos* [LEE-stah day koh-RAY-ohs], though both have become "iffy" services recently. Since PR is bilingual the clerk will be scanning for General Delivery not *Lista de Correos* after he sees your *gringo* face. In the US Virgin Islands it's safest to use a business address. Try one of the services such as St.Thomas Communications in **Crown Bay Marina**.

Reckon with US to Bahamas, one week, unless it looks like a parcel; US to Puerto Rico, 4 days; US to Puerto Plata, one to 2 weeks; US to the Virgin Islands, maybe never. The USPO General Delivery will hold US mail only 10 days, foreign mail one month. Other countries are more or less stringent (several weeks in France, Venezuela indefinite).

How to Send the Mail

Never make letter mail in bunches look like a parcel! Tell your forwarder to separate the mail into 2 or 3 small envelopes so yours doesn't get shuffled off as a package to customs or parcel post for 3 weeks. This is especially possible in **Nassau**. You should know exactly how many envelopes are coming so you don't wait around for the third packet that never comes. If Aunt Lizzy rebels at sending 2 empty envelopes because there's only one letter to send, but your instructions are always send 3, then fire Aunt Lizzy and hire Uncle Claude.

A tip about avoiding local taxes on parts shipped into **Puerto Rico**: send it *Priority Mail* or *Air Parcel Post* to *General Delivery* to small locations that presort in Miami. Examples are Boquerón, PR00622; Salinas, PR00751; Fajardo, PR00740; or Culebra, PR00735. Uncle Sam refuses to collect local taxes, but large traffic points like San Juan, Mayagüez and Ponce have resident PR tax men who whomp you with 6.6% and delay delivery. Priority Mail may also help ensure delivery in the Virgins. Never, *never* send checks so they can be seen by handlers. <u>Anywhere</u>. If they can't be cashed they can always be sold at discount to someone who thinks they can be cashed.

UPS is notoriously difficult for transients to deal with throughout the Caribbean.

Federal Express bends over backward to help in any way. FedEx is at 793-9300 in **Puerto Rico**. With **FedEx** you can call collect for pickup or inquiries to a *real person* who *can* answer your question.

It may sound nautical to address yourself as:
— Captain John J. Courageous
— Aboard the good ship S/Y Chicken Little
— General Delivery

Your mail will almost certainly be stacked under <u>Captain</u>, or <u>Aboard</u>, or sent to the Little's household. Try this for better results:
— John Courageous
— General Delivery

Aside from the pretentiousness of such nautical addressing it makes you an easy mark. What do yacht people ever get except checks and bills? Their kids never write.

As you paw through the mail boxes yourself at the various bars and hotels along your route you will notice how nonuniform all those yachtie addresses are and how difficult they are to sort sensibly. If you have problems, then think about the third world postal employees who might not spell as well as you, nor scan as well as you, nor have an inkling that addresses can be so complicated.

NOTE: in Latin America, the middle name is often the main name for sorting. So leave out middle names unless you are John X. Smith.

TELEPHONE

It's usually easiest and cheaper to call collect or with **credit card**. You can dial direct from any street booth almost anywhere, including the **Dominican Republic**. You may obtain **telephone credit cards** in the US without having a permanent home phone installation. You are billed according to usage, but there may be monthly limits, such as $100. This is sufficient for most cruisers unless, like Superman, they're running a business from the phone booths of the world.

Most Caribbean islands use the country for North American, 1, followed by area code. The area code for the **Bahamas** is 242. The **Dominican Republic** is 809. **Puerto Rico** is

787. The Dominican Republic does not accept credit cards over the phone. In both the DR and PR if you start speaking in English they will answer you in English.

Most telephone companies in the islands offer fax services, and many permit you to hookup and send Email via your laptop. When you strip your calls of all the howdy-do's you usually have only a message to transmit and the **telefax** is unequivocal and lots cheaper.

Telephones in the Dominican Republic

Telephone communications are excellent in big cities. Use any street booth to dial collect, direct (0 - area code - number), and speak in English when the operator comes on to give your call instructions. Use the phone company's office (CODETEL) if you want to pay. Many businesses have competitor booths such as TRICOM with direct dial anywhere in the world. Just dial 1 and your number. When you hang up an English bill will be prepared for you by computer. CODETEL also has telefax service at their offices that's too cheap not to use. Buy your kids a fax machine for Christmas, and save on your phone bills.

Telephones in Venezuela.

Country code is 58. USA DIRECT services are available by dialing 800-11120.

As in St. Lucia and Martinique, the phones in Venezuela are becoming credit card oriented. You buy a thin plastic card with magnetic stripe at various outlets, mostly tourist locations. You insert this card into the phone machines in lieu of coins. A digital display tells you how much money the card has left on it as the time of your call ticks away. Neat.

Also neat and useful is the fact that the decrement by which your card is ticked down is left on the card when you're done, never decrementing to zero. Don't throw away those used up large denomination cards. They're worth a pile of local calls which, of course, have smaller decrements.

On the mainland in Venezuela and not at a tourist resort these phones are hard to find. One must usually go to an IPOSTEL office and wait in line to place the call. The personnel are usually friendly and helpful but the system has its shortcomings. I recall Moscow being better equipped and organized in 1973 — and that's saying something.

LANGUAGE

Don't let the myth of **language barriers** undo the enjoyment of your cruise.

I remember turning an aisle in a St.Thomas supermarket. Across the room were two gaily dressed old geezers by the fruit shelves. They were waving at me. One had a camera around his neck. Half way across to them I realized they were a clever life-sized cardboard cutout advertisement. I felt quite foolish.

Most of us cruising the world experience local life like I did these two dimensional cutouts, unless, with luck, a local befriends them. Cruisers seldom get to read local newspapers. They seem uninterested in any subject outside their immediate yachtie environment. While in Dubrovnik I "read" the papers every day. Local language, newspapers, politics and so on, lack reality and can't interest them.

In non-English speaking countries many cruisers excuse the lack of any but superficial interest with the old *language barrier*. Most, in fact, stay aboard waiting for weather rather than discover what's going on ashore or traveling inland. Many pay too much for everything and later whine they were "cheated". These cruisers never fulfill a good piece of their cruising goals.

With most of my adult life spent outside English speaking countries I think I have a qualified viewpoint on the matter. Simply put, *you erect your own language barriers*. Here's my experience. I have lived or worked in many countries where I did not speak the language. I studied 7 languages, and I came to live in 4 countries where I used the language well enough to make a living. Yet, I always got along *best* in the countries where I didn't know the language!

If you don't do the local language, people expect less of you and help you more. They have more patience with you, going out of their way to guide you. People are more interested in you. If you speak their language, you are more of an interloper in their society, not a visitor. Yes, humans practice prejudice everywhere. Parents show great interest when daughter brings the foreign exchange student home for dinner, but the excitement really gets big when she brings one home to marry! As a visitor not able to use the language at all, you have *privilege*. As a visitor trying to pick up a few words, you have sympathy, and honor as well.

If you seriously want to talk well in a foreign language, go ahead and make a serious try. Be prepared for a mind wrenching, personality bending experience. Languages carry culture, and learning them requires personality change. Acquiring language often causes physical pain. It takes a long time and requires exhausting effort, yet it never can be 100% successful, despite what you've read in spy novels. It will give you great satisfaction, but it shall change forever your ability to be an interesting visitor everyone wants to help.

Get out and see the world while cruising. Don't erect your own language barriers. Wiggle your eyebrows, wave your arms, point to things and words and have fun. But don't ever say to me, "It's *easy* for you. You speak the language." That's *just* why it's not.

TRAVELING IN GROUPS

One of the nicest parts of cruising the *Thornless Path* is that you see the same people again and again. Cruising in company, you can share your **SG&T** time with others. Headed south from **Georgetown** I've often been in company with from 5 to 15 yachts. These trips weld friendships and make what is always a delightful trip south, even more enjoyable.

STAYING TOGETHER

One thing I always make clear to sailing companions is that I paddle my own canoe, do my own navigation, select my own anchorages, and when I grab a **Weather Window** and go, it's my own decision for my boat. I encourage everyone else to do likewise. My boat is my little universe on a savage sea, and she and I function as a team completely different from any other vessel and crew. This is no doubt true of all yachts and their crews. Unless there is an emergency at sea, we neither slow down to nor catch up with other boats, thus compromising the teamwork between crew and vessel, and perhaps forcing an unnatural rhythm to her functioning at sea. I suspect many problems on the path south are precipitated by this phenomenon, and by the subconscious reliance on other boats. (*Well, if I miss the weather, one of the other guys is sure to have it.*) Proper respect for the sea and your vessel come first, demonstrations of camaraderie, second. Sailing in company, get advance permission to dawdle or leap ports ahead. So, sail alone, even in company.

BUDDY CHANNELS

Many boats sailing in company stay tuned to a "buddy channel" instead of VHF Channel 16. I have seen one yacht sunk and many others suffer narrow escapes while the "buddy boats" blithely sailed on in ignorance of repeated warnings on Channel 16. Chatting on low power on Channel 16 while on the open sea will not bother ships in the area. On the contrary, you both will be glad to discover that you're within two miles of each other and didn't know it. Using buddy channels while under way in or near harbors, where dangers proliferate, is even more unwise.

FLEET OPERATIONS

One method of group cruising is to emulate a loose confederation of sovereign states. After all consultations are done, each captain must make his or her own decision, sharing it with the others out of courtesy, but not for approval. That's not to say, of course, that you can't change a decision upon hearing a wiser one made by someone else. Contact is maintained by radio and by common experiences in port.

If you are bound to stay together, then emulate the fascists whose emblem was the Roman *faces*, or bound bundle of spars. Appoint someone Navigator and someone else Admiral of the Fleet and make them responsible for putting voice to consensus. Democracy at sea can be dangerous. Picture a fleet of neophyte cruisers at sea, all strung out like a gaggle of geese, asking each other on the VHF whether to reef or tack while assuring each other of their like-mindedness, regardless of each vessel's differences. I see them every year. Each boat thinks another boat is leading. The one in the lead doesn't know he's leading. He thinks he made a wrong tack and left the group. Whinnie The Pooh, off to discover the north pole, was better organized than most cruising groups I've heard on the VHF. Committee decisions, without a chairman to promulgate them wind up not being made. In port, preparing for a storm, that can be dangerous. At sea it is purely deadly.

THE EXPERTS

Freedom seems to be the common denominator behind most people's choice of the cruising life. But freedom bears responsibilities not known in our modern socialist societies. Among the most cherished freedoms are those of carrying water, washing clothes by hand and trudging miles to the market in the dust and the heat, all the neat stuff our ancestors got to do. The freedoms to be your own blacksmith, carpenter, physician, plumber, weatherman and mechanic comes as a shock to most new Caribbean cruisers. Our ancestors had to be those things and more on their isolated homesteads. So must cruisers today. Rather than face up to those responsibilities concomitant with remote cruising, I prefer to jury rig until I get to an 800 number phone and call for parts. Then I practice component replacement, until all goes right again. But whether help is at hand, I prefer anyway to handle the problem myself. Usually anything you do yourself beats turning to the *experts*.

Like the mule hand in the old Wagons West shows, I stand aside and chuckle at the game as people get stung year after year. Here follow some experts I see repeatedly on the Wagons South show, along with the folly of trusting them instead of yourself.

THE WEATHERMAN

Pained by days of waiting for a Weather Window in Luperón, I dinghied to the town dock to buy a newspaper and spend another day at the ready. I was going *downwind* too! I had not before waited more than a few days to go downwind. Everybody enroute north wore thin in patience. As I rowed through the anchorage I passed a fellow jubilantly hauling at his anchor rode. He was an airline pilot by trade, one of those good looking, clear eyed, straight toothed solid men with the great airside manner and the calm, resonant voice. ("We've lost only two of our four engines folks but, not to worry, this aircraft is designed to fly on zero motors.") He had been reading the weather to the more timid types on channel 16 every morning. They trusted him. He was their *weatherman*.

"Cleaning the rode, Jack?" I asked.

"Heck no! Great window! We're off!" he exhaled between pulls. He hadn't learned to let the catenary pull the boat, he was still using the coronary.

"Window? I heard there was 25 knots and a gale system crossing Cuba."

"No way! Northeast 15 behind the front! A reach the whole way!" he puffed. The anchor came up with a bang on the chocks, and, callused by years of gratuitous advice forcefully cast back in my face, I wished Jack a safe and happy trip. I stroked on to the dock and got my paper.

Back aboard, I threw aside the newspaper and reread my full transcripts of the Off-shore Reports. As I thought I knew, but which Jack had made me unsure of, there were three gale systems. One pulled the front that had gone through the day before, another was pulling a front down on us that should arrive the next day. A third gale center out of Cuba headed northeast right over Caicos to our north. I searched for the words "northeast 15 knots behind the front". They were there, just north of Puerto Rico: *behind the front that was already history for us.*

Three boats pulled out with Jack. One went ashore in the Raggeds. The Bahamas Defense Force pulled off the mate who flew home to mother in Toronto from Deadman's Cay. The skipper dragged himself into Georgetown 3 weeks later severely dinged. I left two days later. I had 10 to 15 knots, clear skies, full moon, anchored every night, without going to shore. I had 12 days of the finest fishing vacation I remember sailing to George-town. I had waited 11 days, and it was a window for the records.

Jack was beached at Landrail Point when I got there, making a new rudder out of construction scraps. A gaggle of tourists and a few yachties surrounded him to hear his tales of *The Ultimate Wave,* and how cleverly his master seamanship and knowledge of the weather saw him through safely. When he finally reached Georgetown, he taught courses on celestial navigation for $5 an hour.

Do you think you need Jack to be your *weatherman?*

THE MECHANIC

Ace was a "cruiser down on his luck", as people say. He ran a marine electronics fixit shop from his boat, which was way down on its luck. Ace did pot. His girlfriend did other things. They got by. I call these guys dirtbaggers, but what do I know? Ace did fast work. In fact, he could get a rebuilt unit faster than Fed Ex could fly. He simply went to his warehouse which was the fleet of boats he was "boat sitting", cleaning, and odd jobbing. There was always a replacement part somewhere. He was eventually caught and spent a few days in jail. His boat had $50,000 of stolen electronics tucked away.

Once a cruiser asked me if I could recommend Ace. "No," I said, "he's a thief."

Now, con men are convincing and charming. If they weren't, they wouldn't have the job. The cruiser liked Ace anyway. He went to Ace and told him what I said. Next day there were 20 gallons of water in my fuel tank. I found it while crossing the path of an incoming cruise ship. The motor quit with a clogged high pressure pump. The idiot cruiser got his, though, when the cops took the GPS Ace had "fixed". Now he had none.

Do your own work, and never ask *me* to recommend any mechanic but yourself.

THE SAILING MASTER

Many folks who think they know all about sailing may know nothing about the sea. In the old days of sailing there was a position of Sailing Master aboard ship. The captain looked to him to provide expert instruction to effect the maneuver he wanted to make.

For three years Dashing Dan darted all over the Caribbean. To the Med and back, in and out, up and down, damn the torpedoes, he was the star of the Herb show every night. If it blew 40 knots and was more than 200 miles, Dan went.

I take the south coast of Puerto Rico a few miles a day in morning calms, rather than wait out a 20 to 25 knot forecast looking for longer windows. Anchored at **Gilligan's Island** one year, I heard Globetrotter Dan calling a crusing couple anchored in **Cabo Rojo**. They had a small child aboard. Dan was sailing down the west coast in the island's lee. He cajoled the other boat to join him on a night sail to Ponce.

"You've got a *well found boat*," he hammered, "you're a *sailor*," he challenged, "I *know* this coast. It's not bad at all." Dan said he was reaching in 11 knots of wind in a flat sea. Of course he was sailing south down the west coast of Puerto Rico and had not yet turned the corner to the east into the full trade seas. Thoroughly intimidated, the father agreed to come out and play. I thought of the little girl aboard. I called repeatedly on the VHF, but he couldn't hear me. I stayed tuned.

Within 5 hours Dan was ankle deep in motor oil, feeling the bilge for a dropped bleed screw without which he couldn't start his engine. "Comes with the territory," he croaked on the VHF. The smaller boat's skipper left the air for 15 minutes, then came back on groaning. He'd been tossed across the saloon. Luckily, he only suffered a few contusions. Wife and child had packed themselves between mattresses on the stateroom deck. Both boats crept into **La Parguera** at 8 a.m. after a 12 hour run of only 9 miles. Earlier that morning I had eaten up my usual 10 miles in a 2 hour calm.

Dan disappeared from the Caribbean scene some time ago, but new Dan's arrive every season. Don't listen to Dan. As the song says, "he's a devil, not a man".

THE LOCAL

A magazine article appeared detailing the drubbing a boat took on a passage. Early in the article the writer made clear that he had discarded my sailing directions in favor of *local knowledge* from a tired cruiser who had been moored at the same spot for 5 years.

I knew that cruiser well. "Sam" was a nice guy who, tired of cruising, took a local job and was moored to that harbor for good, never to go farther. Each time he had tried to venture out he did the wrong thing and got hammered. Over the years "Sam" had collected stories, however, from passing cruisers and from occasional nearby reefings. In other words, all this *local knowledge* he had came from beginners passing through or from someone who made tragic mistakes.

While this guide's advice comes from dozens and dozens of my own successfully safe and comfortable passages, the fellow who wrote the article went with the advice from "Sam", the "local", who must *know*. He got hammered. But he had an epic tale to tell.

Some local cruisers remind me of the rednecks around the bait box on a fuel pier in Florida. "How deep is it at the dock?" I hailed. "Lossawada, lossawada!" they chorused. "Yes, but how many *feet*?" I persisted. "Big boats come in here allatime," they assured. *Morgan OI41's* probably, I thought. "I draw 6.5 feet!" I hollered. "**LOSSAWADA!**" they yelled, getting belligerent now that their expertise came under question. I spent the next 8 hours 14 feet from the fuel dock, hard aground. I got no fuel, but I got "lossa" dings from all the really "big boats" that came to fuel up beside me.

HARBOR HASSLES AND HASSLERS

HARBOR CONDITIONS

The ports of the Dominican Republic are the first Developing World ports seen by cruisers from the north. **Puerto Rico** and the **Virgins**, both deeply on the dole from their US owner are reasonably affluent. The tiny islands of the **Leewards** and **Windwards** have sufficient charter and beach hotel operations around their ports to somewhat disguise their campestral nature. Not so the DR. But if you wanted it like home, you could have stayed there.

The large province of Puerto Plata which stretches from **Luperón** to **Cabarete** (where the windsurfer championships are held), has a pure tourist economy. There are more hotel rooms in this one province than there are in all of Puerto Rico, mostly within the 50 mile long province east of **Cofresí** (name of a pirate who based himself there).

Cruisers in the DR contribute nothing to such an economy, therefore the situation in the DR harbors is unlikely to change. Enjoy your stay, but don't waste your time grousing about the conditions of harbors to whose commerce you add little. Undeveloped ports are a growing rarity for the cruiser. Enjoy the DR's while they last.

DOCK BOYS

Throughout the Caribbean the loafers on the docks and in the harbors will hassle you for work which they may not do or errands they may not run. Some will ruin your laundry if you let them and gouge you in the bargain. The bad actors of the breed are guys who have been spoiled by "ugly Americans", mostly paid delivery crews in town for a crack at the red light district. These crews push out their absent owner's dollars like Bible tracts at the airport. Therefore some of the dock boys respect neither your common sense nor your wallet. So sailor beware! Meanwhile, there are people who can do useful chores. Some dock boys want to sell courtesy flags, and I don't deny them the business if I don't have one. If you employ someone for chores or errands, especially dock boys, specify short, specific tasks with firm, fixed prices. Have each task finished and paid for before going on to the next task, assuming you still want him to work for you. Finally, if a dock boy thinks you've agreed for a service from him, *never* change dock boys before the first one has been paid and discharged. You may find yourself in the middle of a labor dispute right out of Marlon Brando's *On the Waterfront*.

A NOTE ABOUT "BRIBES"

Every season I hear the ridiculous chatter about *mordida* (Mexican for bribes: a "bite") in the DR ports. It usually starts with the age-old Dominican expression for people returning to the island from abroad: "Did you bring any presents for me?". When adults say it, the response is usually something like, "Half of what you have for me!", and a great deal of laughter ensues. After a few $20 "presents" the surprised official becomes accustomed to the insolent response from the tourist. He goes with the flow, and tips become routine. If you "tip" egregiously in Latin America, don't cover your bonehead behavior with wild tales of "being forced to pay bribes". That could be a slander to your hosts and, under Napoleonic law, an arrestable offense. You won't get a bullet for not coughing up, but you will get respect. Just say a friendly "No", then share a beer or lunch with him next day. If you feel you must "tip" officials, try it as a delayed favor, not a *quid pro quo*. Regardless what you've seen on old Viva Zapata movies, it is rude to offer a bribe. Doing

Cap Haïtien boat boy at the marina.

favors for friends is the Latino way. Also, if you do tip, have your tip ready, don't fish around for it.

Both in Venezuela and the Dominican Republic, the men of the *comandáncias* are often stationed far from their families, and travel money comes out of a pittance of a salary. Improvements to shore and harbor facilities largely go unfunded by their government. In Venezuela, you can resolve equivocation by going through a shore agent at little extra cost after factoring in transport and trouble. Upon checking out in the Dominican Republic, offer a small recompense (e.g., 1 or 2 beers) for the guy who types the *despacho*. Give it to him at the same time he hands you the paper. In other words, *before* he asks but *after* the service is rendered. No fishing around and no time for haggling: he's already said thanks. You shall understand why he should get a tip when you see the typewriter.

The Yacht Dock at Puerto Plata with Isabel de Torres in the background.

SECURITY

Tales of Caribbean rape and pillage have titillated youngsters since the 1600's when the maraudings of L'Olenois, the **Corsaire**, and Morgan, the **Privateer**, first hit the British bookstalls. Most long distance cruisers are adventurers and, to some extent, children, at heart. Their titillation runs wild upon occasion and their stories of piracy and skullduggery on the *Thornless Path* are among many false dangers. Like cloud shadows on the banks, if you spend your time trying to avoid them you risk running into a real danger.

PERSONAL SECURITY

There are bad actors all over the world. Pirates are just bad guys potting at targets of opportunity upon the wastes of the sea, or in the alleys of the waterfronts. You're not in the Sulu Sea or the Red Sea, however. Your chances of running into a pirate in the Caribbean is even less than your chances of stumbling into one off Key Biscayne. Ask any European and you'll discover that most of the civilized world thinks America is among the most violent nations on the planet. Unfortunately, there is much to substantiate that opinion. Your exposure to personal assault, on your boat or ashore, is less almost anywhere along the *Thornless Path* than it is in any yachting center in the United States. Having said that, there are yet some caveats which may make for a more pleasant cruise.

AFLOAT

Avoid pickup crew. The Caribbean is full of hitchhikers, both American and European, especially in the large yachting centers. Some are simply doing what used to be called *Le Grand Tour* between college and the start of a career. Others are simply doing you. If, after thorough investigation, you do take someone aboard, hold the person's passport and enough of his or her money to fly them back to their native country from your boat's destination. An even better filter of their real intentions is to do like the South Africans and some Europeans. Charge the crew for their room and board and the trip. Let the leeches pay or go get their own boat. Unbelievable folly has been met with pickup crew.

Avoid casual tours of your boat. What a thrill for that nice school girl to see a yacht. But she goes to school with not so nice school boys. A yacht has been a remote concept for them, unassailable as the homes of the local rich. Innocent talk at school, God forbid a fullblown Show and Tell, may make your snug little home familiar and assailable.

In anchorages without normal VHF traffic, leave your VHF on at night. It's your telephone. This may sound silly, but don't let anyone board your boat at any time for any reason unless they present indisputable documentation of their right to do so. Have deadlock bolts inside below, lock yourself in and wail on any radio frequency you can find.

Beware of *asymmetrical* cruisers. There are hustlers in the Caribbean without apparent resources and with hollow stories that don't fit neatly with accent, age, physiognomy, boat's and personal appearances. Yachties took turns inviting to dinner a good looking young fellow who had run out of funds. "And just imagine!" they gushed at me, "He's off around the world with no charts, no navigation aids and hardly a dime. What spirit! A real nice guy." He looked like a leech to me. After he'd left for the wide world, a rash of burglaries occurred while everyone was at a potluck. It was blamed on the locals. One yacht claimed a $10,000 loss and quit cruising. Mr. nice guy turned up in Central America fully equipped, saying he'd got the stuff cheap in Manzanillo. *Manzanillo?* I met rafts of cruisers down islands who still thought he was a great guy, and they were sincerely glad he had found the right equipment to go round the world. Aren't all con artists great guys?

ASHORE

City waterfronts everywhere are close to rundown sections with poorer, sometimes desperate, inhabitants. Walking alone down unlit streets with flamboyant tourist garb, a bulging hip pocket and half a bag on from some happy hour isn't smart. In **Cumaná**, Venezuela, you're dead meat. Bracelets and necklaces are best left behind. You may know it's only costume jewelry, but does a 12 year old gutter snipe with a razor? Literal cut-purses running through a crowd in Caracas can bisect the strap on those belly bags yacht-ies wear, neatly slicing your kidney in the bargain. It's happened.

On the other hand, it's not always so grim in the third world. It used to be that in **Puerto Plata** and Belize City, a naked sixteen year old virgin with fistfuls of dollars would attract only admiration. And you should have seen the alleys of Belize City at night in 1981. Times have been hard throughout the developing world. Skullduggery is up everywhere. Until you know for sure, act as prudently as you would at home. No more nor less.

Instead of your passport, carry a photocopy of your passport and of the page with the relevant visa stamp. A stolen passport can make a royal mess. On the other hand I've known respectable senior citizens who have spent a night in the pokey because they couldn't prove they weren't wet backs to the Venezuelan National Guard. Instead of a wallet or purse, carry a sheet of paper with every number you ever needed, credit cards, telephones, citizenship, clearances, passports, whatever. Then wrap your folding walking around money over your credit card and slip it into a flapped pocket.

BOAT SECURITY

There are as few anchorages on the *Thornless Path* where I feel I must lock up my boat as there are towns in America where one can leave one's doors open. Most places, if a local inhabitant breaks through your locks he'll cause more loss through damage to teak joinery than he will through the trinkets he's likely to walk off with.

Only boaties take boaty things. Remember that when you anchor next to the dirtbag boat full of hippies in a lonely cove. Such "cruisers" do exist in the Caribbean. Avoid these boats and their crews. If they need a snatch block they'll snatch yours. Unfortunately for world unity, some nationalities more than others tend to spawn boats like these.

In countries with acute economic stress petty theft by locals can occur upon occasion. You can hire boat watchers while you're away but they can sell you out to the pilferers, or pilfer for themselves. You may be asked to hire one anyway, like you're asked to hire a punk in New York City to "make sure nobody slashes your tires". But that's rare in the Caribbean unless you are in the wrong place to begin with.

How and where you moor the boat when you are away from it will provide you with more insurance than any insurance company or commercial guard service can offer. During extended absences, unless you can put up in a guarded marina, securely anchor the boat in a weather safe anchorage, far enough from young swimmers from the shore, near enough to be seen by the casual observer, and in amongst other yachts whose owners you know and trust. Leave them instructions for access to the boat as well as for charging the battery, feeding the parakeet or what-all else.

Alarm systems, like those in suburban America, turn in more false alarms than real. But if you're a gadgeteer and have the money, by all means, have the fun of installing them and spoofing your friends with all the hooting of horns and strobing of lights. Any local intruder, not knowing what to expect, is likely to think that this display is all quite normal boat behavior. One boater I know has a neat switch over his bunk. When he throws it, a brilliant flood light mounted high forward in the saloon blinds anyone in the cockpit, the companion way, or messing about inside. Like a stun grenade: effective, simple and cheap.

FIREARMS

If you have firearms, be trained in their use and know when to use them. Never brandish a firearm. If you take one in hand it should be to use it. It's use is not to scare but to kill. Pretty serious stuff. Firearms aboard can be a hassle while clearing in and out. See also **Customs and Clearances**.

The problem lies in threat assessment. Sober, nonprejudicial judgment is necessary. But that's rarely possible in a strange, poverty stricken land, where people speak a different language with excited jabbers and ominous overtones. It's hardly possible in a dirty town where everyone's a different color than you are and they all stare at you, point and whisper. It's certainly difficult when you're roused out of a sound **SG&T** induced slumber after a long, hard, adrenaline drenched beat to weather by someone who looks like a Huk guerrilla. Impulsive resort to a firearm is invitation to tragedy. Probably yours.

DINGHY SECURITY

If you haven't learned dinghy security in the US waters, here's some tips to help you from **Nassau**, onward. Motor and dinghy theft is not a problem where locals with a yacht dinghy would stand out like a dugout canoe in a Connecticut yacht club. Theft will occur where there is a ready market for either the motor or the dinghy.

First, use chain or coated stainless cable of minimum size 5/16", minimum length twelve feet. Alan's Rigging in Yacht Haven, **St.Thomas**, makes up superb dinghy security cables. Chain is better as you will see below. Padlock or permanently secure the chain to a permanent steel fitting attached to a hard surface of the dink (transom, for instance), _not_ the towing eye of an inflatable dinghy — thieves will simply cut them off. I know of one case in **Samaná** where they cut off the transom. Even if your motor is locked securely onto the transom, run the chain through the motor handle as well. Finally, lock the chain to some permanent fixture ashore with an eye to tide and current. You may want an anchor out to keep from sawing against a pier or going under one at low tide. If you don't, you may come back to a crushed motor when the tide rises.

Lock your dinghy to the boat, coiling excess chain in a bunch on deck so it doesn't go overboard unless pulled upon. The thunk, thunk, thunk of the links going over the rail is your alarm system and enables you to catch the varmint in the act and while still in the water. Depending on the sternness of your response, you won't have trouble at that anchorage for the rest of your stay. I've found flare guns neatly scare everyone in the anchorage as well as the varmint, and they certainly light up the scene of the crime well and call the attention of any law enforcement which may be around and pretending not to notice. Flares also continue to burn in the water, catching the crook in a ring of light.

If I'm concerned about a dinghy thief in the night, I leave my stern light on (it's separately wired), a cockpit anchor light on, and I have a cutlass and a flare pistol handy. Once I squeezed intersecting streams of muriatic acid and ammonia from their squirt bottles. The effect was devastating to the machete wielding bandit in the water. A friend prefers a "wrist rocket" sling shot with ball bearings. One fellow I know brought back a blowgun from South America with some pretty serious darts. I've thrown rocks from the cat toilet for double insult.

If you have big motorized davits, use them to haul up your dinghy and motor every night. Another method is to arrange a three point bridle with its lifting ring centered to keep the raised dinghy and motor level as you haul the rig up to the rail with your halyard.

Make the bridle out of stainless cable, or it may be chopped readily with a machete.

Plaster your dinghy and motor with reflective tape so you can find it when it drifts away at night. It also becomes a less attractive target for thieves. An inflatable in the Virgin Islands becomes less attractive to thieves (other boaters), if it is plastered with multicolored patches and 5200. One of my best dinghy trades was a flawless Avon RIB that looked like it had been through the battle of Trafalgar. I never had to lock that one up.

Finally, at crowded dinghy docks, leave your dink anchored well off with thirty or so feet of painter run to the dock. Neophyte cruisers often snug their painters to the dock and tip their motors up. As the tide changes their props become bucking and slashing scythes which will cut your bow section to ribbons. I usually make a dinghy dock with a stern anchor out, actually an undeployed grapnel. A rock can do as well. I land perpendicularly to the dock a distance down from where I want the painter tied. The dinghy then lays off roughly that same distance, well free of the crowd. It can be retrieved at any point by dragging, since the anchor, or rock, isn't grabbing hard.

INSURANCE

Insurance helped me when I rammed an uncharted subsurface rock in the Skagerack. It came through when a hurricane took off my bowsprit and taffrail. Then, after many years of self-insured bliss, I went with the Seven Seas Cruising Association's recommended agency. Despite A.M. Best ratings, platoons of government inspectorsand $1100 of my financial support, the underwriter went belly up 3 months after I signed up. That accounted for 11% of my net income that year. I went self-insured again.

Like the stock market, invest in insurance only what you can afford to lose. With all the boats around, and all the scams the insurers let by, rates have gone through the ceiling.

The companies increase profitability by policy restrictions only a New York actuary could come up with. Some refuse coverage between lattitudes 12 and 22 during hurricane season. Others demand you get below 16 degrees before June. I asked them to refund the 6 months not covered, or to stop their policy clock from ticking between June and November, if I stayed in the forbidden zone. The companies I queried said, "No." Doesn't sound legally defensible for a regulated industry, but who am I to challenge government.

I do, however, challenge the wisdom of chasing Mom and Pop through the islands and across the sea to places with little storm protection and crowded harbors. Feeling pressed to get south, many cruisers bust their gear and propulsion systems if not theirselves. One fellow made it 30 miles into the "safe zone" only to die of a heart attack the next day. His "risk" amounted to a doubling of his deductible if he got totalled by a named storm. I estimate he had a risk of 0.00012 probability of losing $3000. All because he let an accountant in a Manhattan tower do his navigation for him.

ANCHORING IN THE CARIBBEAN

Many folks who have sailed a bunch have not anchored much, though they may think they have, myself included, until they get to the Caribbean, especially by short hops. I spent some time interviewing a family who had sailed 15,000 miles round the world in 3 years to end it all on the **Cayos Caribes**, motoring to a waypoint given to them with great care and precision by a "friend"; a waypoint *inside* the cut itself. They had anchored less than a dozen times in 3 years. They took long legs and hung out for long periods to refresh their kitty when they stopped.

Cruisers new to the Caribbean may find the following tips useful.

ARE YOU A GOOD NEIGHBOR?

The best neighbor in an anchorage is the one that's silent while you are anchoring or weighing anchor. Let the new boat anchor in peace. I sometime get gratuitous complaints that I'm too close to someone's boat while I start to lay my first anchor. Then the guy sees the second anchor deployed and my boat lays on a wide vee 100 feet off his quarter.

Anglophones particularly worry about Francophones whose sensitivity radius is much smaller than theirs. I personally prefer Latin closeness to Anglo aloofness. Anyway, Anglos have a perception problem. The French may anchor closer, but I notice they do a good job of it, if not better. *Charter*phones are feared by all, and with good reason.

A good neighbor does not call you on the radio nor dinghy over to talk to you while you are in the act of anchoring or weighing anchor. Sometimes I go to the shortest possible scope, hoist the mainsail, then haul anchor before she starts to drag. People sometimes dinghy over to meet me just as a gust takes the sail and the boat starts to move. I try to be friendly while maneuvering under sail in a crowded anchorage, but I'm afraid I sound rude. Isn't it better to get to know each other during all the days together in harbor?

A good neighbor doesn't offer help or advice unless asked. I take my time. I don't strain myself or my boat. Sometimes it's a two-cupper: two cups of coffee to let the chop unglue the anchor while I flake the chain out to dry. Once a guy they called "Animal" stormed aboard uninvited. He dashed up to the bow where I was one-handedly plucking a few slack links, coffee in the other hand. "Here!" he shouted, shoving me aside, "Let me show you how to put some *ass* in that thing." While I was still trying to figure out what hit me, he popped the anchor up right through the teak grating on the bowsprit. Satisfied, he hopped back into his dinghy beside his admiring surfer girl and sped off, waving at me with a big grin, while *Jalan Jalan*, untimely loosed, drifted broadside toward a pier with her bowsprit platform in splinters.

BRIDGE COMMUNICATIONS

This is a subject that ought to be under a heading of *Marriage Counseling*. Mom and Pop on their retirement cruise have never been so close for so long in forty years. Now they're farthest apart only while they're anchoring. And that's only thirty feet or so.

Pop stands at the wheel because he's so technical, while Mom stands at the bow anchor because she's got stronger hands. Some prefer to reverse the roles. One or the other signals and the miscommunication begins.

It can take another forty years to develop hand signals and the concomitant divided responsibilities which are needed to choreograph the delicate ballet of anchoring successfully in all conditions and in front of the usual audiences who are pretending to look the other way. If you can't do it alone at least follow these rules.

The bowman (-woman) should do all signaling from the same position always and with the same hand always while holding the forestay with the other hand to ensure its immobility even more than to ensure bowman's stability. Signals needed are:

> left, hard left, right, hard right , center wheel, ahead, astern,
> more power, less power, stop, @^$*%>#!!!

There are already too many commands so don't add any.

The last command is optional but preserves harmony in the more untested relationships. Roadman signals work fine. So do crane operator signals.

To avoid nasty equivocation keep all fingers together.

To really do it right get one of those walkie talkies on headsets. You can build them into beanies with the boat's name on them. That way they can't be seen by the audience who will think you're just plain proficient.

One couple I saw do this really looked great while silently anchoring with this advanced communications equipment. At least until Pop suddenly screamed at Mom from the bow, apparently apropos of nothing, "I said starboard, dammit!"

LAYING ANCHOR

Yachts that drag into you in the tight anchorages invariably seem to pay more attention to sailing than to seamanship. Ninety-five percent of seamanship lies in the art of *keeping the boat from moving* and only five percent in making it go. Below are some aphorisms which, when taken together, go some distance toward describing the art of anchoring between Florida and Venezuela.

Don't anchor near boats with damaged topsides.

Don't anchor near boats with performance hulls or rigs.

Chances are they are five-percenters and have only five feet of chain. They dance all over the harbor in any breeze. I watched one hull-sailing full circles all night long. He had two anchors, thank goodness, and the boat wound itself down like a cuckoo clock and took off on the other tack for another fifteen circles.

Small boats (under 50') are best anchored by one person.

In this way one person will know what was done at the time of anchoring and the knowledge will not reside somewhere between the wheel and the pulpit with neither station actually being responsible. This rule can save marriages as well.

Preparing the boat to fall off in the proper direction before laying the anchor is best the responsibility of the person who selects the spot and lays the anchor, not someone at the helm who doesn't quite know where the spot is or how the anchor may soar to it. It also calls for knowledge of the boat's characteristics of way, its momentum, and how easily she faces or crosses the wind.

While anchoring single-handedly, however, it is essential that the maneuver to station the slowly swinging bow over the spot selected be well timed to enable the walk forward from the helm to the pulpit to be accomplished with a certain seamanlike decorum, rather than a headlong, cursing rush.

Anchors should be set by wind and current first.

Not by someone behind eighty horses unable to see what's happening, unless there is no wind or current. Burying types such as Bruces and plows, dig in by wiggling and worming with the action of the sea and tug of the chain. If you apply full tractor power to them before they've hooked, they will revert to kind and plow a furrow. Watch for drag by picking a range (not other boats) perpendicular to the extended rode. Also, a grasped rode can telegraph dragging to your hand. If the wind is up, it may be difficult to set even a Danforth in mangrove mud (e.g., **Salinas, Luperón**) or hard marl (e.g., **Bequia**). If you can't arrive early, before the wind comes up, you shall have to motor foreward at low revs so as to maintain slow enough sternway to permit the anchor to set.

Anchors are to be *laid*, not dropped, thrown or swung.

Laying an anchor implies touching its crown to the bottom, gently *laying* it biting side down, and controlling a smooth backward drift in the direction of the expected flow of wind or current, while *laying* the chain in a straight line behind the straightly *laid* anchor. *Lay* enough chain to ensure pull on the anchor will be directed along the bottom, which you gently hook. Pay out more rode and dig it in harder. Repeat and test with motor. Sailors who routinely talk about <u>dropping the hook</u>, you will find, often have hooks instead of proper anchors and usually simply <u>drop</u> them, heavily trussed in a bundle of rope and chain.

All anchors benefit by being properly laid, but Fortress and Bruce types most especially do.

Let the yacht come to rest before paying out more tackle.

Pay out the final bit of scope, or, as the case may be, snug it in, only after securing the yacht and tidying up the deck. That will ensure more time for her to reach rest condition. The seaman who takes longest to get his yacht settled on her anchors is probably the sailor doing the best job of anchoring.

Dive on the anchor, if possible, to check it.

If necessary, set it by hand. While you are down there check your neighbors' as well. I was cruising in company with a good friend who is a professional diver on the oil rigs. In deference to his skills and my taste I started on the **SG&T**s while he dived on the anchors. He found a neighbor's anchor lying sideways on the bottom. "Impossible!" shouted the salty-whiskered downeaster while posed cross-armed and bantam-like on his taffrail. "I set that anchor with 55 horses!" My friend set the fellow's anchor for him in order to protect our own boats.

Anchors should be selected for bottom and boat.

In the appendix are tables which demonstrate the holding power of some anchors, ground tackle strengths, and data which you can use to figure the loads generated on your anchors and rodes while riding out a Class 1 hurricane in a protected hole. The data may surprise you.

Use about a pound of anchor for every foot of the boat. A 45 pound Danforth would suit a 41 foot boat, but not as a single anchor if wind or current can switch. Danforths, while capable of tremendous holding power, do not reset themselves well and the stock can go afoul. Heavy burying type anchors such as the CQR or Bruce work well on almost all bottoms and tend to reset themselves. They don't foul as easily as Danforth types. Use Danforth types in mud or grassy bottoms, making well sure the points are dug in. In a blow, Danforths hold best pound for pound. No matter what the Danforth folks say, don't use a short length of chain. It may function in theory but, in the Caribbean, any nylon rope less than one inch shall most certainly chafe through on the bottom, if not by coral, then by broken rum bottles.

For rocky bottoms use a heavy prayer.

Use enough chain: *long* **enough and** *big* **enough.**

Consider first that the chain's catenary must never be able to reach the anchor itself so as to exert upward drag on the shank — even in the most violent conditions — *especially* in the most violent conditions. Second, ensure that any rode attached cannot come into contact with the seabed or obstructions on it (coral heads, rocks, wrecks and broken rum bottles).

You might consider including enough chain so that chafe at deck level does not occur, i.e., all chain. Also, the catenary of an all chain rode makes a good shock absorber. If you use all chain, attach a nylon rode snubber as long as necessary to quiet the action. Absolute minimum chain length should be five feet for every sixteenth of an inch of chain size, i.e., twenty five feet for 5/16 chain, thirty feet for 3/8, etc. An alternate rule of thumb is to use between 1 and 1 1/2 boat lengths.

For full displacement boats, add a sixteenth of an inch in chain size for every ten feet of boat's length above twenty feet. Thus, for LOA's 20-29 feet use 5/16", for 30-39 feet use 3/8", for 40-49 feet use 7/16", and for 50-59 feet use 1/2".

For all chain use a scope of three to five times the depth of water <u>added to the distance from sea level to anchor roller</u>.

For chain and rode use a scope five to seven times the depth <u>added to the distance from sea level to anchor roller</u>.

To reduce the amount of scope required in tight anchorages, consider extending your anchor snubbers from a bow eye at the water line.

To reduce vertical snatching loads on the bow, buoy the rodes before leading them to the bow.

Considering using two anchors.

The actual uses of the Bahamian Moor, one anchor against each expected change of current direction, are few: tidal bays, coves, creeks or rivers. These are places where currents can be strong and regularly reverse with the tide.

Nine out of ten of your anchorages will be in harbors or against beaches where these effects are minimal. So why use two anchors?

Because everyone around you does and if you don't you'll find your bow poking into someone's bedroom in the middle of the night.

Because you expect a switch in the wind or a front to come; or worse, because you *don't* expect it.

Because the harbor you're in goes absolutely calm at night and you want to prevent the boat from walking around your lone anchor, droodling chain all over and under it, so that when the morning wind rises you drag onto the beach, towing a ball of tackle.

Because you're the first one in harbor in the Virgins and you expect 40 partying bareboaters to plunk balls of chain all around you in the middle of the night and you want to keep your elbows tucked in.

Because you don't want to wind your rode around a coral head.

Because you're in the anchorage for the first time and aren't quite sure about that wide open fetch to the Southwest.

Because you're leaving the boat unattended.

BUT, if everyone else is swinging on one anchor, go with the flow and set only one yourself so they don't bash you.

Beware of local knowledge — the locals may not know.

On the incredibly steep and rocky shores of some islands, the conventional wisdom is to tie your stern to a palm tree with a bow anchor sort of resting on the slope a hundred or so feet below. Well, if you have a deep draft, barn door rudder, you may lose it. The boaters next to you with the expert advice may be down from New York on a charter and the boat boys never managed a boat anyway.

WEIGHING ANCHOR

The following may seem old hat. But sit any morning in harbor and watch the scene while folks up anchors. Before observing too long, you'll want a tot of rum in your coffee.

When weighing anchor, keep the chain *vertical*.

Doing this ensures two things. First you will approach the anchor along the chain's lie and in a pace commensurate with safety and the proper stowing of the tackle. Secondly, you are unlaying the links of chain right up to the anchor's shank, ensuring that you don't dislodge the anchor until ready and it won't skitter and roil around the seabed fouling things like other people's rodes.

The chain can be kept vertical under the bow by:

never powering beyond the catenary, instead let the *catenary* pull the yacht forward, *not the coronary*, and

using the windlass only to pull up slack links, not to pull the yacht

So: when walking the yacht up her ground tackle: *let the 'canary' pull it.*

Keep station until the anchor clears the water.

The bane of all anchorages is the morning clod who, upon sensing the anchor has broken loose, turns his head aft and yells "She's up!", and off the yacht drifts downwind, with a giant grappling hook beneath her soaring a few inches off the bottom, headed almost surely for your rode. Even bane-ier is the knucklehead who powers about the anchorage with an acute angle of chain stretched behind the bow while the crew tries to wrestle up the taut chain and anchor before they snag — you guessed it — *your rode!*

As mentioned in the chapter on **Luperón**, in the Dominican Republic, the mangrove anchorages in the Greater Antilles have a colloidal mud bottom which makes the anchors-up drill a messy, sweaty job. It's always best, as noted in the section on *Staging*, to do the cleanup the day before leaving. Wherever possible, depart fresh and rested from a clean, short rode. That's one harbor hassle that won't upset your departure timing.

Setting or weighing anchor is always easiest before or after the trades blow.

LEARN TO USE OPEN ANCHORAGES

There are various criteria to choosing anchorages while you are passage making. If your **Weather Window** starts to close on you earlier than you thought it would, you may get stuck in your anchorage for a considerable time doing another **Wait for Weather**. One wants a good bar, for instance, like Ted Bain's Ocean View and Kay's Bar in **Rum Cay**. Ditto, the fine fishing and diving found there. Another consideration is comfort. A rolly anchorage can be miserable if suffered for more than a day out of necessity. And then, there is safety. A landlocked anchorage would be best according to conventional wisdom.

But wait a minute! You're tucking into an anchorage while *enroute*, you're not setting up winter camp. Conventional wisdom may not always serve you on the **Thornless Path**. Weather-shore open anchorages may be the best in **Trade Wind** conditions where the wind direction is rock steady, or in subtrade conditions where it at least seems so. An anchorage such as Plana Cay in the Bahamas makes daysails out of an overnighter when the trades are stabile. Many folks endure the balance of the hurricane season at **Bonaire**, anchored with their bows over a narrow, sand-over-coral shelf, and their sterns staring at Mexico, while hanging over a bottomless cliff. Except for potential backwinding around the month of October, this is a fine arrangement.

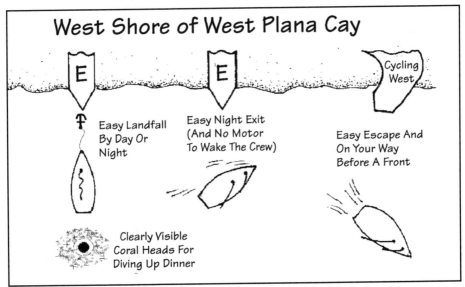

Benefits of an Open Anchorage

Ideally, a weather shore anchorage should be deep sand with lots of productive coral heads or rocks under keel depth. The skipper can anchor to windward of a good fishing spot and let out rode until the stern sits over his dinner. Plans for an arrival during favorable light conditions should of course consider that favorable light is needed under-water to skindive up your dinner from the bathing ladder. This is usually before four o'clock. The dinghy can stay in the davits. Filling this bill are such anchorages as **Santa Maria** (Long Island), **Conception Island, Pittstown Landing** (Crooked Island), **West Plana Cay, Betsy Bay** and **Start Bay** (in Mayaguana). Those roll-free anchorages so often sought out by the mate may be deathtraps. The landlocked harbors of **Attwood Harbor** (Acklins) is a deathtrap in a northerly, for instance, as can be **Calabash Bay** (Long Island) in anything but east. Besides, who can sleep without some rocking?

MAJOR PROVISIONING ENROUTE

Between Florida and Venezuela provisioning a yacht is expensive and often difficult. Puerto Rico and the Virgin Islands have American supermarkets, but all you ever need from an American supermarket are **Joy** dish soap and GLAD **garbage bags**. Joy is usually not available anywhere and garbage bags outside the US are often poor strength. Most places enroute south will be more expensive than the US. Sometimes 2 and 3 times more expensive. There are two exceptions to this bleak picture: the Dominican Republic and Venezuela. Venezuela can be better for many items but it is at the <u>end</u> of the route, not "<u>en</u>" it. **Puerto Plata**, though an undesirable commercial harbor, is a provisioner's Mecca. But based in **Luperón** you can shop **Santiago** almost as conveniently as Puerto Plata.

The Imbert-to-Santiago bus can drop you close to either Supermercado Pola or Nacional, both as good as the Publix or XTRA chains in Florida. The large and modern hardware and department store, Ferreteria Bellon, is across from Supermercado Pola. Lunch at the Pez Dorado, Santiago's finest restaurant. It's on the park by the cathedral (Calle del Sol 43).

KNOW VALUE

Actual prices will not be discussed in this guide because inflation and debasement of currencies (notably the US dollar) cause prices to fluctuate within only a few months. Generally speaking, one can buy goods which are made locally in the Dominican Republic for export to the US market (Libby's, Victorina, Campbell's), for a percentage of the prices charged for the same items in standard US retail outlets. The actual price percentage you will find depends on many economic and political factors. For instance, a can of Campbell's soup may have been imported from the US, not made locally. Hatuey crackers, though usually quite cheap, may skyrocket if the United Nations buys them all up to give to Haiti. Knowing value before you even ask the price will keep you out of a lot of trouble.

First you have to establish a known value such as your favorite bottle of catsup. Then find out what that item costs locally. You now have a percentage to apply to anything.

> Victorina catsup costs the equivalent of 40 cents US and you paid $1.00 in the US for Heinz. Ergo: 40/100= 40% of US prices for locally manufactured products.

> If you got a beer and a pizza in the US at a not-too-swank place for $8.95, then you should expect the same to cost a Victorina Catsup percentage in the DR, or, 40% of $8.95 = $3.58 equivalent of pesos.

This percentage shall be more or less good to use in pricing almost anything of local origin. Restaurants, pizzas, Coca-Cola, etc., but not car rentals. They don't make cars in the DR and cars may cost more than double the US price because of import taxes.

BEERONOMY

I have practiced an economic theory based on beer since 1970, and it has worked all over the world. In any country in the world you can appraise the "oughta-be" value of goods by ratioing against the price of a *standard cold beer in a workingman's bar*. If a beer at a tavern near the station is a buck at home, and a good suit is 250 bucks at home, then a good suit where you are, barring any government interference with taxes and subsidies, shall cost you 250 cold beers bought at a workingman's tavern. You can learn a lot from the window of a shoe store, too, but I'll keep that for when we meet down island.

CASH

Even in the Dominican Republic, **cash** is available for **credit cards** from automatic teller machines outside banks and shopping centers in major cities, and for **American Express** cards at any American Express office. If getting a cash advance from a commercial bank, inquire about any fees they might charge. In Venezuela you may not know what rate was used until months later. You may be better off getting cash before entering Venezuela. You can do this with a VISA card in **Georgetown** from Scotia Bank with little or no fees, or from the Barclays at **Providenciales, Turks and Caicos**.

Currency exchange is regulated in both countries. Both government and private banks, if chartered to exchange money, will do so within a point of each other. Exchanging on the street is illegal, and you may run into fast change artists.

If you carry a lot of cash, don't flash a roll. Keep it in separate pockets. Purses and "belly bags" may get ripped off with a razor in Venezuela. Not too comfortable if it is tightly strapped. So travel light when out and about, and use flapped pockets.

FUEL AND WATER

Water should be taken on whenever available. Always bleach water with 1 tablespoon bleach per 30 gallons of water. Always filter the fuel with a **Baja Filter** (see Glossary) if you can get it, tee shirts if you can't. One year I had FIVE motor stops at sea due to clogged fuel filters. In **Abraham Bay** I bucketed out all the fuel from the tank and gleaned 4 pounds of sand and gravel. The last fuel stops had been in Ft.Lauderdale, Nassau and Georgetown. The same thing happened to *Moon Lady* two years before in the same place.

Between Georgetown and Venezuela I tank up at **Luperón, Ponce Yacht Club** and **Crown Bay Marina**, St.Thomas. Usually I need fuel at those points, the fuel is usually clean, and the docks at Ponce and Crown Bay are easily made by a single hander. At Luperón the dock boys will jerry jug clean fuel from the town's station, ferry it aboard and siphon it through your filters into your tanks. The cost, including their labor, is less than what it would be in the Bahamas, and you shouldn't motor that coast with a less than full tank.

Some places, **Puerto Plata**, for example, you may pay a significant premium for your fuel if delivered at dockside. Often it is delivered in rusty barrels which are rolled down the dock to ensure you get a fine emulsion of fuel and iron oxide. In Puerto Plata you can jerry jug from the Texaco station and get filtered fuel at a fraction of the price charged at the dock. At **Samaná** there is a dockside pump, but it may be difficult to get to it due to the crush of boats, and there is a significant surge.

Treat your water with chlorine and never tank from a line after a recent loss of pressure.

PROVISIONING IN THE DOMINICAN REPUBLIC

The average yacht can easily save a lot by provisioning here, and for cruisers, a dollar saved on provisions is a dollar earned. These savings cannot be realized unless you buy by the case in distributors' warehouses instead of at the pokey little *super mercados* and *colmados*. I always meet skippers kicking themselves all the way down islands because they didn't make room to buy in the Dominican Republic. If you don't speak Spanish, it may seem difficult for you, but it's really quite easy. Follow the instructions given below for single item and caselot purchases.

TRANSPORTATION WHILE PROVISIONING

Take a *motoconcho* instead of walking. These are motorbikes which sport a banana seat for a single passenger behind the driver. In **Samaná**, they tow a rick-shaw sort of conveyance for 6 and try to put 10 aboard. Flag one down with an arm motion which, in America, would mean "slow down". You pay per ride. A ride is a *bola*, [pronounced BOWL-la] and is any length run between 2 points in town. Each *bola* is about a third of a beer, and it sure beats walking. See the section called *Beeronomy*. In Venezuela it's easy. Take a taxi. But get the fare before boarding!

SAMPLING BRANDS

You may get the itch to move on before you've sampled the local goods. It is therefore important to forego restaurants for a couple of days early in your stay and shop single items from the *mercados* to find out what you like before shopping for case lots.

Compared with large economies the reader might be used to, the economy of a small country like the Dominican Republic will fluctuate wildly with world conditions as well as with local policies. Even local goods may often be temporarily limited and therefore prices go up and shelves go bare. Seasonal production also reckons. Therefore, a buying trip is necessary to get individual items in order to sample for both quality and price.

Buy only locally made labels. The only exception to this rule are some occasionally good prices, due to trade concessions, on Spanish imports, some of which may be bulk shipped and bottled locally (olives, mushrooms). The quality of local products may be uneven between brands in the DR, but not as dramatically uneven as in Venezuela.

Sample several individual products before deciding what to buy by the case.

BUYING INDIVIDUAL ITEMS

In **Puerto Plata**, take a *motoconcho* to either the *Supermercado Tropical* on 27 Febrero or *Supermercado Silverio Messon* on Seperación, to look for good buys when you only need one or two of each item or when you are sampling products before buying a case.

These markets are relatively clean and provide a good selection of local products. You must ask for what you want. One fellow complained to me that the DR had no bacon. He was too shy to ask. It's called *tocineta* [toe-see-NET-ah]. He assumed it would be in a vacuum packed package like Oscar Mayer's, with the slices of bacon splayed out like a poker hand. In the DR, meats are usually kept the way they were when our mother's went shopping. They're wrapped in white butcher's paper among a bunch of amorphous packages in the cooler. It is whole and requires slicing by the guy in the store. For that reason, it's usually also better tasting.

Ask to taste anything you can. Certainly sample cheese and salamis before buying.

In **Santiago**, there is a section called *Hospedajes,* similar to the old Les Halles section of Paris (now the Pompidou museum). Here you wander among piles of fresh fruits and vegetables and run between blocks of provisioners to compare prices. Go first by **guagua** and **carrito** to case the place. Later, rent a van and driver to bring back your haul. Have lunch at Pez Dorado, on the park next to the church at the top of *Calle del Sol.*

Have a dictionary handy if what you want is not listed in the word list in this book. Here is a list of <u>DR products</u> which, when they are not entirely diverted to export, are usually high quality at low price in the DR:

— dried milk (*NIDO*) and espresso grind coffee (*SANTO DOMINGO*)

— Worstershire sauce [*Salsa Inglesa*]

— vanilla

— soy sauce [*Salsa China*]

— strawberry jam

— guava & pineapple marmalades

— Rum (the *Añejos* at 12 year, specials are 15 year)

— Gin (Bermudez is excellent)

— local Scotch is McAlbert's (*caveat emptor*)

— Creme de Cacao and other liqueurs (Advocaat is *Ponche Nutrititivo*)

— cooking wines

— cigarettes

— some of the world's finest cigars

— warm-stored margarine [*Manicera*]

— *MasMas* chocolate bars or others to your taste (for watch snacks)

— salamis and cherizos (try the *INDUVECA* or *El Cid* brands and <u>taste first!</u>)

— large loaves of cheese called *QUESO DANESA*

— red ball Gouda cheeses (white cheese only), can be warm stored

Coffee comes in vacuum packed tins, in 10 oz. bags or in small sealed packets good for several cups of coffee each morning. Buy a "greca", the hourglass shaped aluminum pot, to make the coffee with. Control the strength by controlling the amount of grounds.

Buying Case Lot Goods

After you have tried out different brands, make a list of what suits you and what can save money with power purchases. In **Puerto Plata** take a *motoconcho* to any of the *almacenes* for case lots. *Almacén* [alma-SANE] means warehouse. Go early to the Santiago section called *Hospedajes.* There are many wholesale warehouses in Puerto Plata or **Santiago** that do a large business with hotels. Take a look in any walk-in coolers in the *almacenes.* Remember they have a furious trade with the fancy foreign tourist hotels. You may be surprised to get fresh asparagus and artichokes for dinner.

Usually there is a broken case lots section. Here you can buy items which you won't want in full cases and at the same time you get to see pretty much what they have in all those cases stacked outside. If you don't see what you want, crawl back into the alleys of the boxes and look. If you don't understand what's in a case, ask them to break it open and show you. If there's something you want which is not there, ask, and they will break a case and give you a prorated case price on units.

Cans

I have fished cans out of the forward bilge after 3 years aboard in the tropics and found them still legibly labeled and delicious inside. Varnishing cans is a waste of time if yours is a basically dry boat.

Eggs

I've had unrefrigerated eggs aboard as long as 2 months and found them delicious, although they don't foam as much when whipped if you don't turn them. Of course, you must buy only unrefrigerated, fresh eggs; refrigerated eggs go bad quicker. Unrefrigerated eggs are easy to spot. They have chicken poop on them. Instead of waxing your eggs, try turning them once in a while to keep the yolks centered. Like many cruising customs of yore, modern yachts and ubiquitous staples eliminate varnishing tins and waxing eggs.

Chickens

A word about eggs and chickens in the DR. You may see barbecued chicken for sale which is scrawny, and eggs which are more like bird eggs. If they are *huevos criollos* [WAVE-ose cree-OH-yose], or criole eggs or chicken (*pollo* [PO-yo]), snap it up. They're more expensive but you'll find out what chicken and eggs were like in your grandfather's time, before factory methods.

WHAT TO BUY

First of all, only you know what you want. I love French cut green beans and I use them with mushrooms, onions and mayonnaise for great salads when I can't get fresh veggies. You may hate French cut green beans and mushrooms.

Fresh Fruits and Vegetables

The same should be said for fresh veggies as was said for fuel and water: buy them whenever they're available. And wash them before putting them aboard. Also be sure to take away all cardboard which may bring aboard cockroach eggs.

Building boats by eye in Haiti

avocado	*aguacat*	banana	*guineo*	breadfruit	*buen pan*	key limes	*limones*
plantain	*plátano*	cashew	*cajuil*	chayote	*tayota*	cocoa	*cacao*
coffee	*café*	grapefuit	*toronja*	guava	*guayaba*	manioc	*yuca*
mango	*mango*	passion fruit	*chinola*	orange	*naranja*	papaya	*lechosa*
peanuts	*maní*	pear	*pera*	pineapple	*pióa*	potato	*papa*
sapodilla	*zapote*	sour sop	*guayab*	sweet potato	*batata*	tomato	*tomate*

In Puerto Plata or **Samaná** (and all down islands) get to the market early. In Luperón you shall find varying quality in all the little shops and on the streets. Find the lady that has the best of what you want, then find out when she gets it in fresh. Try out the different root vegetables that fed our ancestors before the Idaho white potato and mass production methods drove them from North America.

For a huge, cheap lunch, go into the market kitchen where the workers eat and order up. You'll be aghast at the apparent lack of hygiene, but you won't be sorry.

Dry Staples

Have smallish dry staple containers aboard. Rice, sugar, flour, beans, meal, and so on, are readily available almost everywhere and at prices better than in the US. Trying to store too much flour or rice will have you throwing it away when the insect eggs hatch, that is, unless you have pounds of Laurel (bay leaves) to put in your canisters. *Almacén Sandra* in **Luperón**, right behind Lucas' restaurant has good clean dry staples, including fresh shelled Spanish peanuts. You may need to clean the rice and beans of small stones and stems. When visiting Florida I found myself cleaning a bag of beans as was my Caribbean habit. After discarding more than usual the amount of small dirt clods and sticks, I was surprised to see it was a bag I had bought in the U.S. So much for superior food standards.

In the Caribbean you will find that flour is not always "enriched", rice is not always "polished", sugar is not always "refined" and not much is "new and improved". But it just might be tasty and good for you.

Bread and Dairy Products

Bakeries, or *panaderías*, are ubiquitous in Spanish countries where they make fresh *pan del agua* ("Cuban" or small French breads) twice a day. More expensive, but some-times of better quality small town products, is *Pépé Postre*, with bakeries in **Puerto Plata** and **Santiago**.

The *yogurt* in the DR is great and extraordinarily cheap by the gallon! It's a little lemony and comes like a thick milkshake. Ask for *yo-GOOR* or *Baruga* [bah-ROO-gah], which is the brand. Home made yogurt is available in Luperón from a small store across from the police station.

Meats and sausages

The DR has the oldest *beef* culture in the western hemisphere. You will often get tough and tasteless beef in restaurants and in stores and conclude that DR meat is awful, a complaint often heard from yachties who just didn't know what to order and how. Beef filet is often only sold by the entire filet, but at a price that you can't believe. Good filets are prepared the European way and are aged and blue. Other cuts of good beef are also European style and are lean looking to North Americans.

Cheap beef is called *res* [race] and is often tough. The secret to buying good meat is to not go cheap. It's already cheap, there's no reason for shaving additional pennies which will only get you poor quality. Buy the most expensive filet, *filete* [fee-LAY-taye] *lomillo* [low-ME-yo], and you will be very pleased. *Solomillo* [SO-low-ME-yo] is sirloin. Smoked ham, boiled ham and smoked pork chops are also good. Best sources in Puerto Plata are from *Erica's* butcher shop, next to the University, or the *Italian Super Market*, or direct from the *INDUVECA* delivery van when you see it on the street.

If you can, get a *Saronno* ham to hang aboard. This is the Spanish version of the Italian Parma ham. It may cost you ten times as much in Spain as in the DR, but the masters that make it in the DR all come from Gallícia.

Miscellaneous

Old-time stuff hard to find in the States is readily available in the DR. You can find real sail canvas and blue denim for boat and personal use in the DR. You can eat fancy as well as *tipico* in the cities. In **Puerto Plata** try *Roma II*, or go to **Long Beach,** a *motoconcho* ride east. In **Santiago**, it's at the *Pez Dorado*, the golden fish. In **Luperón**, try *Almendros*.

Refurbish your medicine chest without prescriptions, often cheaply.

Like most small, poor countries, the **Dominican Republic** cannot afford to tie disease curing drugs to doctor's prescriptions, nor can the people afford to buy drugs abusively. Therefore pharmaceuticals may be available without prescription, if you know what you want. The pharmacist will gladly show you the book so you can translate your antibiotic, or whatever, to generic, and back to product name as available there. The European seasickness pill, **STUGERON**, is sold here. It works without side effects.

Drugs needed commonly for public health can be subsidized and cheap. Exotic items may be more expensive than at home. But if you need to replace drugs used up during treatment aboard, then this is the place. Also, pharmacies in Latin countries traditionally handle dangerous chemicals as well. You may be surprised to find acetone, muriatic and cooking alcohol available in quantity only through certain pharmacies.

Siesta [see-ACE-tah]

All the stores close for the noon to 2 p.m. **siesta**. Take your lunch on the park. The central park, or *parque central*, [el PAR-KAY Cen-TRAHL] has a special flavor of its own. Watching the parade pass by is great entertainment while you breakfast or lunch on the porch at *Cafe Central*; pig out in the ice cream parlor on the corner; eat 25 cent hamburgers from the street vendors (they're called *Riki Takis* [REEK-ee TACK-ees]); read world newspapers available at Libreria Félix; get your shoes shined; listen to the firemen's brass band at 8 p.m. on Sundays; fill propane tanks next to *Cafe Central*.

Street food

I know I've got it coming to me, but going on 30 years living abroad in the strangest of places, I've rarely been ill from street food. Once was a long time ago at the grand restaurant of the Palace hotel in Biarritz. In India, one would expect to become ill from the *nazi* balls (rice balls) the peddler rolls in his hands and pops into ancient hot grease. Not so. Perhaps the super hot oil does it. Latin countries have superb little puffed, stuffed pastries (*empanadillas* in PR, *pastelitos* in the DR, and *empanadas* in Venezuela). In Puerto Plata, buy your *pastelitos* from the baritone vendor who sings his wares. He says that the meat filled ones have "mice meat" in them. But he means "mincemeat", I'm sure.

{PS: the wrinkled old lady who begs in Puerto Plata is crazy and really well to do}

PROVISIONING AND REPAIRS IN PUERTO RICO

Larry's Playa Marine in Salinas has the best stainless stock in Puerto Rico, plus nearly everything else. If you can't wait until Salinas, there is a marine store at the Ponce Yacht Club's boatyard, and the Centro Nautico store is within walking distance from the Yacht Club.

Ponce has the most amazing warehouse a yachtie can ever visit: Rubber and Gasket of Puerto Rico (843-8450). They have sheet rubber, Teflon, Lexan, and any kind of **hose** you want, including stainless flex, and they fabricate. Everything can be had in Ponce, **Stainless** fabrication is at Accurate Tooling (AT Metal, 788-4090) on Hostos in Playa Ponce. Also on Hostos, nearer downtown and across from an awesome statue of an unchained slave, is the little shop called Tornicentro del Sur (Southern Screw Center, 259-4419), with a world class collection of stainless fasteners.

To reprovision, tie the dinghy up at the fisherman's cooperative dock, asking them first, of course. Walk a few blocks into the industrial park nearby. There are a half dozen godowns arranged in two large lots, each fronted with high loading docks. Go to RAFA'S CASH AND CARRY in the northeastern godown. This is a caselots warehouse for hotels and restaurants. Grab a dolly cart and heave on all the canned goods cases, sausage, cheese and booze you want. Take a look in RAFA's hardware discount on the same loading dock. When done, drop a dime in the phone outside and call a taxi to deliver you and your provisions to the dinghy for only $3. The number's on the wall.

In the godown behind Rafa's is a fuel and hydraulic hose shop. In the lot across from Rafa's, the northernmost godown has a store taken from the dreams of the mechanically adept skipper. Benitez Carrillo has vee belts, bearings, gears, seals, motor controls and every ball bearing known to man, even your roller furling's. If they don't, they'll deliver it next day. The magnificient Plaza del Caribe Mall is a short ride (or a long walk) from the yacht club. Next to it is an XTRA super market like in Florida. KMART and SAM'S are also a short taxi ride away.

Shop these stores while in Ponce, but do the installation in Salinas.

REFITTING AND REPROVISIONING IN VENEZUELA

If you've been lucky there will be few broken and bent parts as a result of your travels. You can pick and choose what to refit at the terminus in **Venezuela** to prepare the yacht for going back or proceeding on to the Panama Canal. If you've been unlucky — a bent shaft, for instance — you will have a list of things to do which are absolute musts to make the yacht sea ready again.

Venezuela is the terminus for this guide and it is used in the examples below. Nonetheless, the guidelines are valid for most of the Caribbean where most economies are in or close to crisis and shall undoubtedly remain so.

I usually shy from recommendations of specific shops and services. These tips rarely survive the test of a few months, so beware of those you do get, from me or anybody.

Specific prices are likewise not given. Prices go up, quality goes down and businesses go broke. Ten unthinking yachties in a row grinningly declaring, "Wow! That's cheap!", will make even the most straight arrow mechanic revise his pricing policies for *gringos*. He has kids to feed. So get your specific tips on shops and items to purchase (or not to purchase) from several cruisers with recent information, not from any book.

Transportation while refitting and reprovisioning is not a problem as long as **taxis** remain cheap or the dollar dear. Find out what each trip should cost in approximate terms before hailing a cab and find out what the driver will charge before entering the cab. *Always.*

DECIDING WHAT TO REFIT

If you are lucky and have only "wannas" instead of "haftas" to buy or fix, some generic advice will help. First of all, whether you seek services (awning repair?), workshops (straightening shafts?), retailers (awning material?) or groceries, go for the possible. Find out what's available and reasonable rather than pursuing preconceived goals which may get you in trouble.

For example, one cruiser I met thought **Venezuela** wasn't so cheap. They had to import their Sunbrella awning material. Had they investigated further they would have found the

British equivalent available at one sixth the price, out of Hong Kong via Japan and the Venezuelan oil trade.

To understand what's possible one must understand something of the Venezuelan economy. First of all, Venezuela is a large, rich country with undeveloped natural resources, excepting oil and aluminum. They nationalized these, along with all their subsidiary industries, from the Americans over the last 40 years and they have not developed a much wider industrial infrastructure since. The chances of doing so faded with the world oil glut and the dive in oil prices in the early 1980's.

So here you have a modern country the size of a good chunk of the United States with 20 or so million relatively educated (if only by television) souls expecting the good life promised by the beer ads and not finding it.

Carlos Caraqueño (car-ah-KAY-nyo: a resident of Caracas) can't get his shaft straightened because it's too expensive for him. He's told his economy's woes are due to the bloodsucking usurious northern bankers (that's you, by the way) to whom his country's reduced revenue must go in payment of the old high interest rates on ancient loans which didn't help their infrastructure anyway. Agree with him or not, that's the reality he lives in.

Meanwhile, due to the accident of currency markets, Bob Boatie stands beside Carlos Caraqueño in the prop shop in Cumaná and shouts, "Wow! That's cheap!" 'Way to go, Bob. When Carlos goes back to his awning shop, if he's like you or I, he'll really gig the foreign yachts with his prices, and perhaps, with his quality as well. Therefore ...

RULE ONE: use non- yachtie sources wherever possible.

— Go to the hardware store farthest from the marina.

— Get your dinghy anchor at the fishermen's supply store.

— Don't go shopping in white shorts, a goofy hat and a regatta tee shirt

— If you can, grow a Pancho Villa mustache and talk Venezuelan.

Venezuela is a favorite source of Japan's oil for which contracts are negotiated with increasing creativity on a rolling basis almost monthly. Since oil and aluminum are about the only commodities Venezuela can sell, and they need to import just about everything else, the mixture of currency and trade concessions gets frenetic. For example, if Japan gets a break on the oil based exchange rate, they'll sell their outboards to the Venezuelan fishermen on that rate instead of the floating one. Or how about Yamaha sets up a fiberglass factory in the mountains to use Venezuelan petroleum stocks to make boats for the fishermen with Indian labor so the mountain folk don't continue to jam the slums in the cities where there are no jobs for them? If you were Carlos Caraqueño, you'd go for that.

However, when Carlos sees you, the usurious banker, carrying away one of those neat Yamaha fiberglass boats bought at prices subsidized by his labor and resources, and he still sees you demanding your interest, he might get mad and call the militia. When the militia boards your boat they may not be too courteous since they're not always recruited from the best Venezuelan families and they may lack your sophistication and education. The various militias are, after all, like the American CCC in the Great American Depression, a source of employment for the unemployable during the Great *Venezuelan* Depression. They will understand, however, that you are double dipping in their wounded economy and that you are avoiding the export tax on subsidized articles. The export tax would have

45

paid back the subsidy and brought prices of your purchases up to world levels. In their eyes you can be quite a scoundrel. Try grinning at their combat boots and shouting, "Wow! It was so cheap!" Or, you could have followed ...

RULE TWO: know current import/export restrictions.

The economic trials in Venezuela make it a great refitting spot and many bargains exist. Understanding their problem better will not only protect you from doing something illegal but will also open up some purchasing opportunities you might not have thought about.

— Epoxy resin is made in Venezuela, but catalyst is imported. Sometimes epoxy is nearly as cheap as water, other times it's unavailable at any price.

— Ever wanted to replace your charging wires with good "00" gauge battery cable but 20 feet of cable made up into 4 different lengths with small ring connectors cost too much money since the battery shop in Fort Lauderdale took 35 dollars an hour to make them up? Battery cable is one of the hidden resources in the bottom of the Venezuelan heap of industries supporting mining and drilling.

— Need pipe? Tools? Stainless welding? Been thinking of a "jungle gym" to support all the stuff you need to mount high up aft? Awning supports? Take a look at the fabulous grades of polished and corrosion resistant aluminum tubing available and the high tech welding methods they use.

RULE THREE: refit from the strengths of the economy.

While in Venezuela, consume the products and labor of the land. As in Phoenix, Arizona, they will not be yacht oriented. As a matter of fact, outside of Cowes, La Rochelle and Fort Lauderdale, very few places are. Aluminum, oil (a year's supply of 2 stroke oil) and oil stocks products (Imron, polyester resin, enamels, urethane varnish). If electronics were on your agenda, go back to the US or to a free port and order from Europe where you'll get decent quality.

Furthermore, think of all the things you have been doing yourself and not purchasing due to unavailability of qualified labor and materials throughout the islands to the north. You may be in a mental set, normally good for a cruiser, that says "do it yourself." This may not be good for you in Venezuela.

Therefore…

RULE FOUR: let the Venezuelans do it, and consume like a Venezuelan.

— You sew your own courtesy flags? You may be spending more by using your own thread and machine. Some years ago I had my curtains replaced with beautiful cloth backed with reflective coating for 6 dollars. The seamstress was the wife of a restaurant owner who also did children's clothes.

— A can of tuna made in Venezuela may cost a small fraction of what you paid for each can of tuna on board.

— How about your personalized stationery? Your yacht's visiting cards? Visit a commercial print shop and be amazed at both quality and price, and you will also get the copper printing blocks to reuse in the future.

— Tee shirts with your yacht's logo? The artwork and the silk screens are delivered to you with the shirts.

— Say you don't use fancy restaurants? Try one and you may be eating out every night for less than what it would cost to consume your own stores. Please tip the musicians moderately and don't shout, "Wow! That was cheap!" Your patronage of their businesses is appreciated without insulting their currency.

Currency in Venezuela has certain complexities. When I was there in 1972 it was enormously expensive for someone with dollars and the Venezuelans thought nothing of hopping a jet for a shopping trip to Miami to hunt bargains among their poorer cousins to the north. I remember admiring the Venezuelans then for their industriousness and success. How times change!

Now that the shoe is on the other foot, don't expect to be admired for the industriousness which made you a successful cruiser. Latin pride, or *orgullo* [or-GOO-yo] mitigates against it. Furthermore, not all Venezuelans have benefited equally from their country's bounty. As in your own urban societies there always lurks the alienated or conscienceless few to take advantage of what they can.

These days the lurking is pretty good, so ...

RULE FIVE: don't flash your money.

When going to the bank to exchange **cash** or to get cash from a credit card pretend you're in a spy movie and case things out pretty thoroughly. Sit a while on the sometimes sumptuous sofas in the bank lobby both before and after your transaction. Watch for loiterers in the street or even in the bank lobby. Upon leaving the bank, stop to do what shopping you can to divest yourself of some of the cash. Leave stores by entrances other than ones through which you entered and use devious routes back to your boat, throwing in a couple of changes of public transportation.

Think I'm exaggerating? What do you think all those gun slits outside and inside the banks are for? Finally,

---

RULE SIX: leave high finance to the Swiss gnomes.

If you think you understand how the currency game works and you place your bets at the bank accordingly, changing nothing this week and lots of it the next, be aware that how you spend your cruising chips doesn't attract attention in Zurich.

Published exchange rates don't always tell the story. Rates can be floating, fixed, commercial, tourist, bank, central bank, export, import, etc. -- and foreign quotes of rates are meaningless in country. The Bolivar may cheapen against the dollar by a factor of 3, but if inflation raises prices by 4 you've just lost 33 percent of your money. Government controls make timing of purchases which depend on import materials bought with hard currency (e.g., rubber dinghies) very difficult. If you wait for a point more on the exchange you risk running into a sudden order backlog which puts delivery off beyond your **VISA** expiration.

If, like I did one year, you decide to gain the billing time of your credit card, effectively buying the Bolivar short, you may run into what I did. The Central Bank decided to hold all **VISA** transactions until a more favorable exchange rate was available and after debt renegotiation with the World Bank. That was *four months* later. Not allowed under the VISA rules? Call Chase Manhattan, and while at it, call up the central bank of this sovereign nation and tell them you heard they can't do it. Otherwise, follow ...

THE GOLDEN RULE : take cash and convert it as needed.

That way you'll average out your gains and losses and you'll avoid institutional interference with your transactions. You'll buy only the things you can use and won't be suspected of profiteering. You'll consume more on the local market, such as restaurants, and you will be happier. So will the Venezuelans.

Enough examples are given in the previous pages that you should have a good idea of what kind of opportunities may exist and how you can go about identifying the specific ones available during the time frame of your visit.

Shafts can be straightened in **Cumaná**, by the way, as well as propellers repitched. Haulout work is addressed in the *Hauling Out* chapter. Opportunities for reasonably priced and quality refit jobs will change from time to time with the swings in the troubled economy and the government efforts to regulate them. Simply using those opportunities which the economy and the government conspire to make attractive will more than occupy your time without trying the impossible, or worse, the illegal.

Travel in Venezuela

Some bargains will not change, such as **Margarita** for clothes and duty free jug wine, **Cumaná** for industrial supplies and services, **Puerto La Cruz** for consumer products, restaurants and entertainment, and, shades of a younger America, <u>travel</u> by any means which requires great amounts of fossil fuels.

Jet air fare in Venezuela, despite recent price increases, will continue to be one of the greatest bargains around. Firstly, because they have oil and it is relatively cheap. Secondly, because there are enormous distances to travel in South America and thirdly, because there is so much worth touring.

One cruiser I know put the boat up in the marina in **Puerto La Cruz** and spent 6 months touring South America. Even if you don't go so far afield, a trip to **Mérida** and **Angel's Falls** is too good to pass up if you're at all a tourist. By all means leave your boat in a marina while you are gone if you are on the mainland. From Margarita you can have friends look after the yacht in the **Porlamar** anchorage in front of the *Concorde Hotel*.

A neat way to visit the mainland from Margarita is to take a ferry over and a plane back. Now you've sampled travel in Venezuela with minimum investment and without later having to take time out from your stay on the mainland which might be a busy one if you've got a lot of refit to do.

Provisioning

National edible stores can be slightly cheaper on the mainland because you avoid the transport costs of bringing the goods to **Margarita**.

Because shortages will come and go, hitting almost all items but rum and tobacco, it's best to provision wherever you can. The super markets are large, convenient and "Americanized". For example, veggies are Saran-wrapped in little ozone-destroying green plastic trays. The better products are in a *deli* section where you pick a number. Shopping carts are huge and so are the women in curlers compulsively grabbing the impulse buyers' goodies in the check out lines. Very Americanized indeed.

CaDa supermarkets are ubiquitous and on **Margarita**, *CM* (*Centro Madeireño*) is very large and has a great bakery next door. As in the Dominican Republic, you can get *Pan de Agua* here but they call it *Pan Francés* [PAHN frahn-SACE] which makes sense. If in **Pampatar**, there is an excellent little bakery right by the anchorage. As in the DR, <u>you must sample each brand before buying</u> a bunch. Unlike the DR, however, where there is a fairly consistent level of quality, Venezuela is a large market with worldwide sources and quality (or <u>taste</u>, if you prefer) can be a problem.

Try a couple of different brands of corned beef for a test. One will be worse than dog food and the other better than Hormel. And both the same price! Coffee is excellent and cheap, but don't get caught by the troops with 30 pounds aboard if it's on their list.

In Venezuela I've found it more convenient to provision a little at a time while eating out lots. By the time your visa is up your boat is full and you never had the hassle of major provisioning nor attracted undue attention by carting off crates of stuff.

Finally, as in the Dominican Republic, if you need to replace drugs used up during treatment aboard, then this is the place. Also, you will find acetone, muriatic and cooking alcohol available in quantity only through certain pharmacies.

NAVIGATION AIDS

Most cruisers are consumed with getting to a certain place at a certain time. For this they heavily invest in all sorts of navigational equipment. The real art of navigation, however, is to *not* be in the *wrong* place at the wrong time. This should be your criterion for choosing navigational aids.

CHARTS AND GUIDES

Modern yachtsmen are confronted with the problem of too much information being available. Years of cruising in the Third World where documented navigation aids are few, and Europe, where there are too many, have led me to make the following recommendations which are listed in priority order.

YACHTING GUIDES

— **Guides**, this one included, are out of date the moment they are printed. Look for guides that give you less tips on where to do your drinking and more detail on anchorages, landfall marks, sea conditions, etc. The fathom lines rarely change but, except for Lerman in the Peace and Plenty, bartenders change frequently.

— Guides like Nancy and Simon Scott's *Cruising Guide to the Virgin Islands*, Doyle's *A Cruising Guide to the Leeward Islands*, Doyle's *A Sailor's Guide to the Windward Islands*, or Doyle's *Cruising Guide to Trinidad, Tobago, Venezuela and Bonaire*, are essential. The venerable Hart and Stone, now Hart and Hayes, *A Cruising Guide to the Caribbean and Bahamas* is still a great book. The more guides, the better, since each author has a slightly different viewpoint. Land guides such as *Island Expedition* (Bahamas), are also invaluable for getting more out of your cruise.

MEDIUM SCALE CHARTS

— These are the **charts** which get you between guides, or guide sections. For instance, if you already have a guidebook, a single chart each of the **Leeward Islands** and the **Windward Islands** is sufficient. A single chart covering all of the **Virgin Islands** is all that's needed in addition to the guidebook. A single chart of **Hispaniola**'s north coast is sufficient and a chart of the **Mona Passage**, showing **Cabo Engaño** on one side and **Puerto Rico**'s West Coast on the other, is desirable (DMA 25700). This latter is available, along with charts of **Puerto Rico** in a waterproof yachtsman's version.

— The scope and shallows of the **Bahamas** requires good charts in addition to the guides. Fortunately, the *Bahamas Chart Kit* is all that you will require.

— **Imray Charts** and Sailing Supply's **Waterproof Charts** are superior to **DMA** charts because they offer the scale a yachtsman is interested in. They often show landmarks of interest to the small boat skipper making for small harbors. They also have a format which better fits small boat nav tables, and they have excellent color contrasts.

PILOT (also ROUTING) CHARTS

— I keep a pilot chart on my chart table at all times. It is used only occasionally for plotting Caribbean crossings, tracking **Tropical Storms** and planning passages with the current and wind data it provides. However, it is used every morning in the Bahamas to plot the **Cold Fronts** and every morning in the **Caribbean** to plot the **Tropical Waves**. It is the single most used chart aboard and is covered with pencil marks and coffee rings. The best buy the US Government ever offered is the chart table sized book of twelve *Pilot Charts of the Central American Waters* at the price of only one regular chart.

LARGE SCALE CHARTS

— These are charts which cover small geographic areas. Except in the Bahamas, these **charts** are only necessary where you intend exploring areas not shown in available guides. *The Bahamas Chart Kit*, along with a guidebook, is sufficient for all navigation in the Bahamas. Recent versions of the *Virgins Chart Kit*, on the other hand, provide little information beyond what is available in one medium scale chart and the Scott guidebook.

ALMANACS

— These are of great use as reference works aboard. (What *is* the breaking strength of 5/16 BBB chain, anyway?) I have found that a single copy of *Reed's Nautical Almanac* from any year provides more useful information than *Chapman's* and *Bowditch's* combined.

TIDE TABLES

— In the English Channel I was never without my **tide** tables and current guides. The tides were, after all, 34 feet at my moorings, and the currents reached 9 knots! In the Caribbean there's nothing to know outside the information on the Pilot Charts which doesn't vary year to year. In the Bahamas the daily tides are broadcast several times a day on standard AM broadcast radio. The tidal differences on **Nassau** rarely exceed one half hour in the open anchorages, and tidal anomalies, such as on the banks, are all local knowledge, rarely in the guides. I've found Hans Pieper's Shareware *Tide Prediction Program* accurate for open anchorages.

— None of this is really necessary, however, since most places you can assume **high tide** *is at 8 o'clock* local time everywhere near open sea *on the day of a* **full moon.** So you can add 52 minutes a day thereafter and do without tide tables.

NOTE: The south side of the Greater Antilles and the Virgin Islands have diurnal tides with a higher high and a lower low instead of two lows and two highs.

SMALL SCALE CHARTS

— These charts cover large geographical areas. They make great wall decorations at home; at sea, I have only those needed to plot crossings and major passages. *The Bahamas Chart Kit* is sufficient for both large and small scale needs. Charts of **Turks and Caicos** are now available. Charts of the entire Caribbean, such as a Pilot Chart, does nicely for the rest. See *Turks and Caicos* for more information.

THE BARE MINIMUM

COMPASS

I had sailed for years with no more than a **compass** and a **log**. After cruising a while I found that even the log was a luxury. Knowledge of your boat's speed settles into your bones after only a few weeks of cruising. You can navigate surely and safely forever with only a compass by careful and frequent position plotting, attention to leeway, current and tidal currents, and by *introducing intentional errors* in order to ensure which side of a feature you make your landfall. Even the compass needn't be all that accurate, since who can hold a perfect course anyway, what with all that bobbing around?

Old fashioned binnacles look nice and are useful for taking bearings of ships. But, they are rarely visible from comfortable positions while seated. Your compass should be mounted where you can see it comfortably from your sailing position on either tack while cruising. Bolt upright behind or beside the wheel is a racing position. The cruising steering position has a little more Zen in it. For instance, I sail scrunched up in a ball in the same corner of the cockpit on both tacks, never behind the wheel. Therefore I use a bulkhead compass.

The compass should have a large, legible scale which is well illuminated, not just bright. Some compass lights illuminate everything but the card's scale. Ideally you should have a compass which is rapidly damped. This usually means a larger and more expensive model, but not always.

Swing your compass from time to time, even if it's compensated, to confirm your compass' deviation table, and make sure you are using this year's variation.

LOG

Mechanical sumlogs, taffrail **log**, or any device which keeps a digital track of miles run is a great check on the navigator. They all fail, however, and there is no substitute for the skipper knowing intuitively how fast his yacht is going through the water.

Before the impeller is tangled in seaweed or a shark eats the rotor, take the time to calibrate your sense of the boat's speed by the old chip log method. Select a fixed length of deck viewed from your sailing position. Time bits of foam passing between perpendiculars of that length, checking results with actual speedo readings. Speed in knots is twice the meters travelled divided by the seconds taken.

$$\text{Speed in Knots} = \frac{2 \times \text{Meters}}{\text{seconds}}$$

Practice makes perfect and eventually you will know with a glance how fast your boat is going in all conditions. It is an old principle of navigation that the more regular and frequent your plots are, the more sure your course. Without a sumlog, plotting intervals should become shorter. This is due to the fact that you have got to estimate average speed over the last interval and, the shorter the interval, the more accurate your estimate.

SEXTANT

The last time I used my **sextant** was crossing the Atlantic in 1979. In the Bahamas and the Caribbean they're only useful if you really know how to use them on clear and starry nights. I have a friend who could pull off a 3 star fix faster than my Satnav prepared one. He couldn't beat a GPS, however. Solar and lunar sights don't usually provide the kind of precision required to navigate among islands. If you are island hopping, the distances are not great and landfalls are unmistakable and inevitable in the Caribbean. On the other hand, if you are crossing the Caribbean Sea, or you are masochistically beating over the ocean to **St.Thomas**, great accuracy isn't really called for, but the sextant can be useful to confirm drift. I'm afraid sextants have gone the way of the slide rule. Still, they're neat. Every skipper should have one to play with.

In the passages described by this guide, your time and money is better spent on chart work and a good compass. You don't want to be like the "professional" delivery crew who gave up their charge on East Reef, Mayaguana, having spent all their time playing with their sextants and none of it on avoiding a lee reef. The day after the paid crew of 3 deserted their ship, by the way, it was taken off the reef whole by one salvor using the boat's own ground tackle. He turned the key and motored off with the boat.

ELECTRONIC NAVIGATION AIDS

Safety at sea is not bought with expensive equipment nor fancy calculations. Both are subject to operator error and other failures in a crisis. As Eric Hiscock was fond of saying, "The price of safety at sea is *eternal vigilance*".

If all you really need is a chart and a compass, then why spend the money on fancy electronic navigation aids? Well, the older I get, the mistakier I get. Once I missed the Dry Tortugas entirely. A pair of pliers left under the compass gave me a deviation of seventeen degrees.

Nature also makes mistakes, often enhanced by the bureaucracy. Each year there is a budgetary wrangle between the Air Force, NASA, and the Department of Commerce over hurricane surveillance responsibilities. It usually isn't resolved, but they begin to cooperate by late summer and cease abruptly on November 1st. If you don't believe it, watch the newspapers carefully as June 1 approaches.

December 19th, 1984, the **NWS** forecast continuing fine weather. We up-anchored and sailed for Georgetown from the north shore of Caicos. They came back 6 hours later with a hurricane warning for **hurricane** *Lilly* which they placed exactly 90 miles off my stern and blowing me northwest into the islands. *Lilly* was a small, tight 'cane, out of season and bearing no telltale feeder trails. She broke up early but spawned several days of gales throughout the area. *Lilly* was only a hiccup for Mother Nature, of no interest on Capitol Hill, but a major surprise to small boats.

When that hurricane forecast was received I was already on the run before it, surfing down ten footers with the log pegged at eight knots, and me, between curses, wondering what the heck was going on. For 36 hours we slowed our progress toward Exuma Sound, which, with only raging cuts to leeward, would be a **deathtrap** in those conditions, by zigzagging down breaking waves in continual darkness.

My oval of navigational uncertainty became so big, I still don't know if we passed the Plana Cays and the surrounding reefs on the west or the east. Three months later I had a **Satnav** on board.

In general, the more navigation aids, electronic or not, the better. Bless you for being affluent enough to afford them, clever enough to select the right ones from the welter of black boxes on the market, and patient enough to maintain them. Which devices will serve you the most on the way south? This list follows, like the last one, in priority order.

DEPTH SOUNDER

The **depth sounder**, or **fathometer**, is a much under-used tool among yachties. This navigation aid is only second to the compass. A reliable digital depthfinder in the cockpit is great for coasting. Tack in to 20 fathoms, tack out to 50, and so on. Additionally, there is some evidence that sounders left on, even when off soundings, deter broaching marlins and whales from coming up under the boat.

Finding your position off a coast where everything looks the same is child's play by using the **Chain of Soundings** method.

Chain of Soundings Method

This is a method of navigation that many of us use unconsciously while coasting in order to confirm the boat's position. With chart in hand, keep mental track of the soundings shown on the fathometer. If the readings of the fathometer do not agree with your expectations gained from the chart, you have reason to wonder where you really are.

By sailing a straight line and taking soundings at regular intervals one can arrive at a "signature" of the bottom which usually identifies only that line over that bottom. A somewhat complex, but unequivocal, way of doing it is to plot the readings to scale on a piece of clear plastic or tracing paper. Then move the tracing about on the chart until you have a match. Of course the bottom must vary, and sometimes the line is long and you have to get it all done before you've left the area and become lost again. As long as I am on soundings I prefer to just make mental note of the fathom lines as I cross them and never lose my chain of soundings in the first place.

VHF

Required. Get lots of channels. See *Using the Radio.*

AM/FM

Of course you have AM/FM aboard with cassette or CD player. You should also have a hand sized portable with a rod type extendable aerial in the emergency locker. If you have to abandon ship you can listen to all the religious stations that dot the Caribbean. But more important, you can use it as a highly reliable radio direction finder, homing in on island rock stations. Reception will be loudest when the aerial is perpendicular to the rhumb line to the station. Perhaps the combination of direction and religion will save you.

AUTOPILOT

I believe exhaustion has caused more accidents at sea than any other human factor, and like the "rapture of the deep", exhaustion takes its toll before you notice it. The **autopilot** is an absolutely necessary piece of equipment on any cruising boat. The trip to windward can be tiring enough without having to face the tyranny of the wheel. Autopilots are available today for ampere-poor sailing craft which have minimal current requirements: 3-5 amperes on duty, negligible current draw on standby. Most sailboats can sail themselves close hauled with a lashed helm and balanced rig, but the autopilot handles motorsailing better than a crew could. If you have both refrigeration and an autopilot, a fixed mount wind generator can handle the load to windward. Downwind you may not get the zaps from either alternator or wind generator to keep both the autopilot and the refrigerator going. For returning downwind you might want to snap on a self steering device such as the *Aries* wind vane.

SSB RECEIVER

For following the **National Weather Service** reports and the various cruiser nets you must have a radio capable of receiving **SSB**. A cheap portable with a "BFO" switch which can receive the frequencies is usually sufficient. Before you pay $300 for a SONY look at more professional gear which may even be cheaper in the long run and give much better reception. I had two of those small portable units which corroded. One of the older, larger models, however, lasted for years.

GPS

They come in a variety of models. Cheap is best. You both save money and eliminate confusion during operation. All GPS units seem to have the worst human factors built into their consoles since spark advance was eliminated from steering wheels. "Hooboy!", says the engineer, "if we connect the freemis to the gizzis, and you press these six buttons at once, you'll get the Gregorian date expressed in hexidecimal." "Grrreat!" explodes the marketeer, and into the machine it goes.

The more expensive models are loaded up with inane "functional add-ons". These are dohickeys the manufacturers make to keep up unit price in an expanding market. As an example consider 900 waypoints. Unless you're a fisherman or a smuggler on regular and complicated routes, you shouldn't need more than a few waypoints. Where you came from, where you're going (with a couple of options), a couple of real waypoints, and the location of a weather feature on which you may want range and bearing. Leave one or 2 waypoints to play with, and you've justified 10.

When road-based transportation installs GPS receivers *en masse*, then relatively low-cost, low-function units will be available to the yachtsman. Until then, they are expensive.

Plugging in your auto pilot for following routes of waypoints can be hazardous to your health. Course alterations remain the captain's perogative even in these modern times.

GPS Cautions

— Check every waypoint with charts when you enter it and adjust for sea room.

— While coasting, make your own fixes regularly by compass bearings and confirm with the GPS. This ensures your continuous recognition of land features.

— While planning or executing a crossing, keep **estimated positions** (EPs), *not* DRs (**dead reckoning**). EPs include current, leeway, tide, magnetic variation and magnetic deviation. Steering a straight line across the bottom may be the longest way to go for either sail or motor, especially in reversing tidal streams.

— Ignore entrance waypoints given by "helpful" yachties down to the hundredth of a mile (20 yards). The future shall see many yachts motored onto reefs while headed to an entrance or sea buoy waypoint. Get out your chart. Step up to a mile off of the entrance, and make that your waypoint, from where you will go on visual.

— A yachtie in **Luperón** took his dinghy to the little red ball inside the reefed entrance. Holding his hand on the buoy, he took several GPS readings and averaged them. Next morning he called southbound yachts on the SSB. Proud as Columbus, he told them of his venture with the "Luperón seabuoy" and advised them to replace the arrival waypoint in this book with his "more accurate" numbers. Among his hearers were other wannabe explorers who relayed the historic news. In the next month three boats went on the reef right in front of the hotel, the first ever in Luperón. If you cannot resist "super accurate" waypoints, discard your GPS.

— Use the same datum as the chart, or calibrate each chart as you use it by recording waypoints while positioned at charted features. Note the correction vector on the chart and apply the offset to GPS use (e.g., "0.25 nm NNE").

Never believe claims of accuracy, nor confuse accuracy with precision.

SSB Transceiver

If sailing in company and leap frogging each other this helps you keep in touch with your friends. It also helps you keep up with the rumor mill which is grinding between the cruisers on your path so you don't feel such a stranger when you arrive. Be careful about weather information received, however, as well as talk of piracy, revolutions, the sky falling in, and so on. Remember this is an entertainment medium. Pure marine SSBs with fixed channels are usually very powerful. The new breed of synthesized digital ham transceivers are less powerful but can be modified to permit marine transmission.

WEATHERFAX

There is too much information made available through the fax for the average cruiser. Even the scheduling problem can turn into a nightmare, what with large area charts, detail charts and satellite photos. Therefore, the best solution for the cruiser is one which combines the fax with a computer (as if your life wasn't complicated enough already). With a connection to a database you will be able to store only the images which relate to your navigational problem. Your computer will enable you to escape the machine while it regurgitates its endless rigmaroles on unusual sectors of the planet. If you have a computer, you can receive and store weather charts, satellite pictures, and even get the telex of the verbal **NMN** report. Finally, if you're a HAM, you can participate in bulletin-boarding through your radio. Gadgets are great. If you can afford them and if you can use them, go to it. But always get the NWS offshore report just the same in order to know what the experts think.

Compared to the **NWS** radio advisories, the fax data tends to cover very large areas. In reality **weatherfax**es transmit the source materials of the NWS forecasters you hear on the radio. Those guys have studied for years and went on to earn an incredible buck reducing their macro plots of micro data to a carefully considered verbal report with which mariners can make decisions within local areas. To second guess their interpretations seems dangerous. To do so at the exclusion of their analyses may be deadly.

RADAR

As with all electronics, think of your ampere usage and make sure you can handle it. Some can suck juice like a water maker. In the Caribbean, the radar isn't for fog, it's for confirming landfalls, finding buoys (whenever there are any), and 'lordy, lordy', plying a windward coast so close you can shake hands with the natives. For the singlehander, a well tuned four mile radar with a "fence" function may help keep watch on crossings.

RADAR REFLECTORS

Though not electronic, these devices need mention. *Yachting Monthly* showed the futility of anything but welded radar reflectors and the Japanese "goat's eye" solid type in a study done in 1978. We repeated their tests in Antibes the next year and got equally dismal results. Even the manufacturers produce reflectors that can't be mounted in the proper "catch water" attitude. I had used a fender full of aluminum chaff once until I discovered my mast steps were a better target. Radar transponders would be great if only you could get the radar officers to look at the radar within the time you've got between acquisition and collision. Besides the Japanese sphere, there is a Norwegian reflector, a small tube, which is reportedly quite good.

To calibrate your boat as a target, talk to seagoing tugs. They usually keep a good radar watch and the ones I've met will enjoy helping you.

If you haven't got a *tiki* aboard you might as well hoist the old radar reflector, it's marginally more effective than a *tiki* in avoiding collisions. Better to keep a good watch.

LORAN

Great for finding Ft.Lauderdale. Super for crossing the Great Bahama Bank. Depending on your machine's algorithms and tuner fidelity, Loran's can be reasonably accurate in the Exumas by using the TD's with corrections. Below the Exumas, the Loran stations, like Voice of America, if received at all, can give biased information and that's dangerous. An acquaintance swears his worked all the way to St.Thomas. But he also claims to sail 35 degrees to the real wind.

Radio Direction Finders

Unless you have a double loop, mast-mounted antennae tunable to AM, FM and VHF, forget it. In the Caribbean, there aren't enough airports and no marine beacons. Anyway, those low frequencies are only good for homing since any fix available from three shore based senders will have a cocked hat larger than the gap between you and the shore. I buried my last RDF in the North Sea.

Radar Detectors

They work, but ships often don't use their radar in the open sea, and if you're coasting or in a shipping lane, you better darn well keep your own lookout. Besides, these things chirp at such distances that you're never free of an alarm despite no ships in sight. If you squelch them to eliminate ships over the horizon, the controls are so rinky-dink you will squelch out the guy who is about to run you down.

HAM Radio

It certainly gets you invited to a lot of hamfests. And think of the telephone bills you'll save if you were going to have any. Whether a *Rowdy* or a *Good Citizen*, you will find a team to root for on the various *Deputy Dawg Shows* HAMsters run. During emergencies the HAM nets are of great help. Listen in to Hurricane Net 14325 LSB.

USING THE RADIO

VHF

FM Radio Telephony, or **VHF**, has reached an interesting stage of development. Rules for using the VHF were developed for poor reception. When Alpha wants to call Bravo, Alpha should say "Bravo, Bravo, Bravo; Alpha, Alpha" and Bravo should reply "Alpha, Bravo; *nn*", where *nn* is the number of a working channel to which they both repair.

Now that VHF provides high quality reception at a cheap price, every boob has one into which he speaks as would Thomas Alva Edison speak into the ear of Victorola's dog if he had expected the dog to speak back to him.

What's worse, today's Bravo has invented a lottery in which he asks Alpha to "Pick a channel". If he doesn't, then Alpha asks Bravo to do it. Although they call each other several times a day, they will usually pick channels which neither has. This is a noncommittal opening gambit used by VHF lottery players for whom tic-tac-toe is too advanced.

Bridge players will say "six eight" but not press the mike button until the word "eight", thus finessing the other guy into sitting on Channel 8 picking channels with no one. You can always tell a cruiser who plays chess. He will force Alpha to pick a channel first and then say "No, I don't have that, try another" until Alpha hits a good one. Then he talks in HAM codes and International Signals Code over the telephone. These guys also tend to call themselves "THE Bravo", which, incidentally, is against the rules in a few countries and not liked by the Coast Guard unless your transom says "THE Bravo". Guys that say "THIS IS THE Alpha" need severe correction. Guys that say "THIS IS THE SAILING VESSEL Alpha" should have their radios confiscated.

These are the same guys who play CAPCOM MCC (Capsule Communicator, Mission Control Center) and say "Affirmative" and "Negative" and "Roger That" 3 times each to a boat two hundred yards away. Deke Slayton took endless ribbing when he slipped up on acknowledging a complex transmission from space with "Roger ... uh ... that". He never repeated it. But today there is a whole new generation of Captain Videos to repeat it and other airwaves eating clichés — endlessly. Myself, I pretend to be Glenn Ford at the controls of his screaming Saberjet calling to his wingman . . .

In most anchorages VHF users are in good hail of each other on low power. In **Providenciales**, with 200 land stations and 50 boats, or worse, in **Georgetown** with 50 land stations and 400 boats, just following the normal rules with power down and squelch up will reduce traffic and hasten communications enormously.

The above discussion, as well as the following list of DOs and DON'Ts may be extended to the use of Marine SSB radios as well. *Please* don't clog the calling frequencies as did this actually recorded exchange, edited for brevity as it is.

A: Bravo, Bravo, Bravo. This is the Alpha. The Alpha.

B: Alpha, Alpha, Alpha. This is the Bravo. Bravo. Go ahead, Al. Got you 5x5.

A: Bravo, Bravo. Good morning, Ted! Have you got a frequency? Pick one.

B: Yeah. How about 6-alpha? Let's go to 6-alpha, 6-alpha. You copy?

A: No. I haven't got that one programmed. Not programmed. Pick another.

B: Oh. OK. Just a minute. . . . . How about 6-Beta? Let's try 6-Beta.

A: Yeah. Let's try 6-Beta. If not, come back here. 6-Beta. What's the frequency?

Here's a list of some *DOs* rarely *DONE*.

— turn your power down

— find an idle channel before talking

— talk normally, sideways to the mike

— wait thirty seconds for Bravo to answer

— get off Channel 16 with minimum chatter

— use the language your mother taught you

— make each transmission brief

— repeat only if asked

Here are some *DON'Ts* which are *DONE* more often than not.

— Don't call yourself anything but your name

— Don't talk HAM or CB, good buddy. QSL.

— Don't eat your microphone

— Don't repeat everything twice

— Don't use channels permanently assigned (e.g., USCG 21-23, commercial telephone 24-28, bridges 9 & 13, or local taxis, hotels and water sports outfits)

— Don't sit on your handheld's transmit switch, blocking all traffic for hours

— Don't chastise non-English speakers without understanding them

Don't be a Deputy Dawg. That's the guy who sits by his radio and busts in with chapter and verse of the Law of the VHF. He takes up more air time than casual abusers because his dictums are always followed by storms of support from the *Good Citizens* around and Bronx cheers from the *Outlaws and the Rowdies* in the harbor. Unless *Deputy Dawg* is a duly authorized official of the country whose air you are using, you can tell him to take his Barstool Regulations and . . .

CAUTION : never use "buddy channels" to the exclusion of Channel 16.

I recall the two yachts off Montecristi which crossed the steel cables of a 1500 foot tow at night, while the tug's skipper bawled on Channel 16, and I desperately dialed around to find their buddy channel. The hawsers could have sawn the boats in halves, sintering fiberglass and flesh in a heartbeat. It took instead a small bite from a skeg.

EMERGENCY PROCEDURES

Channel 16 is used for all emergency traffic as well as for calling and initial contacts. For this reason, your VHF should be left on and monitoring Channel 16 when not in use. There are three levels of ship's safety broadcasts: *securité* (say-CURE-it-TAYE, French for "safety"), *pan* (PAHN, Greek for "everywhere") and *mayday* (MAY-day, kind of French for "help me").

Broadcasts of navigational hazards come after the word *securité* said 3 times. For example, a sea mark out, or off position, or a tow restricting passage in a channel.

Broadcasts of lookouts for personal safety follow the word *pan* said 3 times. For example, when the Coast Guard has lost contact with an overdue boat, or when you have lost the ability to maneuver, but life threats do not exit.

Broadcasts of imminent danger to life proceed from the word *mayday* said 3 times. If your boat is sinking, if it's on fire, if someone has been lost overboard, or if there exists any immediate threat to life, do the following:

Ensure the VHF Radio is on Channel 16.

Clearly and slowly pronounce, "*mayday, mayday, mayday*".

Say your boat type and name, "sailing vessel (or trawler, or motor yacht) *Boatname*".

Clearly and slowly give your position, "one mile south of Esperanza on Vieques", or "latitude 1804, longitude 6528".

State the emergency simply, "sinking, sinking", or "man overboard, man overboard".

People handling emergencies at sea often get too busy to stand by the radio. In this case repeat the full *mayday* several times, hammering on position and type of distress. Force yourself to speak clearly, slowly and with a <u>minimum of words</u>. Everyone shall understand "man overboard" even with static and intermittent reception. No one can grasp the nature of a rapidly shouted "my husband was looking over the stern and fell in the water and I can't find him".

SSB

A yacht followed me out of **Luperón** when I took a window that I knew had a certain risk of collapse. While rounding **Cabo Francés** I heard him radioing a friend that he intended to stay in the open anchorage of **Rio San Juan**. That was my intention as well, until I heard the 6 p.m. weather and listened to Herb on *Southbound II*. The window was indeed collapsing. A stalled front had begun to move, leapfrogging itself in virtual velocities of 35 knots. I headed direct to Escondido, thinking to rest up and look at the weather again in the late evening. If the phenomenon continued I had just enough time to boogie around the corner into Samaná for refuge, something I couldn't do If I paused at Rio San Juan. Being caught out in either harbor in bad conditions could be disastrous.

Stupid me, I did what one must never do. I offered gratuitous help; something guaranteed to get you bit in the backside. I called the yacht behind me and advised the skipper of the weather changes and of what I intended to do to ensure my comfort and safety. He said he hadn't listened to weather all that day or the night before. Not for lack of a radio certainly, he was chatting to the whole world all during my run down the coast.

I arrived in **Escondido** and promptly went to bed, knowing I might be roused early from the anchorage by a bad weather report. The alarm woke me at the appointed hour and I tried to get the weather. None. The other yacht was now parked next to me, and he was gabbing on the band close by. I stayed up for the next 6 hours trying to get NAVTEX, SITOR, MORSE, SATPICS and at the end, NMN VOX again. Each time I began to get a report he started blabbing with relatives on nearby HAM frequencies or with cruisers over marine SSB. I couldn't raise him on VHF. His was off though he was in an isolated harbor with only two boats, and it should have been on for security. I finally got pieces of a report. The advancing front had slowed. My normal departure time was now only 2 hours away. I got no sleep. While I raised anchor, the guy doubled the insult. He popped up and wanted to know what I'd heard on the weather!

Do not tune up on any frequency on or near one which might be in use. Do not transmit on the same band that nearby boats might use to receive priority traffic.

RADIO TIMES AND FREQUENCIES

Atlantic Std. Time (UTC-4)	Station Call Sign	Freq. 1	Freq. 2	Freq. 3	Freq. 4	Broadcast and Source [see also Listening to the Weather]
530	NMN	4426	6501	8764		NWS Offshore Forecast, Portsmouth
600	WAH	4357	4381	8728	13077	All Forecasts, St.Thomas
	VOA	5980	6165	7405	9590	Voice Of America with news to 0800
630	WVWI	1000				VI Radio Sailor's Report (MTWTF)
635	Arthur	3815	HAM - LSB			West Indian Weather Net -- Barbados
655	WOSO	1030				San Juan weather hourly after news
700	BBC	6195	11865			World News to 0930
	BASRA	4003				Bahamas Air Sea Rescue weather net
	USB	6215				Antilles Cruisers net (all the way down)
705	4VEH	1030				NWS Offshore Forecasts, from Haiti
710	WVWI	1000				VI Radio Sailor's Report (MTWTF)
	BAR	790				Radio Barbados forecast
745	WWNET	7268	HAM - LSB			Waterway net US/Bahamas with WX
800	BON	800				Caribbean forecast, Bonaire
	ZNS1	810	1240	1540		Nassau weather
805	ZBVI	780	AM M-F David Jones WX			and ea. $^1/_2$ hr.; 745 Sats.; 945 Sundays
830	ANT	930				Antigua EC Forecasts (also at 18:25)
	David*	4009				Caribbean weather net with David Jones
845	David*	8104				Caribbean weather net with David Jones
900	WOM	4363	8722	13092	17242	NWS reports (and at 1900), after tfc list
	Maurice	6945	HAM - LSB			French weather net (also 13970 at 1900)
1000	WAH	4357	4381	13077		All Forecasts, St.Thomas
1200	NMN	13089	6501	8764		NWS Offshore Forecast, Portsmouth
1400	WAH	13077				All Forecasts, St.Thomas
1600	BBC	5975	6175	6195	7325	World News every hour to 2400
		9590	9915	11865	15400	....................other BBC frequencies
	Herb*	12359				SOUTHBOUND II, VAX498
1800	NMN	13089	8764	17314		NWS Offshore Forecast, Portsmouth
1900	BBC	5975	6165	9915		excellent financial news, again at 2005
1930	RNI	6020	6165			Netherlands Int'l, good English reporting
2000	VOA	5995	7405	9455	9775	US news with Caribbean report
2200	WAH	4357	4381	8728	13077	All Forecasts, St.Thomas
2330	NMN	4426	6501	8764		NWS Offshore Forecast, Portsmouth

* See chapter, *Listening to the Weather*

Distress & Calling	2182	4125	6215	8291	12290	16420	HAM Hurricane Net is 14325
Alpha	2065	4146	6224	8294	12353	16528	22159	NAVTEX San Juan FEC SITOR WX:
Bravo	2079	4149	6227	8297	12356	16531	22162	516.8 USB at 0600 then every 4 hours
Charlie	2638	4417	6230		12359	16534	22165	NAVTEX Miami FEC SITOR WX:
Delta	2738	†	6516	††			22168	516.8 USB at 0800 then every 4 hours

Expanded Ship to Ship Working Frequencies:
  † **4 MHz**: *from* 4000 to 4057 *every 3KHz.*
  †† **8 MHz**: *from* 8101 to 8110, 8116-8122, 8125, 8131-8191 *every 3KHz.*
Other working Frequencies: 18840, 18843   are **18** Alpha, Bravo
                              22171   is **22** Echo
                              25115, 25118   are **25** Alpha, Bravo

HAULING OUT

Possibilities to haul in the Dominican Republic exist but generally are not to be recommended. Multihulls and bilge keels can use the beaching facility at **Manzanillo** with good effect. Some materials are available in the hardware store in **Dajabón,** otherwise bring your own. Good labor is also available. A railroad lift exists in *Bahía de Cariñero* (careener's bay) in **Samaná, Columbus'**s old careening spot. You'll be quite historical if you haul there. You will be hysterical by the time you launch. Of course anything is possible with all materials and tools onboard and careful attention and guidance from the skipper. In an emergency there is a railroad **haulout** in **Puerto Plata.**

Puerto Rico is dotted with boatyards. You will have no trouble finding one for a quick haul and paint. For more extensive work, as always, shop around before committing.

If leaving your boat for the summer, consider hauling out and leaving it at **Ponce Yacht Club** (expensive), or **Palmas del Mar**, near **Humacao,** or *Puerto del Rey*, in **Fajardo.** *Puerto del Rey* is the largest marina in the Caribbean and very well equipped.

Las Croabas, Puerto Real and **Isleta** have little or no facility for long term storage but are good and fast haulouts. At Palmas del Mar, your boat can be laid up either ashore or afloat and the yard has a marine store with yard owner Hans Grossen as helpful as he can be. **Las Croabas** (*Varadero de Fajardo*) is do-it-yourself and usually cheapest.

The Yards in **Tortola**, *Tortola Yacht Services* at **Roadtown** and *Nanny Cay Marina* at **Nanny Cay** are quite professional. You may also haul or store at *Virgin Islands Yacht Harbor* at **Spanish Town** on **Virgin Gorda.**

Further down island you will find *Bobby's Marina* in **Phillipsburg, St. Martin**, the *Rodney Bay Marina* in **St. Lucia,** *Castries Yacht Service* in St.Lucia and *Prickly Bay Marina*, **Grenada**. In the past Castries has been reasonably priced, and you will do most of your own work. **Rodney Bay**, on the other hand is a well equipped and convenient yard with owner Arch Marez graciously officiating.

In the eastern cruising grounds of **Venezuela** there are two commercial steel boat building yards in **Cumaná.** The *Astilleros de Oriente* yard has a 100 ton Travelift, they do sand blasting in a pit dry dock so it doesn't usually spoil your brightwork and they are capable of any work whatsoever. They are short on English, however, so most of the yachties wait in line to take the railroads up at *Varadero Caribe*, also in Cumaná, which sand blasts everywhere but where they are long on English. Further east in the **Gulf of Cariaco is the Navemca** yard.

Speaking of haulout facilities — Cap Hatien Boatyard

63

Be aware that security at Cumaná requires remaining in the *Cumanagoto* marina while you wait your turn to be hauled. Instead of waiting in the marina you may go across the **Gulf of Cariaco** to anchor in the little bays and bayous. You may have better security there but you may lose your place in the yard's queue.

Puerto La Cruz has regular yacht yards with Travelifts (*Centro Marino de Oriente,* and *Amerigo Vespuccio* and *Enbuco* Marinas). Beware of lax security if you park the boat on the *Amerigo Vespuccio* side while waiting to be hauled. *Centro Marino de Oriente* (CMO), security arrangements are quite impressive. There are 3 levels of secure storage with vicious dogs patrolling the third, or inner, level.

Xenophobia has cost yachties more money and trouble than has divorce.

If **IMRON**-ing your boat, get your own paint at the Dupont store in either **Cumaná** or **Puerto La Cruz**. It will be cheaper than letting the yard get it, and you will be sure to have an exact match in the colors. Each store's personnel are extremely helpful. The yards are capable of beautiful paint work at half the costs found in the Virgins. Nonetheless, results can be quite uneven, perhaps dependent on the interest shown by the owner:

Too much supervision may be worse than too little; none can be disastrous.

Venezuela manufactures DuPont's **IMRON**. As a result of the local petroleum industry, the costs are much less than the US costs. Over the years I have brushed on Imron coats from the dinghy at **Bahía Mangle** in **Chimana Grande**, **Puerto La Cruz**, and in **Laguna Grande** in the **Gulf of Cariaco** for only 2% of the yard costs (1% Virgins). From 5 feet away you would never know it wasn't sprayed.

MOTORING TO THE CARIBBEAN

The way south not only has lots of motoring opportunities but today's yachts have lots of motor to do it with. Motoring while cruising to windward, however, is a different kettle of fish than motoring out to the sea buoy to set sail on a Saturday afternoon. Half your motoring will be close to all out revolutions. Half will be low revs while generating zaps for your refrigerator to run on, or to drive your engine driven compressor. If you escape the daily drill of generating electricity because you've got a diesel generator aboard, you may be in for double trouble with two motors.

Many good books are available to help you with diesel problems and their prevention. Here are some tips how to avoid problems, or plan for the inevitable ones when they come. Once again, these tips are only associated with the special punishments a diesel takes while cruising to windward.

MOTORSAILING

Every year the **Thorny Path** claims its crop of sailing purists and sportsmen. The typical enthusiast starts from **Great Inagua**, or **Mayaguana**, for instance, and sails directly for **Samaná**. After an exciting morning's beat into 4 to 7 foot seas with 12 foot breaking rogues, our heroes return to a grueling afternoon's beat into the same. After going through the carefully posted watch schedules a couple of times the crew begins to realize there won't be any clubhouse showers at the end of the day nor will there be any prize banquets and parties. Just the sour bunk to return to, sodden by the seawater spurting through the crack caused by separation of hull and deck.

As the challenge of the whole thing melts into a funk with expensive repairs at the end, Captain Courageous flicks the starter switch and goes over to motorsailing. If he can. Chances are the incessant pounding has sloshed up the muck at the bottom of the fuel tank and the engine won't start. That's why it's called the *Thorny Path*, folks! And that's why you should know the *Thornless* way.

Now, *Thornless Path* adherents not only select their passages and their **Weather Windows** for short and easy legs (see "Strategies for Passage Making") but they know the following basic rules of motorsailing and don't cavil at applying their auxiliary.

Switch the motor on when you need it to maintain the minimum average speed you had assumed in planning your landfall, and consider *falling off* to a safer, more comfortable tack.

When the engine is up to temperature make a flashlight tour of the engine room. Look for spotting from oil or water leaks and fog from exhaust leaks. Check the bilges at the same time. Repeat every hour or so.

Keep the jib up only if it helps you point better.

Keep the main up. Tack a bit if you're dead into the wind.

Know how much heeling you can take to avoid: sucking air through the raw water intake, causing an airlock in the cooling system and engine overheating; or siphoning seawater into the engine, if you have switched off while the anti-siphon valve is tipped under sea level.

Ensure the exhaust outlet is never under water while the engine is cooling. Following seas or heeling may cause seawater to be drawn up over the exhaust swan neck, flooding the engine. For downwind passages in the **Trades**, install a handy ball valve at the exhaust outlet. But remember to open it again when the engine is cool! Try tying the start key to the valve handle.

Always let the engine cool to its lowest operating temperature by running awhile at idle before cutting it off.

Ensure a goodly air supply to the engine by opening hatches if you have the usual tight and airless installation which was not meant to be high-revved for many hours in the tropics. You may need ducted fans to carry more air to the engine.

MOTOR MAINTENANCE

If you can't maintain your own diesel motor, stay home. There are few marinas and most of the "help" available is likely to leave you worse off than if you had done it yourself reading a shop manual.

BEFORE YOU LEAVE HOME

If you have been used to leaving the car for maintenance at the corner garage because business never left you the time to do your own maintenance, now is your chance to change. If you're really on the *Thornless Path*, you've got nothing but time. Get a shop manual before you leave home and do your own maintenance. When you screw up, you at least learn and won't do it again. If you let someone else do it, you will pay for the same screwup time after time. Review the next few pages. You may want to do some refit before leaving home.

The best preparation you can have is a course in diesel mechanics. Simple short courses are available almost everywhere through manufacturers such as Ford and Detroit (Perkins), or through your local adult education center. You can get independent of mechanics simply by going to your local high school one evening a week for 8 weeks. Some courses last only a single day. If you are not mechanically inclined, don't think you can't do it. Diesel engines are actually extremely simple. All you need is patience and a little logic to follow down and cure a problem.

The vast majority of engine problems on the *Thorny Path* come from contaminated fuel. You can finesse most of these problems by carrying a **Baja Filter** (see Glossary), using a good fungicide (not too much), and by preparing your installation with adequate filtration. What is adequate at home is not sufficient down south. Besides the manufacturer's engine mounted canister filter and the engine's lift pump filter, you should have at least one other filter and a water separator mounted between the tank and the engine. Make sure the filter elements are not decomposable by the fungicide you use.

It will be a good idea to mount a switchable fuel pump to get a few more hours of engine life when clogged fuel filters cause engine surging (fast RPM-ing) which is inevitably followed by engine death — the infamous **Surge And Die** syndrome (**SAD**). This installation also gives you a method of cleaning your tank without having to bucket out the fuel and strain it through tee-shirts.

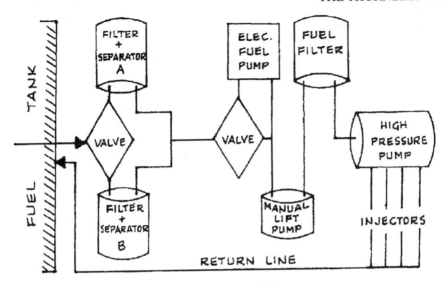

Keeping Your Fuel Clean

Not only does this installation give you better protection but the electric fuel pump gives you the ability to overcome clogged filters in order to make port. When you hear the engine start to surge, put the fuel pump in-line and switch it on. Once in port, you can also use the installation to clean your tank.

SPARE PARTS

If you have recently installed a new engine you may consider saving key elements of your old engine for spares: head, high pressure pump, water pumps, injectors, delivery pipes, exhaust elbow, starter motor, alternator and instrument senders. However, the following minimum spares should be aboard before leaving home. Products which meet your engine specifications probably are not available until Santo Domingo or San Juan.

> — complete gasket set
> — alternator
> — fuel filters (6 each)
> — oil for 6 changes
> — fungicide for 300 gallons fuel
> — vee belts (3)
> — water pump impellers (2 each)
> — oil filters (8)

THE DIRTIEST JOB IN THE WORLD

Changing oil on a diesel engine is undoubtedly the nastiest part of cruising. The job can be made somewhat easier by thorough preparation before starting. Flipping settee cushions looking for the new oil filter is best done before your hands are covered with black goop.

Invest in a filter wrench and lots of 3-ply garbage bags before you leave. Also have a good stock of old newspapers and save those plastic gallon jugs with which to dump the old oil. If you don't have a scavenge pump, have a funnel standing by (a cut off bleach bottle top works fine). Even better, install a petcock in place of your pan drain plug.

Good, strong garbage bags are almost unobtainable outside US territory. Have a year's supply on hand.

Scavenge pumps are fine for getting most of the old oil out but they don't get the gunk in the bottom of the pan. Accumulation of this stuff is what ruins your engine. It is usually best to get the last of the old oil out through the drain plug in the bottom of the pan. If your installation has an angle which prevents complete drainage you should consider having a new hole drilled and tapped in the pan.

It's a good idea to flush the engine from time to time. As an alternative to a mineral spirits flush every couple 100 hours you can flush each time you change oil by using one more quart of oil than necessary. After draining the old oil and before taking off the old filter, add one quart of fresh oil. With the fuel cut off (engine kill switch "on") run the starter for 20 seconds, pause a few minutes and do it again. Drain the engine again, change filters and add the new oil. This procedure will cost you a quart of oil every time you change but it may add thousands of hours to your engine's life.

As with many engine jobs, your cleanup is easier if you start the job with a little **Joy** dish soap rubbed under and around your nails.

MOTOR FAILURES

Every skipper has his own style going to windward. Some motor more than others. The trail south is littered by broken engines which were abused by skippers who didn't **Wait for Weather,** but bucked right into short, steep seas for dozens of hours with the throttle wide open. The boat manufacturers generally do not anticipate this use of the auxiliary engine when they install them. Neither do boat owners generally ask much of their engines until they meet the conditions going south. You should check your engine's specifications for the heel angle it will tolerate and don't exceed it for long periods.

Below are listed the usual engine failures one finds on the *Thorny Path* south. You can make it a *Thornless Path* for your engine by either modifying your installation before leaving home, or not leaving port in the conditions which abuse your engine. A truly **Leisure Sailor** will do both.

Fuel System

Motoring into heavy chop will thoroughly emulsify whatever is in your fuel tank and, if the tank is nearly empty, give your fuel pump a good gulp of air between sloshes.

The **SAD** syndrome (Surge And Die) will come from air being sucked into the system as well as clogged filters and water in the fuel.

If running dangerously low on fuel, you can supplement diesel with mineral spirits from your lamp oil supply. You can throw in some transmission oil to thicken the brew if you use more than a couple of gallons. I know a German engineer who made port with a mixture of vegetable oil, engine oil and gasoline. Shake well before using. And don't forget the oregano if your engine's Italian.

Dirty fuel is all you can buy in the Caribbean so plan on having it. Use a **Baja Filter** when adding fuel. See sketch on page 67 for a description of a good filter and pump installation to combat the problem.

COOLING SYSTEM

Your engine can overheat for hundreds of reasons, but motoring to weather in tropical heat exposes you to all of them. When it happens, which it will, check:

— weed clogged raw water through-hull fitting

— gulping air while heeling and pitching (airlock)

— clogged raw water strainer

— raw water strainer too small for flow volume

— water pump impeller going or gone (salt or fresh)

— water pump belt slipping or gone

— heat exchanger clogged

— thermostat jammed.

Most raw water pumps have a weep hole in the shaft housing between the pump seal and the engine oil seal. If you don't have one at the bottom of the housing, bore a quarter inch hole to permit weeping. This will prevent water from getting through your oil seal, which is meant to keep oil in, not water out, and ruining the engine. Most weep holes are small. Salt and corrosion will seal them up, preventing them from doing their job.

Powering off sandy ground in the Bahamas can etch pump shafts and undermine the seals. Volvo motors have high pressure raw water pumps guaranteeing an effective sand-blasting of the shaft. Water in your engine's oil, due to blown pump seals or gaskets, will show up as milky streaks in the jet black dirty diesel motor oil. If it just started, look for drops of condensed steam clinging to the bottom of the oil filler cap after running hot.

If you waited until you had a gully washer pouring into the oil galleries, watch for a fountain of hot gray oatmeal-like stuff to come foaming out of the blown oil filler cap. Better you check for the water droplets on the filler cap before it happens.

EXHAUST SYSTEM

The most dangerous prospect for your engine is intrusion of the sea into a cylinder through an open exhaust port. Water can get into your exhaust manifold by several means, not limited to those already discussed in *"Motorsailing"*. Corrosion in the exhaust elbow's water injection jacket will not be noticeable from the outside but, with some installations, it is possible for water to drip back into the manifold this way. Know how your elbow is constructed and check it before leaving.

If you have a water muffler such as the wet exhaust VernaLift type, make sure the tank is large enough to hold all the water from a full swan neck. The volume of water in your swan neck is the length of hose to maximum rise multiplied by half the inside diameter squared (Vol = Length x πR^2). Make sure your swan neck is high enough to motor heeled in high seas and your outlet won't spend a good deal of its life under water.

Throw away those bronze anti-siphon valves and replace them with plastic ones. While you're doing it, raise the anti-siphon valve and its U-fitting higher than the level of sea can conceivably come without your boat turning turtle.

Chafe, the bane of the windward yacht can hole your exhaust hose. That's not mortal but it sure is messy. One prevention that's easy is to always idle your engine until the operating temperature has bottomed out before cutting it off. If you attempt to start your engine and it doesn't budge, count your blessings. The attitude of the stroke when it stopped was such that the flooded cylinder compressed before another one fired. Water being basically incompressible, your starter can only sit there and hum a tune. Had a dry cylinder fired your engine would be scrap.

Many of these problems occur on yachts on their first real sea trials motorsailing the thorny path. If you elect to bash into it and cause these problems, it will be apparent by the time you reach the **Dominican Republic**. Get new parts out of **Santo Domingo** and fix it before going on. If you continue in the same style, the next 200 miles to Puerto Rico will be the *coup de grace* for your engine. You can find anything in the DR and the labor, if you use it, is cheap and can be good.

If you have seawater incursion do the same thing you did when you dropped the outboard motor overboard. If you haven't done that yet, not to worry, you will soon.

1. Take off the injectors until you find the flooded cylinder.

2. Crank to expunge the water.

3. Pour in some diesel or mineral spirits and crank again.

4. Put back the injectors, bleed the fuel system and get underway again.

Different from resuscitating an outboard, you don't have to change the gear oil in the lower unit. There isn't any.

ELECTRICAL SYSTEM

This guide does not intend to provide a treatise on boat electrics. Many fine reference works are readily available to thoroughly confuse you. The intent here is to give you warning of what's unique to **Passage Making** south. What you will see for sure are charging problems and more charging problems. You can have wind generators, solar panels, automated battery charging systems and generators separate from the auxiliary. You'll still have charging problems. Especially if you have an electric refrigerator with less than 6 feet of insulation and more than one cube's ice making capacity. The wind won't blow, the sun won't shine, all your charging connections will corrode and generate more heat than they carry electricity, and your diodes will blow.

Law of boat electrics: Consumption expands beyond the capability to supply it.

Carry a spare alternator and get the burned out one fixed or rewound in the **Dominican Republic** or **Venezuela**. Anywhere else is prohibitively expensive if it can be done at all. In **Puerto Plata**, hop a *motoconcho* and tell the driver to take you to *Manuel, el Eléctrico* [man-WHALE, ail aye-LECK-tree-koh]. Don't ask the dock boys.

The most frequent cause of electric failures is chafe. Before you leave home do a thorough review of all wiring runs. Invest in good metal jawed cable ties and tie them everywhere. Make a wiring diagram of the whole boat including motor and instrument panel.

Have a good multimeter and know how to use it to debug the system. If you rewire anything use one or two gauges heavier than called for and use tinned stranded wire. Label everything and turn square corners with the runs. In short, failures will happen. Have a system that can be quickly debugged. Have aboard *Spa Creek's 12 Volt Doctor's* and *Alternator Handbook*s.

Here's a gift: while cleaning up your engine's wiring, install a momentary switch on the hot line to the starter solenoid as it runs through the engine room. You'll use this for bleeding the fuel system at the injectors.

CUSTOMS AND IMMIGRATION

I am convinced the customs and immigration officials of the world meet every February in Den Hague to formulate plans for confounding guide writers. They get merit points for attending seminars in changing procedures rapidly. Find a good bartender or a cheap gourmet cafe and they'll be around at least six months, long enough to make the final proofs. Then the bartender will run off with the cook the day you go to press. Customs, however, has a plan. They change it every ten boats that enter. If someone tells you, "Here's how you clear customs in Gerfunknik!" you are probably better off doing the opposite of that which is suggested. That said I'll try my best to ease the experiences for you.

TIPS ON CLEARING CUSTOMS EASILY

In general, your experience with clearance officials will be dependent on your presentation. Have your boat and yourselves presentable. Have your papers in order: ships papers, passports and clearance out (*despacho* or *zarpe*) from your last port. Crew lists help in Spanish speaking countries or if you use agents. Most other countries ask you to fill out their form.

Smile, be honest, friendly and courteous. *Don't ask questions*. Look bored. Never bribe. You may get in trouble and once started it never stops.

The customs guys all over the world are trained to use their sixth senses. If you're tired from the trip and harried by the hassle of mooring in a strange place you may give odd responses to them. Get some sleep before dealing with guys who are just doing a job. Reread "Pirates!". Clear into ports which "specialize" in yachts, or anchor around the corner with your yellow Q flag flying, and get a good night's sleep before entering.

In places where they don't have many yachts you must realize that you are an intrusion on their management of a port and are a pain in the neck for low paid working men. If you think the Dominican Republic, for instance, is in dire need of your big time cruising kitty bucks, and they should receive you like a major relief to the national debt, then think again. Puerto Plata Province gets up to $200 a night from each passenger aboard the constant stream of jumbo jets laden with European and Canadian tourists. Some waiting may be required as there is only one man available from each of the Customs, Port Authority and Immigration Services. They may be handling a freighter or a cruise ship or be at lunch or a girlfriend's, so just be patient.

FIREARMS

The most abused word among American yachties going south is *"confiscation"*. When one yachtsman sues another for damages after anchor dragging and dock whomping in a storm, the sued boat is put under a lien to prevent it from leaving port, the easiest way to avoid paying the damages. This is a normal and, for fellow boaties, often entertaining practice at all US marinas. When it occurs in **Puerto Plata,** or **Cumaná**, the **SSB** channels buzz with talk of the locals "confiscating" yachts. Also, while headed home to the DR, I often meet disgruntled gun nuts headed north. Like Yosemite Sam, they wave their arms and stomp about and yell, "They **CON**-fiscated mah **WEP**'ns!"

All countries can hold onto your arms and even your bonded stores while you're in port, the US included. They may decline to check your arms depending on their own criteria such as the length of your stay, the length of your hair, security of your bonded locker and so on. The US, where military assault rifles are hawked on every street corner, doesn't bother. Puerto Rico usually won't, but the USVI will.

The **Dominican Republic** and **Trinidad** usually bother. Once, in Samaná, during a particularly rabid spate of motor snatching, the comandante told the yachties to keep their guns and put them into service to save him the trouble. The DR will normally check your weapons at each port of entry. They are not *confiscated* and are always returned promptly in good condition. Once I even had mine cleaned (because they'd fired it). The **British Virgin Islands** and **Turks and Caicos** often want to check in your firearms as well, especially if you intend to stay a week or more.

If you sit long at a dock where gun-checking goes on, you shall rapidly become aware how some yachts carry enough arms to look like mercenaries out to overthrow the local government.

Often enough boats have had their fancy weapons turn up "missing" when they went back to clear out. I've never heard of that happening in the Domincan Republic nor in Trinidad. The best insurance against such official piracy is to use the same procedure advised above to avoid hassles: check in at yacht-only ports of entries wherever possible. Better yet, don't have any arms aboard your vessel.

Finally, make sure your clearance-in papers are correct with respect to serial numbers and ammunition counts. If it's all checked on the way out and mistakes had been made, you're in for a major bureaucratic nightmare. Bullet counts are often off by one and corroded serial numbers are easily misread. Get it right on the way in.

EVERYBODY'S DIFFERENT

THE BAHAMA ISLANDS

Clearing into the **Bahamas** is getting more expensive. Coming from the south it's usually a freebie. Recently, however, the antidrug smuggling effort has required boardings and charges have been added for use of marina docks. Clearing in at the **Nassau** fuel docks while watering up and refueling can be cheaper. Clearing out of the Bahamas isn't necessary, and they don't want to do it. Show your clearing in card at your next port. Refer to *Gun Cay* and *Cat Cay* sections for more recommendations relative to the Bahamas.

TURKS AND CAICOS

The procedures in these islands vary from season to season and even from island to island. Once, coming from the south, I was cleared in by a lovely young lady of high school age in the government house on **Salt Cay**. Often I was charged nothing at all in **Sapodilla Bay**, but other times it was $3, $5, $20 and $28. Once, in **Turtle Cove**, I was charged a $49 for a 16 hour visit to the country to pick up a crew member.

The founder of the old Sapodilla Bay Aquatic Center asked me to accompany him to a meeting with the head of immigration. He wanted to discuss the rules for clearance and the requirements of the yachts using his facility. We were told that the rule was to charge overtime and transportation for officials (even if you transported yourself to them and not vice-versa) if your boat, upon arrival, was within their territorial limits outside their office working hours of 0830-1200 and 1300-1630. A little arithmetic and chart work will show these conditions shall be met 100% of the time. He grinned, and the meeting was over. My host left the island not long after. If things have changed since going to print, not to worry, they'll change again.

The officials, the expatriot inhabitants and the yachties at **Provo** will all press on you the *inflexible gospel* of how it really works the day you arrive, as though it always has and always will work that way. They'll tell you, "Oh, that's just one person's experience one time." It's been my experience *dozens* of times. Just smile and pay. See also the section on **Sapodilla Bay**.

HAITI

Ports of entry on the north coast are **Cap Haïtien** and **Fort Liberté**. At each port you will be boarded by 4 or 5 officials. One must be firm in allowing only one member from each bureaucracy aboard to inspect one's papers, else the whole town will be roosting on your settees. Coffee in the morning or a cold drink in the afternoon is appropriate while all the paper work gets accomplished. Any firearms will be taken for safe keeping until you leave. The costs of clearing in will depend on the yacht but in any case should be only a few dollars unless you arrive on a Sunday or outside office hours, which are variable. There are usually no costs for clearing out.

Cap Haïtien is a large commercial port which has seen busier days. A yacht will have no problem getting full attention clearing in. Moor on the south side of the main pier between any freighters on the east end of the long quai and small fishing vessels on the west end.

Fort Liberté has had the same *Capitain du Port* for many years, M.Herns Calixte, whose office is at the foot of the old town dock. The skipper should dinghy in with his papers and ferry out the officials if they haven't already found transport. The dinghy dock of the *Bayaha Hotel*, a 200 yards to the south may also be used and offers the convenience of a good ladder.

THE DOMINICAN REPUBLIC

Bear in mind that the DR is not a yachting country. For many years it maintained itself drug and violence free by applying maritime conventions rigorously. As far as procedures are concerned your yacht is a tanker. **Luperón**, opened specifically for yachts, is an exception to this attitude. In other ports they are more like the US. They clear foreign vessels in and out of every port and, *theoretically*, you are allowed to go ashore only where a customs house exists. If you're nice, the local guy will invite you ashore anyway.

If you can't manage the dock in a stiff breeze, the skipper should row ashore alone with all his papers and without his firearms and follow the instructions of the uniformed, and normally armed, person in charge (i.e., not a khaki clad dock worker hoping to get a job washing your boat).

With courtesy and understanding it will all be handled easily. For instance, don't wave at them and go below for an extended time. Stay in sight and use your actions to communicate clearly your preparations to come ashore to the official doing the waving.

Once in Puerto Plata, I heard a yachtie complain that the *Comandante* was irritated at him. No wonder! He interrupted his breakfast to do them a courtesy between visiting a tanker and a cruise ship and the idiot yachtie went below to have a shower and his own breakfast before coming ashore. Needless to say, under those circumstances the *Comandante* and his officers wander off out of the sun and don't eagerly come back for you.

Anyway, if you follow this guide you arrive in **Luperón, Puerto Plata, Samaná** or **Manzanillo** in the *early morning calm* when you can easily make the piers, if necessary, and easily get your anchors set. Often the officials prefer you anchor out.

The little cards they gave you when you came into the Bahamas work as Bahamian clearance out devices while entering the DR, but if you go into **Turks and Caicos**, you should have clearance out from there.

There is a tourist card charge for each passport entering the country by any means. It is $10 for 90 days in country. Sometimes they run out of forms, and it may become free. Of course the SSB nets will report it was free, so the next yachties to pay $10 a head can report up and down the islands that they got ripped off by gun-toting officials. There may be a port fee for each boat entering the country. In Luperón it was recently a gratuity.

To extend your visa simply take it to the immigration officers before it expires. They'll extend it without question and no charge as often as you like, unless you are an undesirable. They're nonchalant about how long you and your boat are there because, [a] you spend money, and [b] if you're a bad actor, they'll find out and make you wish you'd never come. See also each section on the individual DR ports.

PUERTO RICO

Non-US vessels, and vessels with nonresident *aliens* aboard (what Americans call foreigners, I'm afraid), must check into Puerto Rico at official ports of entry, which means **Mayagüez** on the west coast. This is an industrial harbor with poor facilities for yachts. By noon the wind is up and your position might be uncomfortable. Arriving in the early morning, or even before morning with the good ship's buoyage which marks the port, you will be able to clear in and get out before the wind is up. See the section on Mayagüez.

US vessels can clear Customs in **Puerto Rico** by phone from their landfall.

Call US Customs between the hours of 0800 and 1700 at the following locations.			
Coast	City	Location	Phone Numbers
west coast	Mayaguez	commercial pier	831-3342, 43
south coast	Ponce	Playa Ponce	841-3130, 31
east coast	Fajardo	Puerto Real Customs House	863-0950, 4075, 0811, or 0102
north coast	San Juan	Muñoz Marín Airport	253-4533, 34, 35, 36
Vieques	Isabel	airport	741-8366
Culebra	Dewey	airport	742-3531
St. Thomas, USVI	Charlotte Amalie	ferry dock	
St. Johns, USVI	Cruz Bay	ferry dock	
St. Croix, USVI	Christiansted	dockside	
Outside office hours call the Customs office in San Juan at 253-4533 or 253-4536.			

Reportedly one can try a toll free number also: 1-800-474-9253.

While Customs, a profitable bureaucracy, goes out of its way to provide courteous and efficient service at the convenience of the returning citizen, US Immigration maintains a confusing, often belligerent, stance despite many attempts to obtain clarification. Specifically, Immigration states they have "the right to inspect the passports" of returning citizens. One lone Immigration officer in Mayagüez interprets this to require the physical presence of crew *and boat* in Mayagüez harbor. His policy to demand presence of the boat is unwritten, unique in my experience, and it is arbitrarily enforced. Landing at

Boquerón and taking a *público* to Mayagüez if necessary is not allowed on his watch.

Otherwise, Customs will advise if they want your boat present when you call them. Customs requires a current sticker (*a cruising permit* for *citizens!*) in both the USVIs and Puerto Rico. They'll tell you where and how to buy one if you don't have one.

US VIRGIN ISLANDS

US vessels coming from Puerto Rico don't need to clear into the US Virgin Islands, but they do need to clear going back to Puerto Rico, because the USVI is a free port.

BRITISH VIRGIN ISLANDS

In the **British Virgin Islands** check in at **Jost Van Dyke** or at the Virgin Gorda Marina at **Spanish Town.** Never check in at **Roadtown** and avoid the Customs at **West End, Tortola,** like the plague. In both of these places, 2 out of 3 trips will go smoothly, but one of the 3 will find you tangled in a fine mess of charter people and cops. There are various official money-making schemes afoot in the BVI's which may catch yachts in charter boat snares. Get all the current stories in the USVIs before leaving, and, check in at my recommended spots of Spanish Town or Jost Van Dyke to avoid hassle and extra expense.

THE LEEWARD AND WINDWARD ISLANDS

The British Lesser Antilles islands usually give more hassle than French or Dutch. France never charges, but they can be sticklers for ship's papers, the islands being a real part of France and, thereby, the Common Market.

Clearing in and out from the English speaking islands is a new procedure every year. At best, the officials in the main harbors are brusque. At worst, they intentionally hassle you, not for money, but for the fun of it. This is only true in the English speaking islands, however. It's best to steer clear of commercial harbors and their official hassles. Go instead to the tourist harbors like **English Harbor, Antigua,** or **Rodney Bay, St.Lucia**. There you will usually be greeted by less antagonistic and more tourist-friendly officials.

If making a rapid passage down the islands and *not going ashore*, there is normally no need to check in. Fly a Q-flag all the way down as a declaration that you haven't cleared in. No one can accuse you of sneaking around if, by chance, an official with his hand out boards you while you are at an anchorage for a single overnight .

Costs for cruising permits seem to vary each year, or perhaps with the official. Some countries choose to levy these, others don't. Some levy "cruising permit" charges depending on your estimate of the time you will spend there. Going ashore one night only while passing St.Vincent could cost you some bucks. Once again, check into the tourist spots. In **St.Vincent** that would be **Bequia**. Recent information should be sought for the area, but for the official policy ask an official for a written description.

Clearing in and out of **Grenada** can be done at the crumbling *Grenada Yacht Services* facility in the lagoon. If you can't find anyone, dinghy over to the bonded port area on the east side of the main harbor. See below for getting a Venezuelan visa here.

VENEZUELA

Clearing in and out in **Venezuela** can be complex with many places to go and everyone, including the taxi drivers, with their hands out, for servicing yachts. Agent services are often available for yachts. For a few dollars they will take care of everything for you while you drink beer under a palm tree. I recommend using them for anything rather than face the hassles. In **Puerto La Cruz,** call Marisol on VHF channel 16. In **Pampatar** inquire at the beach restaurant. In **Porlamar,** call VEMASCO on VHF channel 16.

Venezuela has an economy in crisis which is government controlled (perhaps that's why the crisis). From time to time things happen like soldiers in combat boots boarding you and telling you that you have too much coffee, or beer aboard. Keep your cool and give them what they want: often just some coffee or beer. And a chance to see a yacht. The alternative is to learn all the export controls before shopping, and they can change monthly.

Venezuela Entrance Visa

Venezuela has in the past required an entrance visa. Recent changes of law promote yacht tourism by permitting boats to seek tourist visas and boat permits upon arrival without previously having received an entrance visa (similar to tourists who arrive at airports).

To Get the latest official procedures while in Puerto Rico:
Call the Venezuelan Consulate in San Juan. It is on the 6th floor of the Mercantil Plaza Building, Ponce de Leon Avenue on the south side of the bridge between Hato Rey and Santurce.

San Juan Consulate: 787-766-4250

You may also fax the *comándancia* for all *Capitanías del Puertos* in Carácas. If a voice answers, tell them to put on the fax tone or to give you the number of their fax (*tono de fax, por favor*, or, *cual es el número de fax?*)

Directorate of Capitanías: 011 (58) 2-509-2722, or 011 (58) 2-509-2881

The actual duration of your stay in Venezuela shall be established at the border when they stamp your passport. Stay beyond the specified duration, and you shall be asked to pay fees to extend your stay in country. The boat's permitted time in country also shall be established at the time you clear in. You shall be issued a cruising permit. According to the *Dirección de Navegación Acuatica* in their instruction to the *Capitanías* of all ports on 28 July 1997, you may request 6, 12 or 18 months stay for your yacht, and you shall be assessed a fee of 10,800 Bolívares for each period of 6 months or less: around $20US for 6 months, $40US for a year. Yachts may leave the country for up to 45 days without affecting their cruising permits. Over 45 days, however, and you lose your permit and must apply again. See Chris Doyle's Venezuelan Guide for up to date details.

Trinidad

Call ahead to the *Trinidad and Tobago Yacht Club* on VHF channel 16 for the latest scoop how to enter. It changes. For a while now it has been at Chaguaramas. If not there, and with no advice to the contrary, act like a big ship as follows:

After entering **Port of Spain** harbor, motor eastward close to the docks, past the sea-going tugs, until you see the ricketiest, tackiest little wooden wharf to be seen. It will front a small wooden building where Immigration hides out. Follow their lead for the rest of the procedure in clearing in. See Chris Doyle's Trinidad & Tobago Guide for up to date details.

It can be hilarious if you've got your sense of humor. If not, don't go. Port of Spain has growing yacht traffic, and a large number of functionaries from many ministries, all looking to serve you (or at least fill their day). Each official knows some of his department's procedures but none of the others', nor will he know the overall procedure. Rather than ask, "Where do I go from here?", it's best to take your currently assigned factotum by the arm and say, "Can you show me to the next step, please?" He or she may use the opportunity to schedule a car from the government car pool which will take another half day. You get a free tour of the town with pleasant company. Don't knock it.

Nonetheless, the officials at Port of Spain are the nicest you will run across in the whole Caribbean and the people all over the island are uniformly cheerful, friendly and outgoing. Don't be scared off by their high crime statistics unless you are married to a Trinidadian. Most violence is domestic.

RETURNING TO THE US

They've flipped on us again. This time *in our favor*: something must be wrong. Returning citizens call 1-800-432-1216 to get cleared by telephone, or to get further instructions. Aliens (human ones) who chance to land outside an official port of entry could try the same number to get information on what steps are necessary.

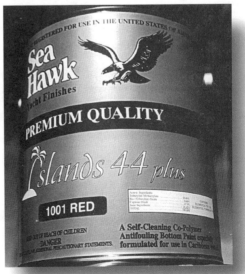

STRATEGIES FOR PASSAGE MAKING

<u>NOTE</u>: Assume *prevailing conditions* (see Glossary) **unless specified.**

The intention of this book is to help cruisers plan <u>windward passages</u> on the way south, *not* to give the cruiser a precise road map and timetable for the cruise. Its guidance on passage routing gives the cruiser safe and comfortable passages between cruising grounds.

Descriptions of the islands, and the anchorages themselves, are provided to support the sailing directions when required. There is no intention to rehash information adequately covered in the guides for the Bahamas, the Virgins, the Leewards, Windwards and South America. Use them to cruise those areas. Use this guide to transit between them.

When you have tired of cruising one area, and you are ready to move on to the next, you must have a specific strategy in mind while planning the passage: a strategy to move you to windward from point A to point B with *safety* and *comfort*: a **thornless** passage.

This section of the Guide provides cruisers with the planning strategies essential to creating their own **Thornless Path** between their chosen landfalls. These are the rules of the **Leisure Sailor** which, when inflexibly adhered to, create a delightful cruise. Seemingly rules of elementary seamanship, which we all should know, all the disasters I have met while going south have generated from the failure to obey any <u>one</u> of these axioms.

WAIT FOR WEATHER

I am always amazed at retired cruisers, who, with nothing but time, and having piddled around in harbor for weeks, even months, suddenly break into hives if they can't go *<u>right now</u>*! Others insist on going "next Tuesday", or "on the 22nd". Year upon year, like the *Tortoise and the Hare*, I find myself passing cruisers who are all holed-up with repairs and breathing hard.

These are the folks whom earlier I would watch go stir-crazy waiting for a break in the weather. They give up their wait and go to sea because, as they say, "It's rolly here."
I would change to a less rolly anchorage.

Or they say, "it's best to take bad medicine all at once."
I would try not to take any bad medicine at all.

Seasoned salts say, "We've got a strong boat."
I've got a strong boat, but there's a weak me inside it.

The stoic downeaster usually says "We've seen worse!"
I remember all my worses all too well. I won't repeat them.

And everyone uses the "well, we were with a group and ..." excuse.

If you want good passages rather than good excuses, learn to interpret the weather forecasts, sea conditions and **land effects**, and thoroughly understand the concept of *weather windows*.

WEATHER WINDOWS

The word *window* was often applied in the manned spaceflight program to indicate a favorable conjuncture of complexly interacting variables, the solution to which required detailed analysis and great precision. It began with familiar concepts of windows for launch, orbit insertion and reentry, but soon spread to all the esoteric disciplines of that great endeavor. I may have aided its currency in the cruising world, and it annoys me to find it most often used with shallow understanding.

In or near the **Trade Wind** belt, the weather is cyclic and regular. There are periods of low, or altered, activity in the Trades which are *windows of escape* from normally strong windward weather. They can be used by the thornless cruiser. **Weather Window**s are the conjuncture of favorability in the cyclic wanderings of four different parameters:

> **wind strength,**
>
> **wind direction,**
>
> **height of wave *and* swell,** and
>
> **direction of swell.**

In combination with perturbating weather features, a window may both widen in favorability and lengthen in time. Short windows are for short hops. Long windows are for **several short hops.** Long hops should be reserved for windows both long and wide.

The basic problem is how to cruise to windward without beating your brains out or performing marathon stunts against any of these conditions while they are adverse.

Depart only when favorable conditions prevail and shall be sustained for a day longer than you need to make safe harbor.

This will be when the winds **back** or **veer** to permit reaching or running, or, if you must beat, when the easterly **Trades** have moderated to less than 15 knots with seas 3-5 feet.

A **weather window** starts *only after swells have abated*, but when it starts, take the leading edge of it and *don't delay*. If you really want to attend one more beach bonfire, or one more dance at the Peace and Plenty, or you already invited the boat next door for cocktails, then enjoy yourself and wait for the next window so you can sail in leisure. Don't drink up half the **Weather Window** in harbor and bank on the second half holding up for you. Take a new window rather than risk getting the current one slammed shut on your tail.

A **Wait for Weather** means taking advantage of the periodic switching of the prevailing easterlies between northeast and southeast due to the wandering of the **Trade Winds,** and, in winter, by the passage of **fronts**, or, in summer, the passage of **tropical waves.**

If you feel you haven't got time to wait for an appropriate **Weather Window**, if you feel pressed to make your next cruising ground as soon as you can, closely examine your motivation and play it off against your reasons for cruising, and more importantly, your safety. If you press on in 20 knot Trades and 5 to 8 foot seas in a 35 to 40 foot boat with a small auxiliary engine, you are pleading for disaster to overtake you. When it doesn't, you haven't cheated it, it will only be that much more of a disaster next time.

Some waits may last longer than a week, but rarely. It may seem that a window will never open. Both 1991 and 1994, for example, were years in which the *Christmas Winds* came as they should, but they stayed into hurricane season. Even in those tougher than usual years, cycles of moderation appeared regularly, if less frequently, than usual. The

Offshore Forecast, the one you should be listening to, showed 2-3 day windows of 15-20 knots, 4-7 foot seas at least twice monthly. It is more usual to have frequent windows of 10-15 knots, 3-5 foot seas, in the summer months; 10-20 knots, 4-6 foot seas, in the winter months. 1997 was a vintage year for windows, many of which went unrecognized.

The weather you wait for may not always look that good to you at first glance. See **"Grim and Gray is Great Going"**. Good sailing days are like good lovers, as my mother used to say: "They're like buses. There's another one right around the corner if you're looking for it." And if you're not looking for it, or don't know what to look for, you'll spend your life getting neither. You must *know* what to look for.

KNOWING WIND AND WEATHER FEATURES

The path travelled, the island harbors selected, the safety and comfort objectives of the thornless path described in this book are each singularly dependent on the skipper's knowledge of, observation of and advantageous use of the effects of wind and wave *at the margin of land and sea*, especially the **night lees**.

Stop reading now. Take a short course on weather features and land effects by reading in the Glossary at the back of this book. Start with **sea breeze** and thread through the cross referenced boldfaced definitions to **nocturnal wind, land breeze, gradient wind, surface wind, inshore wind, coastal front, troughs, ridges, high** and **low pressure centers, depressions, tropical waves** and more.

Are you finished? Have you read and understood them all? Now take a test. Do you know all the ways the observed surface wind can differ from the forecast gradient wind at sea? How much it can differ in inshore waters, and why? Do you know all the reasons why the wind in harbor differs from the **inshore wind**? Do you know how banks affect the weather? This book cannot teach weather. It's author is still learning. Perhaps you need any number of good books on weather for sailors. You shall never understand **weather windows**, nor take necessary advantage of **land effects** until you know these basics cold.

LAND EFFECTS

The islands through which your boat threads disturb the flow of the prevailing tradewinds in differing but firmly prevailing ways. My sailing directions count on your rigorous use of these **land effects** to ensure safe and comfortable passages. Refer to the definitions in the Glossary for each of the terms used in the discussion below.

Cape Effects

The wind blowing across a cape is squeezed by the cape. The same volume of air passing a smaller space must, of course go faster, or the air behind would stack up clear back to Africa. The wind around **Cabo Macoris** [CAH-boh mah-co-REES] and **Cabo Francés Viejo** [fran-SACE vee-AYE-ho] will be fiercer at the capes than well beyond them. At night, the capes in the DR may have no wind at all, whereas **Cabo Rojo**, in Puerto Rico, under prevailing easterlies will have open sea conditions at all times as forecast in the **Offshore Reports**. Since the wind follows the contours of a cape, it may appear to be right on your nose all the way around. This occurs even in light night conditions. Don't despair, the real wind is less than what you see at the capes themselves. In the DR, if you start out to round a cape in the evening, the wind won't always be on your nose when you've left the cape behind.

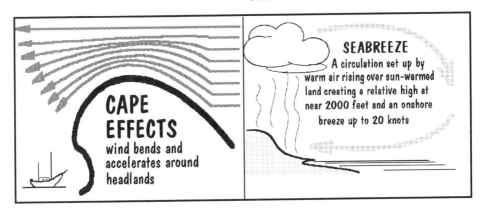

Bank Effects

Least understood by cruisers are the effects that are produced by *banks* such as Caicos Banks, Great Bahama Bank, Exuma Banks, the banks between Long and Great Exuma Islands, between Crooked and Acklins Islands, and even the 90 mile bank upon which the Spanish, United States and British Virgin Islands lie. *Shallow banks act like land.* In other words, banks will store heat during the day and give it up almost as easily as land during the night. A **night lee** can build in light **gradient winds**. The yachtie who arrives at Sandbore Channel at the entrance to Caicos Banks at 9 a.m. thinks, "Boy! The old NWS is wrong again! You can see clear to the eastern horizon, and we've got hardly any wind." Only half way down the 8 mile channel by 11 a.m. he and his unhappy crew buck into 25 knots and 3 foot chop while in only 8 to 10 feet of water. You should know ahead of time that the 60 mile wide Caicos banks stop the wind at night but let it rip in the daytime. If you get there by 6:30 a.m., you can motor into **Sapodilla Bay** in a flat calm by 8:30 a.m.

Coastal Acceleration

Gradient wind will try to follow a coastline upon encountering an island. The **surface wind**, slowed by friction with the surface, will "trip up" the wind above it causing mixing with colder layers. This mixing causes cumulus cloud to form and the surface wind accelerates. If striking the coast at an oblique angle, the surface wind will also accelerate as it bends to the coast, similar to what happens when rounding capes. The total acceleration can be as much as 5 to 10 knots. The sun heats the land and the **sea breeze** sets up. By 2 p.m. the combined effect of coastal surface wind and sea breeze can be ferocious compared to the gradient winds offshore as forecast on the **Offshore Report**.

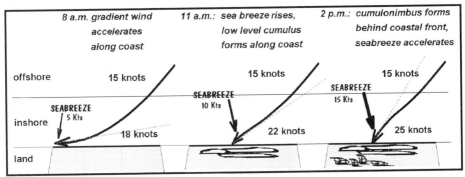

Coastal Fronts

The **sea breeze** circulation creates a line of cumulus that follows the coast at a fixed distance dependent upon the force (velocity) of the surface wind. These systems can get extensive enough to create a weather subsystem beneath them. For example, when mild fronts approach Georgetown, everyone expects the usual clocking of the winds with the forecast 10 to 15 knots out of the southwest. They chug off to anchor in the lee of the western shore only to have the wind pipe up at a brisk 20 knots from the east and leave them hobby horsing in a severe chop on a lee shore. What happened? It's really simple.

First, when the **gradient wind** starts to clock, it goes southeast over Long Island at 5 to 10 knots where it begins to stumble on Long Island and its banks. Then the wind clocks south over the 60 miles of **Ragged Islands** banks to the south and west of Long Island, and it continues to be balked. It can't get through to cool off the Exuma beaches, and in Georgetown the **sea breeze** starts its day. When the wind clocks to the southwest it arrives in Georgetown heated by 90 miles of banks stretching to Cay Sal to the southwest. It lacks the velocity to knock aside the Exuma coastal front which was produced by the beaches that it is too hot to cool. Result? The **sea breeze** prevails, and it is *east,* from **Exuma Sound**. To add insult, the coastal front gives the baffled yachties a Bronx cheer by dumping rain on them. With stronger fronts, of course, the clocking wind will prevail.

This is about the time of day Phred says to his wife, "Dammit Hazel, the blamed old **NWS** is wrong again!" Phred expects the forecast winds (gradient winds) to prevail despite the islands. Later he carries his virus of doubt to the rest of the anchorage on the VHF, using his confidently sonorous and mellifluous voice. From then on they they ignore the NWS **Offshore Reports** and listen to what Phred thinks of the weather. The group proceeds through the islands with Phred instead of the NWS. These are the guys who, when they catch up with me down islands, tell me, "We never saw less than 30 knots on the nose!" while I never saw more than 15 on all my passages.

Permutations

No book can fairly describe the infinite variety of interactions between **gradient wind**, **weather features** and **land effects**. The earth's weather presents a chaotic system which the science of thermodynamics cannot fully predict. For that reason the NWS gives its forecasts in 12 hour windows of decreasing probability. Every 6 hours they slide the windows forward and update the reports. These are the baselines from which you make your own forecast, and from which you shall predict your **weather window**. You need a thorough understanding of how to use these probabilistic models in order to stop asking, "Why don't I see what they forecast?" and start saying, "This is what I'll probably get".

Some reasons you don't see what is forecast are: (1) that the **gradient wind** is too strong to let the **nocturnal wind** assert itself; (2) that the **sea breeze** strengthens the **coastal wind**; (3) that the strong **sea breeze** masks a weak **coastal wind**; (4) that a stalled **front** or **trough** has created a *windbreak* between the **coast wind** and the **gradient wind**. In the DR or PR, if this last reason is true, the weakened **gradient wind** cannot overcome the **night lee**, and you may have your window.

Mid April to mid June the dying fronts and early weak **tropical waves** can create extensive troughs. Mid October to mid December, similar troughs can occur. These can be used to make progress down islands from the Bahamas because they tend to break the trades in the Greater Antilles. This phenomenon is described in two diagrams in the *Picking Windows* section of the *Luperón to Sosua* passage on the coast of the DR.

THINK BEAUFORT

FB	knots wind	descriptive term	SEA CRITERIA	waves in feet
0	0	calm	sea like a mirror	0
1	1-3	light air	ripples, but no foam crests	1/4
2	4-6	light breeze	small wavelets with glassy crests	1
3	7-10	gentle breeze	crests begin to break, glassy foam	2-3
4	11-16	moderate breeze	fairly frequent white horses	4-5
5	17-21	fresh breeze	long waves, many white horses	6-8
6	22-27	strong breeze	extensive foam crests, some spray	9-13
7	28-33	near gale	sea heaps up, foam blown in streaks	13-19
8	34-40	gale	spindrift forms, clear foam streaks	18-25
9	41-47	strong gale	tumbling crests, dense foam streaks, spray may affect visibility	23-32
10	48-55	storm	long, overhanging crests; great patches of dense foam streaks; surface of sea appears white; tumbling of sea is heavy and shocklike.	29-41
11	56-63	violent storm	sea completely covered with long white patches of foam; everywhere the edges of the wave crests are blown into froth; bad visibility.	37-52
12	64+	hurricane	Air filled with foam and spray, sea completely white with driving spray. Visibility very seriously affected.	45+

The Force Beaufort Wind Scale

Work in **Force Beaufort**. It accustoms you to consider overall sea conditions including recent or pending changes.

The **Beaufort Wind Scale** encompasses both wind and wave. For instance, a nice 10-15 knot breeze in the morning after three days of 25-30 knots is <u>not</u> Beaufort Force Four. The waves will be 3 to 5 feet over residual swells of 8 to 10 feet! The Beaufort ratings assume relatively stable conditions.

In the winter months the prevailing easterlies run between northeast by east and east-southeast at Force 5 to 6. In the summer, May through October, they run east-northeast to southeast by east at Force 4 to 5. If either a southeast or a northeast wind is forecast on the **Offshore Report** of the eastern Caribbean, look for a significant weather feature such as a tropical wave in summer, a front in winter, or an unusually strong high or low to weather of the zone. The trades hardly ever blow true northeast or southeast.

The route south is littered with swells from the 3000 mile fetch of the Atlantic Ocean, superimposed with swells from distant storms and, of course, waves from local wind and chop from currents. These all slow windward progress and make for uncomfortable sailing when compared with similar wind strengths at home. Cutters and spoon-bowed sloops may carve through these conditions better than clipper or schooner bows. The going can be extremely rough. Cutters may have their expected way cut by 20%, clippers by half.

Here's a good Beaufort rule of thumb for all hull configurations in these waters, assuming settled conditions for the next 36 hours. Starting with a rhumb line dead to windward, add one Force Beaufort for each compass point working aft from the bow until reaching Force Six. For example, if 48 hours of light airs are forecast with a few ripples on the sea, you may motor to windward. If it will blow 17 to 21 knots aft of your beam, with a few white horses, you'll have a good sail.

Force 5 forward of the beam is for the jocks in their yellow slickers eating cold beans from cans. The **Leisure Sailor** sails in swimsuit and eats pate from china (Corningware unbreakable?) plates.

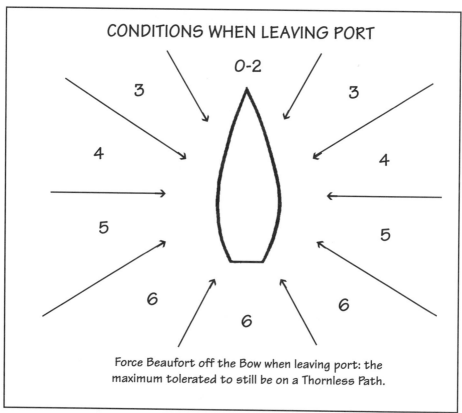

CONDITIONS WHEN LEAVING PORT

Force Beaufort off the Bow when leaving port: the maximum tolerated to still be on a Thornless Path.

Expressed in degrees (**D**) of the wind off the bow, the **Force Beaufort** (F_B) you want is equal to or less than:

$$2 + D/30, \text{ max. } 6F_B, \text{ or, for the purist, } \textbf{half the square root of D}, \text{ max. } 6F_B.$$

Never start out for any distance in a Force 6-7, but if one develops on the quarter, ride it all you can and don't shelter. It probably won't grow stronger. Finally, if you need a slicker and you can't sail in a bathing suit, you should not have left harbor at all.

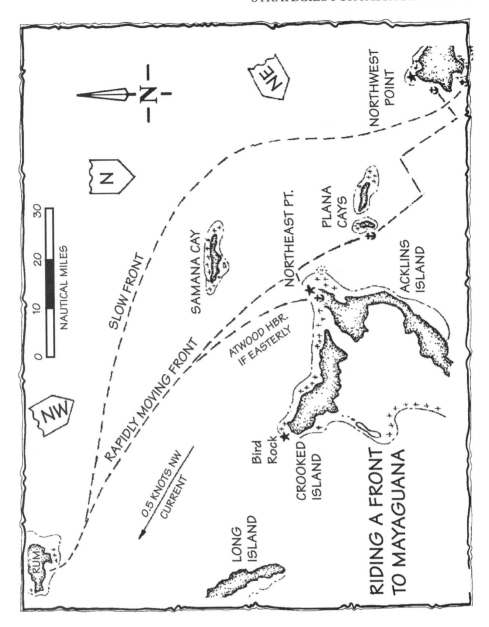

RIDING A FRONT TO MAYAGUANA

GRIM AND GREY IS GREAT GOING

In the winter months it is possible to ride the **front**s down to the Caribbean. In early winter there's a new front every week. By April you'll be lucky to get two good ones. They not only get less frequent but they get slower and weaker late in the season. If you're lucky they'll slow and stall as they sweep down on your little boat, giving you days of pleasant, if somewhat gray, reaching and running. Even luckier if the stalled front backs up as a warm front giving you two rides for your money. Stalled **fronts** and **troughs** north of Hispaniola and Puerto Rico always give a chance to proceed, though perhaps damply, and with swell.

Harbor Telltales

In this guide the unmodified word "wind" always refers to the gradient wind forecast in the Offshore Report, not harbor wind nor local effects.

It is not wise to guess the weather from harbor anywhere but the Bahamas. Even some places in the Bahamas, where there are massive banks and land areas to weather of you, the real wind is not observed. For example, in **Landrail Point, West Caicos, Providenciales,** and **Rum Cay's Flamingo Bay,** or Georgetown in anything but north through east (southeast from there is a 60 mile fetch over land and banks). On the north and south coasts of the Greater Antilles, in prevailing conditions, the harbor wind can be at times greater (i.e., gustier) and at times much less than the wind just a half mile offshore. In **Boquerón** it can blow 15 knots from the west, while, only five miles away on the south coast, it is blowing 20 knots from the east. In **Salinas, PR,** the wind will be zero at night, while outside the reef, only one mile away, it will be blowing 20 knots. Each anchorage and harbor has unique and complicated variables which contribute to its diminishing, increasing or changing of the direction of the real wind. Therefore,

---
***ignore all harbor wind from Georgetown south,* except for the telltales of the cycling of the Trades.**

The point is to watch the cycling of the wind's direction and strength and take your exit only on a down-tick of a cycle, taking advantage of reduced wind speeds and southerly trends. Listen to both the *Southwest North Atlantic* and the *Eastern Caribbean* reports on the **National Weather Service** broadcasts on **NMN** (see *Radio Times and Frequencies*) Portsmouth Coast Guard Communications station, and go when the winds permit a comfortable and safe trip. On the north coast of the Dominican Republic, for instance, moderated **prevailing conditions** should be less than 15 knots and south of east at best. The island shelters you from the eye of the wind, and the night effect is greatest.

To watch the winds, you should construct a table such as the one presented in the section on *Crossing the Mona Passage.* This is a good technique to track the winds and establish a baseline from which to discern "up-ticks" and "down-ticks" in the strength of the trades. (The data in that table are, of course, for departure from **Samaná**, not Puerto Plata or Luperón.) Always use the **NWS Offshore Forecast** winds. Apply "English" to the forecast winds only if you are in an area which is on the borderline of two forecasts, or near a significant weather feature. For example: If you are at 73° with a forecast of

W OF 73W WINDS E 15 TO 20 KT. and E OF 73W WINDS E TO SE 20 TO 25 KT.

then assume your winds are E 20 knots. You shall not normally be so simply equidistant from different forecast segments. Then you should use weighted averages, favoring the segment you are in but giving *English* to it for the segment you are near. Though a little complicated when there are 3 segments at play (e.g., the **Mona**), it is well worth doing. Always, of course, leave harbor on the *beginning* of a downtrend in the wind strength cycle, never at the middle or near its end.

Below are a few examples of harbor telltales I've found work. Coupled with your tracking of the cycles in the wind outside the harbor as given by the National Weather Service, the additional information you receive from these telltales will give you a sure indicator of your position on a cycle. You will have a confirmation of both the time of opening of your weather window and its possible duration.

On the south and north coasts of the Greater Antilles, in normal trade weather, and in the absence of perturbing weather features such as fronts and waves, the trade cycles are indicated by the daily progression of the time of rise of the morning winds in harbor.

In **Puerto Plata**, one friend suggests watching the mountain. If the clouds haven't reached the mountain by 11 am, he says, you can go. In **Salinas**, PR, watch the clocking of your flag from northeast to southeast in the morning. It will start earlier (or later) each day and take shorter (or longer) to finish clocking.

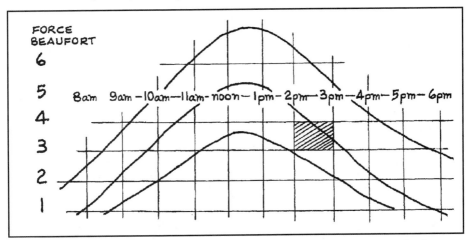

There also are cycles in the endurance of the **nocturnal wind** over the daytime **sea breeze**. Here is a figure constructed in **Luperón** which clearly shows the regular cycle of the winds being masked, but not ultimately deformed, by a **front**.

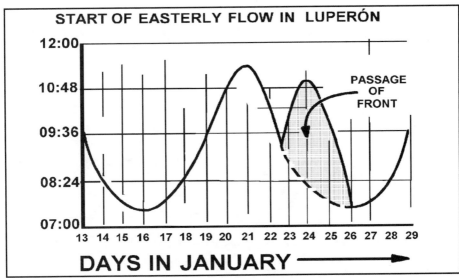

In either **Luperón** or **Puerto Plata** observe the clocking of the winds each day and the cycle of their strengths day to day. The prevailing easterlies come back down to earth along about 9 in the morning along the coast, much earlier at sea, and farther out, they never lift. They reach a maximum between noon and 2 p.m., tapering off to a calm as early as 5 p.m. or as late as 10 o'clock at night. If the maximum strength during the day is, say

Force 5, and it's down to Force 3 by 3 p.m. (having raised to no more than Force 3 by 9 am), get going! The rule, then is: "Force Three by Three". If it's Force 3 by 3 p.m. Monday, leave Tuesday a.m. so as to arrive in Sosua before noon.

FLYING WINDOWS

My waits for weather keep me busy, and radio schedules keep me bound to the boat for 4 hours a day at least. Not for others. Occasionally a bored Type A with nothing to do hangs on my rail during my breakfast, or worse, while I copy a weather report. He usually starts with, "Charlie says it looked pretty good today. Whatcha think?" I should answer, "I don't know because I'm talking to you instead of copying the weather!" I'm learning to harness my tongue. I answer that I don't know, because truthfully, despite all my attention to looking for a window, I'm not sure I've got one until I've left.

That's a way of saying that the more we know, the more questions there are, the more variables at play, the more confusing it can become, and that one sailor's window isn't always another's.

Not long ago I was waiting in **Samaná** to cross the **Mona Passage**. A 12 hour period of 10 to 15 knot winds appeared in the "outlook" section of the **Offshore Report**. It stayed there for 24 hours, or 4 reports. It then moved up to the 12 hour section for Thursday with forecasts of 15-20 knots straddling it for the 12 hour periods of Wednesday and Thursday nights. On a chance of shooting it, I cleared out, shifted to a clean, short scope rode and waited for the 6 p.m. report. It was still there. I was off.

Two skippers, experienced sailors as it turned out, dinghied up beside me while I was raising anchor. (Isn't it always then?) My five days of study couldn't be pressed into a few words. I was working against the sun and against a moving 12 hour window that I wanted to catch just in the middle of the Mona. I told them I was shooting a *flying window*, leading it much like you lead birds with a gun. If the window evaporated by morning, I planned to hole up in **Punta Macao** at the edge of the Mona. I clearly recommended they not go. They'd not done the Mona before. They had no knowledge of Punta Macao. Their boats weren't put away. They weren't cleared out. In short, they were still in their tourist phase in Samaná and totally unprepared to go to sea. All enthused, they raced off to get under way.

I followed my usual ploy, motorsailing the night lee of the Dominican coast. In the morning I dawdled at Punta Macao until the 6 a.m. report. The window was there as advertised! I rode a truly gorgeous starboard tack, flanking the evening thunder storms west of Puerto Rico, in not more than 13 southeast knots. Then, as usual, I drifted down the Puerto Rican night lee to a morning arrival at Mayagüez, playing my favorite tapes, singing all the way, and arriving 32 hours after anchors up. The two behind me spent 60 hours getting hammered. For that story, turn to the passage notes on the Mona.

Reference books:
Kotsch: *Weather for the Mariner*
Jones: *Concise Guide to Caribbean Weather*
Watts: *Instant Weather Forecasting*

HOW TO GET THE WEATHER

While waiting, use the **National Weather Service Offshore Reports** for the **Southwest North Atlantic** until Puerto Rico. Thereafter use the **Eastern Caribbean** reports. Do *not* use the High Seas reports. You may think that's where you are, but that's not where the detail for your zone is given. Refer to *Radio Times and Frequencies* and the chapter on *Making Sense of the NWS Offshore Report.* Do not be fooled into using any other report than the **Offshore Report** of the **NWS**. All the advice in this guide is predicated on the wind strengths and sea conditions as given by this report. More importantly, I have listened to this report, *in situ*, every day for almost 2 decades, and I can certify its accuracy for the route and the harbors covered by this guide.

One "professional" captain I know insists on listening to the Northwest Caribbean forecasts. He, and anyone who listens to him, makes his decisions to leave Georgetown based on conditions prevailing in Jamaica. His nickname is Captain Nogo. He stays and waits because the weather never matches his expectations. No wonder.

Offshore Reports for the **Caribbean Sea** and the **Southwest North Atlantic** are also repeated on standard AM broadcast out of **Cap Haïtien, St. Thomas** and **Bonaire** with additional local details. **Radio Antilles**, *The Big R.A.*, in **Montserrat** has a 5 zone forecast which is excellent.

From Luperón until the south coast of Puerto Rico, use both the **NWS Offshore Report** for the **Southwest North Atlantic** and for the **Eastern Caribbean.** Stitch them together with averaging techniques and with attention to **land effects** on both sides of the **Mona Passage.** From **St. Martin** onward, use Radio Antilles as well. In no case use NOAA VHF WX channel **Coastal Reports** (see Glossary). From Salinas to Virgin Gorda, BVI, you can get all reports, including the **Tropical Outlook** and the **Tropical Weather Discussion**, on VI Radio's VHF WX channel 3.

The **NWS's Offshore Forecast** has the benefit of using a fixed official lingo which permits you to take shorthand notes each day and compare forecasts. It is the changes in the forecasts which interest you, not the particulars of the forecasts themselves. For instance, if you have a forecast of an approaching cold front with a thunderstorm radius of 300 miles, moving at 20 knots, and with 20 knots of Northwest wind behind it, you better batten down for the passage of a reasonably sized front. If, on the other hand, the previous report of this same front gave only a 100 mile radius and a forward speed of 15 knots with only 15 knots of wind behind it, you now know you're in for a Grand Daddy of a blow and you must make adequate preparations. That thing's growing like *The Front That Ate Tokyo*! It is the changes that count.

Getting Hard Copy

I use the 3M Company's Post-It slips that can be stuck up on the bulkhead over the radio. Because the forecasts are repeated in the identical format every day my shorthand notes fill the slips in the same way and they can be rapidly scanned, showing a weather picture developing, or disintegrating, just as those still pictures you flicked through with your thumb when you were a kid made the lady take her clothes off.

If your childhood wasn't that colorful you may wish to employ another method such as recording the broadcast. However, tape quality is usually poor and people who do this tend to not have it written down and can't find it when they need it. Then they play you the whole rotten rigmarole from Georges Bank to Texas while they mutter about which day's recording that is. You can't flip from cassette tape to cassette tape to get the change picture. For that you must have notes. So, if you record, write while you listen anyway, then replay immediately to correct your shorthand. And erase the blasted tapes.

DON'T LISTEN TO YOUR "BUDDY"

Another benefit of knowing the formats and lingo of the reports is that you can separate the wheat from the chaff (nicely said) that's put out by some fellow yachtie on the **SSB** or **VHF**. For example, if Captain Hornblower gets on the horn and knowingly intones the Offshore Report for the Eastern Caribbean as east 15 knots with swells 3 to 4 feet and waves 1 to 2 feet, you know he's full of it! The **Eastern Caribbean Report** does not give swells and waves, it gives sea conditions in overall heights with notable exceptions. What was repeated was probably the coastal report of the airport Met Office in **St. Thomas** or **San Juan**, about as useful to the passage making sailor as the beach report from Miami. One yacht I know left to cross the **Mona Passage** on this advice, hearing that waves were only one to two feet, forget the swells. When he returned to port he adamantly insisted it was the report that was wrong and Hornblower was an accurate source. On the path south your worst enemy may be your best friend.

LEARN TO BE YOUR OWN WEATHERMAN

Study well the chapter on *Making Sense of the NWS Offshore Report*. Know your reports, the lingo and the area covered. And always listen to the same reports every day at the same time so as not to louse up your sense of progression — remember, it's the *changes* that count. Get hardcopy of the NWS **Offshore Report** every day at 0600 AST. Get it right, get it from the **NWS**. In a few months you'll wonder what the mystery was. You'll *smell* the weather windows around the corner.

LISTENING TO THE WEATHER

Knowing the weather is serious stuff, yet 99% of us just don't listen right. The following pages deserve serious study. Also review relevant sections such as *Harbor Telltales, Tracking the Trades, Land Effects* and *Picking Windows*. Know your conditions!

THE MUSIC OF THE TRADES

If you think you're doing a good job of tracking the weather because you listen to Herb Hilgenberg on *Southbound II,* or David Jones on *Misstine*, most of the time, as when you are not out to dinner; because you listen to the **Offshore Reports** almost every morning, making up for mornings slept in by catching the evening report; because you jot down details of the conditions for your specific area, as in "northeast 15 north of the front"; try this:

> — Record a piece of music leaving out one note per measure, change the key on one chord per measure, then delete the introduction, and the refrain.

> — Now ask anybody to name the tune.

That's exactly what 99% of cruisers do, and they wonder where the windows are! Be smart. Write up **NMN** (or print from **RTTY**) offshore reports every morning, and listen to the David and Herb call-in shows to boot. When you can't get the forecasts during storm threats, see the Appendix called, of course, *When You Can't Get Forecasts.*

NWS OFFSHORE REPORT SCHEDULES

AST	Station Call	Freq. 1	Freq. 2	Freq. 3	Freq. 4	Broadcast
530	NMN	4426	6501	8764 13089	17314	NWS Offshore Forecast, USCG, Portsmouth, VA., every 6 hours
600	WAH	4134 4357	4381 6200	8728 8240	13077	St. Thomas VI Radio. All reports. Repeated at 1000, 1400, and 2200
630	WVWI	1000	AM	also at 0710		VI Radio Sailor's Report (MTWTF)
635	Arthur	3815	HAM-LSB			West Indian WX Net — Barbados
655	ANT	930	AM	Antigua forecasts (the best), also at 0805 and 1820		
700	BASR	4003				Bahamas Air Sea Rescue WX net
	WOSO	1030	AM			San Juan, after hourly news
745	WWnet	7268	HAM-LSB			Waterway net US/Bahamas WX
805	ZBVI	780	AM	M-F David Jones and ea. 1/2 hr.; 745 Sat.; 945 Sun.		
830	*David	4009				David Jones' WX net for Caribbean
845	*David	8104				and SWNA.
900	WOM	4363	8722	13092	17242	and at 1900, tfc lists odd hours
1600	*Herb	12359				

* Herb Hilgenberg, formerly of yacht *SOUTHBOUND II*, now in Toronto, gives fore-casts and routing tips for individual yachts. David Jones, the Tortola marine weatherman on British Virgin Islands radio staion ZBVI, summarizes reports and satellite imagery each morning for cruisers throughout the Caribbean.

MAKING SENSE OF THE NWS OFFSHORE REPORTS

For following the National Weather Service reports and the various cruiser nets you must have a radio capable of receiving Single Side Band, Upper Side Band (SSB-USB). A portable shortwave receiver with a "BFO" switch is usually sufficient.

In the Bahamas, the Caribbean and the Gulf of Mexico, the forecast to listen to is the NWS's **Offshore Forecast.** These reports are updated and broadcast every six hours from the Coast Guard's NMN station at Portsmouth, Virginia. The Offshore Forecast is so named because these reporting zones are off the continental shore, not because you have to be 50 miles offshore to use it. The Bahamas and the Antilles are all included in these zones. NOAA or "Weather X Channel" coastal reports available in Puerto Rico and the Virgin Islands, and the NWS High Seas reports are *not* directly applicable to the cruiser making an interisland passage. The NOAA "20 mile out" coastal reports do not give the open sea conditions which, off these small islands, prevail within less than a mile of their north and south coasts which lie on the axis of the **Trades**. If you use the **Coastal Report** you can be buffaloed into going out into 8 foot seas since they report wave heights less swell. The **High Seas Report**, on the other hand, includes a vastly larger area (essentially from Africa to Mexico and from the Equator to beyond Hudson's Bay). A great deal of detail is lost, and the forecasting periods are longer and further out. The Offshore Reports for the Caribbean, the Southwest North Atlantic and the Gulf of Mexico are repeated on standard AM broadcasts out of Cap Haïtien, St.Thomas and Bonaire.

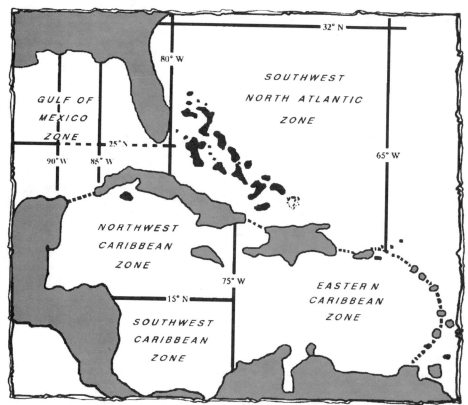

It is the day to day *changes* in the forecasts which should interest the mariner, not just the particulars of the forecasts themselves. Therefore it is necessary to have hardcopy of the reports for several days in succession. You can get the same 'telex' the Coast Guard gets through telefax technology using either specialized equipment or a radio-computer link. You can also prepare it yourself by shorthanding the reports either directly from the radio report or from a recording playback. If you record and playback the weather to make your hardcopy, it must be done on dictating equipment or on a player with a 'pause' switch. The mechanics of the ordinary AM/FM/Cassette machine make the copy process too cumbersome. I prefer to copy directly from the broadcast in my own private shorthand. I use the 3M Company's Post-It slips that can be stuck up on the bulkhead over the radio. Because the forecasts are repeated in the identical format every day, my shorthand notes have the same format and they can be rapidly scanned, showing a weather picture developing, or disintegrating.

If I've been in harbor awhile, I begin listening to the offshore zone reports *ten days* before leaving harbor. That ensures my listening and my shorthand are properly exercised before going to sea. Those ten days also let me develop a sense of rhythm and progression about the weather. In tropical trade wind areas, where the weather is ardently periodic, one develops a prescience for its cycles. I listen to the early morning report. That way I am guaranteed to be on the boat and never miss a report. I've seen no end of grief for cruisers simply because they listen to broadcasts at more convenient times like 1800. Then they eat dinner in town and miss the forecast. They lack a sense of progression since they listen at different times of day and not every day. Or worse, they rely on the guy anchored next to them. It boils down to just plain discipline.

Report Format and Structure

The offshore reports use a fixed format and jargon which shall only be understood by repeatedly listening to the report for the same zone at the same time of day. Warnings of tropical systems come at the beginning of the hour. The Boston and Washington, DC, offices of the NWS give forecasts for the zones under their responsibility, followed by the Southwest North Atlantic and Caribbean reports from the Miami office. Last, the Gulf of Mexico forecast from the New Orleans office is read. Each office's report is begun with a time stamp, the time and date at which the report was released. This is normally just minutes before the broadcast, but if technical problems arise, the Coast Guard may broadcast a report 12 or more hours old. Always note the report's time stamp. The Caribbean forecast comes before the Southwest North Atlantic report. It is divided into three sub-zones which are reported in sequence: northwest, southwest and eastern Caribbean.

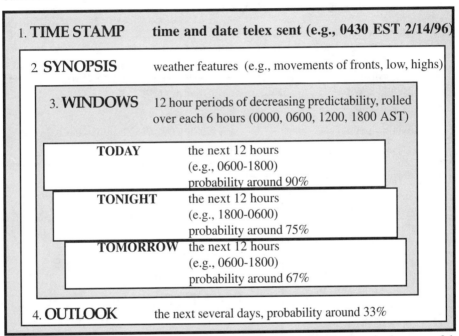

1. TIME STAMP   time and date telex sent (e.g., 0430 EST 2/14/96)

2. SYNOPSIS   weather features (e.g., movements of fronts, low, highs)

3. WINDOWS   12 hour periods of decreasing predictability, rolled over each 6 hours (0000, 0600, 1200, 1800 AST)

TODAY   the next 12 hours (e.g., 0600-1800) probability around 90%

TONIGHT   the next 12 hours (e.g., 1800-0600) probability around 75%

TOMORROW   the next 12 hours (e.g., 0600-1800) probability around 67%

4. OUTLOOK   the next several days, probability around 33%

The forecaster begins with a synopsis of significant weather features in the zone, followed by three 12 hour periods beginning with the time given on the time stamp. Therefore, a new set of three 12 hour periods are forecast every six hours. Then comes an "outlook", or longer range forecast, for the 36 to 72 hour period following the 36 hours already covered. For example "Today, tonight and Tuesday:..." will be followed by "Outlook for Tuesday night and Wednesday", or "Outlook for Tuesday night through Thursday". Reports at 1800 will of course begin "Tonight, Tuesday and Tuesday night", and so on. Each period is described with wind and sea conditions (wave+swell), including precipitation, in all parts of the zone relative to the weather features given in the synopsis. For example, "south of the front and west of 70° west, winds east to southeast 15 to 20 knots, seas 4 to 7 feet; elsewhere (meaning south of the front and east of 70° west to the end of the zone at 65° west) winds east 20 to 25 knots, seas 5 to 8 feet. Scattered thunderstorms west of 75° west." In shorthand:

$$S_F \; W70 \quad E\text{-}SE \; 15\text{-}20 \quad 4|7 \quad \exists \quad E20\text{-}25 \quad 5|8 \quad S\theta \; W75$$

Shorthanding the Offshore Reports

RTTY Hardcopy from February 11 , 1992, NMN at 0615 AST on 4426 USB

00 KMIA 110915 OFFSHORE MARINE FORECAST NATIONAL WEATHER SERVICE MIAMI 0915 UCT TUE FEB 11 1992

CARIBBEAN SEA AND SW N ATLC BEYOND 50 NM FROM SHORE.

. SW N ATLC S OF 32N AND W OF 65W

...GALE WARNING N OF 29N E OF 73W TODAY...

.SYNOPSIS...GALE CENTER ABOUT 150 NM SW OF BERMUDA EARLY THIS MORNING MOVING RAPIDLY NE. COLD FRONT WILL EXTEND S OF GALE CENTER TO __ MVOE TO NEAR 65W TONIGHT. ANOTHER COLD FRONT _ W EJ_CARLOINAS WED AFTERNOON.

.TODAY...N OF 29N E OF 73W WIND NE 35 TO 45 KTS. SEAS 12 TO 18 FT. E OF COLD FRONT WIND SE TO S 15 TO 25 KTS. SEAS 6 TO 9 FT. REMAINDER OF AREA WIND NE TO E 20 TO 30 KTS. SEAS 7 TO 10 FT WITH LARGE NE SWELLS. SCATTERED TO NUMEROUS SHOWERS AND TSTMS OVER THE NE PART. .TONIGHT...E OF 75W WIND NE 20 TO 30 KTS. SEAS 7 TO 10 FT WITH LARGE NE SWELLS. W OF 75W WIND NE TO E 15 TO 20 KTS. SEAS 4 TO 6 FT WITH LARGE NE SWELLS. WIDELY SCATTERED SHOWERS. .WED...WIND NE TO E 15 TO 20 KTS. SEAS 4 TO 6 FT WITH LARGE NE SWELLS. WIDELY SCATTERED SHOWERS MAINLY N PORTION.OUTLOOK FOR WED NIGHT AND THU...LITTLE CHANGE.

Shorthand Legend:

α	area, along
θ	through,thunderstorm
		sea conditions
∃	elsewhere
^	increasing
V	decreasing
»	moving
– –>	drifting center (low)
S$_F$	e.g., south of front
⌂	little change
CF	cold front
F	front
WF	warm front
R	ridge; remainder
G	gale (TD, TS, etc.)
SuMTW ThFSa	
WS	widely scattered
2d	today
2n	tonight
2m	tomorrow
l8	late
am	morning
fr	from
stn	stationary
O	Outlook
lg	large
C	Cuba
bld	building
fw	few
Hsp	Hispaniola
pm	afternoon
wr	near
bec	becoming
bet	between
W	warning

Actual Copy of the Short-Handed Report:

Radio Teletype Copy vs Shorthand

Compare the two copies above, and you shall see that the shorthand version has picked up the garbled transmission that a second cold front is moving SE from the Carolinas in the afternoon. If you don't record the report, it often is worthwhile to listen to a later rebroadcast from commercial stations such as WLO or WOM just to double check your copy from the Coast Guard broadcast on NMN. Shorthand often beats telex.

Using Coastal NOAA Reports

On the east coast of Puerto Rico there is an 80 mile fetch to windward over small islands and shallow, heated water. Conditions here usually conform to the San Juan WX VHF reports. These reports are only good on the east and west coasts of PR. Fajardo, like West Caicos, goes calm at night in light easterlies. The shallow banks to your east provide a land-like night effect. On the south coast of Puerto Rico, the real wind shall be what was forecast for the eastern Caribbean on the Offshore Report. The NWS Offshore Forecast wind, with appropriate *English* applied as required for local variations due to topography or conjuncture of weather features, is what you shall have immediately outside south coast harbors, *not* the observed harbor wind, if any.

Bear in Mind . . .

The boundaries of the reporting zones are *implicit* coordinates.

— The NW Caribbean Offshore Zone lies west of 75W and north of 15N. If, in the report for that zone, the analyst says "North of the front wind NE 15 knots", that does not mean you have NE 15 knots at 20N. The zone stops at the south coast of Cuba. Pretend the analyst is a surgeon operating only on the zones described, and that there is an opaque sheet around the square of operating zone. Nothing outside the zone will be mentioned. An impinging frontal system, if not affecting the zone at this time, will not be mentioned, except possibly in the Outlook section of the report. If you want to know what's coming in more detail, listen to the zones to weather of you (east in the summer, west in the winter).

East to southeast is *not* the same as southeast to east

...nor is it east-southeast. If the analyst has gone to the trouble of telling you "southeast to east", a movement counter to the diurnal flux of the trades, it's a fair bet it's not just a mistake. It means the wind is more likely to back than to veer. Usually this is a sign of strengthening trades. If, instead, "east to southeast" was used, you don't know if that's normal diurnal veer, simple convention to start with the main cardinal point of the compass, or pronounced veering. But that's why you listen every day, right? A veering trade usually portends weakening of the wind.

— Listen the same time each day, and always record the time stamp. Reread *The Music of the Trades* if you don't know why. Often the Coast Guard will replay an old report in the absence of a new one. During Hurricane Hugo this went on for 17 hours. Many thought Hugo was stalled, and they began to venture out!

There is only one NWS

Yachties often compare the value of different sources. Until Martinique, the only source from which everyone starts is the **NWS** data and analysis. Any report you hear *not* from NWS is an *interpretation* of their data.

— When anyone but the USCG computer voice or radio teletype feeds you the analysis, you lose vital information that can cost you dearly. When "*by* Thursday" or "*through* Thursday" becomes just "Thursday" you lose 8-16 hours on calling a front. That can be a 160 to 320 nautical mile mistake! Beware of yachties, even some HAM net operators, who should know better, who repeat "east to southeast" as "east-southeast". You are losing a vital piece of data in your tracking of the cycling of the trades.

WEATHER THREATS

In the Summer and Fall months, it is paramount that the skipper have a storm anchorage less than twelve hours <u>downwind</u>. Preferably these should be three to five hours sailing time. Warning time can be extremely short. Keep a good **Hurricane Hole** close at your back, and look for opportunities to use these systems in your navigation.

WINTER COLD FRONTS

Many northern yachtsman arrive in these waters still applying the term **Norther** to a **cold front**. A cold front in the southeastern extremity of the continental weather pattern is nothing like blue northers up north. Perhaps continued use of the term Norther inhibits the navigator from seeing cold fronts as the very useful friends they really are.

Unlike Western European and North American waters, the building grayness of wind and sea during the passage of a front in the lower Southwest North Atlantic and the Northeastern Caribbean never build to **storm** conditions (Force 10 Beaufort), and they rarely build to a Gale (Force 8). Don't always run for shelter. Get out your dividers and plot your progress south. The rain is warm and you can still sail with or without your bathing suit although you may need a sweater when the front passes and it blows clear and cold. Never a slicker!

A front typically veers the wind from southeast through south, all the way around to northeast. When the northeast wind has blown itself out it will soften and dip a bit below east, a very useful fact to know. As long as the front goes through, the progression through this circle is usually more rapid as the season wears on. When leaving **Georgetown** I often take a full clock of the wind over to **Salt Pond** in Long Island, then I stage myself up to **Calabash Bay** via **Simms** and **Joe's Pond** while it blows northeast. When it begins to dither below east I sail to **Conception**. That strategy sure beats holing out in **Stocking Island**, then beating out into it after its gone. Late in the season you can trim for a broad reach and leave her there all the way from **Rum Cay** to **Mayaguana**, and even as far as **Puerto Rico**, scribing a long arc down islands with the wind's veer. Early in the season the northeast winds may persist for several days after passage of a strong front. Once beyond Rum Cay a front can be used to take you as far as you want to go.

If you want to make it south to the Caribbean and you want to go only in sunny weather, take a plane. Clear weather in the winter usually means 20 knots on the nose and hobbyhorsing into 6 to 8 foot short seas. By including fronts in your winter strategy you can cut weeks off your trip south and at the same time insure yourself a good 3 days to a week of leisurely fishing while doing a **Wait for Weather**.

Rum Cay is an excellent spot to await a front. If the winds are too south of east you may experience a little roll. In that case, you need to have anchored further in to gain protection of the point. See the section on Rum Cay for details.

Between Season Troughs

Boats go up on the beach practically every year in **Bonaire** during the period mid October to late November from unexpected west winds. It should be expected. Fronts begin to make it as far as the western Caribbean in the fall, albeit weakly. **Tropical Waves** (see Glossary) still make it to the western Caribbean, albeit old and frail. The combination of stalled, weak fronts and stalled, dying waves often become **Troughs** (see Glossary) which can stretch from Columbia to the Bahamas. Imbedded storm cells, if not the troughs themselves, can spawn west winds at the unprepared anchorage on Bonaire. It caught me more than 200 miles to the east at Blanquilla one October.

In the other 'tweener season, May to June, the dying fronts and early weak waves can create similar troughs. These can be used to make progress down islands from the Bahamas because they tend to quash the trades in the Greater Antilles. See *Luperón to Sosua*.

Summer Tropical Systems

In the summer months one watches the east for a variety of **Tropical Systems**, the nomenclature of which may sound randomly chosen to the first time listener. Don't be abused, however, the nomenclature used follows a simple progression of severity, and therefore, it is of interest to the cruiser, especially if he or she is uninsured.

Rather than continue to confuse these terms, refer now to the Glossary for the definition of each. Learn what these weather features are now and know how they can be used, rather than confuse and dread them all. First on the scene are **Troughs** and **Tropical Waves**, which come across the Atlantic and may spawn **Tropical Disturbances**. One of these may begin to whirl to become a **Tropical Depression**, which can become a **Tropical Storm**, which often becomes the dreaded **Hurricane**. So it goes.

One season I left **Salt Pond** to take advantage of the weak circulation around a north bound **Tropical Depression** well to the east of us. The words *Tropical Depression* had alarmed some of the other boats into staying put. Upon the depression's passage, strong winds had returned and stayed for a while. After my usual leisurely sail to Puerto Plata, I heard on the ham net that one couple had got discouraged with their **Wait for Weather** and had turned back, that two more had given up waiting and had terrible beats to **Rum Cay** where they were still cornered by the full southeast **Trades** which had come up to their northern limit for an extended visit. One of these was Captain Nogo, the fellow who had everyone listening to the *Northwest Caribbean* reports instead of the *Southwest North Atlantic* **Offshore Forecasts**. His idea of a good **Weather Window** was a breezy, sunshiny sailing day, like in the beer ads. To him, ugly looking days were for staying at anchor regardless of wind strength and direction.

Using Hurricane Holes

Basic requirements

A hole must lock land close enough to run lines to shore against dangerous wind directions. Entrance must be unrestricted at all times and tides. Unless in a bay or estuary likely to empty on the wind, look for a depth a few feet under the keel at low tide. Storm surge will raise your boat, not lower it.

Shallows and island shelving reduce storm surge. If in the path of the storm's right quadrant and holed up near deep ocean (e.g., eastern Antigua) you may suffer the storm's full open ocean surge. Your boat will rise fully exposed above reef and mangrove.

The best holes

The perfect hole does not exist. Nowhere is 100% safe. But you can get close. The boat wants good holding and soft shores to wash up on. Mangroves make the softest shores. They grip the ground with myriad springy roots. The brittle dead wood snaps and breaks easily, but alive, it bends like a palm. A tight bark covers the hard wood like an easily broken skin. A thick mucous layer lies underneath. Strike the tree and it first bends, then its skin breaks. The mucous slides the striking object upward where smaller and more plentiful branches continue the same action. An impinging boat slides up the mangroves harmlessly as onto a Teflon bedspring. Absent overwhelming storm surge, the boat slides back when wind and water abate. Sunshine melts the mangrove stains.

East of **Morocoy National Park** in Venezuela, precious little protection can be found. Yet between Tucacas and Trinidad, yachts will eventually stack sardine like in deep, exposed and rock sided anchorages. With the insurance companies chasing boats south, **Chaguaramas**, in Port of Spain, with its currents, tides and deep water, begs to polish your boat with Trinidad's perennial summer southwesters.

In all the Virgin Islands charter boats and boats with no skippers aboard plug up the harbors during a threat, making the crunch of boats around extremely dangerous.

Salinas, on the south coast of Puerto Rico has nearly two square miles of deep mangroved rivers and bayous in a wetlands national park, far from charter fleets and megamarinas. On the other hand, Vieques and Culebra lie squarely on the evacuation routes of the Virgins and Fajardo fleets.

Samaná has a great hole across the bay but Samaná has never had a hurricane problem anyway. A careful look at the geography will show why: surrounding land masses and mountains defeat the winds even with a direct hit. There appears to be no way for the dangerous semicircle to penetrate the bay undiminished. The same is true for **Luperón**.

Luperón, on the north shore of the Dominican Republic, has impenetrable mangrove bays. There is a small village and good communications. Hurricanes crossing the island lift over the high mountains and disorganize, producing much destruction on the south coast and only rain on the north coast. **Manzanillo**, farther to the west, ranks high in protection but poor in civilization, despite the ever present and ice cold Presidente beer. **Ft.Liberté**, farther west in Haiti, scores well on protection, but bottom on civilization. Yet the Barbancourt *rhum ancien* will acculturate even the heart of wilderness.

What to do

Run! Run every time, and run early. Don't dither. Don't cavil at false alarms. Getting an early jump means forsaking commitments, not letting friends or job distract.

Stake your claim before the 48 hour hurricane watch, then begin to act slowly and deliberately in order to get your nose pressed into the ground within 24 hours of storm landfall. Stay put until the warning lifts.

Always have your boat sea ready in hurricane season. Storms sometimes rise out of nowhere, practically skipping the Tropical Depression stage. Have a clear plan for a hole *downwind* within timely reach. If you decommission your engine for any reason, do so on a hurricane mooring or in a hole.

Rumors and grousing to the contrary, named storms generally follow the instructions of the Miami Hurricane Center. With each report, plot the storm's approach and tie in another line, leaving open the most options possible. Between reports, the work of stripping the boat will loosen the knot in your guts and ease the pain of waiting.

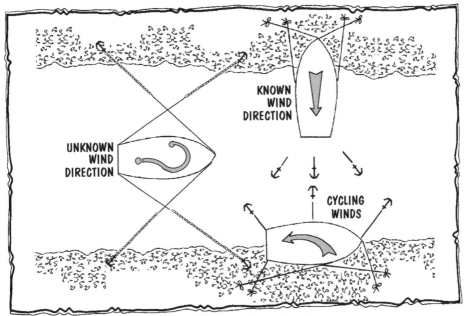

Tying into mangroves for a hurricane.

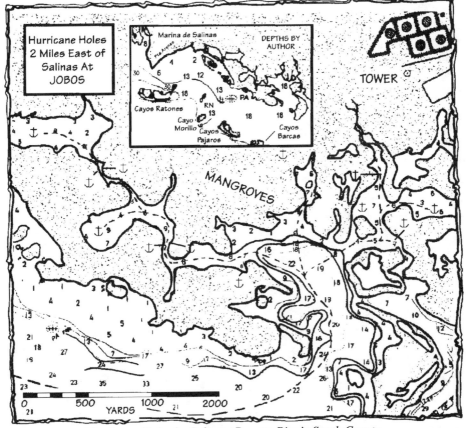

Hurricane Holes by Salinas, Puerto Rico's South Coast.

Stay on or get off?

No absolute answer exists. If you penetrate deeply into mangrove rivers for ultimate protection you can't leave the boat. To leave the boat you must use a hole within dinghy reach of civilization, but not surrounded by drooling looters.

THE DANGEROUS SEMICIRCLE

The **dangerous semicircle** of a **Tropical Storm** is the half of the rotating system which has its winds moving the same direction as its forward speed. Typically, the winds in the dangerous semicircle can be fifty percent higher than the winds in the other half of the storm. If encountering the storm at sea and caught in the dangerous half, the direction of the winds tend to sweep you into its path rather than knock you aside. For example, if you fell in the path of one of those street cleaning machines which has rotating brooms, which side of its rotation would you rather fall? The side which will squinch you forward and into its maw, or the side which will only maul you and spit you back out?

Although you may watch the formation of the 'canes in the Atlantic and you may plot their probable paths two to three days ahead, they still can be erratic. If it is clear that a storm heading west will pass your anchorage to the south, then you don't care if the anchorage is open to the west, and you can put your nose in the mangroves of the eastern shore. If a 'cane is passing north of you and headed west, almost any good anchorage may do. The permutations are, of course, endless and should be chosen for the 'holes you have available. All of these "What If" **Hurricane Games**, like war games, must be played well in advance of a crisis. You must act instinctively when it becomes apparent a hurricane is on its final approach and may not veer. You won't have time to dither.

For more information on storms see the Appendix called *When You Can't Get Forecasts*. But not to worry too much since the odds of a 'cane landing on your little area of the world are slim.

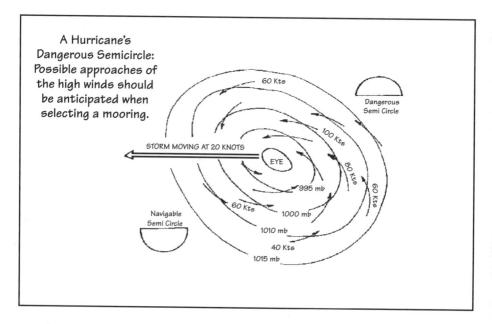

A Hurricane's Dangerous Semicircle: Possible approaches of the high winds should be anticipated when selecting a mooring.

PLAN YOUR ROUTE FLEXIBLY

KEEP TO THE NORTH TO GO SOUTH

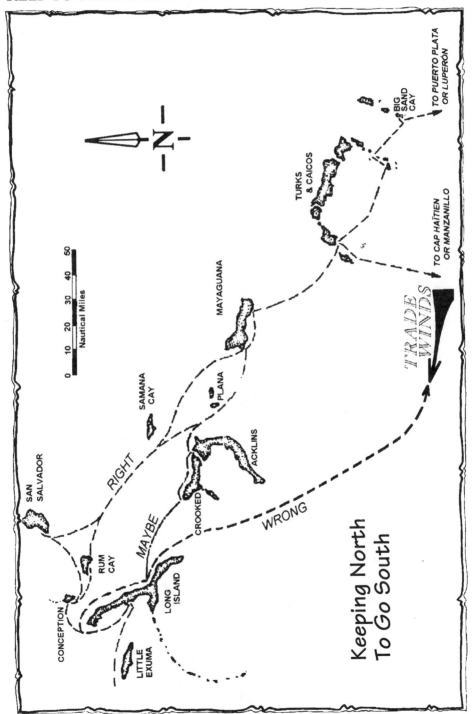

Given a choice of routes, the navigator should give weight to the <u>northernmost</u> to preserve any windward advantage. Since you are heading "south to the Caribbean" this might not be readily apparent. Consider that the "collective eye" of the **prevailing winds** (see *Glossary*) is east to east-southeast. In order to maximize your possible **Weather Windows** you have to widen your angle on the wind. Either you must get <u>over</u> the eye of the wind to sail south-southeast, or you must sail <u>under</u> it to sail northeast. To do the latter requires fitting wheels on your boat to cross Hispaniola, an expensive procedure. I recommend sailing in the islands to the north, gaining easting by using the prevailing south-easterly flow, then spending the windward advantage accumulated by sailing south-south-east.

Remember, you're playing the island **land effects** and the slight switches in the wind. If you are in Great Inagua and your windward rhumb line is east-southeast, the wind will <u>never</u> switch enough for you to lay it. So, when you choose your routes each day, have uppermost in your mind that you *don't give up northing*, just as you wouldn't dream of giving up easting.

There are always the masochists that take the **Great Inagua** route, lured by the easy 65 south-southeast miles of **Long Island** early on the trip. I have sat in Georgetown and seen a 120 foot charter schooner, with English crew, leave for that route. A contingent of yachties followed. After all, didn't those professionals know best? The answer is,

"*No!* They've never done this before."

But, anyway, the cruising couple in their sixties with a 35 footer and a 25 hp engine, let alone the 50 foot ketch with the 120 hp diesel and bow-thrusters, cannot compare to a passel of temporary hires behind 1200 horses dragging the bottomless purse of some foundation. They invariably find themselves slogging directly into the eye of the **Trades**, more prevalent farther south. They also must buck into the mainstream of the **Equatorial Current**, which is three quarters of a knot NNW in the **Crooked Island Passage** and up to *one and a half knots* WNW along Hispaniola, though normally three quarters knots. And in their wake are the broken flotsam of retired cruisers and the jetsam of their broken marriages and relationships. Think I'm kidding? When you get as far as the Dominican Republic, start interviewing yachties that took this mistaken route. You will hear their stout denials that "it wasn't at all a rough trip, it was a good trip, really — glad they came that way, because Rum Cay was too rolly ... ", etc., as I've heard them for years. "Why didn't you wait it out in Flamingo Bay on the northwest corner of Rum?" "Well, we were with a group and ... well ..."

When you're in Luperón, notice how the Great Inagua group preoccupy themselves with what are quite major repairs, compared to your *to-do* list. See Great Inagua on the road back, along with **Hog Sty Reef.** To "go south", unless you are going to Jamaica, *keep north.*

Maque

THINK TWO MOVES AHEAD

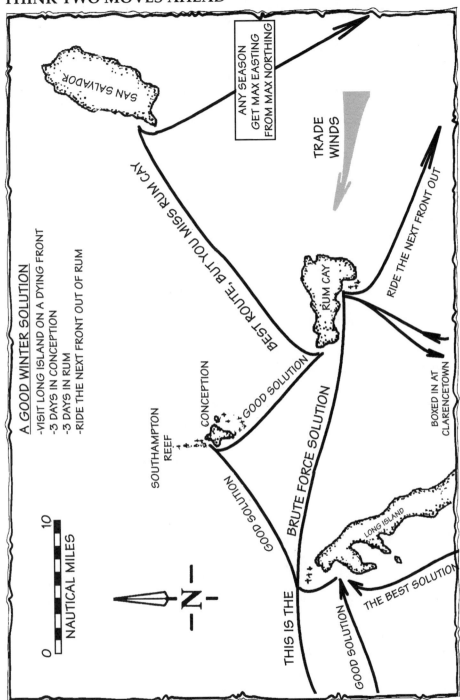

Alternate routes may be longer in distance but either shorter in time or easier on boat and crew.

This rule, and the next three, deal with the strategy for choosing anchorages while wending the Thornless Path under continuously changing conditions. The bottom principle to this rule is to avoid the *idée fixée,* or what the French call being foolishly stubborn.

One acquaintance left the sanctuary of **Salinas** just before Hurricane Dean to sit in its path at **Fajardo**. His logic, as such, was that Fajardo was "closer to St.Thomas" which, *in his mind*, was some sort of terminus, or cusp, in his cruising plans. **St.Thomas** became the "be all" as well as the "end all" for him. His *idée fixée* nearly did end it all for him right there at Fajardo. Dean didn't turn toward Puerto Rico. He was lucky. I guess. A month later he was nailed in Culebra by Hurricane Hugo. As before, he made his "decision" at the last minute, and was practically the last boat to shelter at the overflowing hole.

When planning your next leg, consider not only your **staging** anchorage and multiple possible landfalls, but ensure that you know what conditions will prevail where you are going, and what possible steps you might have to take when you get there. Like moves in chess, your maneuverability at your next position (and your next...) should be thoroughly considered.

— Sailing to **Clarence Town** from **Rum Cay** might end your frustration of waiting day after day for the wind to change from dead east, but it will guarantee you two days of motoring against wind, wave and current, while slogging from Clarence Town to **Landrail** to **Attwood Harbor**. Take two more days of the world's finest snorkeling in good companionship at Rum in exchange for those two days of the wham-bangs spent in mutual disgust. But remember, when it's rolly at Rum, jibsail down the bay and round the corner to anchor in flat calm with good Wind Bugger breezes on the white sand beaches of the western shore. Flamingo Bay on the northeast corner of Rum isn't so shabby in a prolonged southeaster — you can freshen your wardrobe from the Salvation Army wreck there.

— If the wind goes light to 12 knots but doesn't change to the direction you want, you may leave harbor anyway, exercising an alternate plan to go off on the other tack to a different anchorage, at a more stately, close-hauled pace than you had wanted. Or you could motor flat-out to your original goal. Either choice will alter your original plan. Landfall or arrival times have changed. Therefore other contingent conditions have changed: the angle of light for reading the water, the distance to comfortable harbor when your **Weather Window** closes.

— If you wanted to visit **Clarence Town** and you had gambled on a **front** to ride you out of it and lost the gamble, accept your loss like ladies and gentlemen do. **Wait for Weather** a couple of weeks in Clarence Town, or sail back to Rum, or to **San Salvador** to start another, shorter wait there. Going back is OK.

In other words, be flexible with your landfall, even while enroute. And never, of course, *ever* set a schedule or a deadline. Don't hang up on a particular destination as though you had a pot of gold under only one particular rainbow.

PASSAGE ELAPSE TIMES

To estimate the time required to make a specific passage while using the strategies in this book, you must add *time underway* to *time waiting for weather*. When planning a cruise you must consider the time of year since winds will vary depending upon season. You must consider your mode of passage making. Are you a purist sailor? Do you motor, or motorsail, at the slightest *contretemps*? You can not overlap touring, repairing or partying with a **Wait for Weather**. Here is some background to help you adjust these factors for your own crew and yacht, and make your own estimate of passage times.

I have had to whiz through these passages to make business schedules associated with my yacht, *Jalan Jalan*. I was chartering in the north, building a house in Puerto Plata, and refitting each year in Venezuela. Sometimes legs were taken several times a season to work on the house, for instance, between charters. My yacht was uninsured, and I was single handed: caution was the watchword. I traveled as fast as was feasible without negatively affecting the well-being of either the yacht or myself. Many trips I've made were for pleasure, or just aimlessly wandering, which is the English meaning of *Jalan Jalan*.

Jalan was a 15 ton displacement, long-keeled, 41 foot ketch. She had a Perkins 4-108 engine which developed only 37 shaft hp of the 51 rated. She sailed well in ideal conditions, but she has a clipper bow and hobbyhorses in steep, choppy seas. *Jalan* and I tacked directly to windward only in less than Force 4. We accepted a 3.5 knot average, and did not lie about it. Despite those that claim tacks of 35° to the real wind, C. A. Marchaj, (*Sailing Theory and Practice*, ISBN 0 229 64253 5) says 37.5° is the theoretical minimum. With leeway, *Jalan* gave me 50° on the passages described in this guide. I consider that a 35 foot sloop with a 30hp auxiliary and a retired couple aboard will do about as well. With 50° tacks at 5 knots, you will put 14.4 miles under the keel for each 10 miles on a windward rhumbline. With the usual minimum of half-knot Equatorial Current against you, it will be 16.6 miles. To make 5 knots you've got to have a Force 4-5 with seas 4 to 7 feet. You will lose way with those seas. Your leeway may be less than *Jalan's* (one degree for each Force Beaufort). So! A factor of 1.75 keel miles to each rhumbline mile while tacking should not be unexpected for a small boat with a cruising configuration. Don't bet on less, unless you've got a large, fast boat and strong crew. For reaching, running and motoring, reckon as you normally would.

Despite all this data many cruisers ask me to tell them exactly how long a particular leg will take *their boat* (with *them* at the helm, making *their* course and tacking decisions). Well here it is:

— Calculate the speed you make under full motor and sail, against 20 knots of wind, three quarters knots contrary current and short 8 foot seas. Divide this into the number of miles your keel shall travel. Add thirty percent for leeway and optimism. You then have the total hours to wherever you want to go.

If you find yourself actually trying to make these times more often than not, although I wish you well in your cruising, you should closely examine your reasons for cruising.

Cruising takes time. Each stop you make will require rest and recuperation, perhaps some touring or local cruising, and get-togethers with other cruisers. For example, I usually do the 60 or so miles to **Rum Cay** from **Georgetown** by following the clocking winds of a medium front to **Long Island**. When the northeast winds blow themselves out and flag briefly south of east, I go to **Conception** for diving on **Southampton Reef**, then I take the leg to Rum at the end of the **Weather Window**, where I again **Wait for Weather**.

Novice cruisers try to make **Rum** from Georgetown. More experienced crews shoot for **Conception**. Here's the way I did those 60 miles (see the chartlet in *East From Georgetown*), in a relaxed and fun manner while **staging** from Exuma to **Rum Cay**:

DAY	LOCATION OF FRONT	WIND DIR. AND SPEED	ANCHORED THAT NIGHT	ACTIVITY
1	NO. FLORIDA	E-SE 15-20	REDSHANKS	PARTYING
2	CEN. FLORIDA	E-SE 15	FOWL CAY	STAGING
3	SO. FLORIDA	S-W 10-15	SALT POND	CRUISING
4	NASSAU	NW-N 20-25	SALT POND	WAITING
5	OUT ISLANDS	NE 20-25	SIMMS	CRUISING
6	HISPANIOLA	E-NE 20	JOE'S SOUND	CRUISING
7	PUERTO RICO	E 15-20	CALABASH BAY	CRUISING
8	DISSIPATING	E-SE 10-15	CONCEPTION	DIVING
9	DISSIPATED	E-SE 15	RUM-PT.NELSON	PARTYING
10	NO. FLORIDA	E-SE 15-20	RUM-FLAMINGO BAY	SNORKELING
11	CEN. FLORIDA	E 15-20	RUM-WEST COAST	FISHING
12	SO. FLORIDA	E-SE 15	RUM-PT.NELSON	STAGING

That's <u>five miles a day</u> folks! And every mile a pleasure!

Remember, if you aren't partied out by the time a good **Weather Window** opens up, or your favorite serious child is flying down to visit his wastrel parents fiddling their lives (and any inheritance) away in the Caribbean, or whatever reason you have for not taking the leading edge of the first window available, then add more time on your total cruise. Take a new window and don't try to make up time by going when you shouldn't.

In all, the trip from Georgetown to Venezuela can take as little as from two to four months depending solely on luck of the draw during each **Wait for Weather.** That does not, of course include time to satisfy your desire to pause and smell the roses, nor does it account for rest and recuperation which, in my case can be months.

More guesstimates from my own experience, <u>not including</u> touring, fishing nor R&R:

— **Georgetown** to **Puerto Plata** is ten days to three weeks in any season.

— If you visit **Haiti,** add one to two weeks;

— **Manzanillo,** but not Haiti, add a week.

— **Puerto Plata** to **Boquerón**: one to two weeks.

— Boquerón to the **Virgin Islands**: two weeks.

— Virgin Islands to **Venezuela**: 4 weeks through the islands, 2 weeks right across.

STAGE YOUR DEPARTURE

The greatest underestimation we cruisers make is upon the stamina of the crew. We often make judgments based on our younger selves. There is hardly a leg on the way south that can't be shortened by 10% to 30% in time, and 20% to 60% in adrenaline, by one simple practice:

stage to a departure anchorage the day before leaving.

Get away from the crowd. Get near the sea. Get your dinghy up. Go to one shallow hook. Clean up all your rodes. Make sea-ready on deck and below. Take in a reef while at anchor. It will be easier to shake out than to tie in later. Take a swim and a snorkel. Eat a candlelight dinner, listen to music, read a book. Turn in early. Turn out an hour before anchors-up. Watch the dawn, or listen to the night. Hoist a cup of coffee or two. Then hoist sail, hoist that shallow single rode, fall back on the wind, and slide out. You shall be up on the first leg by an hour or more, sometimes much more. And you have an added bonus of a shortened first leg. It sure beats doing all that work just before sailing out with muddy decks and sweaty crew.

In Georgetown, you are four miles ahead of the game if you use the **Fowl Cay** exit.

By going to the Martín Pinzón anchorage in **Luperón**, you save a mile and perhaps several hours, or a whole day if the *comandante's* people have wandered off while you cursed the muck on your anchor. Besides, you can make a night exit from there to avoid the rugged seas as far as **Punta Patilla.** This section of coast is where Hispaniola sticks farthest out into the current, and it's best to wait for the seas to subside.

In **Samaná**, the afternoon winds caroming off the coast can create a terribly heavy chop in the 8 mile entrance channel which usually doesn't lay down until after dark. **Stage** in the morning to the sand anchorage behind **Cayo Leventado.** There you can make a safe night exit after the seas have subsided but still with time to make **Cabo Engaño** by 8 a.m. If you stay in harbor, at least go to a clean, short rode to avoid delays on departure.

In **Salinas**, Puerto Rico, the leg to Puerto Patillas is only 18 miles. The first advantage of **staging** yourself the 5 windward miles in the shelter of the reefs to **Boca de Infierno** only becomes apparent when you do it: the anchorages there are so peaceful, many elect to stay awhile. The second advantage is only apparent to those that don't stage there: the motorsail over to Patillas, though only 13 miles, becomes miserable more than 3 hours after daybreak. This is where Puerto Rico sticks out the most into the current.

In **St.Georges**, Grenada, whether bound for Venezuela or Trinidad and Tobago, stage over to **Morne Rouge Bay** and leave from there.

Stationing yourself on the harbor nearest the pass you want to cross in the **Lesser Antilles** will get you a better sail. It will also get you in before the lunchtime squalls.

Cleaning up and waiting for weather in **Trinidad's Scotland Bay** or **Tinta Bay** on **Chacachacare** gets many miles behind you, and makes a relaxing interlude.

The examples are legion. If you haven't started staging your departures already, spend a few years *cruising*, not *sitting*, in the Caribbean, and you shall spend your last day **staged** at a lonely cleanup anchorage on every step of the path, however insignificant.

It's often a good idea to *stage* into harbors to rest and clean up before clearing in.

LET LANDFALL DETERMINE DEPARTURE

Plan your departure in time to make landfall in favorable light, arriving with <u>several hours</u> of daylight left. The way south is full of windward shore anchorages (i.e., entered to the east) where you will need the sun high and over your shoulder for the first time you enter. A 3 p.m. landfall may dictate a 4 am start. If you've been accustomed to waking at 7 am and having your Wheaties before addressing the world, and you are reluctant to break that custom, then sell the boat and move ashore. Almost every leg of the *Thornless Path* requires an early start in order to benefit from **land effects** that reduce headwinds.

Have a variety of departure plans ready for different breaks in the weather and for different landfalls. Be prepared to cancel all your commitments and haul anchor at the first opening of a **Weather Window** meeting one of your plans. Similarly, never plan a last minute chore, such as one friend who wanted to buy cold milk when the store opened at 8 am. That bottle of milk caused him to miss an earlier departure when the situation changed. He tried to use the change in the weather despite a later start and got pinned down in Long Island. He was still there when I reached **Mayaguana**. Two weeks later, while I was dining in **Puerto Plata**, he had a window slam on his tail and suffered some delamination problems from all the pounding he took. He returned to Georgetown. The lengths of the windows and the lengths of the legs just didn't go together for him. The morals are:

— Plot several routes contingent on breaking weather.

— Depart at the earliest time called for by your contingent routes so that you can make changes underway in response to changes in the weather.

For example, if you're in **Calabash** expecting the wind to go north of east in order to lay **Rum Cay,** and it instead goes to the southeast, *go anyway!* But go to **Conception Island** and depart earlier. Why? You won't be **lee-bowing** the currents and you will have to take an extra tack or two. So you say you're a motorsailor and you'll motor it? Well, even if you don't have to tack sailing tacks, you'll still do motorsailing tacks and certainly make slower progress while pinching the wind than if reaching for **Conception**.

Every delay in departure creates a risk upon arrival.

CONTINGENCY PLANNING

Another moral you won't appreciate the value of until you've done all the trips I have: *leave yourself enough time.* Most of us are fairly adequate when planning contingencies along the route. The discussion above illustrates contingencies of actual landfalls. When most cruisers quote how long it took them to make a passage they usually talk about offing to offing, ignoring the time taken with departures and arrivals. I quote hours of passage making from ready to up anchor to anchors down and set. When planning your route, add in contingencies for getting underway and getting settled shown below.

Reckon on 20% less speed to windward than you are accustomed to.
If you get more, great!

Contingencies Getting Underway...

— the office hours at the customs shack for clearing out,

— the over-the-shoulder light needed to wend your way out of a reef anchorage,

— the anchors-up drills with lots of mangrove mud to clean off oneself and the boat,

— getting the dinghy and motor aboard, and on and on.

One wonders sometimes how one ever escapes some harbors. On the landfall side are other factors.

Contingencies of Landfall...

— there may be reefs to navigate in over-the-shoulder light,

— time to select a safe and shallow spot in which to anchor,

— getting the dinghy and motor down before shoreside closings,

— properly put the boat to bed in a new anchorage with an eye to 2 a.m. anchor drills.

Passage planning must consider timing of arrival at capes as well as at landfalls.

Tally the hours for the above lists, then add a couple of hours of safety margin. You shall discover that navigating some hours in the dark may seem inevitable for almost any passage. I've learned to stage my departures to eliminate night dangers. I've also learned to benefit from the night to make safer passages and safer landfalls.

Entering Calabash Bay under tradewind cumulus at the end of a Long Island cruise. (Use binoculars to find the house with the windmill.)

DON'T BE AFRAID OF THE DARK

Caribbean cruising can call for 8 to 15 hour passages. When one considers all the conditions and requirements upon which getting underway is contingent, it becomes obvious that even an 8 hour windward sail may cause a night landfall.

For instance, I leave **Grenada** for the Venezuelan **Testigos Islands** after sunset to ensure a well lit mid-morning landfall. Rather than push out of **St.Georges** crowded lagoon and busy harbor in the dark, I practice good **staging** by moving my anchorage the day before to an easy night departure site in **Morne Rouge Bay** just outside. I temporarily moor off the windward beach with a clean rode and a short scope. At nightfall I hoist sail in the gentle breeze, lift the shortened anchor aboard and, while making coffee below, I ghost out beyond the island's lee where I can take up my course for Testigos. No rounding up in 25 knots of wind to raise sail with sheets flogging and snarling on the pinrails. No sweating and cursing over fouled and muddy ground tackle.

Bound for Turks and Caicos from the Bahamas, I stage myself in **Mayaguana** to the beach at **Southeast Point**. Leaving at midnight I have a pleasant 15 knot close reach of only 35 miles to **Providenciales** instead of a 50 mile close hauled beat into 20-25 knots apparent from **Start Bay**.

To sail from Turks and Caicos to **Cap Haïtien** or to **Manzanillo**, in the Dominican Republic, I first move from **Sapodilla Bay** over to a **West Caicos** mooring, or depending on conditions, to the entrance of the Caicos ship channel. Before dawn I hoist my reefed sail and fall back on the light night wind from the banks. After I've breakfasted underway, the lee of the reefs gives way and I'm reaching in midmorning trades. That night the loom of either **Monte Cristi** or **Cap Haïtien** lead me into Hispaniola's night lee where the land breeze warms my cheek and crowds my nostrils with the scents of cows, grasses and charcoal fires. I'm tied up at the customs dock in a flat calm even before the officials arrive, and of major importance, I'm cleared and off those docks before the trades come up at 9 a.m. and impale *Jalan Jalan* onto their rusty hazards.

There are anchorages that can be made in the dark also. I have often sailed into **Pittstown Landing**, Acklins, or **West Plana**, both in the Bahamas, by only starlight. **Gros Islet Bay** outside **Rodney Bay** in St.Lucia and **Isabela**, just east of Luperón, are also fine night landfalls. In most of these cases the windward beach is a long sloping shelf of sand without keel hinder. From a mile or more out one can luff into the mild night wind until the sounder shows just a few fathoms. From that point it is possible to idle dead to windward, the clear sand below visible by just starlight. I creep into the wind until the bright white sand beach is off the bow, gently fall off in silent **nocturnal wind** and slowly feed out the anchor. A much easier exercise than in afternoon trades.

I've seen countless cases of the fear of night sails leading a cruising couple into problems. Take the **Mona Passage** for example. Not everyone has the patience to wait for a rare calm in order to transit the Mona in 24 hours, so many cruisers try to make it in two days and one night, because they "don't like night sailing". That may compromise their landfall to late in the second day. Just one pause to replace a blown raw water pump impeller, or slowing down to coddle an overheating engine, puts them precisely where they didn't want to be in the first place: close to land in the dark. I've seen several incidents where crews turned back exhausted after forty eight hours jilling around in the Mona under full trades precisely because they departed **Samaná** in the morning rather than in the evening.

In **prevailing conditions,** a night departure from Samaná permits a lee motorsail down the Dominican coast, a slack northeast tack during the day, and a southeast tack in the lee of Puerto Rico on the second night. Two nights and a day often equals 24 hours of lee sailing and 12 hours of close reaching compared to 36 hours of beating and bucking full trades during two days and a night. There's another reason: there are potentially dangerous thunderstorms which cut loose from the land and drift westward off Puerto Rico in the late afternoons and evenings. Taking my tacks, I slip around and behind these colossal systems. What's more, while they weaken out at sea, their convections provide me some shifting and moderating of the trades even before I feel the lee of Puerto Rico, further reducing my exposure. Again, there is a dawn arrival with plenty of time to clear and get sorted out before the winds get up and make things difficult for a sailboat in harbor.

Every time I cross the Mona I meet boats who start out to do two nights and a day, but in the afternoon they find themselves irresistibly pulled by the direct rhumbline to Puerto Rico. They usually break faith and rev up for a run at the land, often darting into a wall of thunderstorms before arriving at 2 a.m., their landfall navigation aids obscured by a blaze of shore lights. Nerves frayed by the storms, they pick their way into harbor and tumble below exhausted about 4 a.m. They're still asleep while I'm trundling out the dinghy to go clear in only 3 hours later. What did they gain for those 3 hours?

Certain night passages are often mandatory, such as coasting to windward along the north shore of the Dominican Republic, along Puerto Rico's south shore and along the **Paria** peninsula in Venezuela. Besides being a required cruising skill, nighttime navigation has many benefits. You make earlier landfalls, leaving more time to investigate and enjoy your anchorage. You avoid sunburn and glare. Watches are quieter and radio reception is cleaner. Visibility at sea is better at night. Lights loom over the horizon, then stand out sharply many miles away. Ship type, size, aspect and course are instantly apparent. In daytime, everything is a vague blur on the hazy, headachy horizon. Far from being a scary enemy, the dark is more often than not the cruiser's friend.

NEVER MISS A SUNDOWNER

A leisurely gin and tonic at sundown, with the boat all squared away and ready to move again, should end every landfall. This is no frivolous rule. To never miss a Sundowner G&T you've got to plan your navigation with lots of margin for engine stops, adverse currents and so on. In order to make your landfall in time to get down secure anchors, square away yourselves and the ship, and make yourselves comfortable with a drink by sundown, you must make your anchorage several hours before. The **SG&T** (some of my friends leave out the gin) is a reward for good planning. Never miss it.

IF IN DOUBT, STAY OUT

A two million dollar, 92 foot ketch lay on the rocks outside Puerto Plata for three months. It stranded there only one month after launching in Ft. Lauderdale. They went aground early on a clear night at the foot of the light house at the *fortaleza* San Felipe.

Even after scrupulously following all the rules, Murphy's Law eventually will catch up with you. If you can't make the tidy daylight landfalls suggested here, or you are just too uncomfortable with an entrance under certain conditions, stand way out to sea, set the boat to an easy jog in open water or heave to and go below in watches. A properly hove to boat is snug as a baby's cradle. Of course, your **SG&T** at sea should be coffee.

HUG THE SHORE AT NIGHT

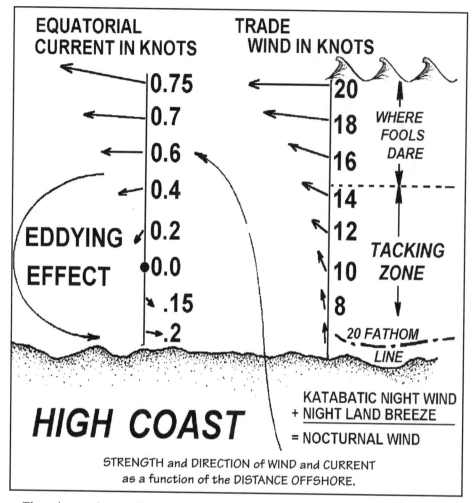

STRENGTH and DIRECTION of WIND and CURRENT
as a function of the DISTANCE OFFSHORE.

The wise navigator, like Columbus, takes advantage of **night lees** on the high windward coasts, which shall prevail in light trades. Modern sailing yachts sail well to windward under these light conditions and in calms they can proceed under auxiliary power instead of behind a rowed longboat like Columbus had to do.

How Far Off?

My standard rules for coasting a hazard free coast are to *tack out until well off soundings*, or until whitecaps are found, then *tack back in until:*

— between 10 and 20 fathoms by day (or eyeball), or

— between 20 and 30 fathoms by night.

This can make for short tacks on a steep coast. If coasting to take advantage of the lee of the land, the strip of relatively calm water is narrow, from 1 to 3 miles. The north coast of the **Dominican Republic** is a case in point.

A Stress Test

Normally I steer a good watch on an inshore tack and go below to read or catnap on the offshore tack, relying on the rougher water to shake me out of the bunk so I can head her back inshore again. One year I was reading below on an outward motor tack while comfortably coasting between **Cabo Macoris** and **Cabo Francés** on the north coast of the DR. An incident occurred which, unfortunately, is common among cruisers headed south.

I was surprised by a barely intelligible call on the VHF. It was from friends supposedly following my advice to hug the coast with me. I marked my book place, heaved the cat off my lap and ambled back over the upright deck to the navstation.

My friend's voice over the radio reminded me of an old Charles Laughton movie where the helmsman is lashed to the wheel during a survival storm. Backdropped by mountainous seas, the terrified man is whipped by buckets of sea water and foam flying horizontally on the screaming wind while the ship groans onto her beam with every wave.

At any rate, that seemed to be the condition of his vessel and crew to judge by the sound effects coming over the VHF and the strain with which he spoke.

"Where the heck ARE you?" I asked.

"A- ABOUT SIX ... MIIIILES ... OOOOUT!" he intoned stoically from the heart of the gale.

"Why not come inshore?" I asked after rescuing my peanut butter sandwich from the cat who almost dumped my coffee cup in her backward scurry.

"We ... WE'VE ... SEEEEN ... WORRRSE!" crackled the speaker.

Earlier, this same friend had insisted on punching on through the day rather than waiting for evening behind the Cabo Macoris headland at **Sosua** because *"people were saying we couldn't anchor there."* I had anchored off Sosua as usual and, after a refreshing four hour nap and a hot supper, I had continued on. Despite his earlier start I overtook him that night motorsailing inshore of him. And, even though I spent most of the next night anchored at **Escondido**, he made port at **Samaná** only a few hours earlier than me.

He was so zonked out he didn't clear customs until the next day while I cleared in immediately and went out to lunch to renew old friendships in Samaná. Later, when I asked him again why he punched on in the daytime and why he didn't sail further inshore, he told me that his wife was afraid to sail at night, which they had to do anyway, and he was wary of the rocks along the shore which his chart told him didn't exist.

If you think hugging a windward coast at night is stressful, then I propose you take a stress test. Convinced you sail as close inshore as you dare? Talked yourself into thinking conditions are not so bad where you are? Take this stress test. Nudge the boat still closer inshore, keeping the depth over 20 fathoms. Nudge it again, then again. With each shoreward nudge you shall discover a strange paradox. Relaxing sea conditions and better boat speed and stability overcompensate the stress of nearing shore. With a good fathometer, you will forget your fear and stay inshore once you have tried it.

Cruising is neither an Outward Bound course nor an endurance contest for retireds. Sailing this coast requires good sense and planning, not a high tolerance for pain. I find the passage along the DR a good trip and I rarely see a white cap. If you round the capes in midday and fail to coast close inshore you will indeed have an evil trip and shame on you. Double shame if you venture out into more than 15 knots of forecast wind, or wind which is north of east, or into large swells left over from storms in the north and east.

When hugging the DR or the PR coasts to windward, don't forget the *cape effects*.

THE PASSAGES

I divide the way south into short and easy passages. The following pages provide advice for plotting and making each passage. When details on anchorages can be found in the guides mentioned in the *Preface*, those details are not repeated here. However, when it is felt that the cruising sailor needs particular information to make the cruise truly **Thornless**, then those anchorage chartlets are included.

These specific sailing directions take advantage of the *prevailing conditions* (see Glossary) at each step, and of their predictable modifications by weather features such as **fronts** and **tropical systems,** and by **land effects,** each of which is defined in detail in the weather sections of this guide or in the Glossary.

Bahamian beacons and lights are, as are all those in the Carribbean, notoriously unreliable. They may be damaged or decrepit, but, wholly visible or no, these are the marks of record you must use.

GPS WAYPOINTS

All GPS coordinates in this guide are given to the nearest tenth of a mile. This should satisfy either WGS-84 (NAD83) and WGS-72 datum. These waypoints were taken on site and confirmed several times each on different occasions. All bearings given have intentionally been made as simple and mnemonic as possible, given the marks they refer to. Every attempt was made to make GPS waypoints with safe searoom, and which coincide with critical compass bearings.

NOTATION

The format used is always **DDMM** (Degrees, Minutes), eliminating the folderol and fritter of ° and ' signs, and **N** and **W** designations for Latitude and Longitude. For example, I write <u>2845</u> instead of **28° 45' N**. Since the area covered by this book is 15-26°N latitude and 60-80°W longitude, there shouldn't be any confusion with this simpler notation. However, if you do get it twisted up, you will no doubt recover your error since 28°45'W is the longitude of Faial, in the Azores, and you probably don't want that right now. In any case, there shall surely be the normal complement of cruisers in Georgetown to rail against the notation. They're usually the ones who don't read the book fore-to-aft, and therefore they miss the keys to its interpretations. Remember,

— coordinate | 2330 |
| 7545 | is Georgetown in the Bahamas,

— while | 7545 |
| 2330 | is Kalaallit Nunaat in the eastern *skærgaard* of Greenland.

All charlet depths are in feet MLW unless otherwise specified.

CAUTIONS

With the full availability of GPS cruisers have taken to giving each other precise coordinates of reef entrances and channel markers. Use these at your peril! In this book all such arrival waypoints are adjusted to give you:

— a safe offing with which to proceed *visually*, and

— a safe approach from sea at any reasonable arrival angle.

An example of a dangerous yet common practice occurred recently. A helpful yachtie, the leader type with a radio voice the envy of every Pan Am Flight 001 captain, dinghied out to the red ball in the entrance to **Luperón**, and holding the ball, did several GPS clickety-clicks. He then broadcast the averaged results over the SSB to all the southbound yachts, touting the data as "very accurate", and calling the ball "the seabuoy". Three yachts on a southeast course (as are most) went onto the reef in the next two weeks. Look at the chartlet for Luperón to see why. That guy's still around, by the way.

And how about the 53 foot Australian yacht lost coming into **Salinas**, Puerto Rico, through **Boca de Infierno**, on a clear night, calm sea, at four knots headed due west, for a waypoint someone had given them for the exact center of the cut. The waypoint was accurate. Take a look at the chart for Boca de Infierno. What were they doing?

I'm sure you have your stories too. Any time you use a GPS waypoint, including those provided by this book, do the following:

— check that the chart's datum is the same as the waypoint's

— move the waypoint to a safe offing in a danger-clear direction, usually seaward

— if uncertain of your chart's datum, calibrate it using a charted mark which is near to hand before using it to create or check waypoints, and draw a difference vector on the chart (e.g., 0.35 nm at 350°)

— proceed visually in all channels, cuts and harbors of the Caribbean or the Bahamas.

Entering Luperón due south on the west side's cliff face.

THE BAHAMA ISLANDS

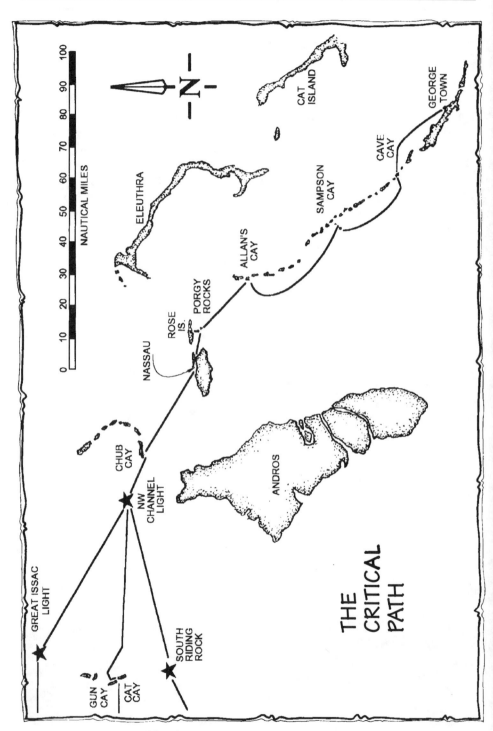

Florida to Georgetown, the critical path.

The route from Florida to Georgetown is more than sufficiently covered by the *Yachtsman's Guide to the Bahamas,* which I strongly recommend. The Guide's chartlets are numerous and accurate for all the upper Bahamas. In addition, you should have the *Bahamas Chart Kit,* published by Better Boating Association and available in most chandleries. Other sources offer great detail for cruisers (e.g., *Explorer Charts*).

The Gentleman's Guide to Passages South is meant to provide information not otherwise available in the guides listed in the *Preface*. It's main contribution is to passage making and other concerns of the hard-core cruiser. Local information is abundant in the other guides. This guide concentrates on sailing directions and arriving/departing the anchorages which are key to the thornless strategies.

Charts for islands from Georgetown to Hispaniola and that great island itself, are less complete in all the guides and therefore more information on these areas is included in *The Gentleman's Guide to Passages South.*

From Florida to Georgetown the cruiser has such vast choices of wholly separate cruising grounds that cruisers could, and should, occupy themselves there many months. However long, and wherever you choose to cruise the upper Bahamas, your best plan would be to make Georgetown, Exumas, by early March. Cruising the Exumas and the near out islands can easily exhaust the months of November until March.

THE GULF STREAM

Wait for Weather in any safe hole south of Palm Beach. For example: **Marathon, Plantation Key, Noname Harbor** or **Hurricane Harbor** in **Key Biscayne**, or **Lake Sylvia** in **Ft.Lauderdale**. Where you start makes little difference except in heading and departure time, but wait *close* to the ocean. For example, waiting at **Dinner Key** Marina may put several hours on your trip compared to **staging** at the marina inside **Government Cut** or **Noname Harbor**. Review the strategy section on *Staging*.

Wait until the **Offshore Forecast** is for south of east winds of 15 knots or less and leave at night from the **Miami** or Ft.Lauderdale area, or before lunch, from Marathon. Never cross the **Gulf Stream** when the wind is against the current or is blowing northwest through northeast. And never cross in conditions over Force 4. An average set of 1 and a half knots at $10°$ True from anchor to anchor works fine. Plot a course for an 8 a.m. arrival at **Gun Cay** or **Riding Rock.**

You can take **South Riding Rock** onto the **Great Bahama Bank** if you plan to clear in at **Chub Cay** or **Nassau**. I've found it all round less hassle to do it at **Cat Cay** while waiting for weather. Then you can go anywhere in the Bahamas without worrying about customs. However, the marinas at Cat and Chub Cays sporadically levy a tie-up fee for the mandatory custom's boarding. The fuel docks at Nassau do not normally charge for clearing in if you fill up with fuel.

If you ride over the **Gulf Stream** on the precursor winds of a front, be sure to be behind **Gun Cay** before the winds go west of south, then move to the west of Gun Cay again when the winds go east of north. A **Leisure Sailor** will in no case be in the **Gulf Stream** while the wind is northerly and over the current.

While at Gun Cay, motor over to the **Cat Cay** basin and check in with Customs and Immigration at their office in front of the dock. Anchor back at Gun Cay or off the channel behind Cat Cay, north of the club. If you anchor west of Gun Cay, check out the ledges on the shore for lobster. The weekenders there from Miami assume it's already picked clean and don't bother to look.

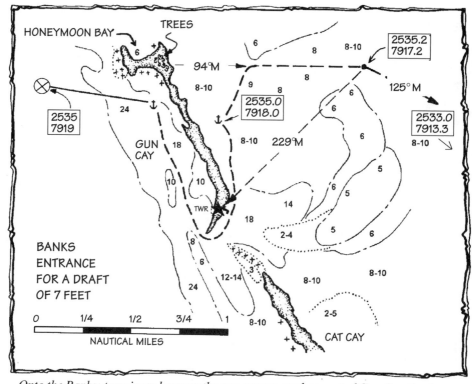

Onto the Banks: to gain an hour on the run across, anchor east of Gun Cay the day before and leave at first light next morning, motor hard.

To take seven feet onto the **Great Bahama Banks,** proceed north from the **Gun Cay** entrance until the clump of trees on the north end of the Cay is abeam. Then turn east to a point one mile east of the trees and northeast of the Gun Cay light. Now proceed on a course of 125° Magnetic for 4 miles. You are back on the rhumbline to **Rusell Beacon.**

THE GREAT BAHAMAS BANK

Try to get to the anchorage south of **Northwest Channel Light** before dark by leaving from the east side of **Gun Cay** just before dawn in good southerlies or westerlies. Otherwise, wait for a calm day and motorsail lickety-damn (see the section on Motorsailing in the *Pointers* chapter). *Staging* yourself to the east side of Gun Cay the previous afternoon will save an hour, effectively shortening the trip by 5 miles.

If forced to anchor on the banks, do so a good two miles south of the lane you are traveling. Set out a bright light, a long anchor snubber, and hope you don't have visitors.

If you are worried about your draft, you can take the northern route around **Isaac Light** in the ocean, or across the top of the banks from north of **Bimini** to Northwest Channel Light, passing a few miles north of the **Mackie Shoal** beacon which may not be there. This is a good, clear route with never less than 10 feet of water. My 6 and a half foot draft always took the route from Gun Cay to **Rusell Beacon** with minimum 2 feet still under the keel. To navigate the shoal area east of Gun Cay with a 7-foot keel, leave on a rising half tide and follow the sketch above.

CHUBB CAY

Anchor off the beach in front of the marina if you are going to check in there. Better anchorages are available at **Bird Cay** or **Whale Cay**, where you also will have a better angle on the wind when sailing to **Nassau**. All of these anchorages are open for easy night exits. Set out two anchors for security from strong westerlies in squalls or thunderstorms year round. Leave around 3 am to get to Nassau next morning with plenty of time to fuss around getting a secure anchorage or to go shopping and tour in the afternoon.

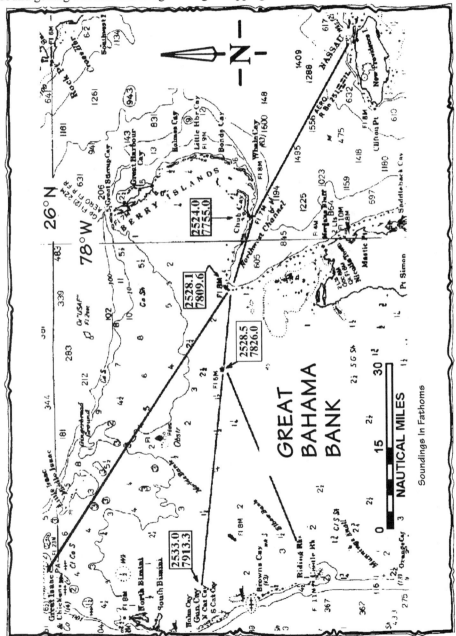

The Great Bahamas Banks to Nassaa.

NASSAU

Some love it, some hate it, but you have to do it at least once. If you arrive at a large port early in the day, you will have lots of time to fool around changing anchorages as may become necessary, and you will generally get a better handle on the town, than if you arrive late in the day. (See *Dinghy Security*). Whatever time you spend in port thereafter is made much more productive by arriving before lunch the first day.

Anchor west of Club Med at the Yoga center. Set anchors fore and aft against the east flood and the west-going ebb. The anchorage off Nassau Shipyards and **BASRA** are fine but often crowded and more available to swimmers from shore. You can land your dinghy at the BASRA dock which is convenient to all of Bay Street. See *Dinghy Security*.

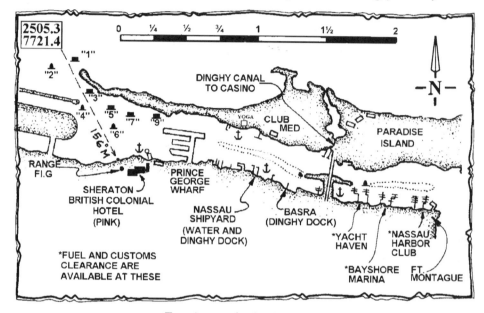

Transient anchoring in Nassau

Leave **Nassau**, for the **Exumas** shortly after daybreak on a day when the wind, if easterly and is less than fifteen knots. Take the direct deep water route to either **Allan's Cays** or **Highbourne Cay** from a point 2 miles east-southeast of **Porgee Rocks**. This route passes between **Middle Ground** and **Yellow Bank**. The water is deeper than charted and the heads are few and distinctive in the high light of late morning to midday, which is what it will be if you left Nassau early. To get a leg up on the passage, or to **Wait for Weather**, as the winds may not be from the direction you wish, **stage** in **Bottom Harbour** on **Rose Island**. To leave Bottom Harbour, motor west at sunup, close to shore, to the entrance to the salt pans, then head True South 0.8 miles until **East Porgee Rock** bears west, whence you turn onto 145° True for 1.6 miles to the departure point east southeast of Porgee Rocks. See chartlet on the next page.

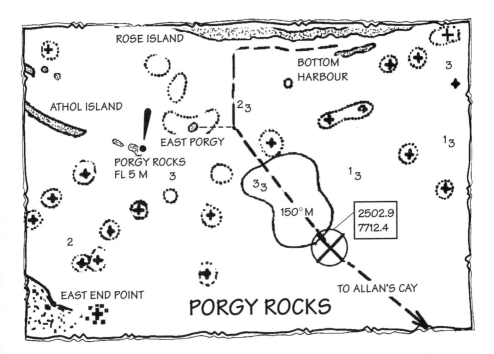

ROSE ISLAND

BOTTOM
HARBOUR

3

ATHOL ISLAND

2 3

EAST PORGY

1 3

PORGY ROCKS
FL 5 M   3

1 3

3 3

150° M

2502.9
7712.4

2

EAST END POINT

TO ALLAN'S CAY

PORGY ROCKS

EXUMA CAYS

You should cruise the Exumas slowly and enjoy every anchorage available. There is no better cruising in all the Bahamas although the **Far Out Islands** offer better diving. These notes, as in the entire *Gentleman's Guide to Passages South,* are for those who have already done their touring and gunk-holing and want to make a rapid and easy passage.

The fastest, safest and simplest passage is to take the **Exuma Banks** all the way down to **Cave Cay**, one of the easiest and deepest cuts and the last cut going south for vessels of any draft. For a rapid passage, do not stop at **Staniel Cay** unless going outside in **Exuma Sound** from there on. There is no reason for a draft under 8 feet to take the outside route. The banks will give you 10 feet or more most of the way, with convenient cays at which to turn upwind and anchor for the night. Drafts over 7 feet are better off exiting the banks at **Conch Cut,** just north of Staniel. Even so, playing the tides and paying close attention to charts of the banks, deeper drafts can go further. Although Staniel Cay and **Pipe Creek** are worthy stops for the cruiser, they are essentially terminals and not convenient waypoints in a banks passage.

The passage down the banks behind the Exumas is one of the best sails you'll ever have, close-hauled on twenty knots of wind without a ripple on the water. Beating was never like this. And never will be again. The water here is ten to fifteen feet deep, unobstructed with coral heads and clear as a swimming pool's. *Even with a deep draft, don't be shy of taking the Banks route behind the Exumas.*

Stage **from Nassau to Bottom Harbour, then jump off from Porgy Rocks.**

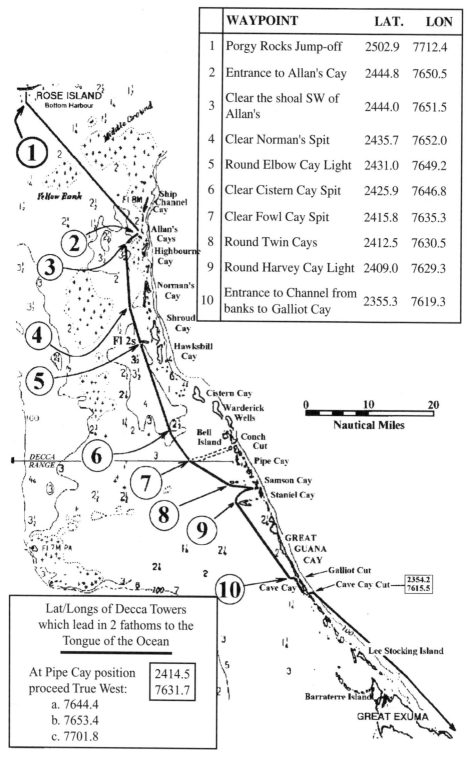

	WAYPOINT	LAT.	LON
1	Porgy Rocks Jump-off	2502.9	7712.4
2	Entrance to Allan's Cay	2444.8	7650.5
3	Clear the shoal SW of Allan's	2444.0	7651.5
4	Clear Norman's Spit	2435.7	7652.0
5	Round Elbow Cay Light	2431.0	7649.2
6	Clear Cistern Cay Spit	2425.9	7646.8
7	Clear Fowl Cay Spit	2415.8	7635.3
8	Round Twin Cays	2412.5	7630.5
9	Round Harvey Cay Light	2409.0	7629.3
10	Entrance to Channel from banks to Galliot Cay	2355.3	7619.3

Lat/Longs of Decca Towers which lead in 2 fathoms to the Tongue of the Ocean

At Pipe Cay position proceed True West: 2414.5 7631.7
a. 7644.4
b. 7653.4
c. 7701.8

Fast Path Down the Exumas: take it slow.

Allan's and Highbourne Cay

The anchorage at **Allan's Cays** is great for staying a day or two. The anchorage off the beach at the middle of **Highbourne Cay** is a good, calm waypoint in settled easterlies if you want to make better time.

Sampson Cay

This is a good spot to get fuel and water as well as being central to an abundance of little anchorages which are suitable for easy starts to **Cave Cay.**

Cave Cay

A draft of 7 feet can approach from the banks during mid-tide neaps on 90° magnetic on the northwest tip of **Little Galliot Cay**. One may also use a transit with the beach on **Big Galliot** just opening on the northwest tip of **Little Galliot**. When in deep water west of Galliot Cay, turn southeast to anchor behind Cave Cay. As almost always in the Bahamas, anchor in shallow water over deep sand with 2 anchors out. In this case, one toward weather threat and outgoing current, the west, and the other toward the incoming current, southeast. Set an anchor light. The mail boats may take this pass at night.

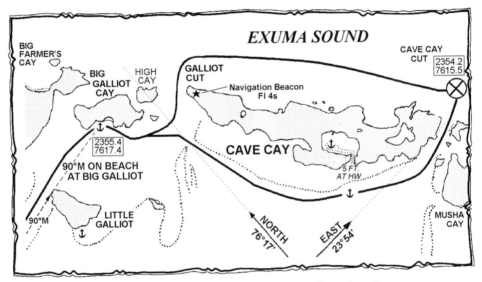

Exuma Banks to Exuma Sound via Galliot or Cave Cay Cuts.

Near slack tide in the morning, charge out the wide **Galliot Cut** or the deep **Cave Cay Cut**, favoring the north side, and sail off to **Georgetown** in a north of east wind of 15 knots. If you haven't got it, wait for it. Better yet, wait for a westerly and reach down to Georgetown in calm water.

Stay and fish awhile if it has been blowing hard east or northeast for several days. You don't want to enter the Georgetown cuts in what they call a **Rage**, where a combination of wave over swell can catch you wrong and broach you onto the reef inside the cut when you try to make the turn. Check out the underside of the fallen rocks on the south shore of **Little Galliot Cay** for yellowtail snapper, or try further south behind Musha Cay. The rocks on the south side of Cave Cay Cut (out of the current) also can be productive.

GEORGETOWN

February through May, Georgetown is the terminus for the apprehensive who are going back home and for the adventurous who are striking out for the southern islands. Mid-March is the Georgetown **Cruising Regatta** started by then Georgetown dentist Joel Fine in 1981. This is an event put on by the cruisers themselves to raise funds for the **Family Island Regatta** in mid-April. It draws 400 yachts, most of them at the end of their Bahamas cruise and at their southernmost harbor.

The Family Island Regatta is the America's Cup of all the races of classic Bahamian sloops and is one of the few remaining old time "Camp Town Races" type of expositions in North America. **Salt Pond** has a similar, though smaller and, some think <u>better</u>, event, 6 weeks after Easter: the **Salt Pond Regatta**. Between all these events you have access to the miniature cruising ground of **Elizabeth Harbor** itself. You can sail over to **Conception Island** or **Rum Cay** or **Long Island** for a week's getaway from the partying at Georgetown. You may, like myself, settle into a habit of Georgetown in the spring and Venezuela for the worst of the hurricane months. A wholly satisfying cruising life with lots of safe, short, *thornless* passages to keep crew and boat in condition, and with good provisioning at both ends (Dominican Republic and Puerto Rico at the northern end).

Georgetown earns the moniker of "Chicken Harbor" every season. Cruisers gab about stopping off at Conception on the way to Puerto Rico, or sailing to Rum Cay in one shot, as though they were just stopping by the convenience market before ramping up onto the interstate. Their biological clocks are still set on high from the hassle of getting the boat ready, from the bustle of provisioning, even from the social whirl among the yachts at Georgetown. One after another finds an excuse to return to Florida and "go south next year": a water-maker filter goes bad, an autopilot is on the fritz. The road south looms long and treacherous.

Unprepared cruisers that take the plunge and head out have their clocks cleaned quickly by the **Equatorial Current** and the incessant **trade** wind. They slow down to island time. They begin to see the wisdom of this guide's constantly drummed advice: **wait for weather**, leave early, get in early, and *never pass a safe anchorage*. Hit all the stops on the way down. Some never get the message. They write the whiny letters to the **SSCA**.

Georgetown abounds in fine anchorages, but unless you are in one of the holes in **Stocking Island** or in **Redshanks**, you will be moving from one to another in the winter months as fronts shift the winds. Redshanks, although remote and isolated, is only an 8 minute ride from town in a fast dinghy. To enter Redshanks with a 7 foot draft run down the harbor on a line 126° magnetic on JR's house on **Man of War Cay**. This will carry you by the reef off **Sand Dollar Beach** anchorage and through the gap in the reef off the **Elizabeth Island** anchorage.

When abeam of the house on the middle of **Guana Cay** turn onto 222° Magnetic until able to distinguish a transit of the easternmost of the Redshanks and the bluff which bounds **Master Harbor** to the northeast. Keep these 2 features just kissing, neither open nor closed, and you will pass a large coral head to starboard which stands in the center of a 100 yard gap in the reef beyond. Leave the last of the Redshanks forty yards to starboard and steer to the bluff, rounding slowly to starboard so as to leave the bluff 100 yards to the southwest. Then steer west until you see the entrance to Redshanks anchorage and pick up the darker colors of the entrance channel's deeper water. Anchor southeast of a ridge-like shoal which runs the length of the harbor in a northeast line. Here deep draft vessels will find from 9 to 14 feet of water in coral sand. Enter 2 hours before high tide with drafts 6 to 7 feet.

Drafts under 6 feet may round the northern extremity of the shoal close to **Crab Cay**. Vessels under 5 feet may try the anchorage even further to the east. The entrance is narrow and shallow but there is up to 3 fathoms and the protection is extraordinary.

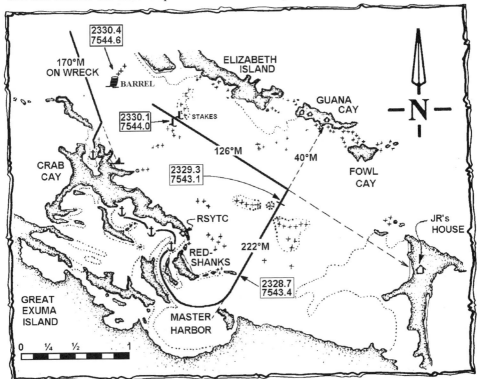

Georgetown anchorage at "Redshanks Yacht and Tennis Club".

For many years the **Redshanks** anchorage has been the locus of cruisers noted for their **Leisure** style. Whereas the **Stocking Island** hole anchorages have their *Volley Ball Beach*, and the monument anchorage has its *Hamburger Beach* at which yachts in the anchorage carry on their community activities, Redshanks has the *Redshanks Yacht and Tennis Club*, a half moon of beach fronting a cliff with many shelf like outcroppings, where happy hours with *hors d'oevres* are held nightly. Many of the same yachts return every year to enjoy the unique isolation in civilization available here, and there is, in fact, a loose sort of club going. When a founding member is not present, one of the yachts will act as Club Commodore, welcoming yachts on the VHF radio.

Past editions of this guide reported the *Redshanks Yacht and Tennis Club* with tongue in cheek, in the spirit of the Redshankers themselves, even reporting the Club's intentions to install a lawn tennis facility. Unfortunately for the game, a German megayacht squeezed into Redshanks after getting reluctant but official clearance from the Commodore. His outrage at finding only a few yachts and ragged rocks inside echoed clear to Nassau.

If you're a diver, a naturalist or isolationist, you'll love the Redshanks Yacht and Tennis Club. Check your tides when you dress for happy hour. The bar might be ankle deep at spring highs.

EAST FROM GEORGETOWN

The **Leisure Sailor** following the **Thornless Path** may find it advisable to do **Long Island's** west coast, in order to get a leg up on the wind and the journey during the winter months. (See the example under *Passage Elapse Times* above). In any case, to leave Georgetown headed south you should position yourself at **Fowl Cay** first. Why? Review the section on *Staging* under *Strategies for Passage Making*.

East from Georgetown: there are many options, take the one that suits the Weather Windows which are available.

If the dawn brings an evil blow with it while waiting at Fowl Cay, retreat to **Redshanks** for a day and attend the Redshanks Yacht and Tennis Club happy hour. Next evening wait back at Fowl Cay anchorage again.

A course of 35° Magnetic through a point 50 yards from the last of the rocks which stretch NE from Fowl Cay will carry you outside to **Exuma Sound**. The **North Channel Rocks** exit will be difficult in early morning light. If bound for **Cape Santa Maria**, take a course of 62° magnetic.

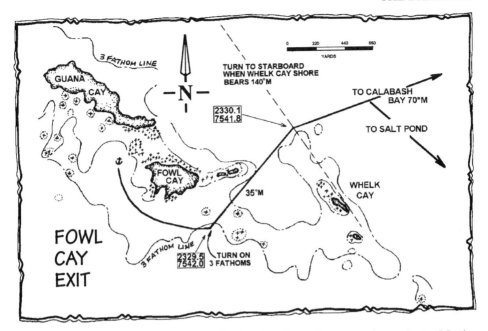

The **Fowl Cay** exit from **Elizabeth Harbor** is a few miles nearer **Cape Santa Maria** and has a better angle on the usual winds than the **Conch Cay Cut** exit. It also has a better angle on dawn light conditions than the **North Channel Rocks** exit. You may shorten a **Conception Island** landfall by several hours if you are already anchored at Fowl Cay at dawn rather than being in the middle of the harbor and taking Conch Cut.

The North Channel Rocks channel can be dangerous as it is directly against the light for anyone leaving Georgetown in the morning and directly up light for anyone entering in the evening. And those are usually the departure and arrival times of sailboats. The north Channel Rocks entrance is basically for power boats transiting in midday. The Fowl Cay entrance is never against the light, is short, and has landmarks close at hand with which to maintain a sure position while transiting. Pilot your vessel despite the waypoints noted. This is a 2 fathom entrance with good visibility which you can *pilot* on a white sand road.

Having positive, near-at-hand landmarks in dangerous cuts is of great importance. One season, we all listened to the breakup of a large ferro cement yacht which, with two other yachts following her, wandered too far from the channel while going out the North Channel Rocks channel, against the light, early in the morning. There just isn't enough positive identification of whereabouts in that channel. It's all water that looks all the same, and a little drift you're not aware of can finish you, especially if you are using a buddy channel while JR is hailing a warning to you on channel 16 (which was the case).

SAILING DIRECTIONS TO SALT POND

If you are ready to leave **Georgetown,** yet the wind continues to blow briskly northeast, then don't hang around Georgetown gathering commitments. Take a sparkling sail over the banks to Salt Pond and say hello to John McKie *(SUNSEEKER)* in **Thompson's Bay**. John has helped countless boats along the *thorny* path over many years from his hilltop **BASRA** station and has detailed knowledge of the whole route.

Leaving **Fowl Cay Cut**, watch set and leeway doesn't drift you onto Whelk Cay Reef as you round it going southeast. Get well beyond the **Whelk Cay Reef** before turning to a course for **White Cay,** on the banks. The course to White Cay is about 120° M, splitting the difference between **Black Rocks** and **North Channel Rocks**. You will be headed for waypoint #1, 2 miles north of the east end of **Hog Cay**. Turn eastward to waypoint #2 where you shall enter a blue water trench bordered on the south by a white bank. Follow the white bank on your starboard hand at 118°M to its end at waypoint #3, then continue on course to waypoint #4 at **Indian Hole Point**.

Round **Indian Hole Point** closely and proceed directly northeast to the **Thompson's Bay** anchorage. Call Dorothy on the VHF *(AQUARIUS)* when you get to Salt Pond and order cracked conch dinner at Thompson's Bay Inn. Top up your water from the old plantation wells ashore.

	LAT	LONG	ACTION
1.	2325.5	7528.0	turn east at **White Cay**
2.	2325.5	7524.0	enter blue trench
3.	2324.4	7520.0	leave white bank
4.	2321.0	7510.0	arrive **Indian Hole Point**, Thompson's Bay offing

Play the Tide for Speed and Depth

For drafts of 6 feet and more, it is best to start onto the banks with an early morning low tide. You should try to catch the slack high tide half way across. Not only shall you get deeper water on the banks, but the stream shall carry you both onto and then off of the banks. The bank tides between the **Exumas** and **Long Island** run east-west in the west and north-south in the east. Reckon on one knot at full ebb. Tides at White Cay shall be about 1 hour 20 minutes later than Georgetown. Salt Pond tides shall be about 1 hour 40 minutes later.

Use the Light

If you leave from **Fowl Cay** (not Redshanks or the Monument) around 7 a.m. you will have fair light south. Parallelling **Hog Cay** and **White Cay** you will again have good light at midday. The sun will be over your shoulder when making for **Indian Hole Point**, the largest and darkest headland visible far to the southeast.

Getting Off the Banks

To leave the banks, sail north in the lee of **Long Island**. From **Salt Pond** north to **Simms**, run from point-to-point about 200 yards off each point. From Simms to **Calabash Bay** stand well off **Ferguson Point** (waypoint #1below), nearly a mile, and sail directly for **Dove Cay** (waypoint #2) until you can see the sandy bar west of it.

A fifty foot wide channel carrying 7 feet at low water will border the bar 280 yards west southwest of **Dove Cay**. Follow it 2 miles to deep water a mile southwest of **Hog Cay** (waypoint #3). Deep draft vessels can benefit by taking the Dove Cay channel with an incoming tide.

	LAT	LONG	ACTION
1.	2329.2	7516.1	clear Ferguson Point
2.	2332.8	7520.3	enter Dove Cay Channel
3.	2335.3	7521.6	leave Dove Cay Channel

CALABASH BAY AND SANTA MARIA

Calabash can be rolly in winds north of east or if there are large northeast swells forecast for the area. East or south of east it is a fine, smooth anchorage. If it looks like the northeast wind is about to go east, tuck in under **Cape Santa Maria** for an early takeoff to **Conception Island**, or fish the point in the morning and go in the afternoon. It's a short and easy sail.

After entering Calabash Bay through the reef continue east to a grassy shoal which stretches blackly north and south in front of you. Turn to the lighthouse built at the west side of the inner basin entrance, turning in toward the houses slightly to a point which bears 325° Magnetic to the point of land to the west, 030° to the lighthouse and 200° to the point of land to the south. There's 8 1/2 feet here. Get out of Calabash if it blows anything but easterly. The chop and swell can be ferocious and will slam you on the bottom.

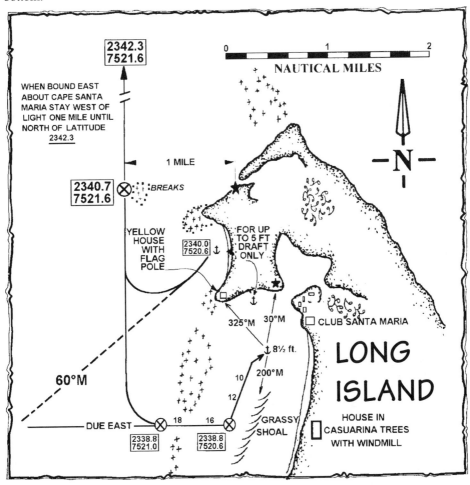

Calabash Bay and Santa Maria Anchorages

129

CONCEPTION ISLAND

If you have easterlies of Force 3 or less make your landfall at **Conception Island** on **Southampton Reef**, anchoring in 20 feet of rock and sand around 2 and a quarter miles north of **West Cay**. Dinghy over the reef for some of the most spectacular reef and wreck snorkeling available in the Bahamas, second only to **Rum Cay**. There are several square miles of reef diving here. With heads towering over 20 feet over white sand bottom, you'll feel like Superman flying between the skyscrapers of Metropolis. The bad guys on the streets below are 10-20 pound groupers, snapper and 5-10 pound lobsters. Look long enough and you'll spot relics of the old wooden ships wrecked on this three mile reef which is invisible from windward. Conception is now part of the Exuma land/sea park whose rules for taking of shells and wildlife are quite stringent. Hone up on actual enforcement policies at the time of your visit. You neither want to despoil this island and reef, prettiest of all the Bahamas, nor do you want to limit your enjoyment of it based on rumored restrictions or out of date publications.

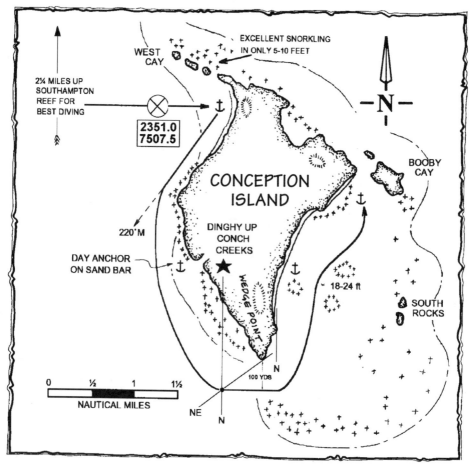

Conception Island: use the east anchorage in a westerly.

Other guides notwithstanding, the eastern anchorage has 18 to 24 feet of deep sand bottom and is an excellent refuge in westerlies. Coral shoals are few and easily seen. Anchor in the corner between **Booby Cay** and Conception. You can move from the northwest anchorage to the east anchorage and back again during passage of a **front**, staying at Conception as long as you like. Enter the east anchorage from a point south of the light and southwest of **Wedge Point**, proceeding due east, 80-120 yards off the Point, and until the north-south line of beach is visible on the eastern shore. Proceed by eye even to the top of the harbor if you wish.

Conception Island is the loveliest of islands in the Bahamas, bar none. Unfortunately, I meet folks every year who, having left **Georgetown**, feel they are now *en marche* and zip right by Conception, or use it only as a waypoint. In such a hurry to get to paradise, they rush right by, never knowing they were there. You can stay at Conception indefinitely, fronts and all, until a **Weather Window** opens which gives you a lay on **Rum Cay** or **San Salvador** as a **Leisure Sail**. Dinghy around the rocks to the shoal pocket east of **West Cay** and north of Conception. The snorkeling is absolutely outstanding and this extensive area of sand and coral is shallow and safe for even nonswimmers in tubes. If you're not up to diving with the pros way out on **Southampton Reef**, then don't miss this snorkeling kiddy park.

RUM CAY

Rum Cay is the best spot, all around, to **Wait for Weather** east of Georgetown — if you're well tucked in. It has the finest snorkeling, fishing and diving you can expect, a friendly little community of under a hundred souls, and good local restaurants and bars. It can roll a little unless you are well sheltered by **Point Sumner**. Whenever I tucked in with a 6 and a half foot draft we didn't roll much here (see anchorages on chartlet). You can always jibsail over to the west coast beach or beautiful **Flamingo Bay** if your **wait for weather** becomes extended, or use the marina in foul weather.

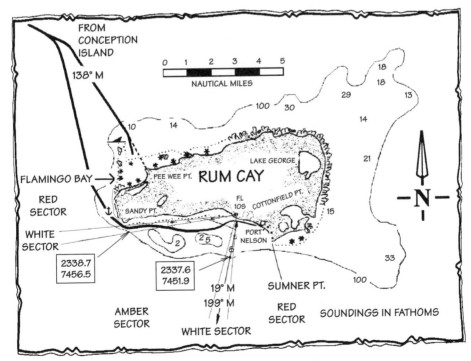

Rum Cay: best spot to wait for a front.

First time entrances here should be made from the south with high sun, or from the west with afternoon sun. For the experienced, a light with 8° white sectors on safe entrance is atop **Cottonfield Point**. Red sectors designate dangerous reefs while an amber sector covers an area with many coral heads. As often occurs in the Bahamas, it may not be lit.

Approach Cottonfield Point on either heading shown. About 800 yards off Cottonfield Point take up a 110° Magnetic heading on houses on the only hill north of the marina between the town dock and **Sumner Point**. When the **Dive Club**'s main house bears 10° magnetic turn to it and proceed to a clear white sand anchorage in 8-10 feet. The **Sumner Point Marina** is a long term project which will see homes sprout along the point. The hill north of the marina, with its houses, should nonetheless continue to stand out as a guide into the anchorage.

A larger anchorage, but slightly less sheltered by the points, can be had by continuing several hundred yards on the 110° course instead of turning toward the club. For shallower drafts, a hole of about one fathom can be found nearer the beach by holding the 110° course even farther.

The dive club closed years ago. It further suffered severe damages in hurricane Lilly. While in operation, the Club developed scuba dive sites where one could get photograped petting 500 pound jewfish. Today, cruisers can hire diver guide Rasta Sean Tynes. Sean used to dive for the Club, and he knows sites for viewing as well as for fishing.

Visit Kay's Bar and talk with Kay's mother, Doloris Wilson, a writer and local historian. Her book, *My Rum Cay Home*, which is used in the Bahamas school system is available at Kay's general store, The Last Chance, just around the corner. Continue inland from there to find BATELCO, with operator Sam Maycock, and the Two Sisters Take Out. Take the road back to Ted Bains' Oceanview Bar, and stop at Toby's Wholesale and Retail Bar across from the schoolhouse.

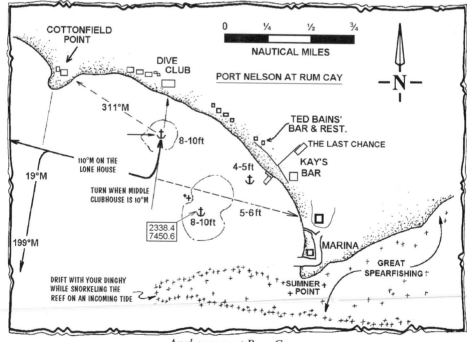

Anchorages at Rum Cay

132

Flamingo Bay on the northwest corner of the island is a beautiful anchorage in easterlies but a **deathtrap** in west and north winds. If you wait there, get out well in advance of any front. To enter Flamingo Bay enter at 138° Magnetic on **Pee Wee Point**, which appears from sea like a rock island, leaving the wreck at the tip of the northwest reef one half mile to starboard. Once inside the bay pick your way through the heads which only become numerous shoreward of a line between the points.

The Haitian wreck northwest of the entrance to Flamingo Bay was delivering a load of Salvation Army clothes to Haiti. It's reported that the skipper ordered the Dominican helmsman to turn left to avoid the reef, which he did. Since the order wasn't countermanded, the helmsman held it left in a broad, circling sweep that ended back where he started but slightly south — where it is today. One used to be able to renew one's cruising wardrobe here, and it wasn't too shabby. Visiting the wreck may help you understand **Haiti** better before you actually go there. Thinking how it supposedly got up on the reef in

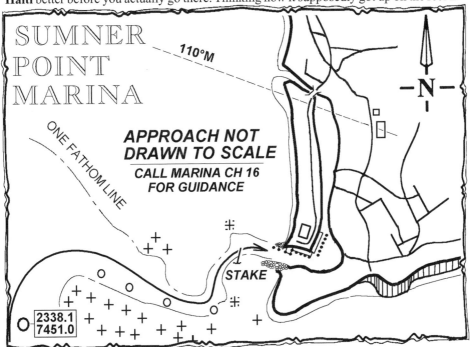

the first place may enhance your enjoyment of the **Dominican Republic**: if you can empathize with the helmsman's "*no problema*" mentality, you'll *love* the DR.

Sumner Point Marina

The marina, operated by Bob, Fran, Bobby, Jeni and Jon, makes a safe haven in severe fronts. They answer VHF channel 16. They take 7 foot drafts at high tide. The style and position of bouyage may change due to storms. If you haven't entered recently, you may want to call to have the marina staff talk you through. They also gladly furnish a free pilot.

The beautifully designed club house has a restaurant and bar with many artistic creations of the owners. The bar is open daily for happy hour. The restaurant boasts gourmet dinners prepared by chef Jon, and graciously served by hostess and host Jeni and Bobby. You may have to wait until Gorda Sound in the BVIs to enjoy both meal and ambiance that meet their standard.

RUM CAY TO MAYAGUANA

From **Rum Cay** you can strike various routes south. Bearing with the strategy to *Keep to the North to Go South*, try to make **Mayaguana** [*my-GUAH-nah*] direct with a **front** in winter, or **Attwood Harbor,** or **Plana Cays,** in light airs in summer (Force 4 or less).

A detour to **Clarence Town** or **Landrail Point** (same as **Pittstown Landing,** or **Portland Harbor**) may be in order. Once on **Crooked Island,** however, a day's motoring to Attwood is almost inevitable and you may stand in technical violation of the tenets of the **Leisure Sailor.** Review again *Keep to the North to Go South.*

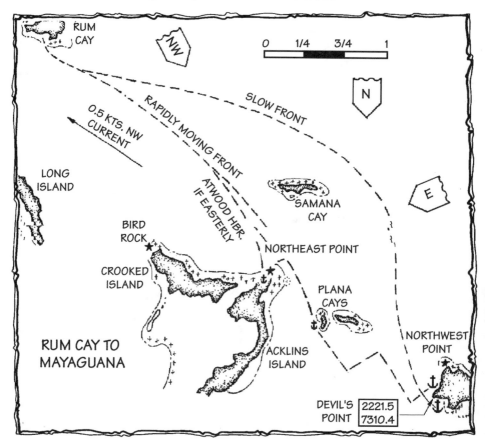

In following a front down to Mayaguana from Rum Cay, take off on the first breath of a southerly wind. By the time you are on a longitude with **Samana Cay** [*suh-MA-nuh,* not *sah-mah-NAH,* in the DR] you will be broad reaching north of the Plana Cays and can reach down the **Mayaguana Passage**, rounding up into **Start Bay** or **Betsy Bay.**

Later in the season, with the more rapid veering of the **front**al winds, you might not be able to turn the corner down the **Mayaguana Passage** before the wind goes east. In that case stop at **West Plana Cay.**

SAMANA CAY

Once, when I approached **Samana Cay** from the south, conditions were just right to provide us with a mirror image of the island, in color, on the bottoms of the clouds of the coastal front above the island. It began, what for me was a series of discovery trips to this nearly unapproachable isolated jewel. If you want to know all about Samana Cay, read the November 1986 issue of the *National Geographic* (Vol.170, No. 5). It is an intriguing piece which proposes Samana as the real landing site of **Columbus** in the new world.

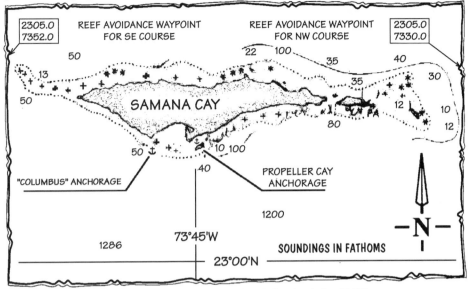

Samana Cay [suh-MAH-nuh]: Columbus's landfall?

Even in **Columbus'** day, Samana Cay was a site of temporary fishing camps where the **Arawak** inhabitants of **Acklins Island** to the south, could get away for awhile (for not always innocent reasons). They would hang out at Samana Cay, drying conch, crabbing and fishing until things cooled off at home and they could return to their settlements — or, as today, make a high speed outboard run over for cigarettes.

Anchor well tucked in at the supposed **Columbus** anchorage on the southwest and dinghy in. This is a very choppy anchorage on sand over rock. Have two anchors down

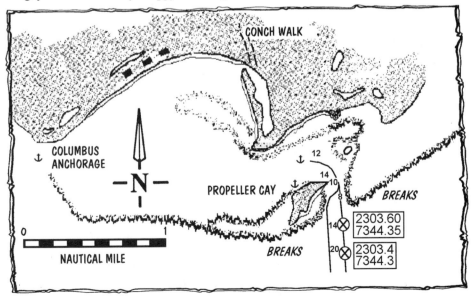

and dive on them for inspection. If your draft is less than 5 feet, you might make it into the bay where the fishing camps are. Lead yourself in with the dinghy, however, and keep a kedge ready!

Samana Cay is pronounced SAM-uh-nuh or sah-MAH-nah, unlike the Dominican Republic harbor, **Samaná**, which is pronounced as the **Tainos** said it: sah-mah-NAH.

Propeller Cay Anchorage

The 45 foot steel ketch *Stealaway* weathered a direct hit by Hurricane Klaus behind **Propeller Cay**, in deep sand, but surrounded by perilous rock.The holding is good. If you take this anchorage, enter in light wind only so there's little chop (Force 3) and in good light (10 am to 2 p.m., sunny). Stay on the white sand, 15 foot wide, 8 foot deep, zigzag channel. The current runs east and west *across* the channel.

If piloting without a GPS:

1. Head magnetic north to the eastern most point of Propeller Cay.
2. 100 yards off the point, round east and north until 50 yards east of it.
3. Continue to round into the anchorage staying equidistant between the point and the rock to its northeast.

With a GPS, head magnetic north from the waypoint shown until 50 yards east of the eastern most point of Propeller Cay, then follow step #3 above.

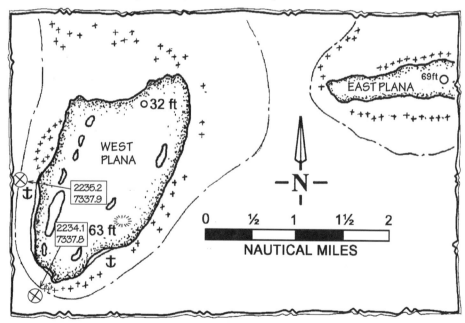

West Plana Cay Anchorage

Plana Cays

Sometimes a fast moving **front** will outrun you and the winds are too far east to continue on comfortably. In that case, head for **Attwood Harbor** or **West Plana Cay**. The anchorage at Plana can roll a bit in southeasterlies but it is snug enough in stiff easterlies.

Proceed east to the middle of the sand beach. When over 20 feet of white sand bottom round to port to anchor at the northern end of the beach, south of a large coral patch.

As you coast to your anchorage, keep an eye on the heads beneath your keel. You want one not too deep and big enough to support a dinner sized grouper and a lobster for appetizer. Anchor about 150 feet dead to windward of the head you choose. After the boat is snug for the night let out enough scope to bring the bathing ladder over the coral head. While the mate sets out the **SG&T**s, the skipper can harvest a bountiful dinner.

If forced to wait a while at Plana don't despair. The beachcombing on the windward shore is as good as at **Big Sand Cay** and there is good diving and fishing by dinghy, or off the beach on the north end of the island. It is possible to take your boat between the islands since there is almost an ocean passage there. You will be in basically uncharted waters however. When the wind moderates, take a sparkling and sporty ocean daysail over to **Betsy Bay** for a good lee over grouper rocks and a tour of the small and friendly village there.

As you round West Plana Cay on the south, the swells can be intimidating since the west northwest-going deep ocean current will be spoiling on the Plana shelf. But once out and away this is a delightful daysail in clear weather and under Force 4 conditions.

ATTWOOD HARBOR ALTERNATE

An alternate harbor for longer waits is **Attwood Harbor** downwind from West Plana. Attwood is not a good spot in northeast wind and a *deathtrap* in anything more northerly. Enter Attwood only in good light from a point one half mile north at 2243.9-7353.0. Proceed 180°M 50 yards west of the umbrella rock on the east side of the entrance. Round to the southeast since the harbor shoals to the west, and anchor in 8 feet of sand.

MAYAGUANA

When rounding Devil's Point (Southwest Point), take it close (40 yards) or the current may whip you out to sea again, and it's a long tacking process around it.

Betsy Bay is your anchorage in southeast wind, **Start Bay** in east to northwest winds. Otherwise use **Abraham Bay**. If only overnighting, the anchorage at **Start Bay** is easily made and easily left. If the next day you decide to stay awhile, move into **Abraham Bay** via the west entrance. Be careful to enter only in high afternoon light, and beware of the shoals and coral extending more than a mile south of **Start Point**.

Follow the reef to the blue water entrance channel a mile or more south of Start Point. Proceed northeast for one quarter mile beyond the reef entrance, then one mile east to a position 200 yards behind the protection of the reef in 2 fathoms of water. To avoid all chop you must snug up to the reef. That also makes it easy to go snorkeling and diving. If you wish to visit the settlement you can take a 7 foot draft up the bay on a rising tide. From the anchorage behind the reef, steer toward the buildings to the north for 3 quarters mile, then steer for the settlement's radio mast, avoiding apparent heads and rocks.

Leave Mayaguana only in settled weather (when the morning's **NWS Offshore Report** is the same for "today", "tonight" and "tomorrow" — see the chapter, *Making Sense of the NWS Offshore Reports*). With prevailing wind directions, sailboats should fill their sails on a port tack from **Southeast Point**. Trawlers should look to swell direction before choosing a point of departure. When the winds go light, or have turned easterly or north of east, take an afternoon sail over to **Southeast Point**. Arrive well before 5 p.m. in order to select a patch of deep sand in 12 to 20 feet at which to temporarily anchor. Do not snug up to the reef and coral heads to avoid the roll. Whatever your departure point, have your SG&T, read a little and catch a nap after dinner. Up anchor late evening to early morning, depending on your estimated time to make the **Sandbore Channel** entrance to **Caicos Banks** by *shortly after daybreak*. See the section on *Land Effects* for why.

MAYAGUANA TO PROVIDENCIALES

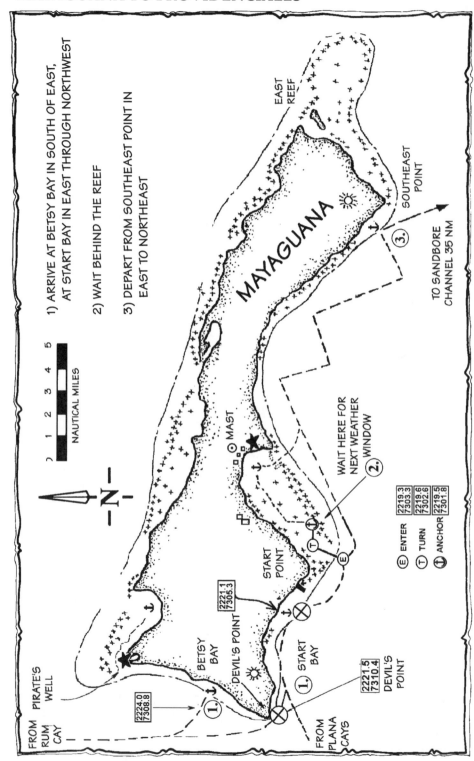

1) ARRIVE AT BETSY BAY IN SOUTH OF EAST, AT START BAY IN EAST THROUGH NORTHWEST

2) WAIT BEHIND THE REEF

3) DEPART FROM SOUTHEAST POINT IN EAST TO NORTHEAST

1 2 3 4 5
NAUTICAL MILES

–N–

EAST REEF

SOUTHEAST POINT

MAYAGUANA

TO SANDBORE CHANNEL 35 NM

3.

WAIT HERE FOR NEXT WEATHER WINDOW

2.

MAST

START POINT

E ENTER 2219.3 / 7303.3
T TURN 2219.6 / 7302.6
⚓ ANCHOR 2219.5 / 7301.8

2221.1 / 7305.3

T

E

BETSY BAY

DEVIL'S POINT

PIRATE'S WELL

FROM RUM CAY

2224.0 / 7308.8

1.

1. START BAY

2221.5 / 7310.4
DEVIL'S POINT

FROM PLANA CAYS

THE SANDBORE CHANNEL

DMA charts and some guide editions to the contrary, the remains of a freighter is grounded on the reef about 2 miles northeast from the north edge of the channel entrance. Sail to the freighter in early morning light until you see the atoll-like reef with breaking seas dividing ocean blue from bright shoal green. Follow the reef south until you come to the half-mile broad ocean blue waters of the Sandbore Channel entrance. Can't miss it! Arrive early morning before the east wind, which comes over 60 miles of banks, begins to honk.

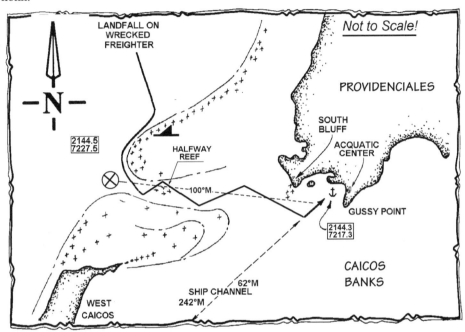

Sandbore Channel Entrance to Caicos Banks.

Motoring or sailing, tack the 8 or 10 miles to the ship channel and enter **Sapodilla Bay**. You will meet supposed *cognizenti,* local and cruisers, who scoff at tacking the Sandbore in morning light, and motorboaters who say you should arrive around midday.

Why tack this channel in the early morning, even if you are motoring? Look again at the chapter on *Land Effects*. In **prevailing conditions** (see Glossary), the 60 mile wide shallow Caicos Banks comprise an extraordinarily large heat sink. It might as well be light color land. If a sailboat doesn't get in before the wind rises, it may have to motor die straight into 20 knots and 3 foot chop in 8 to 10 feet of water for 3 hours at high revs. Arrive in early morning calm. Review *Land Effects: Bank Effects.*

Why tack? If you're sailing east in a light early easterly, you either tack or get a sailboat not yet invented. If you're motorsailing, the sun is ahead of you, but each narrow tack permits good up-light visibility either side of the sun as well as the advantage in boat speed. Once on the banks, there are few real heads, but there are shoals of veggies and a few rocks, most of which are covered by 8 to 10 feet of water. Dodge them anyway for the sake of the odd rock which might be sticking up above the others in a trough. Tacking slightly while motorsailing, you can also keep a watch over your shoulder to know when you've passed **Halfway Reef** and the shoals off **South Bluff**. It looks scarier than it really is, but the above precautions can avoid mishap. Let the experts talk. I zigzag a morning up-light course over *any* shallows, any*where*. More fool you, if you don't, too. With or without tacks, the beat up to the anchorage could take several hours, so arrive early with a sailboat. *Never after the wind strengthens.*

SAPODILLA BAY

Cruisers on a budget can pass up **Turtle Cove** on the north coast of **Providenciales** ("**Provo**") and anchor at **Sapodilla Bay** under the Aquatic Center building. Customs and Immigration can be found at the government dock over the hill to the east or by dinghying around the point. The Aquatic Center is off and on again open and closed under different owners. If open, officials will come down and clear you in there. If closed, you may get bit by a guard dog trying to enter private property. Call "HARBORMASTER" on VHF Channel 16 for instructions.

If you didn't get enough **cash** in Georgetown there are banks here. And, believe it, you will need cash if you stay long in Provo. Also, if you are planning to provision in **Puerto Plata, Santiago,** or **Luperón**, it is probably cheaper to get your cash here in Provo. Some DR banks may charge a percentage fee on **VISA**. A visit to the **Conch Farm** at **Leeward Going Through** is well worthwhile.

Have your anchors well down. Holding's fair to good, but besides the occasional summer squall, a winter front can have leading edges of up to fifty knots from the west. Otherwise this is usually a very good anchorage.

If bound for **Cap Haïtien, or Manzanillo** you might leave through the Provo ship channel and **stage** yourself off **West Caicos** for a 2-3 hours shorter passage. There are buoys off the west coast for the dive boats that are normally not used at night. Remember that hours cut from the beginning of a passage really come off the end of the passage.

Plan to be about twenty miles offshore of *'Cap'* around 4 am. Any uncertainties of landfall will be made up for by the loom of the city in the predawn hours. Refer to the directions for sailing from **Big Sand Cay** to Puerto Plata or Manzanillo, and to the sections on *Approaching Hispaniola, Manzanillo* and *Cap Haïtien* for sailing directions.

Turtle Cove Marina on the north coast of Providenciales, Turks & Caicos.

TURKS & CAICOS

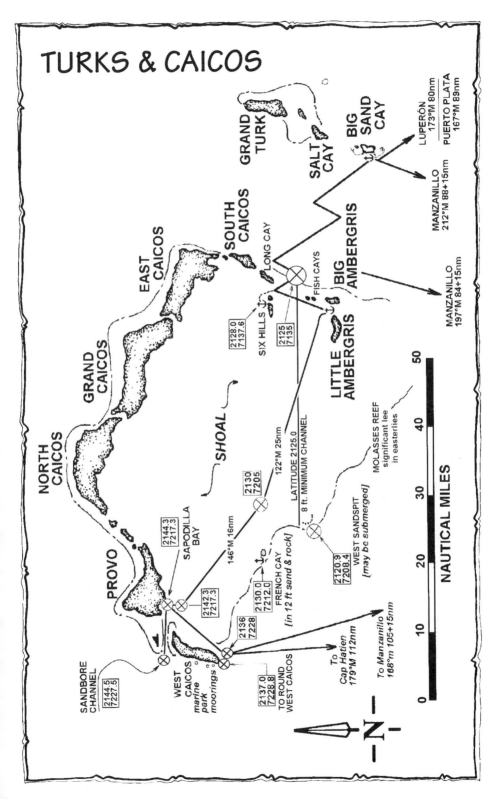

NORTH CAICOS

GRAND CAICOS

EAST CAICOS

SOUTH CAICOS

GRAND TURK

SALT CAY

BIG SAND CAY

LONG CAY

FISH CAYS

BIG AMBERGRIS

SIX HILLS
2128.0
7137.6

2125
7135

LITTLE AMBERGRIS

PROVO

SANDBORE CHANNEL
2144.5
7227.5

WEST CAICOS
marine park moorings

2137.0
7228.8

TO ROUND WEST CAICOS

2136
7228

2142.3
7217.3

2130.0
7212.0

FRENCH CAY
[in 12 ft sand & rock]

2144.3
7217.3

SAPODILLA BAY

2130
7205

SHOAL

146°M 16nm

122°M 25nm

LATITUDE 2125.0

8 ft. MINIMUM CHANNEL

WEST SANDSPIT
[may be submerged]

2120.9
7208.4

MOLASSES REEF
significant lee in easterlies

To Cap Hatien
179°M 112nm

To Manzanillo
168°m 105+15nm

MANZANILLO
197°M 84+15nm

MANZANILLO
212°M 88+15nm

LUPERÓN
173°M 80nm

PUERTO PLATA
167°M 89nm

0   10   20   30   40   50

NAUTICAL MILES

-N-

141

OVER THE BANKS

Bob Gascoin's and Jane Minty's charts of the Caicos islands (Wavy Line Publishing) are excellent. A caution for sailors, however, is that the routes shown are basically for power boats such as used in dive operations. For example, the **Pearl Channel** direct from **Sapodilla Bay** southeast through the shoals is fine, but it is directly into the wind and narrow. Tidal set affects slower, large keel sailing craft more than powerboats, and of course sailboats don't go to windward as well. Under prevailing winds, most sailing vessels should make better time on the route shown on the chartlet, both sailed and motor-sailed.

From time to time there are reports of the central shoaly area having "gone away". These are probably started by cruisers who went more north than they intended, and having been lucky in their trip through the maze. They assume the shoals are overrated. The slightly higher than the rest bulge in the middle of the northern half of the Banks has been there since, according to one theory, a northeast-going space rock slammed into the ocean zillions of years ago, forming the Turks & Caicos. I don't think it will go away so easy.

The route in this guide is chosen for easy-to-remember coordinates, for safety of the vessel without GPS, or with a frail engine in severe cross tidal currents, and because it is tried and true. Other routes may save you a half mile. You might do them safely a dozen times. Then again, maybe you'll hit the odd lump on the first try. Play it right. Play it safe.

Before SATNAV and charts were available, I took *Jalan Jalan's* 6 and a half foot draft across the banks to **Six Hills** as an experiment, going *north* of the central shoals. I waited for calms, and it took two days of laborious backtracking in a sandbore maze. I don't advise it. If you draw less than 6 feet, it is possible to cross to Six Hills from the 2130-7205 waypoint shown on the chartlet. The way from Six Hills to **Turks Passage** must be done by eyeball in good light. It is faster and safer to reach **South Caicos** from Six Hills via Turks Passage.

Though you may not think so, the **Caicos Banks** are on the Thornless Path. That is, it is easier to cross them than to go around them. Leave **Sapodilla Bay** at dawn on a day when the wind is north of east or else *under 15 knots for certain*. To clear out early you may be asked to pay overtime charges, even if the papers are done the day before during office hours. Pay it and go at daybreak. Don't delay departure. You don't want to be caught out on the banks. Leave Sapodilla Bay at *daybreak*.

Cross the banks with a 7 foot draft from a point 2 miles south of **Gussy Point**, proceeding along 146°M for 16 miles to a point 72°05'W, 21°30'N. Then motor lickety-damn in deeper water the 25 miles to **Ambergris** at 122°M.

Leave at dawn to arrive at **Ambergris** well before sundown. Reckon on a 1.2 knot northeast tide set at peak flood (northwest near the Ambergris islands) and use the **Rule of Twelfths** to interpolate your drift (see Glossary). Unless you have a GPS, keep a good **EP** (see Glossary). A **DR** is not enough.

Even though the coral heads are far and few between, it doesn't pay to be complacent on this run either. Sailboats have been known to graze a coral head while in over twenty feet of water. So, with the Caicos Banks, as with the rice pudding in the school cafeteria, it's always best to avoid the dark spots.

If you have to anchor on the banks, do so at the risk of bending your anchor shanks, as I have done, while getting them up in a stiff chop the next morning, or chopping your foot off with the chain wildly snatching at the bow. Best to start out at *daybreak*. But *never* proceed after sundown. How can you, anyway? You've got to have your **SG&T** to stay on the Thornless Path.

THE FRENCH CAY ROUTE

It is possible to carry 8 feet to **French Cay** from **Sapodilla Bay**, exit the banks and reenter between **French Cay** and **West Sand Spit**, proceeding along 21°25' in plenty of water to exit to the **Turks Passage** north of the **Fish Cays**.

AMBERGRIS CAYS

The round the world cruise for a family of 4 nearly ended here scarcely before it began. They rammed a rock just at sundown trying to make the anchorage before dark. Start early and "arrive by 5" at Ambergris and anchor where shown, *not* near the land.

This anchorage looks wide open, but it is good in most conditions and provides bountiful fishing. Anchor in 8 feet of water half way between the islands, one mile east of **Little Ambergris** and one mile west southwest of some fishermen's shacks on **Big Ambergris**.

One cruiser accosted me down islands with a harrowing tale of how he spent the night in 4 foot seas amidst hull-tearing elkhorn coral. He thought this guide irresponsible for recommending Ambergris. When asked if he stayed at the anchorage recommended above, he replied, "No, we couldn't find it because it was getting dark and we had to anchor".

Now this guide specifically warns against anchoring on the **Caicos Banks.** But my false accuser had done exactly that. So, as the night followed Polonius' day, I asked:

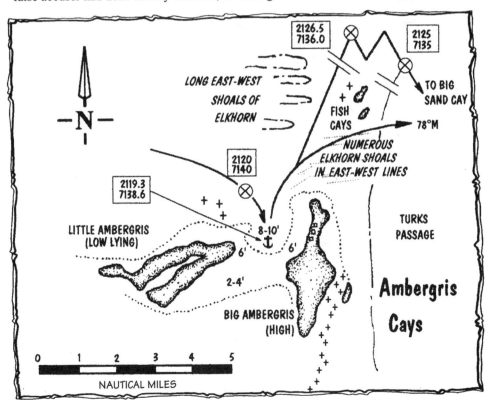

Ambergris transient anchorage

"What time did you leave Sapodilla Bay?"

"About 8:30 or 9:00."

"What were the winds like?"

"Oh, southeast, 15 to 20."

"Couldn't you have left earlier, say, *daybreak?*"

"Well, we were with some other boats."

"Couldn't you wait for a better window, say, 15 knots or less?"

"We really needed to get going. We'd spent too much time in the Bahamas, and we needed to get to the Virgins to earn some money."

Four violations! He didn't leave at daybreak. He left in a southeast Force 5 on the nose. He didn't captain his own boat. And he was in a hurry ... The penalty almost came to fit the crime, but the perpetrator still saw himself as victim.

There are large fields of elkhorn and other coral in this area and you need good afternoon light (before 5 p.m.) to identify them. The way into the anchorage from the Banks, however, is deep (10+ feet) and free of anything but obvious and black and only occasional heads. I have stayed at this anchorage during quite heavy blows, passing **storm cells** and steady, strong **Trades**. It remained peaceful and serene with a light chop. Very surprising, since at first glance it appears wide open and not such good holding. Dive on your anchors, and of course, use two in case of wind shift from showers.

Don't go south of Fish Cays unless headed <u>west</u> in morning light the first time.

From Ambergris proceed to **Big Sand Cay** to take up station on a **Wait for Weather** before jumping off for **Hispaniola**. If proceeding south of the **Fish Cays** watch out for the elkhorn north of the west coast of Big Ambergris. See the chartlet.

The first time you go south of the Fish Cays, go in good light only. There are east and west running "streets" of 3 fathoms depth, but in poor light you won't recognize them.

The current in the Turks Passage can really rip north, so *lee-bow* it.

If you decide to go outside and avoid the Banks, you can reduce the agony by taking the ship channel out and nosing over to French Cay to anchor for the night, then following the reef until the punishment of the **Equatorial Current** and full Trades start.

Upon leaving the banks either side of the **Fish Cays** be prepared for steep and short seas. Wind with tide, you have the Atlantic Ocean trying to climb the wall onto Caicos Banks. Tide against wind, you've got cataracts underwater and overfalls above as the Banks empty themselves into the sea. Outside will be much smoother. For purists, a good sail is north-northeast to the shoals south of **Long Cay**, thence southeast between Long Cay and Fish Cays, long-tacking and lee-bowing the current down to a western approach into **Big Sand Cay**. Do not tack as far south as dangerous **Endymion Rock**. If you short tack, be prepared for an all day sail, although Big Sand Cay is only 20 miles away.

BIG SAND CAY

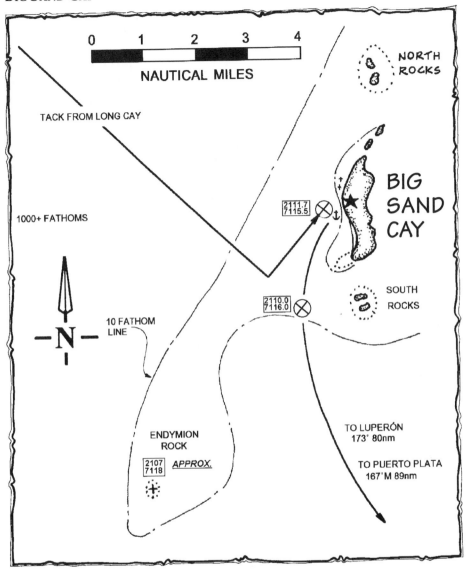

Big Sand Cay and Endymion Rock

See **South Caicos** while you are cruising the **Turks and Caicos** but don't **stage** from there. The anchorages are poor, shallow and rocky, with the exception of behind **Long Cay**, where there's not much room for boats with draft, and it rolls badly in anything but southeast winds. If you need to jerry jug you will have to clear in and out again. **Staging** from here can add a day to the sail to Hispaniola due to the current in the **Turks Passage**.

Big Sand Cay, though a bit rolly, has a large, deep sand anchorage. Thus the "Big Sand" name. Waiting here puts you 20 miles farther to windward and up to a day's sail closer to **Hispaniola** than does any other route (e.g., **South Caicos** or direct from **Ambergris**). Being here also frees you from worry about **Endymion Rock**, 4 feet underwater and not always breaking.

Walk over the hill from Sapodilla Bay (above) to the Customs Dock (pictured below).

Some DMA charts show **Endymion Rock** where **Big Sand Cay** is and other charts don't even show it. Kline's *Yachtsman's Guide to the Bahamas* shows it correctly on the chartlet of the **Turks and Caicos** as does the *Bahamas Chart Kit*, about 7 miles bearing 215° True from Big Sand Cay light which is at 21°11.7'N and 71°15.5'W. Also note the clearly visible rocks, **South Rocks**, about a half mile south of Big Sand Cay. If sailing the windward coast of Big Sand on a route from **Salt Cay**, you can safely sail between South Rocks and Big Sand, swinging wide of the sandy shoals off the southwest tip of Big Sand.

Getting to Big Sand Cay can be an all day tacking sail due to the north setting current in the **Turks Passage**. But those are hours shortened on the sail to Hispaniola, had you begun your trek from South Caicos or **Ambergris**. Approach the island from the west on the light, even in the dark, and anchor in sixteen feet of deep sand about 150 yards southwest of the light. The light is run by solar cells and is usually working. However, the switches often fail, leaving the light to work throughout the day, failing on dead batteries sometime around midnight. As with all lights south of Florida, assume they may not work. If they work, assume their characteristics are wrong because of poor power due to poor maintenance. It is actually all-round best to flat distrust all markers in the non-US Caribbean and the Bahamas, navigating by pilotage. Transits of land features don't wear out.

The best beachcombing in the islands is on the windward shore of this uninhabited jewel. Watching **whales** is great in the month of February where the humpbacks gather to mate from **Samaná Bay** to the **Silver Banks**. In their once-a-year euphoria to get there

the 40 and 50 footers will leap clear of the water, leaving echoes like canon shot.

Big Sand Cay can be departed by starlight with safety. Depart Big Sand, being sure to clear South Rocks well to your port, so as to arrive off the coast of Hispaniola just before daybreak. Your departure time can be as early as 3 a.m. and as late as 4 p.m. depending on conditions and your boat. Knock 20% and ten degrees off what you think your boat can do, however, unless you are facing a dead calm motor trip.

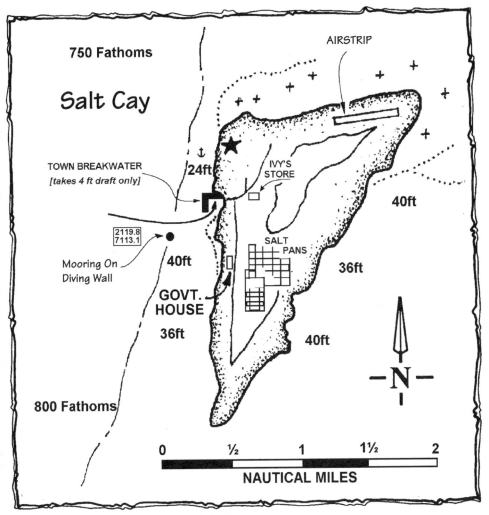

Salt Cay mooring.

An alternate plan after leaving the banks is to sail to **Salt Cay** for an overnight on the mooring there before proceeding to Big Sand Cay. It is worth the visit.

There is a mooring suitable for large freighters a third mile southwest of the small boat breakwater at the town. It's a float with successively large messengers tied to a huge hawser attached to 3 large navy anchors. The mooring is in 40 feet atop a more than 300 foot wall. Scuba divers, don't miss it. Don't anchor off the town. It's just a few inches of sand over rock. Same with the anchorage under the light. You'll bend your shanks in the chop if you don't drag the anchors into a crevice from which they cannot be tripped. Of course, in settled weather, these anchorages can be used with an eye to the wind.

The factotums at the Government House south of the dock have been known to clear one in and out when wheedled well. The people here are super nice.

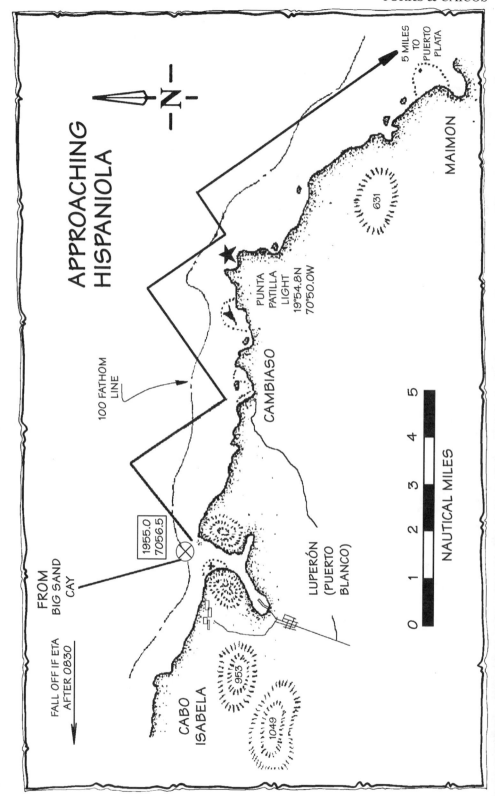

APPROACHING
HISPANIOLA

5 MILES TO PUERTO PLATA

MAIMON

631

PUNTA PATILLA LIGHT
19°54.8N
70°50.0W

CAMBIASO

100 FATHOM LINE

1955.0
7056.5

FROM BIG SAND CAY

FALL OFF IF ETA
AFTER 0830

CABO ISABELA

953

1049

LUPERÓN
(PUERTO BLANCO)

0   1   2   3   4   5
NAUTICAL MILES

148

APPROACHING HISPANIOLA

PICKING A WINDOW

Hispaniola extends a nighttime umbra of calm around itself which can reach as far as 30 miles offshore to the north and 20 to the east. Knowing how this phenomenon works can permit you to make a quicker and easier passage. At night, the huge land mass of Hispaniola gives up the heat it accumulated during the day, while the sea, which has a much longer memory for heat, does not. Think of this as creating a "heat bubble" over the island which shimmers away from the direction of the overall easterly flow. More north in the component of the **trade wind**, and the bubble shimmers south and west, shrinking the north shore's night lee. More southerly trades, and the bubble shimmers further off the north shore, providing sailors a larger lee.

Additionally, the **katabatic** wind, which is the cooling mountain air that slides downhill after nightfall, lifts the easterly flow off the island's coast. The katabatic wind adds to a possible **land breeze,** the opposite of the day's **sea breeze.** The land breeze is caused by the land cooling faster than the sea.

All of these effects create the **nocturnal wind**, which is offshore and can be light to moderate. The island's heat loss and the nocturnal wind redirect the flow of the trade winds over and around the island like a stream flowing around a rock. The effect will start earlier and last longer on light wind days, and start later and end earlier on days with strong winds. Similarly, the effect will extend itself farther to sea on light wind days and stay inshore on hard wind days. The effect is greater after bright hot days and weaker after overcast days.

After hot days you will feel the warm breath of the land on your cheek, and you will smell the aroma of black earth, cows, and charcoal fires up to 30 miles at sea!

Considering all the above factors, and observing the backing and veering of the winds from day to day, the shrewd **Leisure Sailor** waiting at **Big Sand Cay** to lay a course for **Luperón** or **Puerto Plata**, or waiting at **Sapodilla Bay** to jump off for **Cap Haïtien**, or **Manzanillo**, will leave in 15 knots or less south of east to intersect this belt of flagging winds as far out to sea as possible. On the other hand, 15 knots north of east is a fine sail despite a more narrow lee from the land. This calls for some iterative course planning to handle various assumptions of the **land effects**. After an overcast day of strong trades, stay in port. But after a bright hot day of Force 4-5, consider giving it a shot.

The **Equatorial Current** can sometimes be as high as 1 and a half knots in the heart of the stream, but it is usually half to three quarters knot. It works for me to assume one half knot west northwest, door to door.

BOUND FOR CAP HAÏTIEN

Follow the same scheme as for **Luperón**. Plan to be off **Hispaniola** at dawn so as to be in port by 9 am, cleared in and squared away, before the **trades** renew. Leaving for **Cap** from **West Caicos** gives a little more beam wind than the **Big Sand Cay** to Luperón route, and the first 20 miles you have some lee from **Molasses Reef** to the east. The looms of **Montecristi** and Cap Haïtien can be visible up to 30 miles out if there are no power failures. Be careful not to confuse the two, as I did one year, and got into the **Montecristi Shoals**, thinking I was 10 miles out to sea off **Cap**.

Follow the **Provo ship channel** out through **Clear Sand Road**. Clear the southeast spit of West Caicos standing off the beach there about one half mile. The lat-long of the Clear Sand Road, entrance to the banks is 21°36'N, 72°28'W, and the channel stretches 242° magnetic from **Gussy Point**. It's even easier to slip a mooring from the marine park west of West Caicos.

Enter the port at **Cap Haïtien** after 8 am to ensure a non-defensive reception and proceed to the customs dock on the south side of the huge pier constructed by "Baby Doc" to receive the cruise ships which have, so far, not come.

BOUND FOR MANZANILLO

Sail for a waypoint 19°55'N, 72°00'W to ensure you clear the **Montecristi** shoals, then sail eighteen miles southeast to Manzanillo. You can thread the shoals in daylight by sailing due south on **El Morro** behind **Punta Granja**, then following backwards the instructions given in the chapter, *Montecristi and The Shoals*. El Morro is visible at night since it clearly interrupts the loom of Montecristi with its unmistakable mass.

BOUND FOR LUPERÓN

First sail or motorsail, southeast, and eventually you may be motoring flat out for Luperón in a slick, rolling calm. If winds strengthen or are not north of east, then *don't beat into the seas,* but reach across them for the island and tack up the coast in an early morning Force 3-4. The deep bar south of **Big Sand Cay** will give you a couple more feet of sea than you imagine. Get out 5 miles before making definitive judgment of conditions.

When faced with bucking into current, wind and seas, slack sheets and bear off for lee of land where you can tack back up in comfort.

La Sona Verde

Fall Off for Pete's Sake

If you had planned one tack to **Luperón**, but for *whatever* reason a daybreak ETA can't be made, don't be shy to change your plan in midstream. Sail comfortably south, <u>across</u> the waves, for the shelter of the coast. *Don't* continue to buck into it. Then motor-sail up the coast in a lee. The trip will be faster and more comfortable than beating into seas.

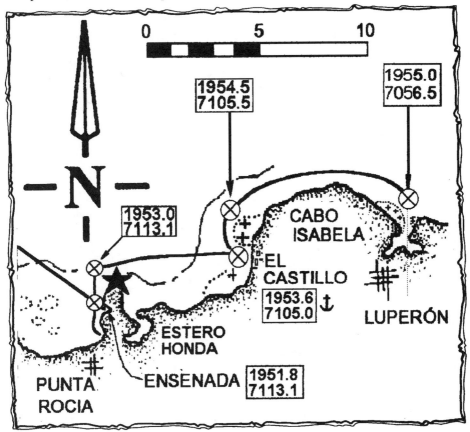

Use Backup Landfalls

I watch 3 out of 5 boats arriving in Luperón add a 3-6 hour nightmare onto what should have been a pleasant 12-15 hour night passage. Some think they're too close to land, and they heave to or drift until dawn 5-10 miles out. They don't believe depth sounders, charts or GPS. All they see is high dark land. Some underestimate current or land effect. Most cruisers underestimate the importance of getting in before the trades begin. If you do, don't try to make up for your mistake by pounding into 8 foot, 20 knot trade seas. Fall off to backup landfalls and motor up in a dead calm 5 or 6 a.m. next morning.

Tuck under **Cabo Isabela** for the day if you get caught out when the trades start. I don't know why, but year after year I see folks ignoring this advice as they often do the advice to avoid roll at **Rum Cay** by jib sailing around Sandy Point to the west beach. **El Castillo** is a basin of 10-12 feet of sand nearly a mile square. Enter as far downwind as you like from the small reef at the northern edge, then round up into the wind, anchor in a fine sandy lee, and visit the digs of the New World's first surviving settlement. If you're set even more, tuck into **Ensenada** behind **Punta Rocia**, both excellent anchorages.

HAITI

ASHORE IN HAITI

Haiti, founded in bloody 1804 as the world's third republic since Rome, has a rich and dark history. Invest in a book on Haitian history. It will enhance your visit ten fold. Start your history lesson with an excellent dinner at the *Hotel Roi Christoph,* owned and operated for many years by Henri-Paul and Joël Mourral amid cool gardens. The mansion was built in 1724 with 2 foot walls and 15 foot high open rooms to house the governor. Worm some invitations to some of the old residences in town. Go when the squalid streets and dingy facades are cloaked in romantic luster from the fuel lamps of the evening. The interiors of the more maintained mansions will astound you with their elegance. Even those that are in half ruin make historians weep.

Haitians, individually, are among the sweetest and most pacific people I have met in a lifetime of world travel. Collectively, however, Haitians have a penchant for screwing up what is the world's third oldest republic (not counting that France is on its *sixth*). Unlike Latin Americans, Haitians cheerfully admit that they do it without outside assistance. You won't find Haitians blaming you for their plight. You will find them eager to share your resources, however, and squander them as they have their own. To prevent undue pressure on your purse, just practice what you do elsewhere, but industrial strength. Especially get all prices down firmly before accepting a service. It helps to speak French badly.

Haitian money is called the *gourde.* That's right, as in gourds, like Indians used to trade. It is pronounced "goo". The first time you are given your change in a gooey ball of old one *gourde* notes you will understand everything. Five Gourdes made a Haitian "dollar", a confusing name whose ambiguity they gladly exploit. *Caveat emptor.*

CITADELLE

If you take a tour of the **Citadelle** and **San Souci**, you don't need to see the pyramids. First, because the experience is comparable, and second, because you won't anymore be able to afford it. The con artists that take you there must have been trained in Egypt. A new cost will arise every step of the way if you don't act to prevent it. Haiti is not cheap, despite its poverty. Perhaps, therefore, the Haitians are accustomed to wringing every *sou* from the tourist. If you ask a price, be prepared to hear astronomical sums quoted by people who haven't seen a penny in months. Not seeing it much, the ordinary Haitian hasn't got a grasp on reality when it comes to money.

To go to Citadelle, get a firm, all inclusive price, due on completion of the tour, before setting out. If you're a good and patient bargainer, it's 15 to 20 beers a head (see chapter on *Beeronomy*) for 4 to 6 persons, half of which is transportation to the second parking level. Once, I hired a car for 6 hours to run over to the Dominican frontier. After a half hour of a-hemming and a-hawing the first driver finally quoted his *discounted* fee of $US150. Another gave us a quote of US$60, and finally Gabriel, a member of the national police, gave us a "reasonable" price of US$40. He offered the added security of having a cop as a driver, he noted, as he patted his monstrous 0.45 pistol!

The *Hotel Mont Joli* still has the loveliest deck in Haiti from which to enjoy your **SG&T**, but rooms are twice the price of the *Roi Christoph,* my hotel of choice. *Beck's* and the *Brise de Mer* hotels are still open. The *Hotel Universel,* downtown, is both air conditioned and relatively cheap. Farther afield is the *Hotel Imperial.* The best buy in the market, although not a great bargain, is still the charcoal roasted cashews. Haitian art, usually cheap elsewhere, is, of course, even cheaper in Haiti. Do not, however, expect bargains in Haiti. For instance, they haven't learned to make bottles, therefore the deposit alone on a bottle of beer may be more than a full bottle in the DR. Never expect to find something like an engine part.

The story of **King Henri Christoph** is a Haitian parable. The Grenada born mulatto slave arrived in Haiti from a shipwreck. In a short time he named himself king of the northern half of the island. He managed 200,000 slaves to build a copy of the French Sun King's Versailles palace at Milot, near Cap Haïtien, and the great work above it, the **Citadelle**. When the work didn't proceed at the pace Christoph wanted, he used the Roman decimation technique, butchering every tenth man in a long line. The work sped up with 90% of the workforce. Under the grand staircase of **Sans Souci**'s grand ballroom is an airtight room into which Henri popped troubling guests. They suffocated while he danced with their ladies. He disciplined his officers by drilling them on the 1000 foot high parapets of the Citadelle, delaying a "column left" for a beat or two now and again just to keep the file still marching on their toes.

The Barbancourt 15 year rum still vies admirably with the best of the Dominican rums. Be careful of the *clairin*, called *vignt deux* (22) by the locals. You may like to make your *p'ti' punch* from *clairin*, but watch it! Haiti is not Martinique.

AFLOAT IN HAITI

Sailing directions on the Dominican coast apply in Haiti. See *Afloat in the DR*.

CAP HAÏTIEN

Plan to arrive off Cap Haïtien at daybreak. Maneuvering at the docks may be difficult when the wind gets up by 9 a.m. The course from the **Clear Sand Road** behind **West Caicos** is 172° True for a distance of 112 miles. Add a half knot of west-northwest current, stir in some leeway, variation and deviation, and add a pinch of caution: several degrees to ensure you aren't set onto the **Montecristi Shoals**.

The lights of the port may not be functioning but the buoyage is good. There are large red and green piles which follow the American "red right returning" rule. Make a daybreak landfall, sailing to within 500 yards east of the old lighthouse on **Picolet Point** on **Cap Haïtien** itself. Proceed down the well marked channel, turning right around the south end of the large pier. Midway down the long dock, between the freighters and the fishing boats, is the Harbor Master's office. Hail the officials at the dock and tell them you shall tie up at the yacht dock, or anchor out as you please, and that you shall dinghy in shortly for clearance.

After clearing in at **Cap Haïtien**, visiting the **Citadelle** or whatever else you find to do there, leave your arms, if any, with the authorities and clear out for **Acul Bay**.

Years ago, when the cruise ships were coming to **Cap Haïtien,** yachties were given short shrift by the officials here. There were no facilities for yachts and you got ripped off for fuel and water and the labor to fetch it. You were hassled endlessly by the kids "seeking work", but to whom a paint brush was a high tech tool. These harmless street urchins scammed quick bucks from ship's passengers, taking them to the market, shopping the *bric-a-brac* and art stalls and generally misguiding them around.

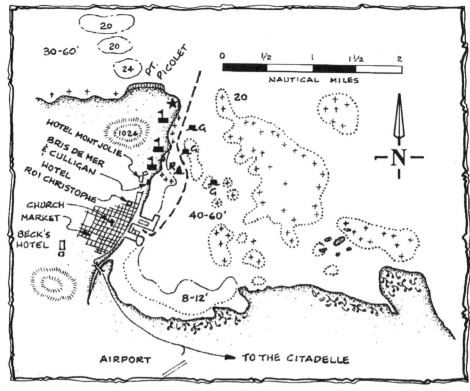

The marina at Cap Haïtien.

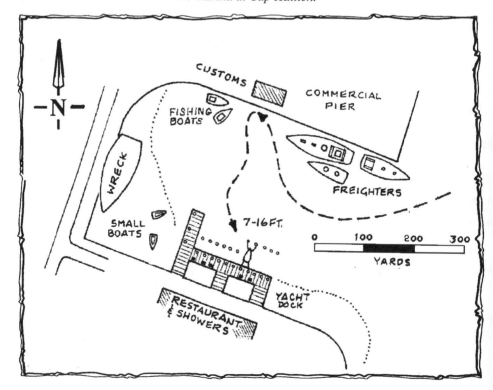

The marina built by Jean-Claude Duvalier (Baby Doc) with sturdy steel pilings and bollards off a long dock has begun to rust and sag sadly.

There are fewer kids pulling at you, fewer hassles and, with fewer cruise ships, officials have more time for yachts.

The marina facilities have been sporadically functional since being started in 1984. Until recently there have been few yachts, no cruise ships and zero tourists. During all its troubles **Haiti** has recently been through, the north coast plodded along with its usual serenity.

Try to tie up to the yacht dock early or late, before the sea breeze comes up, or, after it dies. The dock is unaccountably built across the wind instead of into it. The docks are at what used to be an island. Since the land was filled to create the "marina" it can be assumed that lying across the wind was a specific design. Welcome to **Haiti**, the land of the inexplicable.

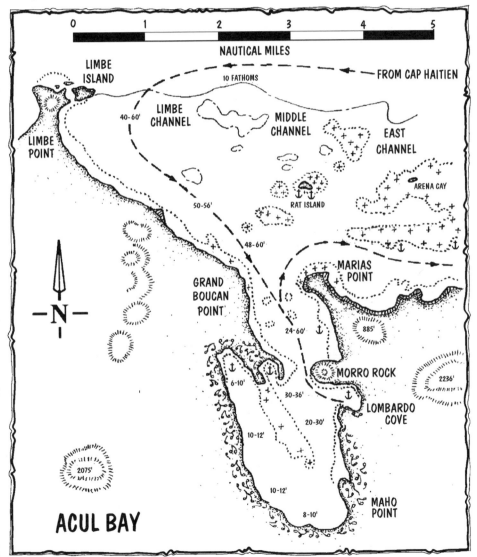

ACUL BAY

The miniature cruising ground of Acul Bay, a fine hurricane hole and only 5 miles west of Cap Haïtien, can easily absorb a week with a different anchorage every night.

Follow the **Limbe Channel** down the west side of the bay, rounding **Grand Boucand Point** a half-mile off, then steer for **Morro Rock**. This will bring you safely up into a good anchorage deep inside **Lombardo Cove** by **Maho Point**. Ashore, see John and Mary (Jean et Marie) for great avocados, grapefruit and coconut. The Haïtien grapefruit is the world's best and you get 20 to a beer (see *Beeronomy*). There's a fine hurricane hole up between **Lunetta Point** and **Belie Point,** and another behind Lunetta Point.

LA BADIE

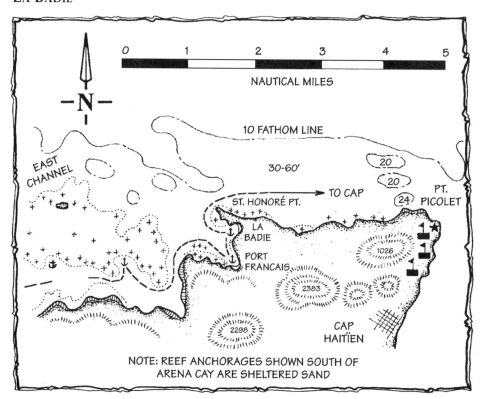

La Badie — still a pleasure

This whole coast, from **Ile de la Tortue** to **Puerto Plata** was for more than 200 years controlled by **corsaires** and **privateers** and the **freebooters** and **buccaneers** they left in their wake (see Glossary). **La Badie** was a famed watering hole and bordello in those days. Today it is host to a cruise ship whose passengers sun themselves and picnic on the white sand beaches twice a week. **Rat Island**, in the middle of the bay has good anchorages in clear water south and southwest of the island. You can snorkel and spearfish the reefs around the island which is an overnight camp for local fishermen.

FORT LIBERTÉ

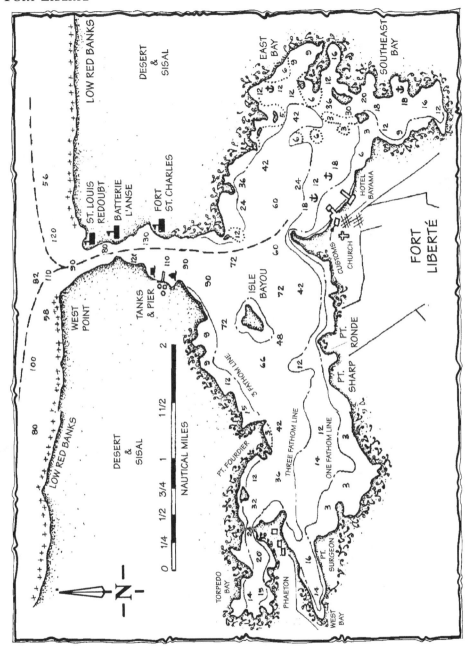

Fort Liberté is an easy and safe port of entry as well as a fine hurricane hole.

Leave **Cap Haïtien** the same way you came in. You want, of course, to leave as early as possible to avoid the hassle of the trades. To minimize any hassles from the officials, talk with them the day before leaving. Show up at the harbor master's office at first light with the yacht moored as instructed when you called on them the previous day. Then press hard for a quick clearance.

Leaving **Cap Haïtien**, turn on a course of 60° True when close under the lighthouse at **Point Picolet,** proceed for one mile or more, then east for 3 miles. This should put you a mile or more north of **Limonade Reef,** where **Columbus** lost the **Santa Maria,** and well clear of danger. Now set a course of 105° True for the entrance to **Fort Liberté** 18 miles distant.

The entrance to Fort Liberté is difficult to spot from sea. This whole area is desert and sisal plantations and everything looks the same. For several miles east and west of it, however, you can safely sail a quarter mile offshore, so go close in to be sure not to miss it. The entrance to the bay is a narrow throat surrounded by low red cliffs and nearly a 100 feet deep everywhere. Once inside the bay, like the approach outside, everything looks the same again, but, instead of brown rock the color is mangrove green.

The entire bay is lined with mangroves. Head for the large stone building with a concrete dock on the east side of the town. This is the *Hotel Bayaha,* run by M et Mme Nyll Calixte. The customs house is by the old town pier a couple of hundred yards seaward of the hotel. *Le Capitain du Port,* Herns Calixte, has been the boss here many years. He will organize the boarding party. Either dock has only a couple of feet of water. You will have to anchor well off and ferry the boarding party from either dock. The hotel dock is more convenient as it is new and has a good ladder.

There is a water point near the customs house, but it may not be functioning. Fuel can be purchased in gallon containers in the town. It is best to come here from either **Cap Haïtien** or **Manzanillo** with full tanks. See Mme Calixte about jerry jugging water from a water point beside the hotel. The hotel has a verandah bar and restaurant overlooking the anchorage. Charges for clearing in depend on the boat but should range to a few dollars only. After clearing you are free to anchor in any of the small coves and holes around the bay and you may stay as long as you like. Leave for Manzanillo, 6 miles to the east, to arrive there around 8 am while it's still dead calm. Once again, do what you have to in order to get cleared and free of the harbor early.

Security

Those concerned about taking their boat into Haiti should not forego the opportunity of a visit by land while the boat lies safely at **Manzanillo** or **Luperón**. Many tour operations exist in the Dominican Republic. Barlovento Tours in **Puerto Plata** do an excellent job. You can also take public transport to **Dajabón** on the border, walk across the bridge at the **Massacre River,** and begin Haitian transport from the small town of **Oanamenthe**

Until firm physical security measures are provided for yachts at **Cap Haïtien**, a member of the crew should stay aboard while at anchor or at the dock. Anchoring out is preferable. You should not expect any personal threat in Haiti, although pestering from beggars may exasperate you, and thievery at night can be expected if made too easy by carelessness.

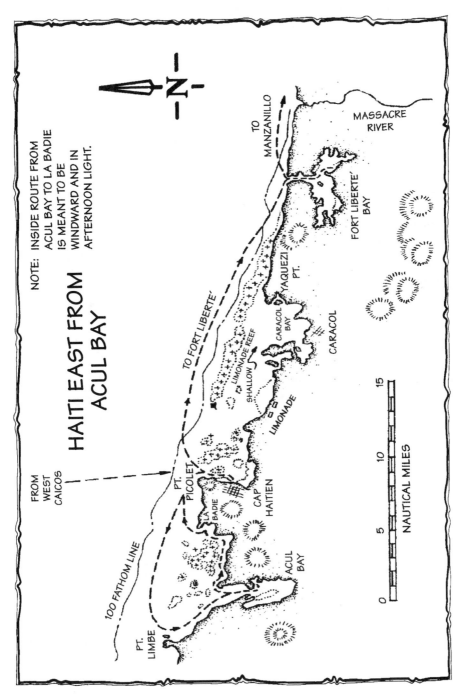

Haiti East from Acul Bay

Coasting east from Acul Bay, you must stop again at Cap Haïtien to pick up a clearance for **Fort Liberté**. In Fort Liberté, you need to pick one up for the **Dominican Republic**. Clear first in **Cap Haïtien** to cruise the bays to the west. See *Tips on Clearing ...*

THE DOMINICAN REPUBLIC

The north coast of the **Dominican Republic** can be the roughest passage for yachts island hopping to the Virgin Islands. But the oldest ploys in sailing, described later in this chapter, can make it quite pleasant. The DR offers astounding opportunities for tourism. You can find a DR English news and information service at Internet http://www.dr1.com.

Embassies and their consular functions are located in the capital, Santo Domingo. Telephone numbers and addresses are in the telephone catalog (*guía telefónica*), both white and yellow pages. Puerto Plata has consular agencies for all three countries.

Canada	689-0002
United Kingdom	567-9159
United States	541-2171

HAITI vs. THE DOMINICAN REPUBLIC

Although Americans are closer to Hispaniola by both heritage and geography, they are normally more confused than Europeans as to the differences between that island's two nations. The Dominican Republic occupies two-thirds of the island with 7 million people, 3 million of them in Santo Domingo and 2 million more in the U.S. Haiti's third has an estimated 7 million, 3 million of which in Port au Prince and another 3 million overseas. The differences between the two peoples are startlingly bold.

The Dominicans talk Spanish, Haitians talk Créole, an extremely corrupted French. Dominicans are Roman Catholic. Haitians are more animistic than Catholic. Dominicans run the gamut of skin color, averaging cinnamon. Haitians are pitch black, with a few mulattos who are off-island as much as on. The history of the two countries is one of bitter rivalry: Haiti invading the DR, the DR slaughtering Haitian immigrants.

Further distancing the two peoples is a practically impenetrable border with only two crossing points. The frontier that divides them is a 20 mile swath which alternates between desert in the north and the south, and *haïtises,* or jagged jungle hillocks, in the middle. The terrain either side of the frontier has been unoccupied through the centuries due to its basic inhospitality to settlement.

While fourth poorest in the hemisphere, the Dominican Republic is wealthy compared to Haiti, the poorest. There are Dominican businessmen in Haiti, but in the Dominican Republic there are only Haitian migrant workers.

ASHORE IN THE DOMINICAN REPUBLIC

Whether touring or seeking parts for your boat, **Luperón** is the preferred port at which to leave the boat to go inland in the Dominican Republic (see *Haiti versus the Dominican Republic*). If you fail to explore this wonderful country with its handsome and friendly people, you will have missed a major highlight of your cruise. Though many Americans do live in or visit the DR, the preponderance of foreign visitors and residents are European or Canadian. Only 30% of foreign tourism comes from the United States. Americans tend to be timid travelers. If you are American, break the mold and see the DR! It has 18,800 square miles including lakes, forests, deserts and mountains over 11,700 feet. Visit it's museums of American culture (the **Taino** museum at *Altos de Chavón*, in La Romana, the *Museo del Hombre,* in the *Plaza de Cultura*, Santo Domingo, and *Casa Real,* also in Santo Domingo), and get to know its gracious people, models of the American race.

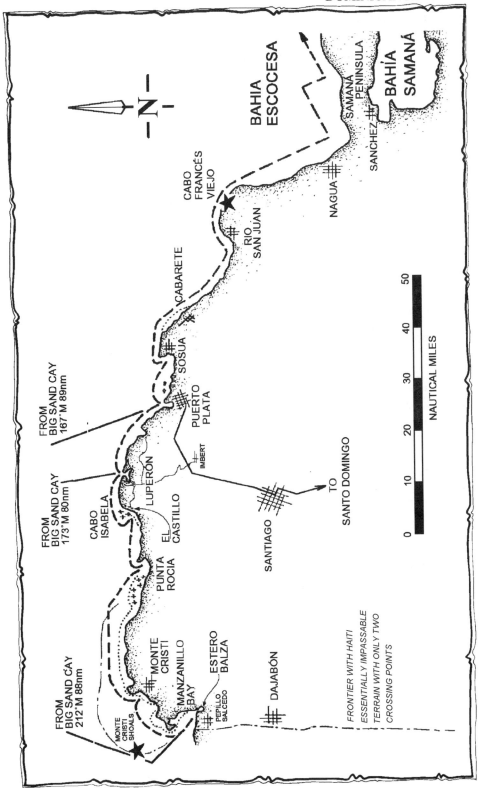

The DR has about 80,000 foreign residents and long term visitors. All of them travel routinely and with safety. Many live in the north coast retirement communities. Many have built retreats and ranches throughout the island. Affluent visitors rent cars. Groups travel by bus. The more adventuresome, who want to meet the Dominican people and experience the country close up, simply wander the nation with backpacks, renting dirt bikes or taking whatever local transport is available from pickup trucks to minibuses.

TRANSPORTATION IN THE DOMINICAN REPUBLIC

Your choice of transport ranges from motorcycles, called *motoconchos*, to pickup trucks to *guaguas*, to large air-conditioned buses with two feature films, and in times past, a bar cart. *Guaguas* are minivans, or tired buses, and a boy who takes money and pushes passengers into place. They travel fixed routes and usually don't leave until nearly full. Passenger cars on fixed routes are called *carros públicos*, or *carritos*. They wait in ranks around the town square, or at terminal facilities in cities, until enough passengers have signed up to nearly fill the car. If you wish to depart earlier or to travel in comfort, you may buy any unfilled seats. For best results, buy the 3 seats next to the driver. While públicos always gather and start from the same place, they usually deliver passengers to where they wish to go at the destination town. Puerto Rico has the same system.

THE TOWN OF LUPERÓN

Luperón is the site of a tourist development project with villas, condos, hotels and marina. There is a large hotel complex on the beach which is run on the all-inclusive plan. Local business people are cheerful and friendly, and you will find them willing to help you with anything. In the DR, *smile*, that's the style.

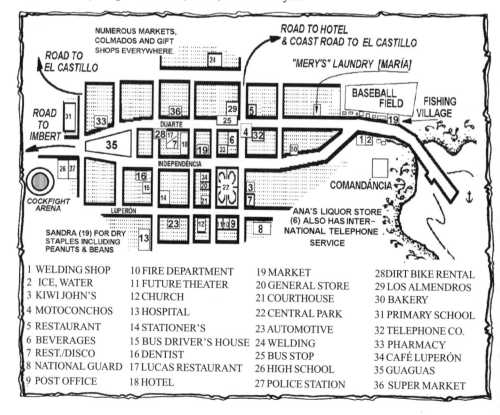

1 WELDING SHOP	10 FIRE DEPARTMENT	19 MARKET	28 DIRT BIKE RENTAL
2 ICE, WATER	11 FUTURE THEATER	20 GENERAL STORE	29 LOS ALMENDROS
3 KIWI JOHN'S	12 CHURCH	21 COURTHOUSE	30 BAKERY
4 MOTOCONCHOS	13 HOSPITAL	22 CENTRAL PARK	31 PRIMARY SCHOOL
5 RESTAURANT	14 STATIONER'S	23 AUTOMOTIVE	32 TELEPHONE CO.
6 BEVERAGES	15 BUS DRIVER'S HOUSE	24 WELDING	33 PHARMACY
7 REST./DISCO	16 DENTIST	25 BUS STOP	34 CAFÉ LUPERÓN
8 NATIONAL GUARD	17 LUCAS RESTAURANT	26 HIGH SCHOOL	35 GUAGUAS
9 POST OFFICE	18 HOTEL	27 POLICE STATION	36 SUPER MARKET

You don't have to stay long in Luperón to do your R&R and provisioning, but it's likely to capture you a while. Luperón is a small rural town, it boasts markets and hardware stores, discos, hospital, police, a dentist, and all the other amenities a civilized place needs including ice cream. Don't mistake lack of sophistication for lack of civilization. You may feel restricted in what you can find in Luperón. A pharmacy catering to just a few hundred people will not likely have just your brand of laxative.

Usually *anything* can be had in the DR if you look and you ask. You shall be surprised what a little persistence will produce. Otherwise, you have to travel to **Puerto Plata** or **Santiago**, or even the capital.

The bank in Luperón is a farmer's savings and loan institution and does not **change money**. Individual tourist businesses, such as restaurants and gift shops, do change money. Altagrácia, at the Bahía giftshop where she runs the CODETEL (32) **telephone** and **telefax** facilities, exchanges pesos for cash and traveler's checks at the going rate. As of this printing the Dominican Republic had one of the most stable currencies in the Americas, according to the hemispheric Chamber of Commerce. It also was slightly undervalued against gold and the dollar. There was no need for a black market in pesos.

Welding (carry your own stainless rods) and carpentry work is available in Luperón. Once a local **carpenter** built my shower grating with a hand saw and pegs. I gave him the teak and the old one to copy. Go to Puerto Plata or Santiago for machine shop work.

The rules for provisioning are the same everywhere: buy singles of everything you think you might like, then cases of what you find you really do like. You can get rum, soft drinks, tonic and beer by the case at Ana's liquor store (6), delivered and loaded into your dinghy, and what Ana doesn't have in stock you can order, including canned goods. Most everything is in local markets if you ask, but a trip to buy samples in Puerto Plata won't hurt. Don Santiago Morrobel's store on the square wholesales caselots and delivers them to your dinghy. Give Don Santiago a list of what you want before the truck goes to Santiago to do his buying for the week.

GETTING OUT OF LUPERÓN

Buses leave **Luperón** daily at 1:30 p.m. for the capital (25). The same bus leaves Santo Domingo every day at 8:30 a.m. and returns to Luperón by 1:00 p.m. To get anywhere but the capital, take a *guagua* to **Imbert** from the *parquecito* (35). Imbert is a town on the highway that connects **Puerto Plata**, **Santiago** and **Santo Domingo**. To return to Luperón from anywhere but the capital, take a bus to Imbert.

Start your experiences touring the DR by renting a dirt bike. Take a ride to **Cambiaso** (see chartlet in the *Approaching Hispaniola* chapter) or **El Castillo**.

Take the *guagua* [gwah-gwah] to Imbert from the *parquecito* (35) in Luperón. The *guaguas* wait under the trees in the park until one is full, whereupon it takes off for **Imbert**, on the Puerto Plata - Imbert highway. These *guaguas* are vans and cost a beer (see *Beeronomy*). For max comfort, sit at the window behind the driver. Have change ready. At Imbert there will be a stack of *guaguas* waiting to fill up to go back to Luperón. They relay back and forth all day from 6:00 a.m. to 8:00 p.m. It's best to leave for Puerto Plata at 6:30 a.m. Much later and you hit the rush hour. After 8:30 - 9:00 a.m. it slows down and you have to wait forever to get a full vehicle. Then you get to town and it's already siesta time and all the stores are closed from 12:00 to 2:00 p.m. The 6:30 a.m. start gives you 4 hours additional useful time in Puerto Plata. It's best not to try to make the 8:00 p.m. *guagua* back from Imbert. It might have left at 7:30! It's best to leave Puerto Plata by 6 p.m.

To get to **Puerto Plata** from Imbert, cross the highway and get into an east bound car

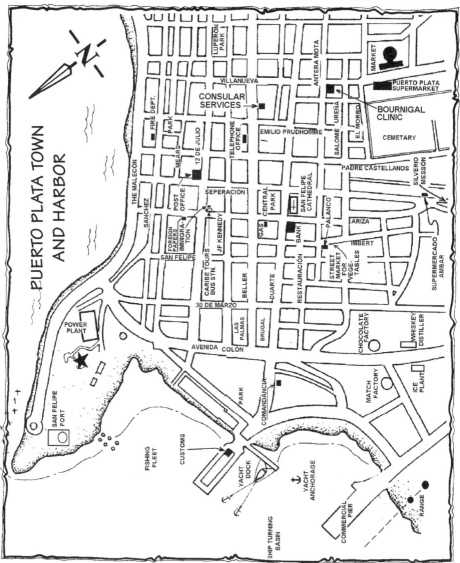

PUERTO PLATA TOWN AND HARBOR

(small cars this time, not vans) waiting to fill up with six passengers, or a bus. These cars are called *carros públicos*, or more current some places, *carritos*.

Arriving by car to Puerto Plata, the driver will take you wherever you wish in town. Go to *el Parque Central* if you aren't sure. Returning to Imbert from Puerto Plata, take a *motoconcho* (moped) to La Rotonda (lah roh-TONE-dah) which is the west bound terminal for *guaguas* and cars. Ask for the **Luperón** car and, once again, it will leave when it's loaded up. The motoconcho costs half a beer. Have the proper change ready! Otherwise you may have to wait to the end of the line before the conductor has got together enough small money to make change for you.

To get to Santiago, get into either a car or bus headed west. In **Santiago**, like in Santo Domingo, there is a "conveyor belt system" of cars marked "A", "B", "E", "G" and "M" which buzz all over town on fixed routes. You ask for *carritos de M*, etc.

PUERTO PLATA TOWN

You may stop and anchor overnight at **Puerto Plata** if necessary, but be aware your security is slim until the port renovation project is completed. With **Luperón** only a bus ride away, there's no reason to take your boat there. Why visit Puerto Plata at all? Because the town and its people are fantastic, and it is a great place to provision. Puerto Plata is the second oldest town in the New World, **Santo Domingo** being eldest. In Puerto Plata you can get almost anything you need, otherwise go to **Santiago,** a city of nearly a million an hour away in the mountains. Luxury busses to Santo Domingo, the capital, cost just a few bucks. The bus terminals are near the central park. *El cheapo transporto* is also available in a range of flavors (see *Traveling in the DR*).

The people on the north coast of the DR, besides being very handsome, are among the most hospitable people in the world. In genes and traditions they benefit from their pacific **Taino,** and **Arawak** ancestors, as well as from pirates and **Hidalgos.** They have a 500 year old tradition of independence from **Santo Domingo,** the island's big city of 2.5 million people. Despite its inherence to a Spanish colony, Puerto Plata was the main trading center for the fleets of *corsaires* and **privateers** who harassed the Spanish for two centuries. For trading with the crown's enemies, Puerto Plata was burned to the ground and sacked by the Spanish themselves. Unlike the stone city of Santo Domingo, wooden Puerto Plata has no monuments of architecture that survived fire and rot. Its heritage as the second oldest town in the hemisphere resides in its fabulous people, not its buildings.

Violence is unheard of on the north coast and theft ashore is rare. If you meet a cad it's usually either a misunderstanding or an itinerant outsider. Except for tourist shops, all prices are the same for everyone and there's normally no haggling. Treat these people as honest and trustworthy and you'll discover that that's exactly what they are. **Guides** are available, official and unofficial, for the non-Spanish speaker. For official guides see Hector or Anaima Echavarria, owners of Las Palmas gift shop across from the Brugal rum factory. Hector is director of the Association of Tourist Guides. Money is changed at various banks at virtually the same rate. You can get **cash** for **credit cards** at most banks or Automatic Teller Machines.

SANTO DOMINGO, THE CAPITAL

Hotels in Santo Domingo

It's most convenient, and most pleasant, to stay the first night at one of the old palaces in the *zona colonial*. I like the smaller **Hostal Nader** (687-6674) at the corner of *Luperón* and *Duarte*, a short walk from where the **Luperón** bus stops. Built in 1514 for General Alvarado, the Spanish military commander, the Nader served as headquarters in Santo Domingo for **Cortéz, Ponce de Leon** and **Pizzaro.** The **Nicolas Ovando,** the palace of the first governor after Columbus is operated by the government, and therefore poorly maintained. It is at the corner of *Luperón* and *Damas*. Nearby the Nader is the privately operated **Palacio** (682-8340), at *Duarte* and *Salomé Ureña*. There are many small hotels with bath south of the *Conde*. These cost much less than the *paradors*. The **Duque de Wellington** (682-4525), on *Independéncia* 304, just round the corner from the obelisk on the *Malecón*, has quite a high standard. It is next to an Italian restaurant and just down the street from a great *panaderia* with a sidewalk cafe for breakfast.

There are big tourist Sheraton and Hilton type hotels on *Av.George Washington*, also called the *malecón* (meaning dyke, or seawall). But the *paradors* are more comfortable and right in the heart of the old colonial city where the shopping and the night life is, <u>and</u>, of interest to cruisers, cost about a third as much.

To reserve rooms or get current rates, call from CODETEL in Luperón. Other hotels are in the Yellow Pages (*Paginas Amarillas*) under "hotels", or in the white pages, otherwise Altagrácia or Nati will help you.

While in **Santo Domingo** I do all the hardware stores, marine places, take care of medical visits, get new glasses, stock up the medicine chest, and so on. It often takes two nights. The first night usually stay at the Nader for both convenience and luxury. On the second night I stay at a small hotel like the Duque de Wellington. On the third, well ...

If I'm rounding up hardware and diesel stuff, I may take a cheaper and less commodious room at one of the neighborhood hotels out in the industrial areas. These may cost a tenth of what the paradors cost. These are accommodations for the less priggish cruiser. Around the world Chinese restaurants, like French Cafés, often rent rooms upstairs for the economical traveler. The standard may vary. Often they have full bath and a noisy air conditioner and cost just a few dollars. The DR is no exception. There may be large commodious beds, European baths and mirrors on the ceiling, when they're the type of room which is mostly used in the daytime. Anyhow, after 8 p.m. they sure are cheap. There's one with a not so firm mattress over a Chinese cafeteria near the best *Gallego* restaurant this side of Gallicia: **Pepin** on *Avenida San Martín*. For a beer more (see *Beeronomy*) there's a higher standard at the *Londres* Chinese restaurant down the street.

There's even a great ice-cream store and a newspaper and magazine vendor across the street from *Pepin*'s. I run my errands all day, then go to Pepin to read the paper over a drink. Late that night, after a great leisurely *comida gallega* accompanied by the Movie Channel, I scrub off the city dirt and crash onto a king-size bed for the night. (I try not to look up.) The security is superb and no traveling commercial man ever had it better.

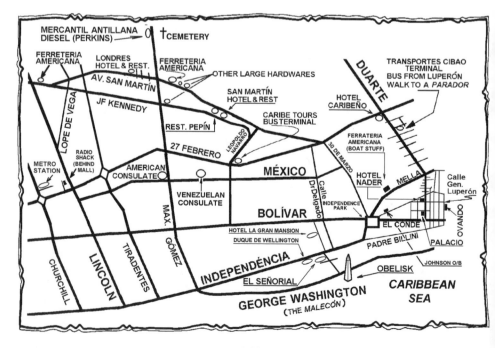

166

Using Guaguas in Santo Domingo

Santo Domingo is a huge Latin American city. It is dirty, noisy and confusing, like New York. But also like New York, you can get anything you want there if you know where to go. Look in the yellow pages to find what you want (yes, they're the same as at home), get a map and go to it.

In Santo Domingo the *guaguas* run like conveyor belts at right angles to each other all over the city. If you know the *X* and the *Y* map coordinates to where you want to go, simply ride one *guagua X* blocks one way, then ride another *Y* blocks on the perpendicular, and you're there. See the city sketch above. *Guaguas* in Santo Domingo run west the length of *Bolívar, Mella* and *San Martín*, and east on *Independéncia*, and both east and west on *John F. Kennedy* and *27 Febrero*. They run both north and south on *Máximo Gómez, Lope de Vega, Avraham Lincoln* and on *Winston Churchill;* north on *30 de Marzo*. This is a complete grid, but there are still more routes. You can hop two of these conveyances in just minutes and be within a block of your destination for less than the cost of a local phone call most places. Taxis cost from 2 small beers to 2 big beers.

MEDICAL ATTENTION IN THE DOMINICAN REPUBLIC

The Dominican Republic has more than 7 million inhabitants. More than 1.5 million Dominicans live in the United States, where traditionally medicine has been the Dominican purview among the trades serving the large US Latin American population. Many doctors retire back to the DR. Some keep homes and practices there. It is not unusual to find specialists practicing in the DR who are on call at major centers in cities such as Houston, New York and Miami. In short, private medicine in the DR is often excellent. I prefer to have all my medical needs taken care of in the DR. There are some whom I could heartily recommend. However, far be it for me to recommend a doctor to anyone, even farther a lawyer (especially in the DR). That said, here is a list of specialists with whom I have dealt without complaint.

Luperón			
Estelvina Felipe	Dentist	see town map (30)	
Santo Domingo			
Doraida Jones Castillo	Dermatologist	566-4424	
Hans Jager	Chiropractor	685-1034	English
Santiago			
Jose E. Marmolejo	Ophthalmologist	583-1377	English
Joaquin Alverez	Urologist	580-1171	English
Puerto Plata:	Bourignal Clinic	586-6850	
Barbour	E, E, N & T		
José Redondo	Cardiologist		English

Medical Tests

The DR, as in most countries but the US, permits its citizens to avail themselves of medical analysis services without the orders of a physician: blood analysis, X-Ray, tomography, sonograms, etc. Standard blood tests are available in Luperón. **Puerto Plata** and **Santiago** have many more sophisticated labs (*Laboratorio de Analisis*). Medical labs in **Santo Domingo** cluster around the streets *Dr.Delgado* and *Independéncia*.

AFLOAT IN THE DOMINICAN REPUBLIC

AN OLD PLOY

For almost 500 years sailing vessels have navigated the north coast of **Hispaniola**, against the very strong winds and seas, by hiding behind the headlands and capes during the day and proceeding close to shore at night where the more moderate conditions permit a slow progress against the wind.

Sailboats coasting against the wind have used this tactic all over the world for longer than recorded history. There doesn't seem to be much difference today, except whereas **Columbus** had to sometimes tow his ships at night with longboats under oars, you are lucky enough to have an auxiliary. The *Santa María*, Columbus' flagship, was lost on the reefs off **Caracol Bay**, east of **Cap Haïtien,** while being hauled in this fashion. After the ship touched they were unable to float her off. All the hoopla over efforts to find the *Santa María* notwithstanding, there shouldn't be much there as Columbus' journal reveals they scavenged the ship down to her beams before leaving her to wave and rock. Even as you would do if you were on Mars and one of your 3 transports were disabled. You would have to make do there with whatever you had. Since **Martín Pinzón** had run off with the Pinta in the Raggeds, half the crew had to be left ashore. The *Santa María*'s materials went into construction of their new shelters at the lost settlement of **Navidad**.

If ever trades cease, i.e., "trawler weather", surface current subsides along the coast. You may then contrarily try hugging the shore *west*bound and proceed cape to cape *east*bound.

GO WITH THE FLOW

The authorities on the north coast will seldom give yachts clearance to any port other than the official ports of entry: **Pepillo Salcedo** in **Manzanillo, Luperón, Puerto Plata** and **Samaná**. This is simply because the DR is a small poor country and cannot afford to place a customs house in every pokey little village for the odd cruising yacht to visit twice a year. But it doesn't mean you're not welcome given the right circumstances.

Don't be like the Swiss I know who tried to cruise the United States. Being a good Swiss, he insisted everywhere on proper papers which followed the letter of the law. None of the American officials were quite certain of the rules relative to Swiss yachts, but he made them research it. My friend got as far as Rhode Island and fled directly to the Bahamas under the weight of harbor fees and the welter of regulations whose lines he felt he had to toe. Though a dear friend of mine, he dislikes Americans and America to this day.

One man, a HAMster, spent weeks chasing bureaucrats all over the Dominican Republic looking for a temporary license before using his SSB marine radio in their territorial waters. He finally received assurances that the usual treaty between the two countries in question provided for a 30 day grace period in which a visiting ship could use its radio. Armed with at least this verbal approval he counted the days he had been in the country. They amounted to thirty-one. He never did use his radio in the DR. The usual Children's Hour and Breakfast Shows went on without him.

I *do not* recommend having improper papers, but, if you want to have pleasure out of your pleasure yacht, I do recommend you ease off on the expectations you place on officialdom and *go with the flow*. For instance, if you ask to be cleared into ports other than the official ports of entry in the Dominican Republic you shall most certainly be told that you cannot do that. If you declare your plans to "stop at" **Sosua**, for instance, you will be told you can't be cleared for Sosua. True enough. With consideration for the language gap, a more careful communication would have you "pausing off" Sosua while the wind and seas around **Cabo Macoris** subside. I always coast with this strategy and have usually met understanding officials along the way. But some understanding of the officials by cruisers is called for as well. Read the section on culture shock.

I have got cleared "with intermediate ports" (*con puertos intermedios*) from **Manzanillo** without problems. I just waived the paper at each new *comandante*. But a simple *despacho* to **Luperón** is all that's needed. For some reason, many American yachties find this procedure a lot of trouble. It's actually less trouble than the Americans put the Canadians to. Still, it leads to a lot of grousing which is quite unfair. From Luperón I clear to **Samaná** regardless of how many stops I shall make.

DEPARTURE TIMING

Coasting the north coast of the DR is much like coasting the south coast of Puerto Rico as far as departure times are concerned. The best strategy is to take the smallest hops possible between the major ports of **Manzanillo, Luperón** and **Samaná**, during 2-3 day **Weather Windows,** while making the best use of the night lees available, and ensuring good light landfalls.

Weather windows to depart **Luperón** need a 3 day window for **Samaná**, or a 6 day window for **Puerto Rico**. The best strategy calls for a stop at **Escondido** where the skipper can review how the window holds and continue onto Puerto Rico if adviseable. See **LUPERÓN TO SOSUA:** PICKING WINDOWS

CRUISING IN COMPANY

It used to be that the only authority in a small village was an 18 year old soldier with a rusty rifle who never saw a foreigner. His consternation at a great fleet of boats showing up on his beach was second only to that of the Nazis in Normandy on the morning of D-Day. Things have changed. The 18 year old now wants a tee shirt.

Nonetheless, remote anchorages continue to offer touchy situations for border and drug enforcement. If cruising in company, do so modestly: no jilling about, yoo-hooing and mooning each other off the town beach. If you're there to rest and wait, then ghost up to anchor unobtrusively, slip below for a rest and wait. Communicate your intention of not visiting the shore by anchoring well beyond the reach of any swimmers.

La Glória in Puerto Plata's Parque Central.

MANZANILLO TO LUPERÓN

Short-leg this coast, hiding behind the capes at **Punta Granja**, or **El Morro**, the table-like mountain at **Montecristi**, at **Punta Rocia** (also spelled Punta Rusia)**,** for its Bahamas like diving, and at **Cabo Isabela**, to visit the penultimately historical site of **El Castillo**.

Manzanillo to Montecristi is a simple 17 mile motor trip. Montecristi to Punta Rocia is 28 miles in a flat calm before dawn. Montecristi is simple and safe to leave at night, and offshore dangers on that leg are more than a mile to starboard at any point in the trip. Plan in each leg to be at anchor by 08:00 before the wind rises.

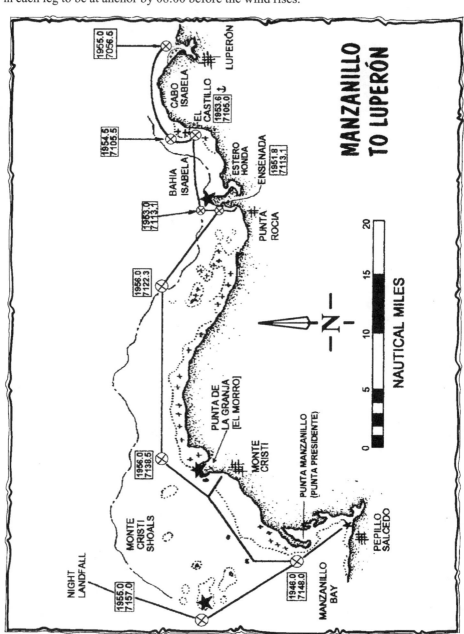

MANZANILLO BAY

Try to be inside **Manzanillo Bay** in the early morning while the bay is calm. It is most convenient to clear in at the old company pier, but in the high chop and surge usual after midday, it is a dangerous place for a small boat. If you cannot arrive early then anchor off the *comandáncia* to the west of the pier and ask to be cleared the next morning.

There is a fine hurricane hole in **Estero Balza,** the little estuary three quarters of a mile east of the large pier on the south shore. Seven foot draft can be accommodated over the bar at high tide, 5 feet at low. If you draw less than 5 feet or you have fair wind and tide to enter the estuary, enter the **Estero** (*ace-stair-oh*, or estuary) before the wind is up, and clear from there by walking to the *comandáncia* at the head of the pier.

Occasionally there is a range of mangrove stakes at the entrance to the estuary, but don't expect it. If it's not there, ask for a guide to enter the Estero. Since the channel can change slightly, it's best to have a pilot aboard if you draw more than 6 feet.

This is a fine hurricane hole and long term anchorage.

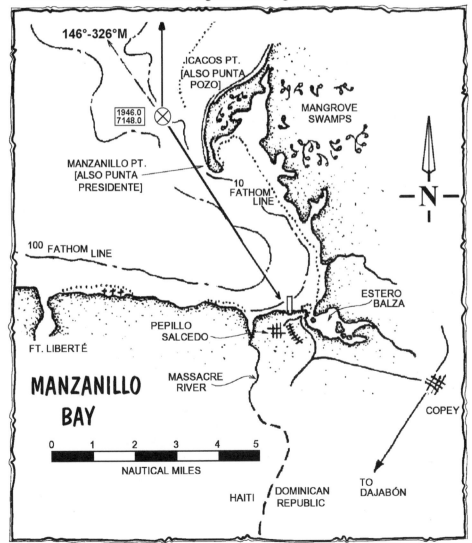

171

PEPILLO SALCEDO

Pepillo Salcedo [*pay-PEE-yo sal-SAY-doe*] is the name of the Grenada Company town built under the Trujillo regime in 1947 by United Fruit. It took 3 years to build the town and facilities before exporting one banana. During the political vacuum of 1965, when the United States Marines were invited to pacify Santo Domingo, the Company gave up and pulled out, leaving factories, equipment, houses and the physical infrastructure of a sizable American town. The government's Project Cruz which was to have rehabilitated the enterprise barely survives and the town languishes with a few bananas being exported and fish being sent inland. The stone houses lining the wide curbed and sidewalked streets shelter hospitable but poor Dominicans. For major shopping one needs to go to **Dajabón** [*dah-hah-BONE*], 20 minutes away in the foothills by the Haitian border, or to **Santiago**.

Fianchi [*fee-AHN-chee*], a former immigration officer, speaks excellent American. He now exports tropical fish. The port exports bananas from inland. The only other industry is an occasionally active historical salvage and diving operation, **North Caribbean Research** (**NCR**), run by Rick Berry with his two sons, Chris and Scott, under license to the Dominican Republic.

Estero Balza

While at **Estero Balza**, see Fianchi for the latest on fuel, water, repairs or secure storage of the boat. He can set you straight on most anything. If not at his restaurant/bar on the central park, or at his tropical fish acquaria across the street, then call him at home at 579-9536. But everyone knows Fianchi. The best store for provisions is on the south side of the central park.

There is a beach bar with the inevitable *Merengue* dance floor at the entrance to the Estero Balza. At the southern end of the estuary Doña Lulu runs the only hotel facilities from her row of cabañas. For bilge keels and multihulls of modest draft, the *varadero* (var-a-DAIR-oh) beaching operation can serve your haulout needs, provided you can squeeze in among the derelicts.

Transportation to Santiago is via Caribe Tours bus at 07:00 and 14:30. They return from Santiago at 10:00 and 17:00.

The sea breeze rises from the northwest around **Manzanillo Point** — **Punta Presidente** in some charts — about 10 a.m., veers throughout the day, reaching 15 knots and above, and dies in the east toward 6 p.m. to make room for the gnats, or *gegenas* [*hey-HEN-nas*]. The bugs are usually gone by 8 p.m., but, nonetheless, have your screens in or plenty of repellent handy.

If you draw more than 5 feet and don't have a fair tide in the early morning, or if you have arms which need to be delivered to the yacht, move the boat over to the anchorage off the *comandáncia* on the west side of the pier the day before leaving and clear out the afternoon before leaving. Row in for your guns first thing in the morning and get underway immediately, crossing the bay before the wind gets up, as it will accelerate around Icacos Point and it will *pen you into the bay* for many hours. Motor across the flat *early* morning calm of **Manzanillo Bay**, north toward the little island of **Tororu**, and when the wind rises, sail to **Montecristi**, tacking in the light morning airs.

Leave the bay in early morning calm or get penned in for a rough sail!

172

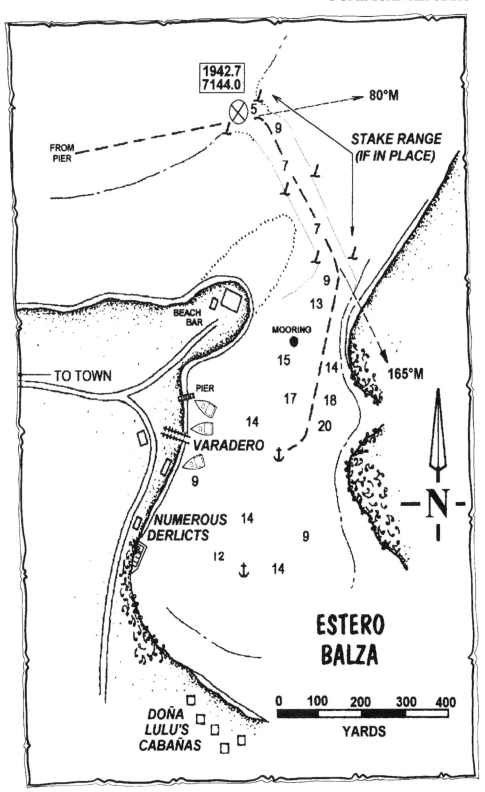

1942.7
7144.0

80°M

STAKE RANGE
(IF IN PLACE)

FROM
PIER

5

9

7

7

9

13

BEACH
BAR

MOORING

15

165°M

TO TOWN

PIER

17

18

14

14

20

VARADERO

9

NUMEROUS
DERLICTS

14

9

12

14

-N-

ESTERO
BALZA

0   100   200   300   400

YARDS

DOÑA
LULU'S
CABAÑAS

MONTECRISTI AND THE SHOALS

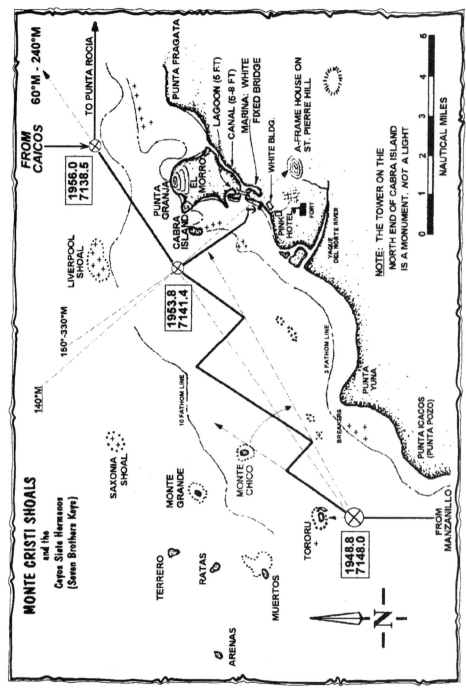

Stay on a longitude through **Tororu** to avoid the shoals off **Icacos Point** — also known as **Punta Pozo** — and **Yuna Point** -also known as **Punta Luna**. When a half mile south of Tororu tack northeast within the angle projected from the island of **Monte Chico** to the north and **Punta Granja** to the east. When one half mile west of **Cabra Island** steer 150°

The brooding ruin of Roi Chistophe's San Souci.

magnetic onto the large white building with the seawall, anchoring 300 yards off the marina in 10 feet. Take a good look around on the way in, you will want your bearings for leaving in the dark. Not to worry, though, its a wide cinch (DMA chart 26141 or 26142).

Many early morning departures are called for in this guide. But that's how it is on the windward way. Masochists can leave later than advised and slog against the **Equatorial Current** in Force 6 conditions and in the midst of the **Montecristi Shoals**. If you're a motorist you can leave **Manzanillo** for **Montecristi** even later, but put the pedal to the metal, Gretel, if you want to get there before dark. If you leave Manzanillo at sunup and sail some too, you'll be in the beach hotel at Montecristi for lunch, sucking on a cold beer. But leave later, and ......

Founded in 1533 by 60 families shanghied by the Spanish from the Canary Islands, Montecristi is a sizable town with a budding ecotourism industry due to its mangrove rivers and lagoons. See Mike Kilburn on Calle Colón at Mike's Hotel, a sort of shipwreck-patio-bar-ecohotel, for local scoop. Extensive salt pans still working between the town and the sea are the only industry. The canal accessing the marina (*el caño*) shall shortly have a haul-lout facility (*varadero*) included.

Although the conch grass harbor at Montecristi is fine in most conditions, it is wide open from the northwest and weather can be expected from that quarter in the winter months.

Leave Montecristi for **Punta Rocia** after midnight with plenty of night lee left, during a forecast

Typical house in Cap Haïtien.

period of 15 knots or less easterly gradient wind. Follow a course of 330° Magnetic from the beach hotel, passing close under **Cabra Island**, until **Punta Granja** is cleared to the east. Steer 62° Magnetic for 4 miles to a point 3 miles north of Punta Fragata. Then steer true east (following latitude 19°56') for 14 miles to the 100 fathom line, thence 126°M for Punta Rocia's **Ensenada** harbor. With DMA chart 25801, a depth sounder for sure, a GPS and even a radar, you may run even closer inshore, still well clear of all dangers.

Punta Rocia

Punta Rocia is a delightful Dominican vacation village with beautiful white sand beaches and extensive Bahamas-like coral reef snorkeling and fishing. A swiss restaurant, a closed hotel and several cantinas dot the shore among the vacation homes. In settled easterly weather one can stop here for many days of diving. If a weekend, look for a fishfry on the beach, and join in. This is the last Bahamas like water you see before **Margarita Reef**, Puerto Rico. Try parking behind **Cayo Arenas** for superb fishing. If in doubt, get a guide from shore. Exit at sunup to make the short 7 mile leg over to **Cabo Isabela** for another day's pleasure and tour of the New World's first successful European settlement.

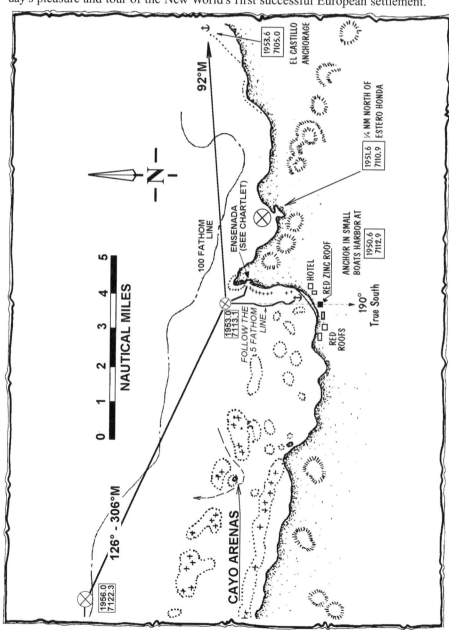

Upon meeting the 100 fathom line on the eastward motor from Montecristi, turn to 122° Magnetic for 9 miles to arrive off Punta Rocia at first light. Be careful not to go too close to the point itself which is surrounded by a coral bottom 10 to 30 feet deep. Proceed True south, or 187° Magnetic, from a point one half mile west of the point's shoreline to a red zinc roof on the beach. Turn onto 120° Magnetic after one third of a mile to enter the anchorage at Ensenada.

ENSENADA

This is an easily recognizable landfall when you've got caught out too late in the morning while approaching Hispaniola from the north, and you want to give it up to continue in the next morning's calm. When entering the **Ensenada** anchorage be careful to go exactly between the coral awash on the south side of the entrance and the boulders on the shore at the north side. When inside, pick a sandy patch between the grass and coral patches and get your anchors well down. If staying here overnight, anchor off the town and leave at sunup for **Cabo Isabela**. To get to the town anchorage proceed south on the red zinc roof for 1.6 miles from the point, then steer to the blue building to its east until in 2 fathoms of sand about 200 yards from shore. The blue building and the thatch roofed building next to it are part of a very nice hotel complex which attracts foreign tourists seeking a more simple scene than can be had at the great resort complexes further east.

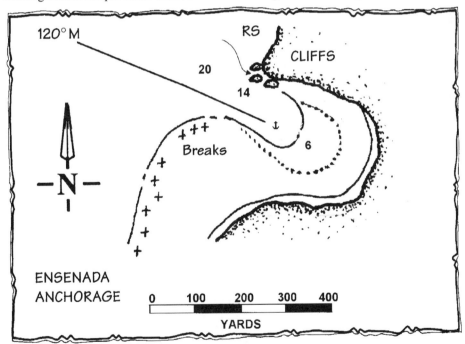

The military will visit and inspect your papers. They may prefer you to anchor off the town, especially if you look like you do drugs. But if you are only here to hide behind the cape during the day and to rest up, you will be exiting before sundown and there should be no problem in staying put if you explain yourself. Exiting from Ensenada in poor early morning light, or moonlight, is not a problem. Simply motor slowly for the half mile on 300° Magnetic, turn north for 1 mile and you're in the clear to head east.

CABO ISABELA

The most *thornless* cruisers shall have made landfall on Hispaniola in **Manzanillo** and shall be approaching **Cabo Isabela** from the west. When motorsailing from **Punta Rocia** in early light, duck inside **Isabela Bay** to avoid strong cape effects and get the most of the morning calm. Approach the beach anchorage due east to avoid the reef a half mile north of it. Your landfall is **El Castillo**, just north of the mouth of the **Bajabonico**, also known as the **Isabela River**. It is a low, red rock promontory which will stand out as the only variation in what is otherwise miles and miles of dark sand beach. Sailing from the north, sail due south and one mile off. Turn up wind and go east to anchor in calm conditions.

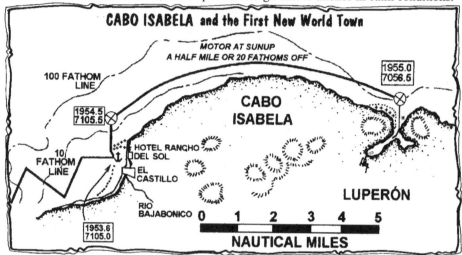

Anchor directly in front of Hotel Rancho del Sol in 2 fathoms and await the arrival of the Navy. They are nice young men, full of smiles, stuck in a lonely outpost with no opportunity for advancement. This is a calm and tranquil anchorage in prevailing conditions. Leave here at sunup for the 10 miles to **Luperón**, swinging wide of the rocks and reef projecting north of the anchorage. A Belgian-Dominican couple, Herman and Sonja, own and operate the Rancho del Sol which has an excellent restaurant. Herman's Prout catamaran and the Kon Tiki glass bottom boat lie on the north side of the anchorage.

El Castillo is the place where **Columbus**, on his second voyage, established the first surviving European settlement in the New World. After losing the *Santa Maria* on his first voyage he had left his crew's troublemakers to establish the first European colony at **Navidad**, behind the **Limonade Reef**. The fact that no one survived cannot be blamed on the Admiral of the Ocean Seas. Based on the later behavior of the Spanish crews in Hispaniola, it's a safe bet they stirred up the Indians some and were probably the last of their breed to suffer due retribution.

The site selected for the first colony at **Isabela,** as you will see, presented free fields of fire on all sides, including over the rocky palisades to seaward. This was a snug redoubt fronted by a 1-by-2 mile patch of sand bottom in a harbor easy for a square rigger to make and leave in all conditions. Close to shore the bottom is shallow rock. Shoreward of 2 fathoms lie rocky "heads" which must be avoided.

Don José María Cruxent, a Venezuelan archeologist runs the digs at El Castillo while University of Florida tries to make sense of the findings. It is computerized archeology because in the 1950's, the dictator Trujillo ordered a crew to clean up the site in preparation for a visit by Spanish archeologists. They did what you might do if a dictator orders you to clean up something. They bulldozed the remarkably intact ruins to a cleared depth of 80 cm. Nonetheless much has been done and the site makes for a very interesting afternoon's visit.

Motor the calm over to Luperón at first light, not later or the 10 miles may seem 100.

LUPERÓN

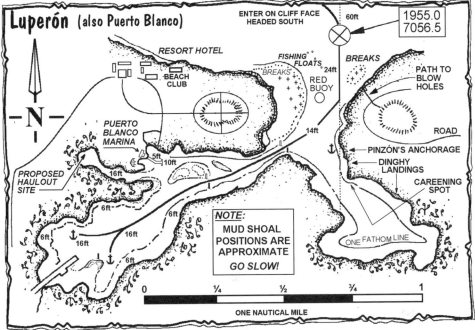

(See Page 115 entrance photo.)

Due to current, landfalls are often well off to leeward when bound for **Luperón** (**Puerto Blanco**). See *Fall Off For Pete's Sake!*, page 151. The significant land feature to be recognized will be **Cabo Isabela**. It should be near dawn and the coast is steep-to here with the 100 fathom line being less than a mile off the coast. After some time in the Bahamas you will be land shy and the mountainous coast will look very close at first. These mountains are quite high: 1049 feet at Isabela which is backed up by a range 3000 feet high! You will see them, even on dark nights, as a high border of blacker against black.

Head due south to the cliff face on the east side of the opening. Come close under the cliffs, leave the red ball buoy to starboard and round into the western harbor favoring the southern shore. Do *not* trust the stakes I show or other markers cruisers will tell you about over the radio. Over many years I've watched these stakes get dragged around for various exercises and left wherever they were. A casual cruiser would assume the marks were being carefully placed and had permanent status. Follow the fathom lines above as well as the stakes. The DR charges US$10 per passport for all tourists entering the country by any mode of transport. Tourists can stay up to 90 days (ask for it) without further charge.

These mile deep bays provide the best yacht harbor on the island of Hispaniola. The low cliff on the east side of the entrance provides a convenient transit with which to enter headed due south. Martín Pinzón anchored off this cliff with the stolen Pinta, trading with the indians for gold. He was found out when **Columbus'** longboat rounded Cape Isabela from El Castillo looking for the Niña's next anchorage. Surprise! Why, there's old Marty!

Eye the place well on the way into **Luperón,** you may be coming out in the dark without a moon. Not to worry, it's dead calm at night. Motor slowly and if you nose into a mud bank you can slide right off into deep water. If you get stuck, you'll just have to prolong your stay in this lovely bay that looks more a Swiss lake than a bay of the sea.

Clearing in here is easy. Do not anchor in the channel running between the two pairs of stakes and to the dock. You can easily find 12 to 16 feet of sandy mud anywhere else. Usually the harbor is free from mosquitoes and *gegenas* (hey-HEN-ahs), or no-see-ums. They may appear for an hour at dawn and sunset, however. If a clearance party doesn't arrive by dinghy, and you get antsy, dinghy ashore and take your papers up to the *comandáncia.* **Guns** may be checked until departure and they may even get cleaned for you. The DR tries to be drug free. **Drugs** land you in jail and you may, properly, lose your boat for possessing them. See the section on *Customs and Clearances.*

The Fernandez family runs a small marina with restaurant and bar on the northwest shore. They accommodate cruiser functions with pleasure, and have water and showers..

The water is good here, but add chlorine before filling your water tanks. Also, wait for the lines to clear after a drop in pressure caused by a break or a power outage. Shame on you if you fail to take either of these measures, even in Florida.

Treat all aids to navigation in the Caribbean with great suspicion.

LUPERÓN TO SOSUA

Most cruisers, especially Pacific sailors, underestimate the Atlantic trades. Around the Greater Antilles there are great variations of depths through which pour voluminous, though not rapid, currents. The tumbling of these large flows across uneven bottom found on the northern edge of the Caribbean tectonic plate can cause steep seas or spurious currents otherwise not warranted by surface conditions.

Sailing or motoring to windward on this coast during full trades is flat out suicidal. For a truly *thornless* passage, the reader should study carefully the effects documented in the chapters: *Wait for Weather, Hug the Shore* ... , *Let Landfall Determine Departure,* and *Approaching Hispaniola* as well as the specific advice given on the appropriate leg. For some signs which tell the tale of a smooth exit when you are otherwise blinded from the conditions offshore by harbor and **land effects** on this coast, see the section *Harbor Telltales.*

By making the tables and figures shown, and by listening to the **Offshore Report** each day, you can attune yourself to the music of the trades, and there will be no question when your window has arrived. Remember to wait the first day of any window for the seas to subside, and don't count on the last day. It may melt away on you.

The sailing directions on each leg may not make sense without understanding the chapters referenced above.

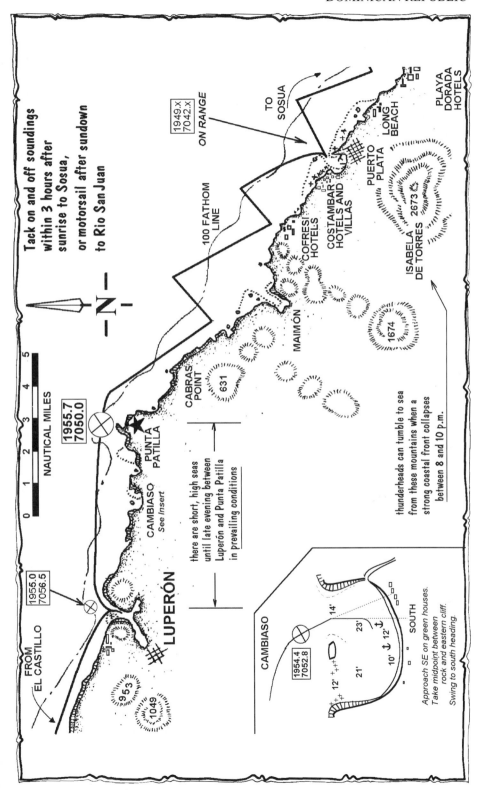

Tack on and off soundings within 3 hours after sunrise to Sosua, or motorsail after sundown to Rio San Juan

1949.x
7042.x
ON RANGE

TO SOSUA

PLAYA DORADA HOTELS

LONG BEACH

PUERTO PLATA

COSTAMBAR HOTELS AND VILLAS

COFRESI HOTELS

100 FATHOM LINE

ISABELA DE TORRES 2673

MAIMÓN

1674

CABRAS POINT 631

1955.7
7050.0

PUNTA PATILLA

CAMBIASO
See Insert

–N–

NAUTICAL MILES
0 1 2 3 4 5

1955.0
7056.5

FROM EL CASTILLO

LUPERÓN

953

1049

there are short, high seas until late evening between Luperón and Punta Patilla in prevailing conditions

thunderheads can tumble to sea from these mountains when a strong coastal front collapses between 8 and 10 p.m.

CAMBIASO

1954.4
7052.8

12'
21'
14'
23'
10' 12'
SOUTH

Approach SE on green houses. Take midpoint between rock and eastern cliff. Swing to south heading.

PICKING WINDOWS

The section of the coast from **Luperón** to **Punta Patilla** is high and rugged with the 100 fathom line being less than 2 miles offshore. If the offshore wind has been blowing less than 15 knots from east or south of east during the day, you usually will have a flat calm motorsail in deep water close inshore before dawn. The secret is to hide behind the capes in the daytime and transit the bays at night, taking the wind that is on a down-tick of a Trade cycle. Go only when the forecast wind is 15 knots or less from behind the island (i.e., south of east), less than 15 knots if blowing east (along the coast), and 10 knots or less if there is an onshore wind. If you want to coast in daylight reduce these wind strengths by 5 knots or more due to seabreeze. These conditions must last 24 hours longer than you think you need. Otherwise, you have not got a proper window.

In mid-October through mid-December, and the spring months May through June, look for stationary **troughs** which stretch from the southwest Caribbean to north of Hispaniola. Year round the approach of weakening cold **fronts** can turn into stationary troughs as well. This phenomenon, shown in the figure below, opens a window for going east along the coast, because a wedge of relative calm is created between the coast and some distance out toward the trough.

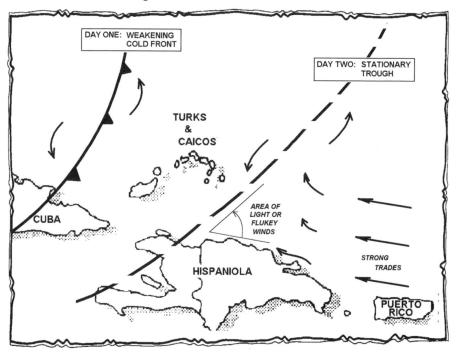

Occluding fronts and stationary fronts can develop north of Hispaniola which give protection from the trades for going east, as shown in the diagrams.

Never try to ride a moving front on this coast. It is dangerous as a lee shore.

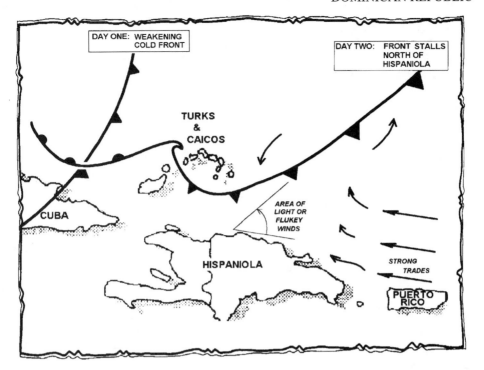

Preparing for Departure

The north coast harbors leave your ground tackle a mud- and growth encrusted mess. You shall have a cleanup job on the ground tackle that will leave you exhausted and in an ill mood for a bad start to sea. You'll need a night's sleep after your labors. The day before leaving, get anchors unfouled and clean the rodes. Lay to a single fresh hook, and make ready for sea. Hire a boy, or use the Pinzón anchorage (see *Luperón*) to scrub prop and bottom for the motoring ahead. This is also a good practice throughout the mangrove harbors in Puerto Rico.

Departures from **Luperón** can be customized to the **Weather Windows** available:

— depart **Luperón** at *daybreak* for an afternoon at **Sosua**. Leave Sosua at *sundown* to arrive **Escondido** before 5 p.m. Depart there to arrive **Samaná** before 8 a.m.

— depart **Luperón** at *sundown*. Arrive at **Rio San Juan** by 8 a.m. Round **Cabo Francés Viejo** that night and be sailing in **Bahía Escocesa** by 8 a.m. for an overnight anchorage at **Escondido**. Depart there to arrive **Samaná** before 8 a.m.

No fixed rule can calculate a fixed departure time for every window possible, but in many years of departing Luperón, all my departures have been either dawn or dusk.

Leaving Luperón in the Morning

Clear out the night before so you can hoist a short scoped anchor at sunrise. Try to round **Punta Patilla** before 7 a.m. to avoid rugged seas which can make up early between there and Luperón. From Patilla take two tacks in light easterlies down to **Owen Rock** off **Puerto Plata**. This should give you protection from **Cabo Macoris** as you short tack up to **Sosua** by noon.

183

Leaving Luperón in the Evening

Don't hurry out of **Luperón**. During **prevailing conditions** (see *Glossary*) rugged seas can build during the day between Luperón and **Punta Patilla**. They may not lay down until some hours after sunset. Wait a couple of hours in the Pinzón anchorage if necessary. Also, from **Puerto Plata** east, the remnants of the day's **coastal front**, untethered from the land by the setting of the sun, float down hill to their destruction at sea as late as 10 p.m. Hang back a bit to miss them. Otherwise you must slack sheets and run off, giving up 10 to 20 minutes of easting for northing.

If you got cheated on the window somehow, don't be shy of turning back to wait for another. Motorsail at night close along the capes themselves. If you don't stop at **Rio San Juan**, be sure to turn the corner and hoist sail east of **Cabo Francés Viejo** by 8 a.m. when the next day's easterly flow shall hit.

PUERTO PLATA PORT

Note that **Luperón** is the preferred port of entry for yachts.

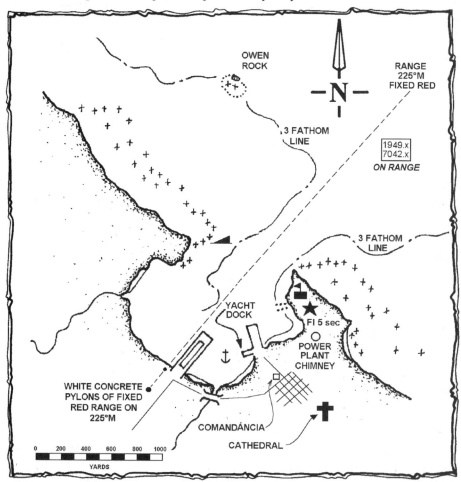

The loom of the lights of **Puerto Plata** will be visible up to 30 miles out if they haven't had a power failure. During the day it can be seen by the enormous outpouring of smoke from the power plant's stack. Again, if there hasn't been a power outage.

The distinctive mountain at **Puerto Plata, Isabel de Torres**, is 2673 feet high and is surmounted with a statue of Christ. Tack up the coast to round **Owen Rock** 200 yards on your starboard and enter **Puerto Plata** by the range before 9 o'clock in the morning. If you've had luck with the weather and arrive off the port at night, use the range. It consists of 2 fixed red lights at the west end of the harbor, just to the west of the long commercial dock at that end. A note of caution, the range lights, although large and bright, are well shrouded, as they should be, providing a narrow beam for you to follow. Keep a sharp lookout when picking it up and stay well off until you do. In daytime, the range can be seen as 2 white concrete pylons with orange tops.

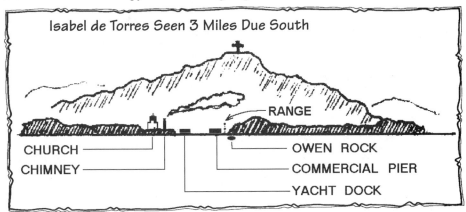

Isabel de Torres Seen 3 Miles Due South

CHURCH
CHIMNEY
RANGE
OWEN ROCK
COMMERCIAL PIER
YACHT DOCK

Go to the dock in **Puerto Plata** only in Force 3 or less. If you arrive in windy conditions, anchor and row in with your papers to see the *comandante*. Move to the dock the next morning. Boats often bunch up in the small anchorage and line the pier like sardines. Damage can occur from surge and big ship propwash. Security on the yacht dock doesn't seem to be anyone's responsibility. Lock up well and follow the anchoring advice below.

When one entered Puerto Plata in the past, one found the dock was free, the electricity was free, the excellent mountain water was free and, when you walked through the gates to the nearby rum factory, the rum was free. Not a bad town at all! The dock is an abandoned concrete pier. "Med moor" to the dock with crisscrossed stern lines, 2 long springs, an anchor 150 or more feet ahead and slightly east and another ahead and slightly west. Keep the boat half to a full boat length from the dock and use your dinghy to shuttle back and forth with a "telegraph" line. Whether anchoring or "Med-mooring", let 3 days go by before trusting the anchor. It's in 20 to 35 feet of colloidal mud and will set itself fine after a spell. If at the dock, take up the slack for 3 mornings. Keep good slack in your stern and spring lines or you'll "rubber band" like a slingshot when a surge starts.

The cinders from the power plant, dry and harmless, float out to sea and over the yachts, perpetually raining black dust. The commercial ship traffic in the small harbor causes the yachts at anchor to knot up dangerously close to each other and often a seagoing tug will wash up anchors with its propeller.

The officials of the port handle yacht traffic with the left hand, so to speak. They often get fed up and can offer hassles of their own to the cruiser who loses his sense of humor. The **Puerto Plata** dock is a free port area and Customs may inspect anything you take ashore. Don't be offended.

Sosua

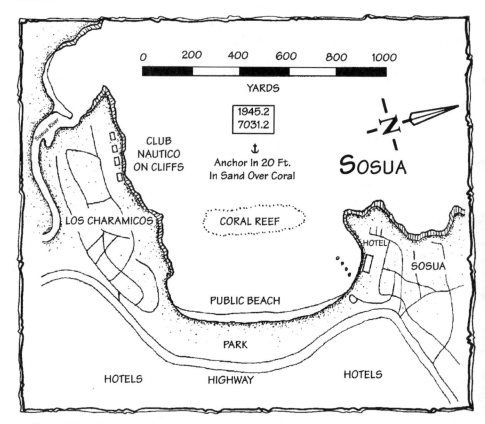

Cleared from **Luperón** for **Samaná**, take a **Leisure Sail** over to **Sosua** [soh-SOO-ah], standing well off the reefs along the shore. Leave Luperón at first light or a few hours earlier, anchoring overnight in the entrance, if necessary. As you approach the airport near Sosua, the cape effect around **Cabo Macoris** will be felt. Get closer inshore at this point to get cover from the stronger winds this effect produces. The reefs here are readily visible. These, and the surfing beaches off **Cabarete**, will be the last shoal shores on this passage. Anchor outside the public swimming beach at Sosua until early evening, not going ashore or anchoring overnight, and forego your **SG&T** toward a safer voyage. Take a nap and prepare a thermos or two and a pressure cooker full of hot *burgoo* (see Glossary). Raise anchor at 6 p.m. and **Leisure Sail** around **Cabo Macoris** until it's no fun anymore for lack of wind. This is usually an exciting sail in the ebb of the day's wind. If there are some white horses, they will be the last you will see that night, and the wind will slacken beyond the cape, assuming, of course, that you picked a good window.

Depart Sosua at first light if daysailing to **Rio San Juan** on extremely light days.

Remember, great fleets of boats anchoring where they're not expected tend to draw more concern from local officials than do 1 or 2. Don't anchor close enough for swimmers to come out and hang onto your boat, thereby making a scene of yourself. If, despite your intentional low profile anchored way out there, a representative of the Puerto Plata *comandante* wakes you up, simply explain to him that you are sheltering under the headland until 6 p.m., and will be on your way when the seas permit.

SOSUA TO SAMANÁ

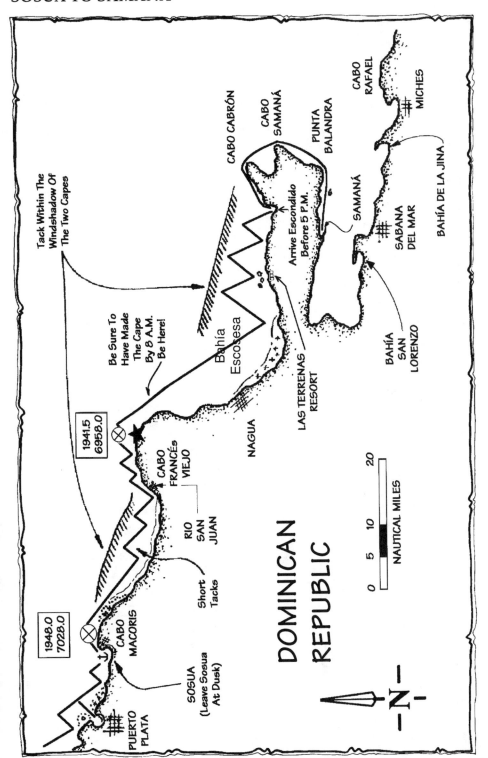

RIO SAN JUAN

This port offers a good lee in *prevailing conditions*: i.e., E-ESE wind with no large swells, no threatening weather features approaching. Arrive here at dawn after departing Luperón at sunset. On extremely light, settled days, it is possible to daysail here from **Sosua**, but don't count on getting those conditions without waiting more than you probably want. Boats bound both east or west can use the little harbor of **Rio San Juan** as an escape hatch if caught out in rough seas between **Cabo Macoris** and **Cabo Francés Viejo**.

Rules of good conduct while nosing around a harbor for which you have no explicit clearance prevail. If you are only one or two boats, you will heighten the prospect of the Puerto Plata *comandante*'s representative inviting you to tour the botanical gardens by dinghy and dine in town. If the young man comes out to your boat on a jetski wearing a bikini and a tanktop, don't be surprised. Ask for his identification, which he will be proud to show. It's waterproof, because he carries it in the bikini.

Wait for the night lee to set in solidly before rounding Cabo Francés Viejo.

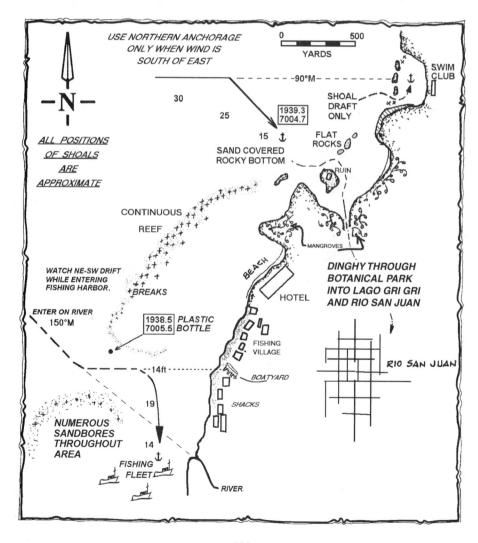

CABO FRANCÉS VIEJO

It seems to take forever to get around **Cabo Francés Viejo**. Hugging the shore makes it easier. If you are one of the latter day Lt.Maury's, no doubt you will use your GPS to discover all sorts of eddies and counter currents. Don't make a fool of yourself reporting them to your buddies back in Luperón. When they get there it may be counter-counter. I've had apparent lifts of up to six knots here sustained for as much as 15 minutes. Curse or praise your private luck, but in no case go public with your discovery of the Lost Current. Like the Mona, the bottom conditions coupled with the **Equatorial Current** cause hydro-thermodynamic chaos, the prediction of which is a fool's game. Refer also to the section on *Cape Effects* under *Land Effects*.

BAHÍA ESCOCESA

Time your passage around **Cabo Francés Viejo** to arrive well into the **Bahía Escocesa** before 8 a.m. It may prove to be near impossible to make the cape later in the day, and you need sea room off **Nagua** to begin an inshore tack in the rising tradewind. One friend who failed to do so lost a beautiful Baltic Trader there. One or two tacks south-southeast across this bay should carry you to the high offshore rocks east of Nagua and west of **Escondido**. From that point east the shore is fairly clear of reefs and one can hug the shore and tack up to Escondido within a band of smooth sea. You should arrive at Escondido before 5 p.m. to ensure good light. The harbor is difficult to spot from sea the first time. You will recognize it by the two rocks lying off the northwest arm of the bay. If it is your first time there you will also need light while going in to convince yourself it is an easy night exit. Of course, it is as easy as a Norwegian fjord.

This is interesting territory. The bay is named "The Scots Woman" while the two headlands surrounding her are named "The Old Frenchman" and "The Cuckold". Furthermore, the bay is thought to be haunted. On several occasions I've talked with sober and mature merchant seamen who told me they have heard the crying of a woman while crossing the bay at night. My first trip (westward) across the bay was at night and we logged a peculiar melancholy that night, attributed at the time to the sorrow at leaving the Caribbean islands behind us. Only years later did I learn of the supposed haunting.

ESCONDIDO

DMA chart 25723 taken from WGS72 datum and US Navy survey of 1977 show **Puerto Escondido** oriented east-west more than 3 miles to the east of what has come to be accepted by boat captains as Puerto Escondido at position 19°19'N, 69°19'W, where its fjord-like entrance is really oriented north-south. The chart's position is actually a refuge for fishing canoes. The chart identifies the village correctly as **El Valle**.

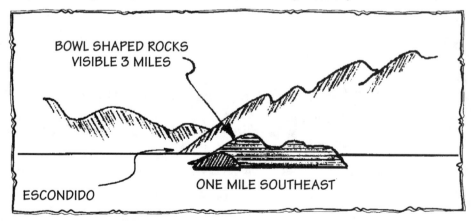

If for any reason the wind has gone north of east, stand well off and take your lumps against the current for a night. Do not either enter Escondido when there are large north swells running. Instead, sail down the edge of the **Mona Passage** about 2 miles off shore (a half mile off in daylight) and enter **Samaná Bay**, heaving-to a mile south of the **Balan-**

190

dra **Head** light, if necessary. Put a lantern out and go to sleep.

In **Escondido** the local Navy shall visit in a dugout canoe rowed by fishermen he must hire but can't pay. They shall ask for handouts because that's the way they are paid. Welcome the officials with identification aboard, not the fishermen. Treat them with dignity and friendliness, but the fishermen have no business aboard your yacht. If you're having your **SG&T** when they come, ask them to join you, perhaps by a small bottle of rum which they can share at home, since you won't be in the mood for onboard guests after your journey. Of course you purchased a case of small rum bottles while in **Luperón** just for this purpose. Didn't you? The official has a hardship post indeed. He might be able to use your old leaky beach cooler to use as an ice box. While finishing your SG&T the locals may give an exhibition of community net fishing from either the beach or canoes.

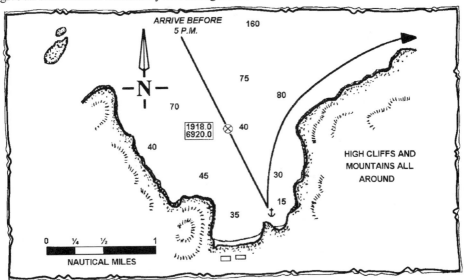

The next morning leave **Escondido**, a broad deep fjord, between midnight and 4 am, following the towering east wall 200 yards off, even using starlight. Motor hard against the cliffs in the flat calm, while scrambling eggs in the galley, up to **Cabo Cabrón**, cutting its cliffs as close as a boat length if you dare. One German reader's English caused him to interpret this literally. Coming out onto the dark deck, his wife screamed at the weight of looming rock and nearly frightened him overboard. Not to worry. I wouldn't have used the allusion had I not actually tried it myself beforehand; although, in *daylight*.

Be sure to round **Cabo Samaná** well off (a half mile) and be sailing south by 9 am. before the trades make it difficult to round the capes and set sail. It is smartest to sail into **Samaná** harbor shortly after daybreak in order to anchor unplagued by the wind, and before the dock has a pestilence of teeming idlers. Have an early **SG&T** in the middle of the day, and toast all the slicker clad yachties huffing and puffing into the anchorage from their offshore trials. Sit in Samaná Sam's and listen to their tales of the ultimate wave. One year I met 5 crews exactly in this way. We had all left **Puerto Plata** together. They motorsailed while I mostly sailed. I was the only single-hander. I had a comfortable, upright and dry trip. Their decks, strewn with drying slickers and cushions, showed the kind of a passage they had. Hard to believe? Every season there's a fleet of hardnose cruisers who carry on offshore. Follow the coasting advice in this guide and you'll be a believer.

SAMANÁ

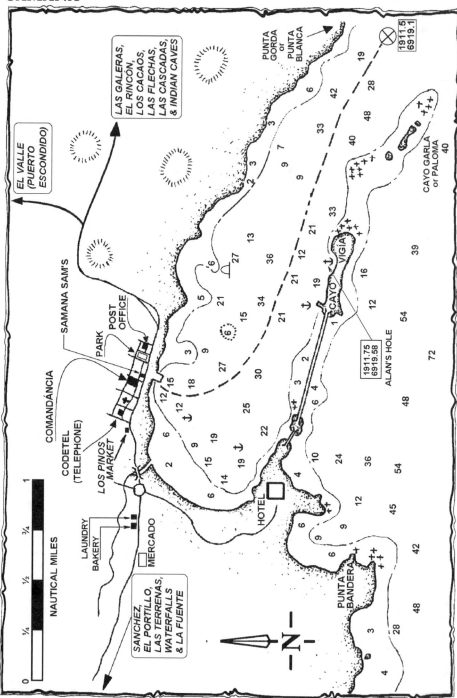

Samaná [sah-mah-NAH] is the Appalachia of the Dominican Republic. Its remoteness both curse and charm it. Samaná was settled in the 19th century by American former slaves from first St.Croix and later Philadelphia. In 1949, the dictator Trujillo built a road into the area, burned down the town and forced the population to heel, making them speak Spanish. With that background it should be no surprise that a visit to **Samaná** is not an in-depth look at the Dominican Republic, its people, nor its culture. It enjoys a certain uniqueness. For instance, remnants of African cultural practices are found in Samaná as in Haiti. Samaná is surrounded by many natural splendors of karst geology. In the caves to the east the **Taino**s made their Messada-like last stand against the *conquistadores*.

SECURITY

In the last years Samaná has become notorious for dinghy and motor theft, even occasional boardings by someone looking for a motor. The **Mona Passage** is to Samaná what the Rio Grande is to Tijuana: a focal point for smuggling to the US. A market exists for big outboards. A secondary market exists for little outboards on which a clever man could parlay himself to a big outboard (in horsepower: 2+2=5, 5+5=10 and 10+10=25).

Many Americans assume the *yola* traffic between here and Puerto Rico is innocent and hungry Dominican refugees desperate to flee their poor country. Dominicans eat better than Puerto Ricans, and they are universally proud of their country, poor as it may be. The only desperation on the *yolas* is with the desperados aboard them. Young Dominican adventurers and law-dodgers may pay $500 to cross the Mona in an open boat. Chinese may pay $3000, Cubans $2000. Police interrogators from former Latin American dictatorships of either the left or right might pay $25,000! Once in Puerto Rico, no one asks who you are. You are free to establish a new life as an American from Puerto Rico to Samoa. Samaná is a terminus for smuggling illegals. It is not a place to leave the boat and tour the island. **Luperón** is more convenient, located centrally on the island, it is near to important cities and airports. And it is secure. Therefore, *as you would certainly lock your car in Tijuana, lock your dinghy in Samaná.* See *Dinghy Security.*

COMMUNICATION

Mail and **telephone** work here, but recall that it's a very remote location and add a few days or even a week to Puerto Plata mail times. Nonetheless, there are times at which the service is surprisingly good. The personnel are friendly, anyway. Transportation within Samaná is very comfortable. Flag down a *motoconcho* which, in Samaná, is a motorized rickshaw carrying 6 passengers, with a canvas roof to keep you dry.

WHAT TO SEE

Samaná has some of the best scenery in the DR. There are three spectacular waterfall sites. Take swimsuits to both. The cascades east of the town are like water chutes which drop to successive baths from a lovely tree shaded river which runs along the ridge above. Take a *motoconcho* or *público* [POO-blee-koh] to the falls 8 kilometers west of town where the 150 foot wide falls slide into a treed gorge down a 100 foot high cliff warmed by the sun. You can bathe in the cool lagoon below and shower under the hot waterfall. Before taking the path up to the falls, buy your lunch of cheese, salami, bread and ice cold Presidente beer from the *colmado* [coal-MAH-doh] on the highway. Take a *público* to La Fuente, west of **Sanchez** for an excellent *tipico* (native style) lunch and a swim in the springs there. You can also organize boat trips to the grottos across the bay in the **Bahía de San Lorenzo**. Samaná is the closest you will come to Bora Bora while in the Caribbean. Some stay the whole hurricane season. Some go ashore and stay forever. But, like Bora Bora, Samaná is painfully remote, and likely to remain so despite all claims to the contrary.

CROSSING THE MONA PASSAGE

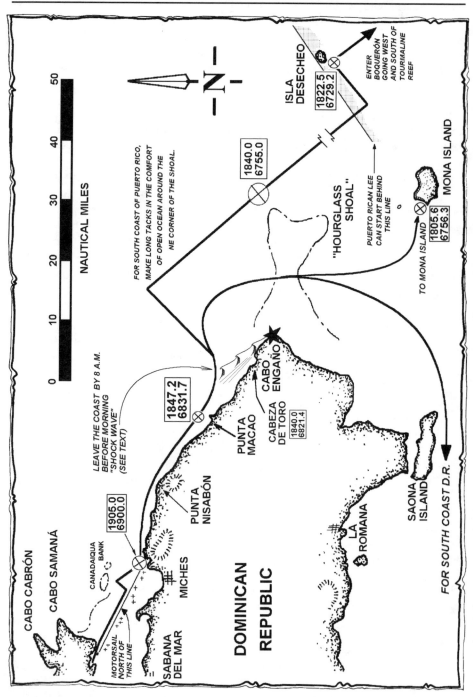

The **Mona Passage**'s reputation comes from stories dished out with relish by delivery skippers motoring dock to dock with someone else's property, or first time cruisers who motor on a straight rhumb line in east southeast greater than 15 knots, right through the shoals, and by still others who collect their data over the bar (or on the SSB Breakfast Show) from cruisers who made the trip only once or twice or under a deadline.

None of these make reliable sources for the **Leisure Sailor** who can afford to **Wait for Weather**, and if cruising isn't Leisure Sailing, what is it? I have crossed the Mona dozens of times in comfort and safety, using the following methods. Along with the strategies for hugging the coast at night on the north shore of the DR, and making little harbor hops at dawn on the south shore of PR, these are not *my* strategy, they are the *only* strategies that work *all the time* against **prevailing conditions**. To do the Mona you can choose from several strategies, one of which *is* mine. It is presented here for mom and pop on their 36 footer with the 25 hp auxiliary, but anyone can use it with multiple benefits.

The **Mona Passage** has unpredictable currents everywhere and rough shoals off **Cabo Engaño** and **Balandra Point**. Thunderstorms, often severe, are set adrift from Puerto Rico's **coastal front** by the cooling of the night. The fooler for newcomers to this area is that the shoals are deep, and one doesn't expect rough water; the forecast was for fine weather, and one doesn't expect a rank of thunderstorms. Both shoal areas and the storm cells can be avoided by the strategy below which calls for coasting, then sailing.

PICKING WINDOWS

Some motorsailors can make the run in less than 24 hours in light conditions. You might sail directly across in under 30 hours when **prevailing conditions** abate for any reason. To find a window *under prevailing conditions*, however, I strongly recommend using the nightly lees on both sides of the channel by taking a window of Force 3-4 easterly with no unusual swell, taking 2 nights and a day to cross. That is, 2 nights of lee sailing and one day of smooth, open ocean sailing. Should you leave **Samaná** in the morning, trying to cross the Mona Passage in one day, there will be no margin for error or problems enroute, and you probably will have the stuffing kicked out of you during the daytime on both sides of the passage.

You can follow a stalled front across in a mild northeast wind. You can motor through the calm of a trough. But in light prevailing conditions, use 2 nights and a day.

The ever cyclic **trade winds** switch back and forth like a cat's tail. Record them until you get a handle on the cycle. Then, remembering to weight average the **Offshore Reports** for both the eastern Caribbean and the southwest North Atlantic, take the first down-tick in the cycle that has sensible wind (see *Harbor Telltales*).

Shoals

Many cruisers don't recognize the shoals on the **charts** because they may be several hundred feet deep and that does not, in their experience, mean shoal. However, the water these shoals are trying to contain comes from the **Equatorial Current** spilling into the **Puerto Rican Trench**, the *second deepest* hole in the world. That's a lot of water and a lot of energy for the shoals to dissipate, and you don't want to be part of it. Stay clear of any area much more shallow than another if it lies west of the Puerto Rican Trench. The first shoal, the **Canandaiqua Bank**, lies south and east of the **Samaná** peninsula. The second area, which I call **Hour Glass Shoal** from its shape of an hour glass lying on its side, lies east of **Cabo Engaño**, directly on the motoring rhumb line from Samaná to **Boquerón**, a sure hit for most delivery crews.

The *thornless* transit of the Mona Passage counts for comfort and safety on tacking away from both areas. The **Hour Glass Shoal** can be a short cut on your way to or from the south coast or **Mona Island** by passing north-south through its "waist".

STORMS

The line of WNW drifting thunderstorms released from Puerto Rico's heat by the setting sun sometimes dissipate to squalls or showers or nothing at all within 30 miles of the coast. Sometimes they grow more wicked and charge like bulls. Some of these storm cells have been the fiercest I've seen in my life. If you have satellite pictures or long range radar, you may know which it is and find alleys between them if they exist. Mom and Pop or me use the plan below to make a *veronica*-like tacking maneuver around the charging bulls as shown below. Power boats can outflank them to the south.

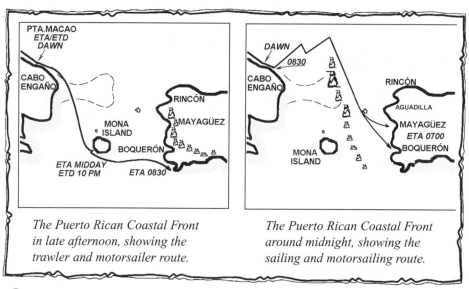

The Puerto Rican Coastal Front in late afternoon, showing the trawler and motorsailer route.

The Puerto Rican Coastal Front around midnight, showing the sailing and motorsailing route.

CURRENTS

United States Navy Lieutenant Matthew Fontaine Maury, the hydrographer who initiated the idea of sea lanes in his *Sailing Directions* in 1859, created a repository of data on world currents and winds which today is found in the American Pilot Charts (British Routing Charts). This data has been confirmed and refined for a century and a half. That doesn't preclude Captain John Courageous of the S/V Chicken Little from differencing his GPS from his speed log and announcing to the world the discovery of a new current. One year a whole fleet out of Georgetown put me on the spot. They radioed me, still in Georgetown, with an insistent request that I sponsor a notification to the US Navy and NOAA that the **Equatorial Current** had reversed itself and was flowing *east*. I put it all down to giddiness of overnighters approaching Hispaniola for the first time. They urged me to act, feeling they had uncovered an incipient North American *El Niño*, and that the world must be warned. To no avail I listed the extensive variety of phenomena at play: logs, GPS, microcode algorithms, standing hull waves playing on their impeller, tide, upwellings, eddies, hydraulic curlicues and hallucination. To end the embarrassment I asked they mail me data logs from each ship with exact times and instrument readings, and I committed to forwarding the data to a disinterested Navy (after all, it was <u>ornithologists</u> who brought the original *El Niño* to their attention). Of course I never heard more.

What's my point? ***If it ain't on the Pilot Charts, it don't exist,*** as far as your course planning is concerned. Plan no currents in the Mona, just *because* they are unpredictable.

LANDFALL

If you have more favorable conditions than you had planned, or if you get edgy and motored hell-for-leather, you may make landfall in the dark. Instead you should motor less and sail more to ensure a morning arrival. In any case, **Mayagüez** is an easy and well marked, well lighted, open roadstead port, and it is the official port of entry.

SAIL OR MOTOR?

Small trawlers, unless they find a calm, should take the Mona Island route. Sailboats who want to motor the Mona may have to wait a month of Sundays to get their 30 hour calm. If you can motorsail in easy conditions, do it, but in **prevailing conditions**, the way across for mom and pop is within a window of 36 to 48 hours of easterly 10 to 15 knots. This mostly comes in summer. In the winter, a mild, or stalled front or trough, or a gale system passing to the north, might provide the same window, or even northeasterlies!.

TIMING

When the guy a day ahead of you radios back that there's a strong northerly current he's just named *Chicken Little Gullywash*, don't alter your plan for crossing the Mona. I see it done every year and every year I see people lose their timing crossing the Mona. They either get off the coast too late in the morning and get pinned by the trades, or they get run down by the drifting storm cells, or, with no GPS, they just get lost. The timing of sailing tacks or of a flat out motor passage, must take into account: (1) the night lees on both sides of the passage, (2) the drifting **coastal front** from Puerto Rico, and (3) the vigor of even light Atlantic **trades** undiminished by either wind shadow or night lee.

Here's an example of what can happen. The first half of this story appears in the chapter on *Flying Windows*. The pair of yachts that followed me out of **Samaná** against my urging spent *60 hours* being hammered in the Mona while I drifted dreamily down the Puerto Rican night lee at the end of a delightful 32 hour easy sail. Why?

I heard them on the VHF (waking me) discussing the lovely sail they were having tacking down the nighttime DR coast: they were playing in the night lee. Meanwhile, I had a serious look at my progress. To control the timing of my passage I needed to step it up a bit. First I took shallower tacks by running the engine at a little over idle. Later, I rolled up the jib and escalated to a motorsail to ensure I was off **Cabo Engaño** at dawn.

It is crucial to be at the end of land and tacking off the coast by daylight because the cape effect (see *Cape Effect*) on **Cabo Engaño** can be murder. I called them and told them this. They said they understood, yet they still didn't budget their time. They weren't even near **Punta Macao** by daybreak, when according to their VHF chatter, every time they tacked out, they were assaulted by the wedge of swift and raging water rounding the cape, and they turned back into "smoother water". If tacking in a sailboat were comparable to making *zigzag stitches* on the ocean, these guys were doing a narrowing *button hole stitch* inside the **cape effect**, getting nowhere fast. I lost them on the VHF because I was *basting a hem stitch* toward the northeast in 12-14 knots just forward of the beam in 4 foot long seas. Their saga continued that night when **storm cells** from the collapsed Puerto Rican **coastal front** hit them. That kept them busy and pushed them back a fair bit. I saw the tops of the storms at sunset off my quarter, where my northeast tack had flanked them. Exhaustion began to help matters. Next on their plate was the roar of the trades around Rincón during the daytime, then came ... Never mind. You get the point.

Get off the coast before the trades begin!

TRACKING THE TRADES

By following the **National Weather Service**'s *Eastern Caribbean Report* you can predict when the **trades** will be lightening up and favoring your tack.

While you **wait for weather** in **Samaná** you may receive the Puerto Rico VHF weather channels (WX). *Use this information at your peril!* You will be crossing open Atlantic Ocean, not coasting the west coast of Puerto Rico.

Do not rely on data received by radio from friends in Puerto Rico. They are less able to gauge the weather from their lee harbors than you are in Samaná, and you can't do it well from there either. You shall hear reports of strong winds in **Ponce**, calms in **Boquerón** — even westerly winds which, in Boquerón are common enough as a southeast Force 5 wraps around **Cabo Rojo** and backwinds the bay. These are all coastal effects in Puerto Rico which don't affect you.

Construct a decision table like the one below and update it after listening to the **National Weather Service Offshore Reports** for the *Eastern Caribbean* and the *Southwest North Atlantic* on **NMN** each morning. Unless you spend a long time in **Samaná**, you must start collecting this data already in **Luperón** or even **Caicos**.

DAY	WIND DIRECTION	WIND SPEED IN KNOTS	SEA CONDITION IN FEET	QUALITATIVE CHANGE IN OFFSHORE RPT.	GO/ NOGO
1	E	10 to 15	4 to 6		
2	E	10 to 15	<5	better	go
3	SE to E	10 to 15	4 to 6	worse	nogo
4	SE to E	15 to 20	4 to 7	worse	nogo
5	E to SE	15 to 25	5 to 7	worse	nogo
6	E to SE	20	5 to 8	same	nogo
7	E to SE	15 to 20	4 to 7	better	nogo
8	E to SE	15	4 to 6	better	go
9	E	10 to 15	4 to 6	better	**gone**

BOUND FOR THE NORTH & WEST COASTS OF PUERTO RICO

A sailing or motorsailing crossing should use the nighttime lees on both sides of the passage. This took *Jalan Jalan* 32 to 40 hours depending on her draw of wind and wave. In a northeast Force 3 you can motorsail more directly across in less time. In a calm you can motor straight across in 24 hours or less. Count on leaving in less than 15 knots easterly and do not go over the windward side of the "hourglass" shoal. In 10 to 15 knots wind, follow the method below and you can do the **Mona Passage** in as little as 2 tacks with little or no roar of the motor <u>and</u> comfortable conditions.

— Leave Samaná on a day when the gradient winds (weighted average of the eastern Caribbean and the southwest North Atlantic **Offshore Reports**) are lighter than usual, preferably east or north of east, and with no unusual swell running. Leaving **Samaná** in the evening will take best advantage of whatever night lee the island extends eastward. Have your rode cleaned and on short scope and the boat squared away for sea. Up anchor about dusk with enough good light left to clear **Cayo Leventado**. There may be heavy chop here in the late afternoon which you can avoid by **staging** yourself to the anchorage west of Leventado. Halfway between Cayo Leventado and the mainland take up a 120° Magnetic course for 19°05'N, 69°00'W (see chartlet *Crossing the Mona Passage*).

— After leaving the land behind, long tack southeast and short tack northeast to **Cabo Rafael**, well east of the shoals off **Miches** on the south shore of Bahía Samaná in the **Bahía de la Finca**. The loom of Miches at night is quite clear as is that of **Sabana de la Mar** across the bay from Samaná. Don't confuse the two.

— The southern limit of a tack to avoid the shoals off Miches is on a line bearing 120° magnetic to a point 19°05'N, 69°00'W. You may have to take a short tack or two out from the coast to maintain the course to Cabo Rafael.

— Close with **Cabo Rafael** 2 miles off, then sail or motorsail the coast on the 20 fathom line (often a mile or less off) to **Punta Macao**. With luck your first northeast tack can be your last and will be taken near **Cabo Engaño** itself as the lee you have been using all night begins to waiver. Punta Macao is a good anchorage in settled easterlies should you want to pause there (see below).

— Plan to be tacking away from the coast before 8 a.m. The acceleration of wind around Cabo Engaño shall form a "shock wave" of heavy conditions offshore of you if you remain inshore too long in daylight.

— Carry on northeast until able to lay a southeast tack to a safety waypoint, 18°40'N and 67°55'W, well off the northeast corner of the Cabo Engaño **Hourglass Shoals**. This is usually smooth sailing in open ocean.

— Storm cells from the decay of the Puerto Rican **coastal front** may sweep westward well to your south. If you carry your northeast tack long enough, your leg down to Puerto Rico shall be under starry skies.

— Carry the southeast tack past a line from the northwest corner of Puerto Rico through **Isla Desecheo**. Conditions usually moderate southeast of that line and you can usually lay either **Mayagüez** or **Boquerón** early the next morning.

— You can pass Isla Desecheo on either side, but if you are headed for Boquerón instead of Mayagüez, be sure to pass west of **Tourmaline Reef**. From Desecheo onward is usually a motor in calms with Puerto Rico lit up like a city seen from the air at night.

— Buoys and lights in Puerto Rico are usually reliable and US standard.

BOUND FOR THE SOUTH COAST OF PUERTO RICO

A *thornless* option takes 3 legs in night lees when forecast gradient wind is less than 15 knots. This is a good run for small trawlers. This option can also be used to sail up to the west coast of Puerto Rico. A careful watch on satellite pictures before and after sundown helps. If there are any dangerous storm cells off Puerto Rico, the sun over the horizon shall light up their high tops on the satpics as they drift off the coast.

— Coast down to **Punta Macao** or **Cabeza de Toro**, and anchor by 9a.m. at the latest.

— Leave anchorage at dawn to arrive **Mona Island** by 9 a.m. Proceed around **Cabo Engaño**, through the waist of the "hourglass" shoal during the night lee, and approach the lee of Mona Island as the trades pipe up.

— Leave Mona Island late evening so as to outflank any storm cells drifting west from Puerto Rico and to arrive at your southcoast destination before 8:30 a.m. (Cabo Rojo, Parguera, Guánica or even Ponce).

PUNTA MACAO AND CABEZA DE TORO

I often jill around right off Punta Macao or Cabeza de Toro, if I get that far, waiting for the morning forecast before tacking offshore. If a weather change favors a wait, I hang out here awhile, but only during *settled easterlies with no significant northerly swell.* There is a Navy station at both anchorages and officials will visit and look at your *despacho* to Puerto Rico. Cabeza de Toro, situated next to the Bavaro Beach Resort, has a fuel dock. This is a good spot to make a nighttime dash down the coast and through the waist of the "hourglass" shoals to Mona Island, arriving before Hispaniola loses its lee. The trick here

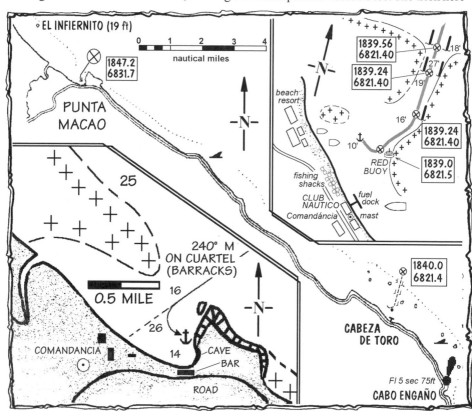

is to get the most of the **night lee** off the big island behind you while catching up with the shrinking lee of the small island ahead.

These two ports are used by the agencies of both the Dominican Republic and the United States in the so-called "war on drugs" as well as in the battle against illegal migration in the Mona Passage. Have respect for the official point of view, and you shall get respect in return for your right to seek shelter. The little basin at **Punta Macao** is the prettiest you shall have seen since the Bahamas. Hoot and holler and skinny dip in the presence of the boys at the cuartel on the beach and you shall surely be asked to leave. A small horarium to rewrite your despacho might help at **Cabeza de Toro**.

MONA ISLAND

Mona Island is a Puerto Rican national park and wildlife refuge with rangers in residence. The anchorage at **Sardinero** is used by Puerto Rican fishermen and vacationers alike. It also serves as a base for the Oceanology branch of the University of Puerto Rico located at La Parguera.

Enter on a range of two white triangular day boards which are lit until 10 p.m. The ranged channel carries 7 feet if exactly followed to a small sand anchorage with 8 feet. Either side of the channel has a few spots of only 5 feet on rocky ground. Coming from the Dominican Republic fly your yellow Q flag.

If there is a decent anchorage under 40 feet outside Sardinero, I haven't found it. With *Jalan Jalan*'s 6° draft I try to leave the Mona anchorage in good tide and good light, and, if necessary to *avoid evening storms* and to *control the time of landfall*, I heave to in the shadow of the island until departure time. Lesser drafts will have no problem here.

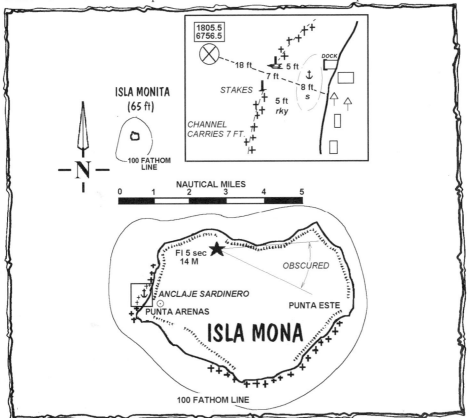

PUERTO RICO

The Commonwealth of Puerto Rico is a territory of the United States. It was discovered by **Columbus** on his second voyage to the New World in 1493. He named the island, called Borinquen by the **Tainos**, San Juan Bautista to honor Prince Juan, the son of Ferdinand and Isabela. Ponce de León, who explored the southeast United States, founded Puerto Rico's first settlement and was its first governor. The Spanish Virgin Islands east of Puerto Rico were alternately ignored or disputed by the European powers during the four centuries in which the main island of Puerto Rico was a colony of Spain. They were all ceded by Spain to the United States with the Treaty of Paris in 1898. Puerto Ricans are U.S. citizens and half are bilingual. The population is the most affluent in Latin America, but in recent years most of it was on welfare. Expect to be boarded by the U.S. Coast Guard. A significant amount of the illegal drugs entering the U.S. do so through Puerto Rico.

PUERTO RICAN REGULATIONS

BOAT AND DINGHY REGISTRATION

Vessels remaining in Puerto Rican waters more than 60 days must register in Puerto Rico. Fees are similar to Florida, e.g., a couple of hundred dollars for a 35 foot boat, plus separate registration for a dinghy with motor.

FIREARMS

Firearms aboard must have Puerto Rican permits after 60 days in country or be impounded. Such permits are impossibly difficult to get without political connections, or lots of time and money, by which time the arms might be missing anyway.

ASHORE IN PUERTO RICO

TOURING BY RENTAL CAR

Like in North America, one must have access to a car in Puerto Rico. If you decide to rent a car to tour the country, it is best to do so from **Salinas** which is centrally located and convenient to the only major highway. Get a road atlas and follow the purple lines, the *Ruta Panoramica*, through the mountains and small towns, staying at designated *Paradors*, usually historic or otherwise noteworthy inns. A good rule to use while driving: stop at every *lechón* (roasting pig) at the roadside, buy a beer and rip off a piece of the *lechón*. It's delicious, you'll meet many good Puerto Ricans, and in this manner you'll only make about 20 miles a day on weekends and holidays.

TOURING BY PÚBLICO

It is still possible to backpack Puerto Rico like you can in the Dominican Republic. There is not, however, the elaborate public transportation system found in the DR. Like North America, nearly everyone has access to a car, and for those that don't, there is still a good *público* system which has been waning as the island affluence waxes. *Públicos* in Puerto Rico use the same rules as do *públicos* in the Dominican Republic (see *Transportation in the DR*). In Puerto Rico they are large honky old American cars with about the same interior space as the Japanese ones used in the DR. The *públicos* in Puerto Rico cost much more than they do in the DR, but they only cram in 5 instead of 6, and like in the DR, you can always buy vacant seats for more comfort. Most small towns have público ranks around the town square. Larger towns have elaborate terminal buildings.

FIESTAS PATRONALES

Summer in Puerto Rico is the season of the *Fiestas Patronales* [fee-ACE-tahs pah-tro-NAHL-ace]. These are celebrations each town throws for itself (and theoretically its patron saint) as a way to liven up the summer and the business doldrums.

The *Fiestas* are sequenced to permit the traveling entertainers, rides and food concessions to appear at every one. Yet each *Fiesta* has its own atmosphere as the town turns on for a full week. The *Fiestas* in the smaller towns will bring back the Fourth of Julys of 50 years ago for older cruisers from Main Street, USA. The larger towns and county seats, such as **Cayey** often have fiestas which ring the central plaza for 3 and 4 blocks deep. Each port in Puerto Rico is either at or within a *público* ride from at least 3 *Fiestas*. Entertainment provided may be world class. You may see José Feliciano or Yolandita Monge.

Useful telephone numbers in Puerto Rico, country code 1, area code 787, follow:

US Coast Guard	Search & Rescue San Juan	722-2943
NOAA Weather Service	San Juan Airport	253-4588
Caribbean Stranding Net		399-1904
US FCC	San Juan	753-4567
Customs	*See chapter on Customs and Clearances*	
Charters	Tropic Keys Yachts, Puerto del Rey	860-6100
	Club Nautico Powerboats, Pto. del Rey	860-2400
Engine/Generator Repair	Marine Energy Svc., Puerto del Rey	863-6965
	Re-Power Marine Svc., Fajardo	863-9786
Services & Repairs	Captain Ron, Puerto del Rey	381-9146
	El Español,. Puerto del Rey	863-6965
	Island Marine, Isleta	382-3051
Marinas with Haul Out	Isleta Marina	384-9032
	Puerto del Rey	860-1000
	Puerto Chico (no hauls out)	863-0834
	Palmas del Mar	850-2065
	Villa Marina	863-5131
Chandlers	Abel Marine, Fajardo	860-0945
	Basic Marine, Puerto del Rey	860-5151
	El Pescador, Villa Marina	863-0350
	Larry's Playa Marine, Salinas	824-5337
	Skipper Shop, Villa Marina	863-2455
Sailmakers / Canvas	Atlantic Canvas & Sails, Pto. del Rey	860-1433
	Isleta Canvas, Isleta Marina	376-9324
	Tradewinds Sail & Canvas, Salinas	824-1611
	Fajardo Canvas & Sails, Villa Marina	863-3761
Towing	Abel Marine, Fajardo (VHF 16)	860-0945

SAILING DIRECTIONS, WEST COAST

Coming from the west one has a choice to approach Mayagüez from either side of **Desecheo**, a barren rock island 10 miles west of **Punta Higüero**. There is room for a single boat to moor in a completely rockbound anchorage on the south coast of Desecheo (pronounced dess-aye-CHAYE-oh, the discarded one). North of Punta Higüero, in the bight of Aguadilla, is an open roadstead anchorage subject to a good deal of surge, as is a roadstead anchorage south of the point at **Rincón**. **Puerto Real** and **Boquerón** are the *only* good harbors on this coast for cruising sailboats.

MAYAGÜEZ

The harbor at **Mayagüez** is for large ships. The pier may cause damage to your yacht, and there is a charge for laying alongside. Anchor between red buoys numbers 8 and 10 on the spoil bank where holding is poor, but the dredged areas are deep and even worse holding. Leave for **Boquerón** or **Puerto Real** before the wind comes up. It can be gusty and onshore in this wide open bay. Therefore arrive before 8 a.m. to be at Customs when they open in order to be under way and out of there by 10 a.m.

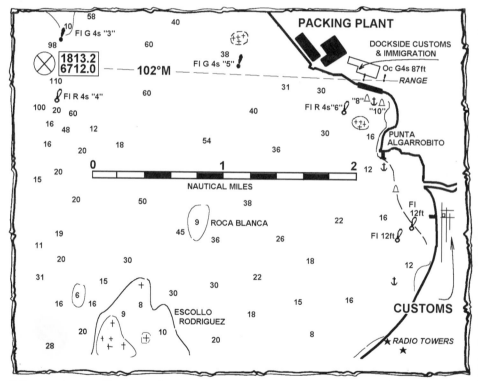

MAYAGÜEZ TO BOQUERÓN

Leave Mayagüez by 10:00 a.m. before the wind is up. This open harbor is subject to williwaws from the hills, especially when the coastal front builds up with large thunderheads. The route to either **Boquerón** or **Puerto Real** is inside **Tourmaline Reef** leaving red nun buoys numbers 6 and 4 on the port hand. *Club Deportiva* is a private marina for motorboats with shallow draft.

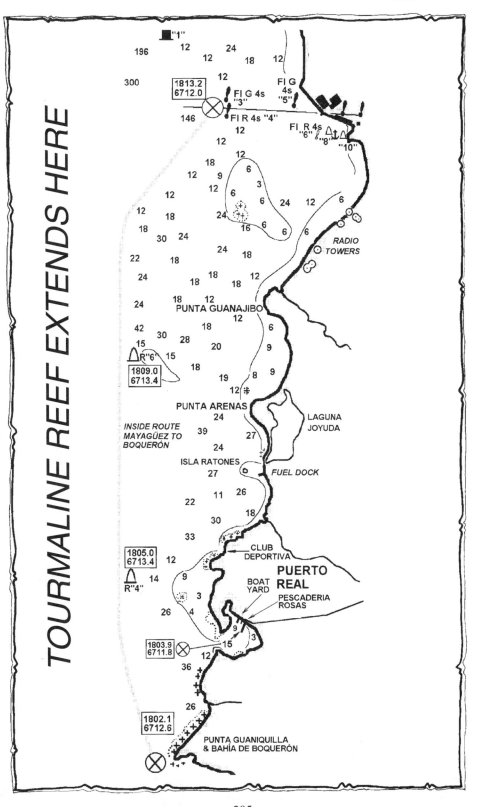

TOURMALINE REEF EXTENDS HERE

■"1"

196
300

12   24
12   18   12

12

1813.2
6712.0

Fl G 4s
"3"

Fl G
4s
"5"

146

Fl R 4s "4"

Fl R 4s
"6"   "8"   "10"

12

12

12

18   12

12   9   6
12   3
12   6   6
6
24   6   24   12   6
24   16   6
6   6

RADIO
TOWERS

18
30   24
24   18

22   18

24   18   12
18   18

24   18   12
PUNTA GUANAJIBO
12

42   30   18
28   6
15   20   9
R"6"   15
1809.0
6713.4   18   8   9
19   8   9
12

PUNTA ARENAS
24

INSIDE ROUTE   39   27
MAYAGÜEZ TO
BOQUERÓN   24

ISLA RATONES
27

LAGUNA
JOYUDA

FUEL DOCK

11   26
22
30   18

33

1805.0
6713.4   12

R"4"   14   9

3

26   4

1803.9
6711.8   15   3
12

36

26

1802.1
6712.6

PUNTA GUANIQUILLA
& BAHÍA DE BOQUERÓN

CLUB
DEPORTIVA

PUERTO
REAL

BOAT
YARD

PESCADERIA
ROSAS

9

Puerto Real

Follow the 2 fathom line paralleling the coast to the south of the harbor entrance. Enter on an east northeast heading passing about 200 yards off the southern side of the entrance. Crossing the bar just seaward of the harbor mouth, you may not see less than 10 feet, but a 6 foot spot exists at extreme low tide.

A small fishing village with facilities for haulout and repairs, Puerto Real, hosts tourists from around the island during the weekends because of its seafood restaurants. Pescaderia Rosas has extended their dock for loading ice and unloading catches. Besides watering and fueling, yachts can berth there for making repairs. Nearby, the boat yard can haul you with their 35-ton Travelift and fix anything that needs fixing. The haul out facility is a fishermen's cooperative with little room ashore, and working boats take preference.

Boquerón

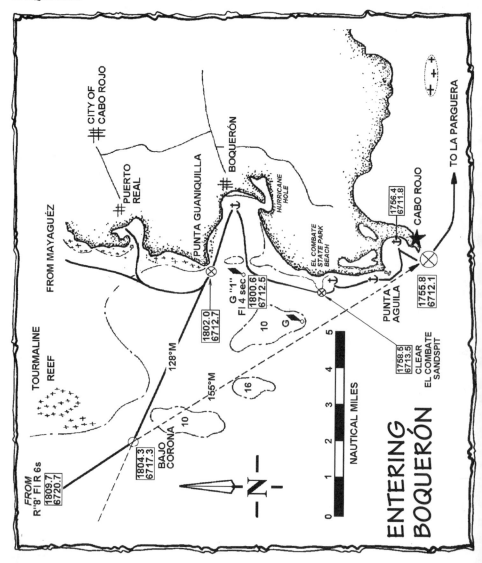

Approach **Boquerón** [boh-kaye-ROAN] along a line of 155° Magnetic on **Punta Aguila**, by **Cabo Rojo**, turning onto 128° Magnetic on **Punta Guaniquilla**, the northern point of the bay. Round the point one quarter mile off, and enter the bay, keeping a quarter mile off up to the anchorage off the town dock. With the shore close at hand as a guide, this is a deeper and safer entrance than the one through the reef in the middle of the bay.

If you haven't already done so, check in by phone in the little park (read carefully the chapter on clearing **Puerto Rico** under *Customs and Clearances*). Sears, K-Mart, Western Auto, WalMart, Burger King, Kentucky Fried Chicken and Pizza Hut are two *público* rides away at **Mayagüez**. However, Ponce has more and better malls.

Boquerón is a weekend haunt for Puerto Rican bohemians, and a beach and beer getaway for the Mayagüez University crowd. Weekends are wild, and the police force is very understanding. There are bars and restaurants everywhere with oysters and clams and tacos sold on the street. Try the conch salad at the *Shamar* beach bar or across the street. Conch is called *carrucho* [car-ROO-choh]. If you never were a sophomore in college, or you were, and you miss it, you'll love Boquerón. Because you've been in the boonies in the Bahamas and the DR for the last months, you will love this Latin version of Myrtle Beach.

But don't confuse this convenient and amusing landfall with the refit and reprovision point you need. Use all those 800 numbers to have stuff shipped in, but as far as provisioning, or local parts procurement or mechanical work, wait until **Salinas** if you can. Caselot stores, big malls, mechanics and parts in Ponce are handier to the anchorage in **Salinas** than Mayagüez is to **Boquerón**.

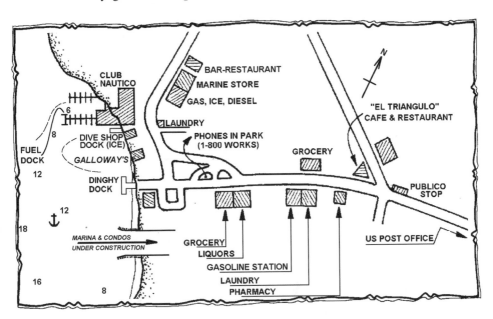

Boquerón, a convenient and happy layover.

SAILING DIRECTIONS, SOUTH COAST

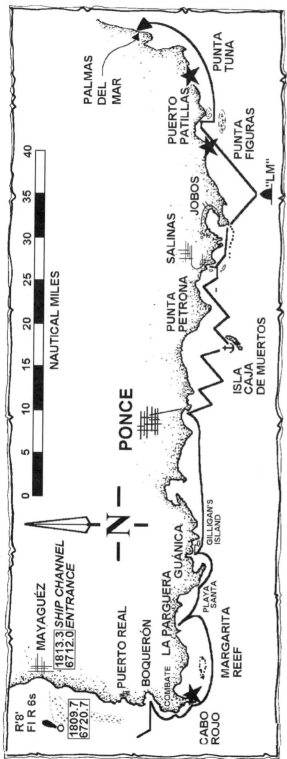

An Australian couple on a circumnavigation told me the south coast of Puerto Rico was the roughest they'd seen. After reading this book in Salinas, they understood why, and the thorns were taken out of the leg from Salinas east.

I have learned the hard way to take at least 11 days to transit the south coast of PR. I prefer 2 to 4 hour pleasant motorsails at dawn to dancing the "Caribbean Two Step" one minute. I begin my coasting by moving from the bay of **Boquerón** in the mid-morning, after shopping, over to a beach anchorage (review chapter on **Staging**). Short moonlit and dawn sails with lots of time to explore the small villages during the day, can be the highlight of your Caribbean cruise. Some anchorages could capture you for an entire season, so plan a slow cruise here.

You can wait until Boquerón to get your Puerto Rico charts. If headed west, they are available in **St.Thomas** at either Marine Warehouse or Island Marine Supply. Detail DMA or HO **charts** of this coast are hard to come by and expensive if you can get them. The **Imray** collection is excellent here and provides the best detail available for the small keys around **La Parguera** and **Jobos**. There are also excellent **Waterproof Charts** of Puerto Rico available in **Boquerón**.

The trick with this coast is to take advantage of the night conditions. Unlike the high north coast of the Dominican Republic, the south coast of Puerto Rico has wide coastal plains which further mitigate the already reduced calming effects of this smaller island. Look for a light offshore wind and a full moon. If you are lucky, or wait long enough, you can get both. If you're lucky it will be a moonlight sail on a flat sea with an offshore Force 3. If you are unlucky, tuck back into the next safe harbor, usually only 10 miles farther on. East winds, and in the winter, northeast winds, may become offshore at night as the central *cordilleras* [core-dee-YAIR-ahs] divide the wind. With the **katabatic** effects added to it, the wind slides downhill and offshore. Don't look for much of a calm extension from Puerto Rico, however. It's a tiny island and you must stay close inshore to get any effect at all. Often the only effect you will get is a shifting of the daytime winds to slightly north of east which is, anyway, on the nose.

Don't be fooled by the apparent closeness of each objective. This coast will be your first encounter with the "Caribbean Two Step": two steps forward, one step back. The Caribbean swell is usually from the southeast and 4 to 8 feet high. More like a chop than a swell, you will swear there are 3 swells within the length of your boat! With a clipper bow the "Caribbean Two Step" becomes more like two back and two to the side. So unless you get that rare offshore breeze be prepared to motorsail close inshore with full main and no jib, while tacking.

If you are clever, you will be leaving each little harbor at dawn, or before, and arriving before 9 a.m., that is, before the trades come back. Row ashore to a *café* and have breakfast, reading a daily (English) newspaper. Go back to the boat for a late morning nap. If you decide to carry on, then before retiring in the evening, lay up a thermos of coffee and a pot of hot **burgoo** for breakfast underway just after daybreak.

When coasting Puerto Rico look for an *Eastern Caribbean Forecast* on NMN (see radio list in the appendix) of *east* 15 knots or less. Late summer afternoon storm cells spawned by the **coastal front** may be intimidating and local winds, especially the seabreezes, or beach winds, may be stronger than expected off the sea as a result of circulation around these towering cumulo nimbuses. If you have a good **Offshore Report** don't let these effects inhibit you. They will all dissipate by dusk when the overall flow as reported in the forecast will reassert itself. If you listen to the **NOAA** forecasts over the San Juan VHF weather channels (WX Channels and AM broadcast, so-called "coastal reports: up to 20 miles offshore"), add 5 knots to the report. If you listen to the United States Coast Guard's Channel 22 reports, you may have to subtract a full day from their validity as they often read the wrong report.

CABO ROJO

When hopping from Boquerón to **La Parguera** it is best to shorten the passage into 2 or 3 smaller legs by moving out of Boquerón in the daytime to one of several anchorages along the public beaches off **El Combate** or **Punta Aguila,** or in the snug little mangrove anchorage immediately under **Cabo Rojo Light**. This is a shallow shore area. Pick your way to within a couple of hundred yards of the beach with a high sun, farther out if you draw over 6 feet. Do a bottom scrub in the clear water there.

I prefer the mangrove anchorage under the light. There is room only for a couple of friendly boats, but I find this site ideal for watching the weather. The night wind over the point is the open sea condition you may expect on rounding the cape.

The beaches at El Combate are a state park with many tourists on weekends. After scrubbing the bottom I'll mingle with the crowds, buying beer and *empanadilla* for a late lunch and watching the monkeys which inhabit the place. They're escapees from a research center and are breeding like rabbits. Watch it, they bite!

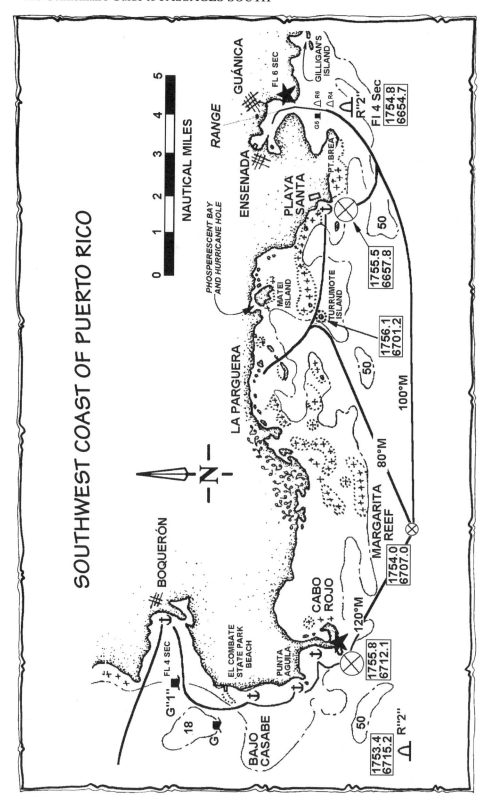

SOUTHWEST COAST OF PUERTO RICO

LA PARGUERA

Jump off from **Cabo Rojo** for La Parguera by daybreak. Never later! Leave your anchorage in the predawn hours by hoisting anchor and drifting back due west, over the same ground you covered on the way in. Skirt **Margarita Reef** in 12 fathoms. Most of the fish traps on the south coast are off there, and most of them lie in 10 fathoms or less.

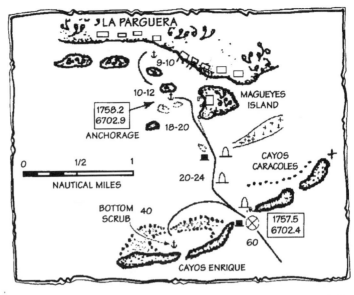

La Parguera [par-GAIR-ah] is inadequately shown on most **charts**. International Sailing Supply's Waterproof Charts and Imray-Iolaire charts are available in **Boquerón** at Schafer and Brown Electronics. They show this section of the coast with great accuracy. Waterproof charts are not only waterproof but printed on both sides. Both are available in Florida as well.

Enter between **Caracoles Cay** and **Enrique Cay** following the buoys. Drafts under 5 feet can anchor in the clear sand lagoon behind Enrique Cay, feeling your way through the reef in good light. There is excellent snorkeling and fishing on the reefs offshore.

To reach the anchorages near town, proceed toward a small boats dock on the southwest corner of **Maygueyes Island** until the larger dock on its northwest corner is visible. This is the main dock of the University of Puerto Rico's oceanographic research station. Continue toward town until abreast of the University's dock, then swing west into the 12-15 foot deep channel south of a row of mangrove keys. Drafts under 6 feet can continue northwest, rounding between the second and third little cay, to arrive in a small anchorage in front of the town. An excellent **Hurricane Hole** is 2 miles to the east, northwest of **Matei Island**. In the right conditions this is also a highly phosphorescent bay.

To leave La Parguera by night, sail that afternoon to **Playa Santa.** Wait there for the nightly lee. Playa Santa is a public beach with condos north of **Punta Jorobado** and 5 and a half miles east of La Parguera. Anchor in 8-10 feet of sand and leave in the dark for **Guánica** or **Ponce** by sailing south midway between Punta Jorobado and the small cay three quarter of a mile to its west.

It may be hard to leave La Parguera. It is known for its freedom loving houseboaters who regularly flout the government, turning its miles of mangrove rivers into a Caribbean Venice. Reef diving, beach excursions, seafood restaurants, *sangria* bars and live *salsa* and *marengue* bands bring many Puerto Ricans here on weekends. A few years ago the town closed its borders to the bottle throwing students and the dykes on bikes crowd. They went to Boquerón, and the adults came back to La Parguera.

GUÁNICA

The anchorage off the town of **Guánica** [GWAH-knee-kah], north of the entrance, is no good. It suffers from heavy afternoon gusts directly through the gap at the entrance to the bay, especially in the summertime. Anytime the wind is south of east, it will combine with the onshore beach wind in the afternoon and roar through the cliffs at the entrance directly onto your anchorage. In addition, this anchorage has a foul bottom with construction material randomly placed, but surely under your tackle. Finally, the old dock there is actually in use occasionally. When it's used, it's used to off-load *fertilizer*, just about the time the wind picks up. Not to worry. There are excellent anchorages off the pleasant little town of **Ensenada**. The anchorage to the southwest can be used much closer to shore than shown in most **charts** and the one to the northwest is an excellent **Hurricane Hole**. *Ensenada* means small bay, or cove, in Spanish. It is an old sugar mill town which became a near ghost town when sugar lost its majesty. It is early 20th century American, even down to oak tree planted swales and slate sidewalks.

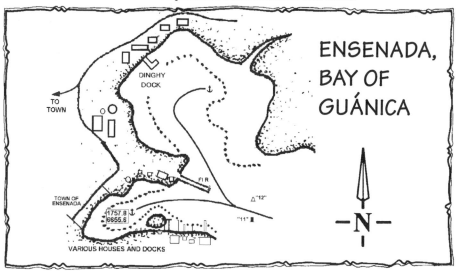

Anchorages at Ensenada in the Bay of Guánica

Exit at night is easy if you looked around on the way in. Leave Guánica at 3 a.m. to arrive in **Ponce** before 8 a.m. Follow the ship channel out. It is light buoyed, wide and deep. Even better, leave in daylight to spend a few days at Gilligan's Island nearby.

GILLIGAN'S ISLAND

Enter from the west by the **Guánica** ship channel. Turn east at the green can marker No.5. Follow the coast 400 yards off, staying in 3-4 fathoms. With a high sun and mild conditions you can enter from the east through the broad channel between the outer reef and the **Caña Gorda** reef, being careful to avoid the shoal inside and west of the channel (see chartlet).

The best anchorage is east against the point where the water is flat and the wind funnels through the last narrow channel, or *caño*, between the mangroves. Anchor out of the ferry wakes on weekends (see chartlet). Moored off the docks of the restaurant San Jacinto and the hotel Copamarina you have access to either *criollo tipico* or fine dining. There may be a slight roll here.

Gilligan's Island is the last in a chain of keys east of **Guánica**. It had been called **Cayo Aurora** after an extraordinary woman who, at the age of 40, escaped misery and mistreatment in the workers barracks of the nearby La Ballena farm, and swam to the island, where she lived off the sea for many years.

Locals who used the island for pig roasts began calling it Gilligan's Island after a 1970's American television show of that name. The island looked like the one on TV, and one of the fishermen looked like the lead actor, Bob Denver. The keys have been appearing recently on charts as the **Cayos Caña Gorda**. Chart makers don't bother to ask locals about the small stuff. By 2050 it shall no doubt have another name, but I prefer Aurora.

Gilligan's Island is now a state park manned by rangers. It's crowded on weekends, but midweek anytime but the summer months you can have its blue lagoons and white sand *caños* all to yourself. Dive Copamarina (809-821-6009) can orient you for snorkeling or wall diving adventures. On weekends you may want to talk to Sr.Fundador Ortiz Matos who sells his stories and local histories outside the San Jacinto restaurant.

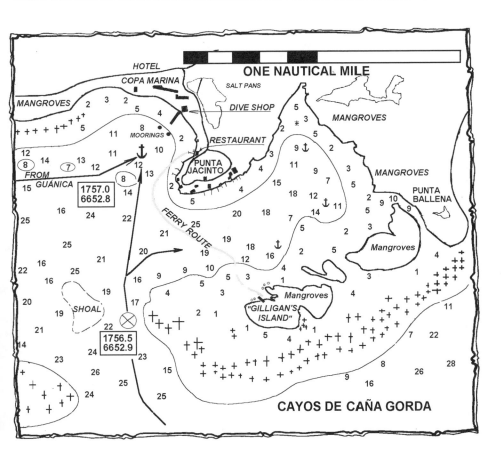

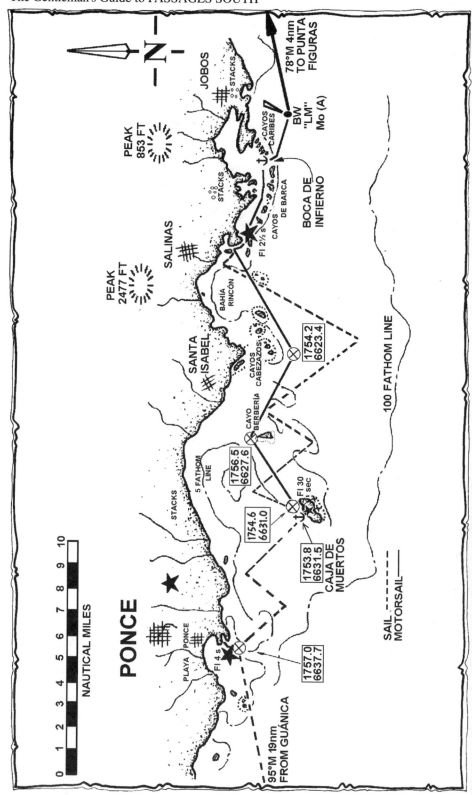

PONCE

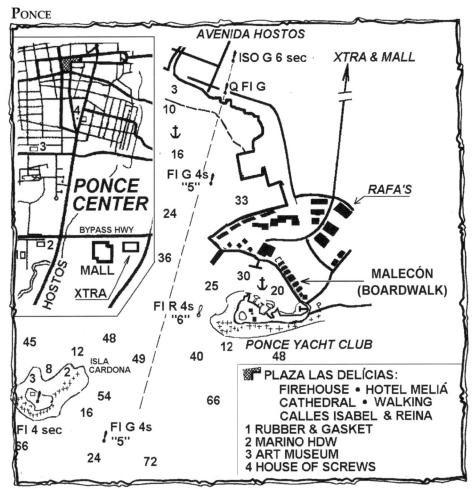

Anchor in the Yacht Club anchorage. The anchorage is deep and relatively small. The Club has a large Travelift and a convenient yard. For a $5 charge per person per day you can enjoy their facilities. The restaurant is open to all. For many years PYC, along with Crown Bay in St. Thomas, has met my fuel and reprovisioning needs. The dock is a single hander's dream in the early morning, and by the time I've put 6 months of caselots aboard from Rafa's, the wind has come up to blow me off it. The fuel, of course, is exemplary.

Ponce [PONE-say], an industrial center with a renovated Caribbean Victorian downtown merits a walking tour. Hypermarket XTRA and the luxurious Plaza del Caribe Mall are on the way to town from the yacht club. A Sam's membership warehouse is west of town on the Ponce Bypass. Ponce is Puerto Rico's second city. It's a working town and you can get just about anything done there. Ponce has an excellent fine arts museum. If you haven't done it, nor toured the town, you haven't been to Ponce. The US Customs house, built in 1842 as Spanish military headquarters, and used from 1898 by the US military, is on the waterfront opposite theold Coast Guard station.

Ferries to **Caja de Muertos** had been cause for loud weekend gatherings in the street and sidewalks across from the Yacht Club. Taxpayers built an old fashioned boardwalk to bring order to the pandemonium, but they succeeded in institutionalizing the party instead. Join the throng and dine from the vendors' *pinchos* [PEEN-chose], Latin *shish-ka-bobs,*

215

fried chicken and *empanadillas*. But unless you're deaf, you won't anchor long here. If you tour the island, do it from **Salinas**. After a tour of the art museum, sail to the island of Caja de Muertos for a Bahamas breather. Missing Muertos means a much rougher trip.

CAJA DE MUERTOS

I always take a morning sail out to **Caja de Muertos,** a state park which has 4 guys in Smoky the Bear hats that live over the beach. The Park Service has installed sand screw moorings, sufficient for most yachts in most weather, to protect the seabed from anchor depredations. The moorings are usually empty on Monday through Thursday except holidays. Puerto Ricans on family outings throng the island on weekends when the ferry is running (it was missing last time they looked for it).

Caja de Muetos, or Coffin Island, looks in the golden light of sundown more like a shrouded and vigiled body than a "corpse's box": toes up, cross-armed chest and backward lain head. The lighthouse was built 20 years prior to the Yankees walking ashore at **Guánica** to take possession of Puerto Rico. It is a perfect example of 19th century Spanish public works architecture.

Paths wind from the anchorages and mooring fields on the west side to the lighthouse on the summit, the snorkeling park on the east coast and the *balneario* (beach and bath houses) near the rangers' complex in the southwest. Hike up to the old light house, visit the Park Rangers for information on the rookery, and visit the snorkeling park.

Stopping at Caja de Muertos is an excellent example of the principle of **staging** (see *Stage Your Departure*). Besides its fine Bahamas-like white sand bottom where you can have a good scrub, the island sits 6 miles offshore, astride the true conditions you will encounter upon leaving. This is one of only 3 spots on the south coast where you have this luxury. Ponce is in a deep bay. If you leave without knowledge of the conditions in the sea outside you may get the collywobbles kicked out of you east of Muertos even though it's blowing less than 20 knots.

Wait for a 3-4 a.m. departure to Salinas. **Salinas** is a motorsail against easterlies. Review *Sailing Directions, South Coast of Puerto Rico* for the conditions in which to leave. The chartlet shows both motoring and sailing routes from Muertos to Salinas. With a fast vessel one could motor direct from Ponce, proceeding east from **Isla de Cardona** light to a point 1 mile north of **Cayo Berberia** and thence 126° True to round the **Cayos Cabezazos** off **Punta Petrona**. I prefer to sail from Muertos by tacking southeast between it and **Berberia** in the light northerly of the predawn hours, then northeast into **Bahía Rincón** in a spectacular sunrise blended with Puerto Rican mountain expresso.

BAHÍA RINCÓN

Coming from **Caja de Muertos**, enter **Bahía de Rincón** on a northeast course which splits the difference between **Cayos Cabezazos** and the **Media Luna** reef 2 miles further east. This will leave **Cayo Alfenique** one mile to port. Proceed east in the sheltered bay, rounding **Cayo Mata** into Salinas harbor.

It's better to commute to the shops and sights at **Ponce** or **San Juan** from safe moorings at **Salinas** [sah-LEE-nahs] than from any other harbor in Puerto Rico. There is a large new *público* terminal in Ponce, two blocks off the main square, from which you can reach any westward destination. The trip to Ponce from Salinas is only one *público* ride. Remember to return from Ponce terminal early enough to catch the last *público*. Find out when that is. It could be as early as 2 p.m. Guayama, to the east, has a público terminal for all destinations north and east.

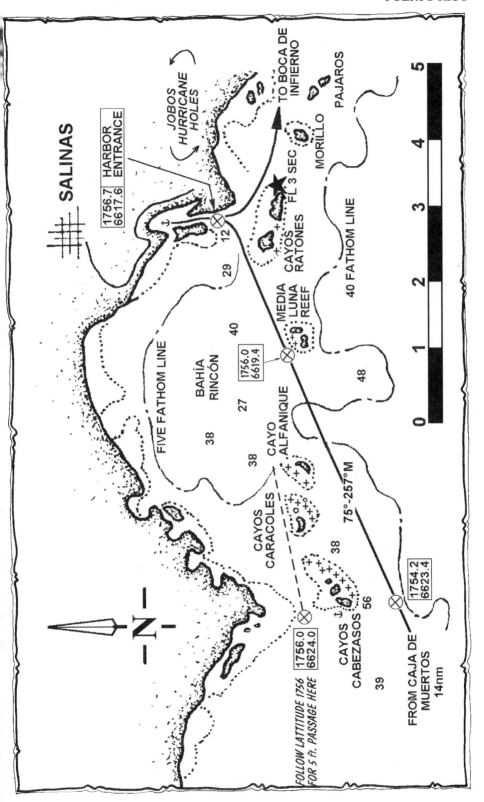

SALINAS

JOBOS HURRICANE HOLES

TO BOCA DE INFIERNO

PAJAROS

MORILLO

1756.7 6617.6 HARBOR ENTRANCE

FL 3 SEC

CAYOS RATONES

29

40 FATHOM LINE

12

40

MEDIA LUNA REEF

FIVE FATHOM LINE

BAHÍA RINCÓN

27

1756.0 6619.4

48

38

CAYO ALFANIQUE

38

75°-257°M

CAYOS CARACOLES

38

1754.2 6623.4

N

56

1756.0 6624.0

CAYOS CABEZASOS

FROM CAJA DE MUERTOS 14nm

39

FOLLOW LATITUDE 1756 FOR 5 ft. PASSAGE HERE

0   1   2   3   4   5

217

SALINAS

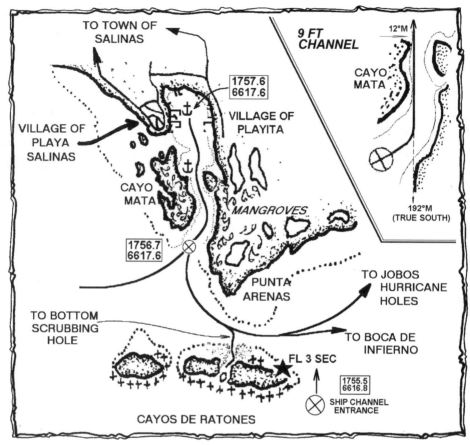

Salinas — stay for the summer.

For drafts over 6 feet favor the channel behind **Cayo Mata** slightly left of center until midway down the island, then favor the channel slightly right of center (midpoint of perpendicular from the shores). Anchor in 10 feet of mud and sand (mostly sand) near the Marina de Salinas. The water is typically mangrove murky. **Salinas** is the best spot to leave the boat while touring. It's a well protected hurricane hole, has a convenient marina, post office, sail loft, and marine store. There's a good bottom cleaning anchorage between the two **Cayo Ratones**. The reefs and keys 5 miles east or west of Salinas provide good diving. See *Hurricane Holes* for details of the mangrove holes at Jobos nearby.

Salinas is a great place for refit. Restaurants abound here both around the harbor and on the bay shore. The town of Salinas is a short, cheap, *público* ride away. In the village of **Playa Salinas** outside the gates of the marina there are no less than 3 hardware stores. The local *colmado*, Rodriguez, is really a marine store. It carries a wide variety of neat marine stuff — even stainless fasteners, fiberglass, polyester resin and 5200, but you have to look for it. For metal repair and fabrication, call H.R. Machine Shop at 824-1098. There are two alternator shops. Refer to the chapter on **Ponce** for other refit tips.

Salinas, my favorite port in the Caribbean, and **Jobos**, next door, are both excellent **Hurricane Holes**. See the chart for these holes in the chapter *Weather Threats*. For that reason alone it is becoming a summer yachting capital.

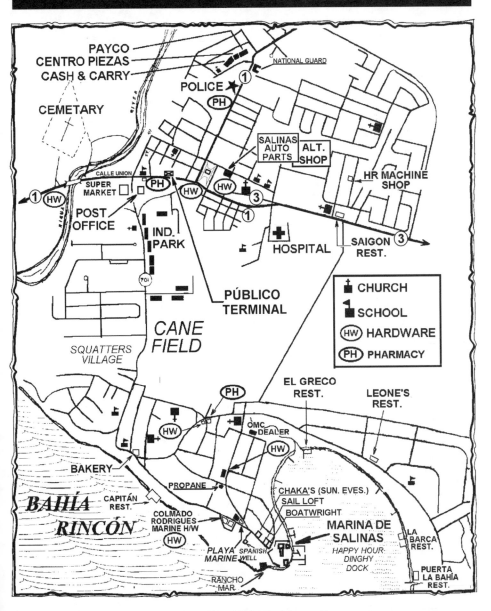

219

From Salinas you can finally get English weather reports on standard AM broadcast from **VI Radio**'s Sailor's Report at 0630 and 0706. See *Radio Times and Frequencies* for other times and stations. Set your wake up radio alarm and forget twiddling the SSB knobs. Listen, of course, for the *Eastern Caribbean Forecast* in the **Offshore Forecast** from the **NWS**. San Juan's English station, WOSO, or "El Oso" [the bear] has reports at 10 after the hour. *Add 5 knots of wind to all coastal reports.*

While in Salinas visit **Caño Matías** [CAHN-yo ma-TEE-us] with your dinghy. This is a pleasant bathing area behind the reef and between the **Cayos Ratones**. There is a small island between the two cayos with a hole on either side of it. The deeper water is on the western shore of either hole. Having gone in once by dinghy you may also bring in the bigger boat. *Jalan Jalan* gets in at 6 and one half feet. Go in at near high water and take the western fork.

If there are northerlies and you sail nonstop for the east coast, leave **Salinas** at dusk to arrive in **Palmas del Mar** the next morning, being careful to not wander too far offshore as the current and confused swells will make your northeast tack across **Point Tuna** difficult. Stay a good mile or more off Point Tuna to avoid the confused seas there as well.

However, the advice of this guide is to continue this coast thornlessly. To do that you have at least two more stops before Palmas del Mar: **Jobos,** where you **stage** and watch the actual outside conditions from a snug mangrove anchorage, and **Puerto Patillas.** If conditions are settled and the wind from east or north of east is 15 knots or less, you can also stop over at the little fishing port of **Arroyo..**

BOCA DE INFIERNO

The long leg to the east coast can be a bear. For shorter, easier legs, position yourself at **Boca de Infierno** [BOH-kah day een-fee-AIR-noh]. When approaching the anchorage take bearings in good light of the Central Aguirre pier which is distinguished by two old fashioned brick chimneys almost in line. Note also the breaking of the reef and the sea conditions outside. You should motor through this pass in *early morning* light conditions; ground swells on either side can be heavy in daytime conditions. As with the anchorage at **Caja de Muertos**, the benefit of waiting at Boca de Infierno is that you can see for yourself what the sea conditions are the morning of your departure. Depart through Boca de Infierno at first light, keeping the *Central Aguirre* pier at a 10° Magnetic bearing. When a half mile clear of the pass, head for the 'Lima Mike' sea buoy 2 miles east southeast before taking up your course for **Punta Figuras** and enter **Puerto Patillas**. I feel one *must* stop at Patillas, but if you don't, keep **Guayama Reef,** off Punta Figuras well to port. The sea buoy (FL R "2" on some charts) off Punta Figuras has been missing for years.

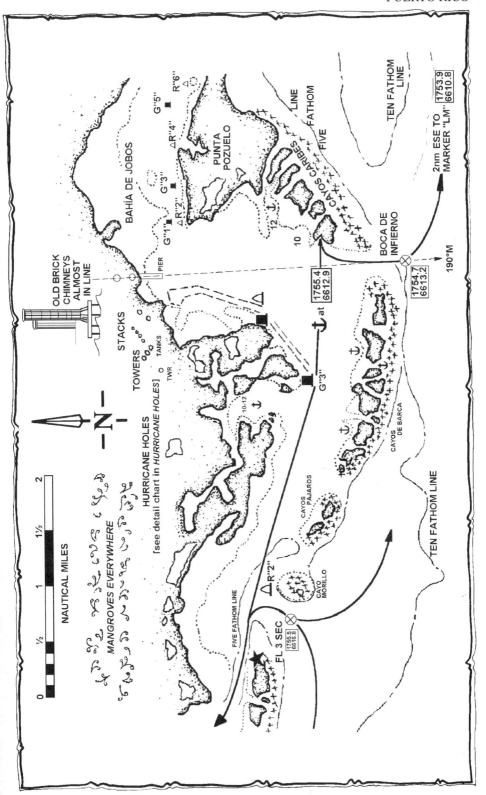

PUERTO PATILLAS

Puerto Patillas [PWAIR-toh pah-TEE-yahs] is a small town, once a small boat fishing village supported by the reef 2 miles offshore. It lies northwest of **Punta Viento**, a low-lying treed point 3 miles east of the **Punta Figuras** light (FL 6 seconds).

Other sources notwithstanding this is a well protected anchorage in prevailing conditions as long as you snug up to windward, which the modern sailboat with auxiliary is capable of doing. Extending southward from the town one mile, to just beyond the point, there are rocky shoals. These shoals extend one mile west of the beach giving good protection to the anchorage in anything but south to west. Approach for 11 miles on a heading of 80°M from the sea buoy [Mo(A) BW "LM"] off **Boca de Infierno**, leaving Punta Figuras one half mile to port. Continue until high cliffs backed by hills are on the north and an A-frame house, just south of a power boat dock, is to the east. You will be in 12 feet of water. Head east to the A-frame house and anchor in 7-8 feet of sand and mud bottom, 250 yards offshore and between the A-frame and a private boat ramp to the north of it. Go slow because of fish traps and old moorings in the area. Dinghy in to enjoy the park beaches along the point and the restaurants on the harbor.

Leave **Puerto Patillas** before daylight to take advantage of the night lee. Be sure to stay south of the shoals by heading due west for 3 quarters of a mile before turning south. Turn east in 10 fathoms for either **Punta de Arenas**, **Vieques**, or **Palmas del Mar**. Stay in the 12-15 fathom, 6 miles long, one half mile wide, trench between Puerto Patillas and **Point Tuna.** The 7 fathom ridge to seaward trips the seas, and the shoaling shore to landward makes up groundswells. The trench, like deep waters in a brook, runs still. You not only shall make better time, but this way you shall avoid fish traps.

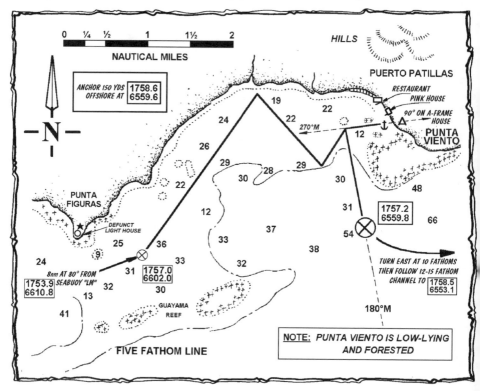

SAILING DIRECTIONS, EAST COAST

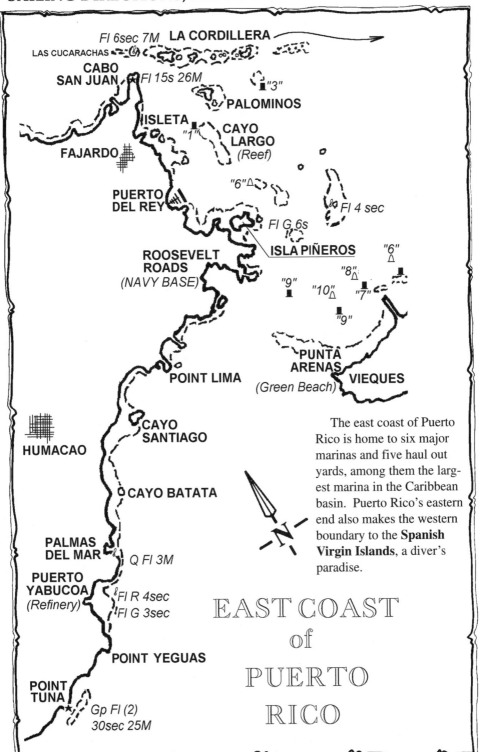

Fl 6sec 7M **LA CORDILLERA**

LAS CUCARACHAS

**CABO
SAN JUAN** Fl 15s 26M

"3"

PALOMINOS

ISLETA "1" **CAYO
LARGO**
(Reef)

FAJARDO

"6"

**PUERTO
DEL REY**

Fl 4 sec

Fl G 6s

ISLA PIÑEROS "6"

**ROOSEVELT
ROADS**
(NAVY BASE) "8"

"9" "10" "7"

"9"

**PUNTA
ARENAS**

POINT LIMA *(Green Beach)* **VIEQUES**

**CAYO
SANTIAGO**

HUMACAO

CAYO BATATA

**PALMAS
DEL MAR** Q Fl 3M

**PUERTO
YABUCOA**
(Refinery) Fl R 4sec
Fl G 3sec

POINT YEGUAS

**POINT
TUNA** Gp Fl (2)
30sec 25M

N

The east coast of Puerto
Rico is home to six major
marinas and five haul out
yards, among them the largest marina in the Caribbean
basin. Puerto Rico's eastern
end also makes the western
boundary to the **Spanish
Virgin Islands**, a diver's
paradise.

EAST COAST
of
PUERTO
RICO

PALMAS DEL MAR

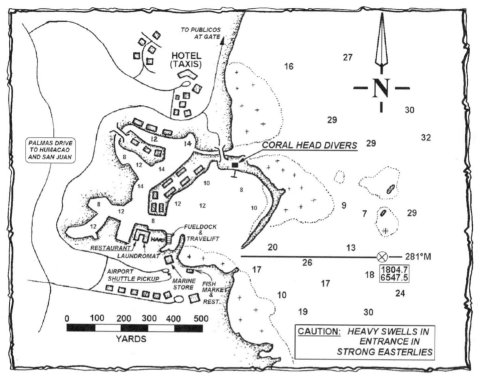

Enter in good water directly from the east. The anchorage may be temporarily used, some guides notwithstanding. There is good holding in 10-12 feet everywhere except the northeast corner which has silted to a depth of 5-6 feet near the seawall, but that's where you want to be to avoid rolling in swell which can sometimes penetrate the harbor.

Palmas is a resort and condominium project along the lines of Puerto Cervo in Sardinia and José Banús in Spain. Golf, tennis, scuba, sport fishing and sail charters are available to owners or guests of the hotel, marina or shipyard. At a condo slip, in the marina, or laid up ashore at the yard, this harbor affords reasonable **hurricane** protection. Boats

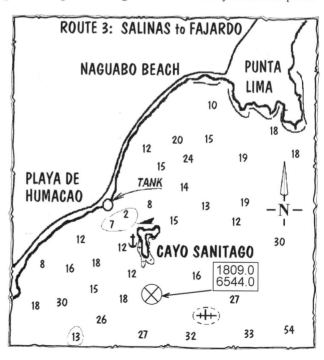

fared well here as hurricane Hugo passed by. If you lay up ashore, ensure for yourself that the jackstands are lashed securely together with nylon warp, and using Spanish wind-lasses to maintain tension. During Hugo, boats on the hard blew over due to inadequate lashings.

Chez Daniel is an excellent authentic French restaurant. A fisherman's restaurant and seafood store is in the southeast corner of the anchoring basin.

CAYO SANTIAGO

Also called "Monkey Island", **Cayo Santiago** is a free range for the Caribbean Primate Research Center. It is inhabited by well over 1000 monkeys, whose crazy antics include biting persistent tourists. Best to stay on the sand beach and enjoy the cerulean water and the abundant snorkeling behind the island. It is not permitted to go ashore other than on the beach. Do not molest nor feed the monkeys. Enter from the south and east.

Day charterers and snorkelers from Palmas del Mar may join you, but this anchorage is normally deserted late afternoons and nights.

Rumors are that a resort marina is planned for **Punta Lima** to the north to compete with Puerto del Rey and Palmas del Mar.

ROOSEVELT ROADS NAVAL STATION

An emergency refuge for all but retired career military and their guests, Roosevelt Roads has a small marina with marine store, limited dockage, med-moorings at the seawall and some moorings. The marina stands by on VHF Ch.16. Telephone (809) 865-3297. Not a safe place to leave the boat in hurricane season.

Turn to the chapter about **Navy Range Vieques** for more on the mission of Roosevelt Roads and how it affects, and helps, the cruising community.

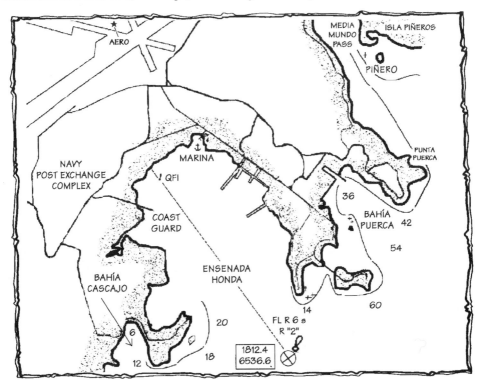

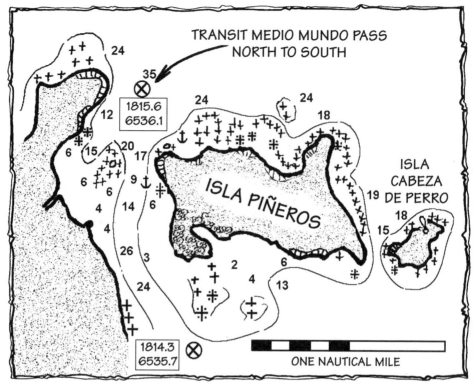

ISLA PIÑEROS

A well protected anchorage which is quite secluded during the week, yet it is only 3 miles south of the largest marina in the Caribbean. This island is part of the Roosevelt Roads Navy Base and the Navy does not allow going ashore. Nonetheless one can anchor overnight for excellent swimming and snorkeling. The cove in the northern reef is a nice lunch anchorage in summer months when the wind is south of east. Enter **Pasaje Medio Mundo** from the north where the rocks west of the pass are clearly visible. The shoal on the island's southwest corner extends quite far and is less visible. It is not recommended to pass between **Isla Piñeros** and **Cabeza de Perro**. Call Puerto del Rey's harbormaster at 860-1000 or VHF channel 71 for information regarding Navy maneuvers.

The Marina de Salinas

226

PUERTO DEL REY

If visiting San Juan or picking up crew, **Puerto del Rey** is the port of convenience. With 750 slips and long term land storage it is the largest and most modern marina in the Caribbean. Atlantic Canvas and Sails is here as well as any yacht service desired. Puerto del Rey's 80 ton Travelift is available for emergencies 7 days a week, 24 hours a day. Call the harbormaster on VHF channel 71 or 16 for a slip or a transient dock, or anchor temporarily in the turning basin inside the breakwater north of the docks. A rental car agency is on site.

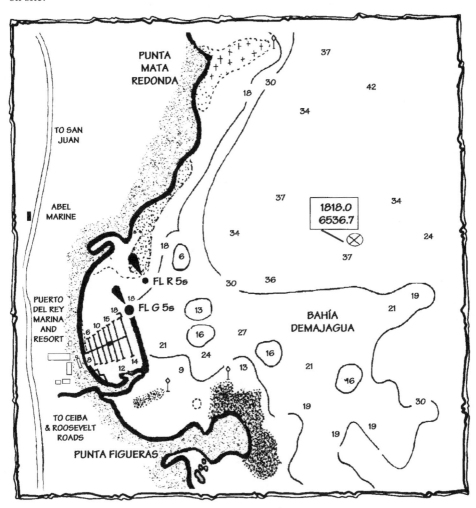

Puerto del Rey Marina and Resort

A yacht will get reasonable hurricane protection here if laid up ashore in the yard. As with any yard, ensure the jackstands get securely tensioned to the boat with Spanish windlasses of stout nylon 3-strand line. Also see the yacht gets laid up in a spot unlikely to require moving around in your absence, thus canceling your good work on the jackstands.

While on the east coast, Puerto del Rey makes a sensible base in which to leave the boat, rent a car and tour the country.

FAJARDO

The district of **Fajardo** caters to yachting enthusiasts from around the world. Major sailing events such as the Heineken International Cup and CORT regattas, as well as the Club Nautico de Puerto Rico's Round Puerto Rico Race are hosted from Fajardo.

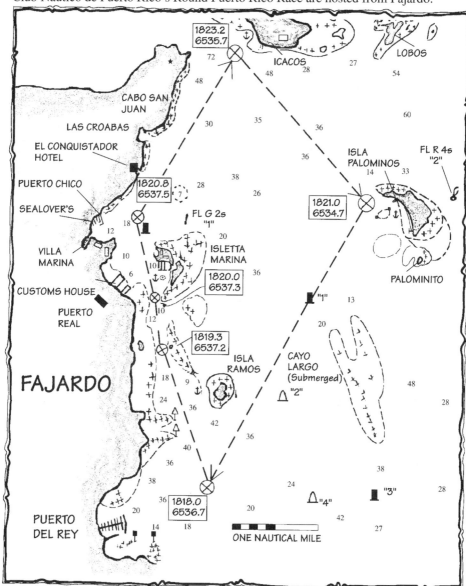

Fajardo lies at the foot of the only tropical rain forest in US jurisdiction, the 28,000 acre El Yunque national forest, where annually 100 billion gallons of rain nurture 240 species of trees. The forest's 3,532 foot peak, El Toro, is visible throughout the Spanish Virgins. Excepting Chez Daniel in Palmas del Mar, Restaurant du Port at **Puerto del Rey** and Rosas seafood restaurant in **Puerto Real**, sailors ashore seeking fine dining need a car. Then it's the family run Mexican restaurant, Lolitas's, on Route 3 north of town. Across the street is a paint store that has the best **IMRON** prices north of Venezuela.

Ports on the mainland can be approached via the ship channel or via the "inside route", behind the keys and the reefs using a careful eyeball method. If taking the inside route, watch for a cross set at the GPS waypoint shown on the chartlet just south of Isleta.

When approaching downwind from the east, be careful to avoid **Cayo Largo.** The ground swells to windward of this dangerous reef are not always visible from their backs.

RAMOS

Ramos is a private island. You may anchor outside the string of floats off the beach with which the owner has marked his territory, but you may not go ashore.

ISLETA

Anchor at **Isleta** west of the marked shoal in the bight of the two islands; close to the marina you will suffer from the ferry wakes. There are two ferry services to **Puerto Real**, one for residents of the condominiums and marina, the other for visitors at a cost. The ferries run from 6:30 to 21:30, quarter after and quarter of the hour.

PUERTO REAL

Except for dredged ferry channels, **Puerto Real** is shoal and windward. It is best approached by dinghy or by the ferries from **Isleta Marina**. Ferries to and from **Culebra** and **Vieques** can be had here. Some provisions are at Big Johns across from the Isleta ferry dock. Dine at Rosas Seafood, a short walk inland from there.

VILLA MARINA

Villa Marina, with 250 slips and a 60 ton Travelift, caters mostly to power craft. Marine stores Skipper Shop and El Pescador behind Villa Marina are the most extensively stocked in the area. On the same street are Fajardo Canvas and Sails, and Re-Power Marine Services for engine, prop and machine shop needs.

PUERTO CHICO / SEA LOVERS

Immediately northeast of Villa Marina are the marinas of **Sea Lovers**, near the beach, and **Puerto Chico**, larger and to the east behind the seawall. Puerto Chico has a fuel dock and handles drafts to 7 feet. Sea Lovers is for smaller craft.

LAS CROABAS

Las Croabas is a government run haulout facility next to a fisherman's cooperative. The reef entrance is well marked and handles 6 and one half feet at midtide rising. This is a cheap and fun place to haul with lots of nearby *tipico* restaurants and bars. Take all you need with you, however. There are no hardware stores nearby.

Touring Note:
A personal tip to cruisers thinking of renting a car and touring the country. unless you stay in the Fajardo area to live and work, as I have, it does not make a good base for the cruiser/tourist (excepting if you leave the boat berthed at **Puerto del Rey** and have a car). **Isleta**, with its ferries and curfews, or **Roosevelt Roads**, with its remoteness, might make good xenophobe hangouts, but they create major inconveniences for the tourist. Cruiser friendly **Salinas**, central to the island's only superhighway, and close to Ponce or Guayama malls and discount centers, makes the most sense.

SAILING DIRECTIONS, VIEQUES SOUND

From Vieques Sound (pronounced vee-AYE-case) until the end of the **British Virgins,** the islands are within sight of each other. **Vieques Sound** is a duck pond compared to the south coast of Puerto Rico. That is, unless you try to cross it in one bound.

For many years I have experimented with *sailing* to windward across **Vieques Sound.** I find that I save a couple of hours by tacking in the area south of the **Cordillera,** where the current and chop is less adverse, into the lee of **Culebra.** However, a strong motor-sailor can barrel down the middle in heavy chop and contrary current with more stress in less time. The south coast of **Vieques** can be tough going to windward in onshore easterlies against the equatorial current. It's best to sail the south coast of Vieques *downwind* and with several stops at its beautiful beaches and anchorages. In short, if you circumnavigate the **Spanish Virgins**, do so *clockwise.*

Cross the shoaly Sound with pleasantly short and easy trips. See the chartlet of Vieques Sound for an indication of the shoals to avoid. Notice that to avoid a visit to **Isla Palominos**, one would have to go out of one's way and bash 9 to 12 hours to windward across Vieques Sound. From Palominos one can use the lee of Culebra and the keys west of it to pleasantly sneak-tack one's way to **Dewey** in only 6 to 8 hours.

CURRENTS AND TIDES

Cruisers in the Spanish Virgins should take special note of set in **Vieques Sound**. Yachties from the Virgins on their first trek to Puerto Rico and back are surprised to find it sometimes takes twice the time to sail east as it took to sail west, something to bear in mind when setting out late in the day from **Fajardo.** You don't want to be caught out among the reefs in bad light! The **Equatorial Current** flows west northwest in this area at a clip of 0.4 to 0.7 knots. When it mounts the shallow plateau of the Sound, sheering forces increase its velocity in chaotic ways. The tide floods west and ebbs east, but on the Sound's north and south borders tidal flow is more north-south as it pours onto or spills off the Sound's shallow plateau. These currents approach 1 knot on flood, a half-knot on ebb. While these effects are not extreme, when taken together, they can lead to unpredictable landfalls and arrival times. Since you want to arrive at reef entrances in favorable light, conservative course planning is essential.

The shallow Sound can whip up a vicious chop in wind above 15 knots which impedes windward progress. If motorsailing, sheet in hard and tack the chop in comfort. With sail up, you'll make better time over ground as well.

STAGING

Start at **Punta Arenas** and take whatever route you wish to get to **Culebra,** just *not direct.* Stop first at **Roosevelt Roads** for retired militaries, the **Fajardo** boat yards for those not hauling in **Palmas del Mar,** or **Isla Palominos** for those wanting to scrub their bottoms and enjoy a Bahamas-like respite before going eastward over the Sound.

A stop at **Culebra,** is required before pressing on to the hurly burly of the commercial US Virgins. Anchor at the little beach behind **Luis Peña.** Carry on to **Dewey** or **Ensenada Honda** next day. Culebra is also a place to wait out summer storms. Some cruisers make a pattern of summer in Culebra, winter in the Virgins, never moving their yachts more than a few miles in an east or west direction all year.

Wait for favorable conditions in the comfortable reef anchorages of **Dakity Harbor** or **Bahía Almodóvar** before moving on to St.Thomas or Puerto Rico. If bound for a circumnavigation of **Vieques,** set sail for **Bahía del Sur** after ensuring a cold Navy test range.

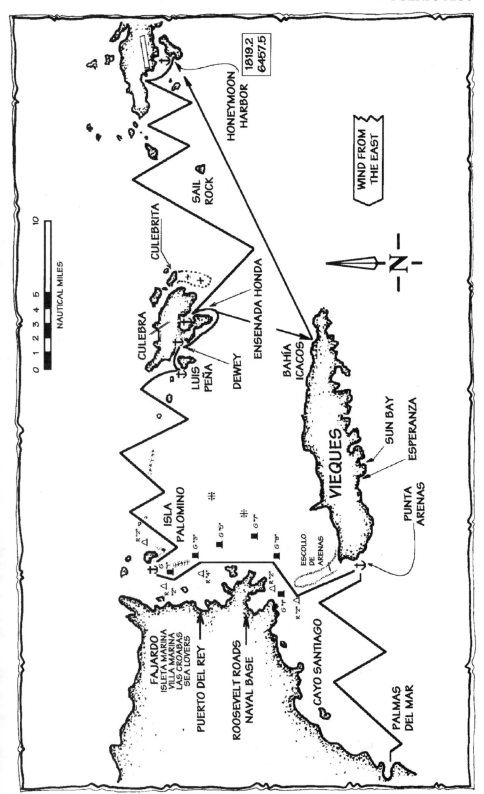

THE SPANISH VIRGIN ISLANDS

The **Spanish Virgin Islands** embrace 400 square miles to the west of the US Virgin Islands. Unlike the USVIs, Puerto Rico has an extensively developed industrial and agricultural infrastructure. But like the USVI, the Spanish Virgins are entirely dependent on tourism, yet they are many years behind in the development of tourism infrastructure. Bad for the typical resort tourist, good for the cruiser. It means unaffected townspeople, undisturbed anchorages, pristine beaches and productive fishing (with a year-round lobster season). Ashore, the Spanish Virgins offer immersion in the Spanish Caribbean with the escape clause of bilingualism and the convenience of US institutions. There are three cruising areas in the Spanish Virgins: **La Cordillera, Culebra** and **Vieques.** Be sure to schedule ample time to enjoy each. Review *Sailing Directions for Vieques Sound.*

NOTE: *Navigating these reefed islands at night is inadvisable.*

December through March, distant northern gales often create swell in exposed northern anchorages, and some day anchorages might be untenable. Fortunately, the lovely harbors of the south coast of **Vieques** and the reef anchorages of **Culebra, Icacos** and **Palominos** are unaffected. Cold fronts that make it this far south are often stalled or have dissipated into troughs which persist for several days. While not good for the avid sailor, these conditions make for fluky winds which in turn create diving and snorkeling opportunities across **La Cordillera,** in Culebra's outlying keys, and on **Vieques'** north coast.

From late July to early September there may be some "bloom" in the water which can restrict visibility for divers. Sailing is great in the cooling summer trades which make these islands cooler and less humid than most of North America at this time of the year. Long hauls to windward are pleasurable, and anchorages are often empty. Like **front**s in the winter, summer **tropical waves** create breaks in the tradewinds, and otherwise exposed diving sites become open to exploration.

April to June is usually too late for strong fronts and too early for organized tropical waves. October and November are, conversely, too early and too late; trade winds moderate and days are clear and sunny. Northerly swells are infrequent and there is minimum chop on **Vieques Sound.** Diving sites and day anchorages have their highest availability during these months.

AM/VHF RADIO WEATHER FORECASTS

Local meteorological and marine reports are given hourly after the news on WOSO San Juan, 1030 KHz AM standard broadcast band. WVWI broadcasts a brief "Sailor's Report" on 1000 KHz AM, at 6:30 a.m. Monday through Friday. This includes the short range NOAA coastal report and the next 12 hours of the National Weather Service's **Offshore Report. NOAA** broadcasts a Coastal Report on a continuous **Coastal Report** on VHF from San Juan, but it is of limited use to the cruiser more than 3 miles east of the Puerto Rico mainland. **VI Radio,** however, broadcasts a complete summary of the meteorological, coastal and offshore reports, as well as the **Tropical Weather Outlook** and **Tropical Weather Discussion** during hurricane season. This is also continuous and on a VHF Weather Channel which is received in eastern Puerto Rico.

While the coastal reports are fine for most islands and anchorages, if you are out on the open Sound in the daytime, or anywhere east or south of **Vieques,** you must listen to the **Offshore Forecast** for the **Eastern Caribbean** on WVWI's Sailor's Report or on VI Radio's VHF Weather Channel; no other report will do.

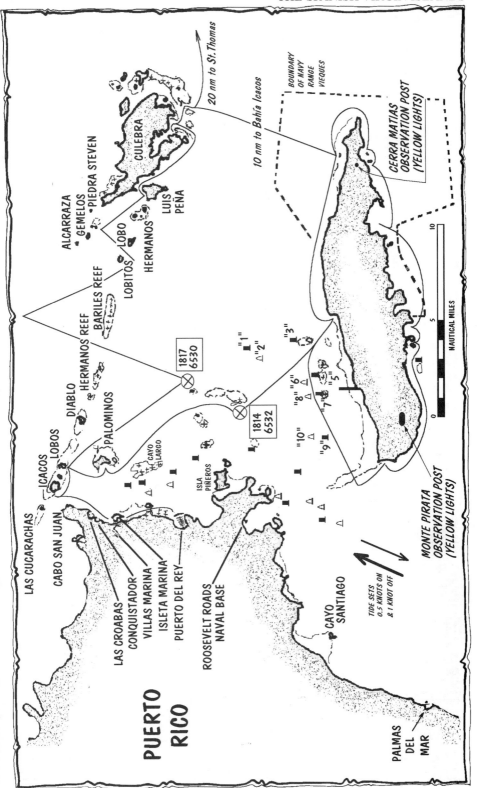

ISLA PALOMINOS

A jewel of a tropical island from which to watch the sun set over **El Yunque** on a last night's return to **Fajardo**. If headed east, **Palominos** is a must to break up what can be a bear of a windward close-hauled leg.

Facilities ashore are leased by El Conquistador resort on the mainland. Anchor between the harbor's central shoal and the island, or close to **Palominitos**, to avoid the wash of the hotel ferries.

Whether running west from the USVIs, or beating eastward on the start of a cruise, **Palominos** is a fine farewell or introduction to the **Spanish Virgins**.

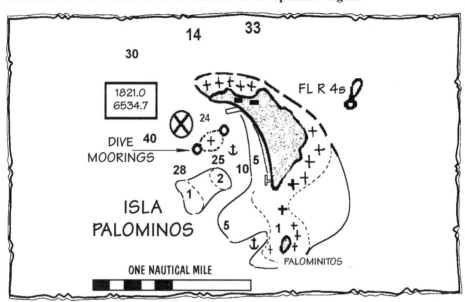

Having overnighted in Palominos, take a morning sail down to **Isabel Segunda** for lunch and a look at the fort. To continue on to **Culebra**, tack up to **Diablo** from behind **Palominos,** continue tacking east along the **Cordillera,** making successively shorter tacks as you gain lee from **Culebra**. Let anchors-down at **Luis Peña**.

See the sketch of **Vieques Sound**.

DIVE OPERATORS IN PUERTO RICO		
OPERATOR	LOCATION	TELEPHONE
Puerto Rico Diver Supply	Fajardo, Villa Marina	863-4300
Coral Reef Divers	Villa Marina Center	860-REEF
Sea Ventures	Puerto del Rey Marina	863-DIVE
Coral Head Divers	Palmas del Mar	850-7208
Culebra Marine Center	Dewey, canal southside	742-3371
Dive Isla de Culebra	Gene Thomas, Dewey	742-3555
Blue Caribe Dive Center	Esperanza	741-2522
Solimar (tank service)	Esperanza	741-8600

DIVING IN THE SPANISH VIRGINS

These lovely keys and islands provide cruising and diving opportunities as good as Anglophone cousins to the east, but they have the added spice of "going foreign".

As a diving destination Puerto Rico is still virgin territory. The Puerto Rico Tourism Company estimates that less than 20% of the snorkeling and scuba opportunities in these islands have been exploited to date. For decades Puerto Rico has been a Mecca for sports fishing enthusiasts. Tourist dive boat operations are a relatively recent development, and charter sail operations have only begun.

The islands are edged with narrow shelves of white sand beaches by rocky cliffs over coral outcroppings, where snorkelers wander and wonder. For the scuba divers, most keys and islands are surrounded by precipitous drop-offs of 12 to 14 fathoms, where the windward walls are brilliantly illuminated in the morning, and those off the leeward anchorages are displayed by the afternoon sun.

One doesn't have to go to the South Pacific to explore extensive coral reefs such as the mile long formations southeast of **Culebrita**. The Spanish Virgins are a submarine photographer's dream.

Lobster season in Puerto Rico, thanks to the animal's continuous mating season, is year round. Catches are restricted to male adults, or females without eggs, having a carapace (antennae base to beginning of tail) of 3.5 inches or more.

For the more adventurous, there is **La Cordillera**, the twelve mile long string of islets, keys, reefs and sea mounts which stretch from **Cayo Icacos**, near **Cabo San Juan** on the mainland, to **Arecife Barriles** west of **Culebra**. Many spectacular snorkeling and diving sites here, and elsewhere in the Spanish Virgins, are available from day anchorages only. When planning each day's activity, you should cast a cautious eye at the strengths and directions of wind, wave and swell. At many of the recommended day anchorages, and depending on conditions, you should keep an anchor watch aboard while the diving party is out. It is of course always best to snorkel or dive upwind and upcurrent of the boat in exposed areas.

Wind strength and direction, and possible swell, are factors to consider in setting a ports and diving itinerary, especially when choosing day anchorages.

VIEQUES

Vieques was a redoubt of **Taino** and **Caribe** indians from which they could maraud the Spaniards, **Vieques** became a refuge for all stripes, from army deserters and runaway slaves to the renegade "portugee", as were called the whites of any extraction who were on their own in the Caribbean. Today the island hosts a fiercely independent and proud population dotted by (sometimes dotty) expatriates.

Circumnavigate Vieques clockwise (see *Sailing Directions, Vieques Sound*).

Punta Arenas

Punta Arenas, on the northern end of the western shore of **Vieques**, is a good stopover either entering or leaving **Vieques Sound**. Depending on conditions and wind direction on leaving **Palmas del Mar**, **Punta Arenas** may be a better first tack than **Isla Palominos**. A good anchorage is 40 yards off a flat crescent beach, which the Navy calls Green Beach, and which is one half mile south of Punta Arenas. Another is just south of a ruined dock backed by a couple of large rusty tanks.

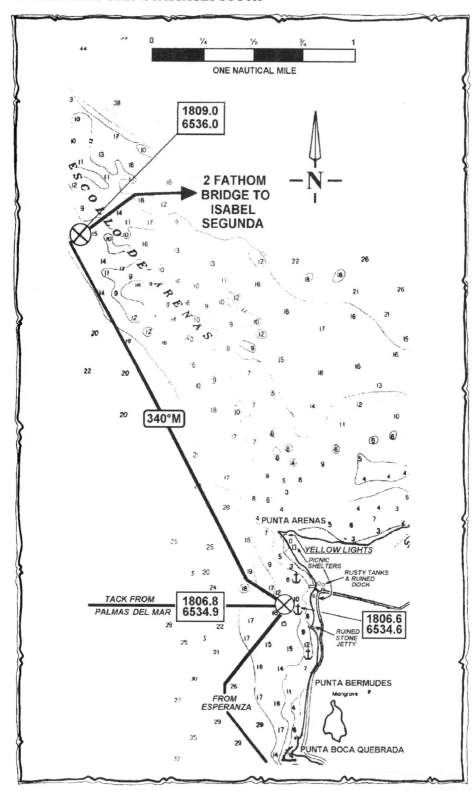

Head east to the point and turn to the anchorage when in 30 feet of water. Pick a grassy sand spot to avoid the patches of sand colored coral ledges here. The anchorage is isolated on weekdays and the water is clear. Great for bottom scrubbing and skinny dipping. Conch and an occasional lobster are available on the rocky shores to the south.

The **Escollo de Arenas** is the name of extensive sandbores with rock stretching north northwest from the northwest tip of Vieques with only 8-10 feet covering them. Be warned: escollo means trouble. This permanent rocky ridge collects storm detritus for the entire Sound. Though it can be crossed without incident, each season some foolish yachtie brags to me that he's gone across the Escollo in a high chop and never saw less than 10 feet. Let him try it ten times in a row! Don't be fooled by these one time experts. Play it safe. Debris on the bottom can combine with 3 foot troughs to give you a nasty bump on some old wreck or steel tank. I usually go around the Escollo except in a calm. It is a pleasant, reaching sail compared to motoring across it.

SUN BAY

This southern anchorage is outside the Navy zone and next to the fishing village of **Esperanza**. Enter the middle of the bay headed north, steering clear of the shoal off its southeast arm. Anchor in grassy sand tight against the east southeast shore to avoid roll in strong wind east or south of east. This is a public beach more than a mile in length. A bath house is in the northwest corner of the bay.

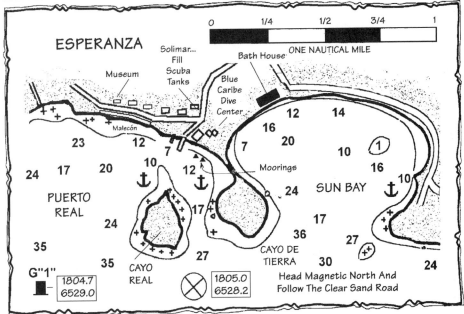

ESPERANZA, PUERTO REAL

Blue Caribe Dive Center maintains moorings at the north end of the anchorage. You may want to pay their fee to use them, since it may be difficult to get a good hold in the fluffy sand and grass bottom in this anchorge. Be sure to check the state of the mooring first, however. **Puerto Real**, the anchorage northwest of **Cayo Real**, can be rolly, but once dug in, the holding is fair in sand and coral. Lunch ashore after a pleasant stroll on the balustraded *malecón* and a visit to the small archeological museum. For fresh seafood, see the fishermen when they bring in their catches in the morning, or when they gather at the town pier to pack them off on the ferries later on. West of **Esperanza**, there is a 2 fathom shoal where seas can build up in strong easterlies or southeasterlies. Official charts notwithstanding, it is marked only by a green can, No. 1, on its eastern edge.

Isabel Segunda

Arrive at **Isabel Segunda** in midmorning in time for a walk up the hill and a visit to the museum and gallery in **El Fortín**, the **Conde de Mirasol** fort protecting the harbor. This was the last fort constructed by Spain in the new world. Have lunch overlooking the harbor on the way down from the fort. A $20 million resort is in the works on the beach west of here. Visit Isabel Segunda now before the tourist boom.

This anchorage can roll viciously. Up anchor in the early afternoon in time to make **Punta Arenas** or **Fajardo** to the west, or **Bahía Icacos** to the east, all with calm anchorages in prevailing winds which are easy to make while the light is still high and westing.

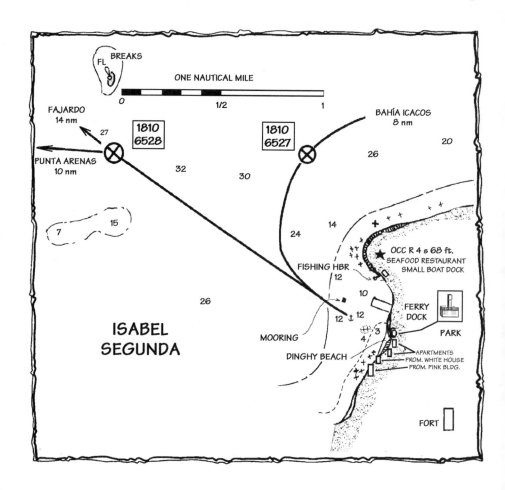

NAVY RANGE, VIEQUES

Many consider these anchorages and beaches the best of all Virgin Island anchorages. They have been left untouched by developers. They have been off limits most of this century, and they have been little used as anchorages since they were formed.

For most of the 20th century the US Navy has used much of **Culebra** and **Vieques** for weapons training. Roosevelt Roads hosts the Navy's Atlantic Fleet Weapons Testing Facility (AFWTF) which controls more than 100,000 square miles of ocean test range, where US and NATO navies use the east end of Vieques for land, air and sea based war games. Nonetheless, the anchorages and beaches are available for use by yachts when the test range is not *hot*, as they say.

Weekends are normally available, but these anchorages may be visited at any time with Navy permission, which is easy to get. The Navy has an advisory service on VHF channel 16, on 3130 Khz. and on telephone 865-5240. Call **RANGE CONTROL** to inquire if the range is *hot*. If, after diligent but fruitless attempts to contact the Navy, consider the range available for your use. If you wander into a closed zone, not to worry, the Navy will graciously let you know in good time. Keep VHF channel 16 on. Observation posts are on **Cerro Matías** (see chartlet for **Salinas de Sur**) or **Monte Pirata** on the island's west end. As a service to the yachting community, **Puerto del Rey Marina** in Fajardo will provide the Navy's weekly Vieques hot exercise schedule. Call Puerto del Rey HARBORMASTER on VHF 16 or 71, or dial 860-1000 by land line.

It is unrealistic to depend on constant harmony between the Navy's use of its test range, your cruising schedule and the weather. A good plan is to launch a cruise of Vieques from **Culebra**. While enjoying superb *culebrense* cruising, watch for a window of favorable weather and no operations in the Vieques Navy ranges. When that happens, which it shall, you'll be off for a memorable cruise. When visiting the beaches, do not go inshore. Do not molest any devices found on the beach — certainly not shells made by man!

Bahía Icacos

Bahía Icacos is a beautifully protected azure bay surrounded by ranks of reefs for both protection and snorkeling. Approach from the west with high afternoon light over your shoulder. The narrow gap between the mainland shoals and **Isla Yallis** has 8 feet of water and is sheltered from swell. There is no clear sand road in this channel, so it is uncomfortable for deeper draft vessels. They may take the 17 foot minimum depth of the channel between the breakers on the seaward reef and Isla Yallis. **Bahía Salinas**, to the east, is a secluded beach exposed to northerly swells through a gap in the reefs. Leave the bay the way you entered by **Isla Yallis,** in the morning and with light over your shoulder.

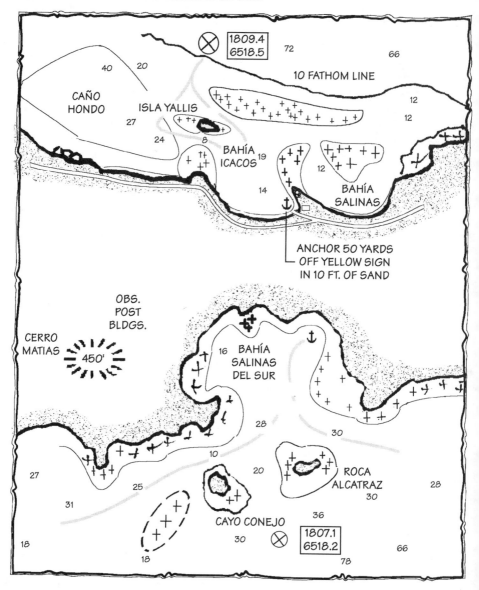

Bahía Salinas del Sur

Under east to north winds this is a calm, beach lined anchorage. Tuck up into the northeast corner behind the reef and select a patch of bare sand to anchor in 10 feet of water. If you use the beach, don't go further inland nor pick up man-made objects.

ENSENADA HONDA, VIEQUES

Ensenada Honda is a wonderfully tranquil and secluded mangrove anchorage and a fine hurricane hole for hurricanes that cooperate and don't blow from the west. Enter northwest by north on the first point of land inside the bay. Turn northeast at 3 fathoms toward a baby mangrove off the tip of the third point. When north of a set of rocks called Los Galafatos ("The Thieves"), turn east southeast for the anchorage. See the chartlet for waypoints

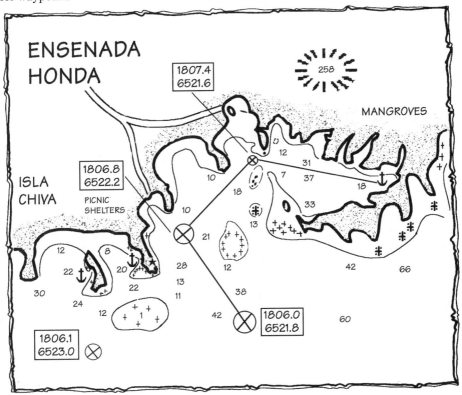

BAHÍA CHIVA

Bahía Chiva is a US Navy beach area with many picnic shelters, the anchorage can nonetheless be quiet and private. Holding is good in fern and fan covered sand. The calmest anchorage is in 10 feet of water in front of the southernmost picnic shelter, close to the beach and covered from swell by the reef west of the point. On the west side of Isla Chiva is a fine anchorage tight up against its northern end, or, for a lunch stop with snorkeling, off the rock crevice at the island's midpoint.

BIOLUMINESCENT BAYS OF VIEQUES

Both **Puerto Ferro** and **Puerto Mosquito** are strongly phosphorescent. If you don't overnight at them, you can visit by dinghy from **Sun Bay** or **Esperanza**, or you can take night tours from **Esperanza** arranged through several local dive and tour operators.

Puerto Ferro

Puerto Ferro is a mangrove anchorage with a narrow entrance and only a 7 foot controlling depth on the bar. A day anchorage is feasible outside the bar when the wind is north of east or less than 15 knots south of east.

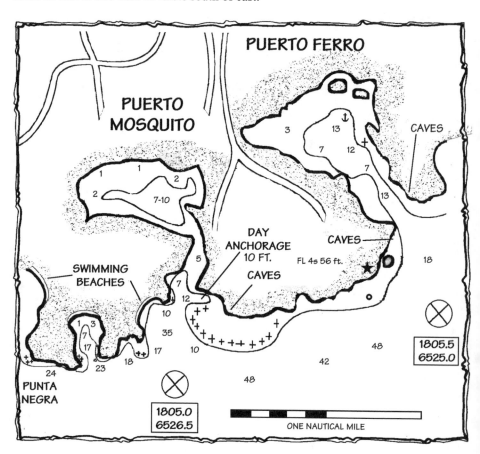

Puerto Mosquito

Puerto Mosquito is accessible only to drafts under 5 feet, or slightly more at high tide (with infinite patience). A day anchorage is available which, under settled conditions, can be used for snorkel trips to the rocks and caves about the harbor's mouth. To the west of the entrance is perhaps the loveliest palm lined, white sand, azure water swimming beach in the Caribbean.

LA CORDILLERA

This 12 mile chain of islets and reefs is Puerto Rico's **East Coast Marine Reserve**. The larger keys can be used to day-anchor the mother boat in the lee of the easterly trades and in shelter of northerly swell in the winter. Diving expeditions can then be run by dinghy to the surrounding reefs and walls. Diving opportunities on the **Cordillera** are constrained in the winter months by conditions of wind and swell. Northerly swell and anything but mild easterlies are unusual in the summer months. In general, look for minimum swell days with a favorable wind of 15 knots or less before choosing your day anchorage and dive sites.

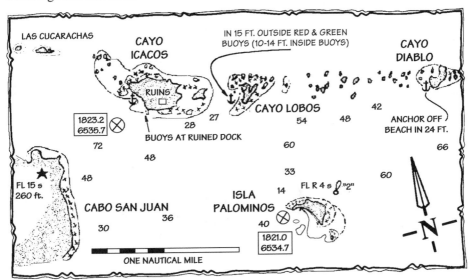

CAYO ICACOS

Arrive at the waypoint shown, then proceed into the cove of deeper water by eyeball, snuggling up to the white sand beach in 7 feet of glass clear water. Under prevailing trades this can be a good night anchorage and provides endless diving, snorkeling and shelling on the surrounding reefs and secluded beaches. It might be a little rolly in winter, however.

CAYO LOBOS

This is a privately owned resort island with a protected harbor marked by red and green floats. Make a day anchorage just inside or outside the buoys and well off the channel, respecting the access and privacy of the owners.

CAYO DIABLO

Shoal draft vessels can work close in to the beach, while deeper drafts must avoid the coral formations and anchor in 3-4 fathoms of clear sand farther out. The rocks and islets downwind can be dived with a reliable motorized tender. Be sure there is enough anchor rode and that it includes chain. This is a day anchorage only, and only in settled conditions of less than 15 knots east. There is a diveboat mooring on the east shore.

CULEBRA AND ITS OUT ISLANDS

Unspoiled **Isla de Culebra** is a winter retreat for some and a permanent expatriate refuge for others. Most people are attracted by its seclusion, its spectacular beaches and the quaint and insular town of **Dewey**.

Unexploited diving opportunities abound in the rocks, islets and full boarded islands centered on Culebra. Dive any number of day anchorages, though swell can affect them in the winter months. Culebra and its outlying islands can absorb the serious cruiser or diver for weeks.

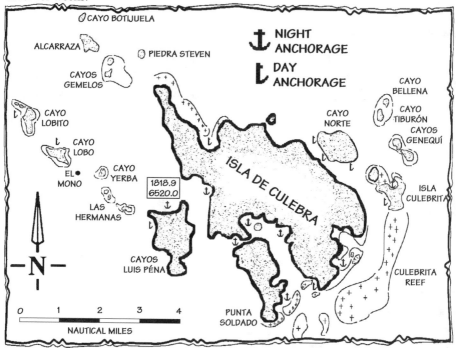

Arriving from Puerto Rico, make your landfall at **Luis Peña.** Arriving from the **Virgin Islands** or overseas, anchor overnight at **Dakity Harbor** behind the reef entrance to **Ensenada Honda**. Proceed next morning to the top of Ensenada Honda to clear in at **Dewey**.

Cayo Luis Peña

In settled easterlies, the beach on the north shore of **Luis Peña** provides anchoring in clear white sand roads between patches of coral rock. Stay in 1-2 fathoms, since the water shoals quickly. The anchorage inside the reef is available to drafts of 5 feet and less. In winter the northwestern point of **Culebra** shields the anchorage from the worst of the northeast swell. Luis Peña is an uninhabited wildlife refuge with hiking paths and secluded beaches. Except on weekends, you are likely to be alone here, where you will toast the sun disappearing spectacularly over the rocky skerries of **Las Hermanas**, backed by the majestic peaks of the El Yunque rain forest.

In light conditions, this is a great place from which to launch diving expeditions in gofast dinghies. To the north are the reefs of Culebra's **Punta del Noroeste** and the offshore keys of **Alcarraza, Los Gemelos** and **Piedra Steven**. Closer yet to the west are Las Hermanas rocks and **Cayo Yerba**.

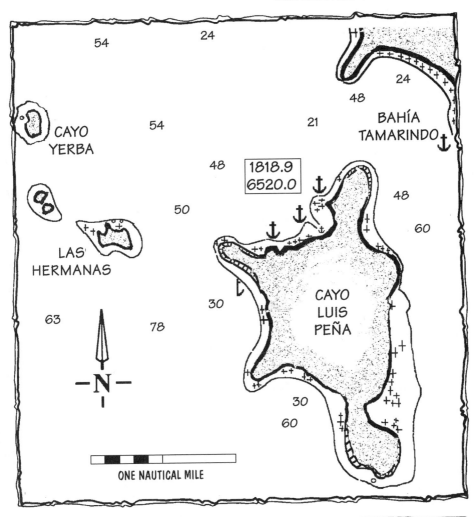

Cayos Lobito and Lobo

Unless you have a large launch, these keys are too far downwind to safely visit by dinghy from **Luis Peña**. However, under settled east southeasterlies with no northern swell, it is possible to use day anchorages at either key. There are both reefs and walls to satisfy snorkelers and scuba buffs. As with most day anchorages, the skipper might want to post an anchor watch aboard while the diving party is out. Dive up wind and current of the dinghy.

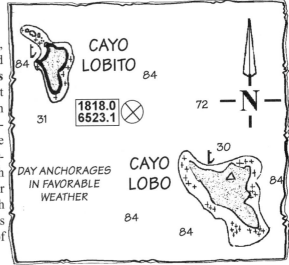

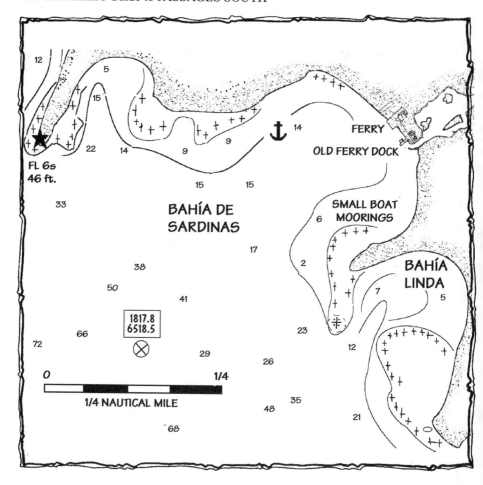

BAHÍA SARDINAS

Dewey can be entered at night by **Bahía Sardinas.** Position yourself one half mile south of the *flashing 7 second* light marking the reefs west and north of the harbor entrance. From there take up a heading of 87° Magnetic on the brightly lit old ferry dock on the south edge of town. Anchor in 12 feet of clear water over white sand to the northwest of the new ferry dock. The ferries stop running after 6 p.m., so your night should be a comfortable one. You shall be conveniently waked by the 7 a.m. ferry, however, should you oversleep. The above advice notwithstanding, it is *not* advisable to be sailing these waters at night.

If coming from the east you shall need to clear **Customs and Immigration** in **Dewey** from the **Ensenada Honda** side. Customs is at the airport, a five minute walk from El Batey restaurant whose dinghy dock is a long ell pier northwest of the anchorage, just north of the high school stadium which is visible from the water. See the chartlet of **Ensenada Honda**.

El Batey has the best sandwiches on the island.

TURTLEWATCH PROGRAM

Playa Resaca and Playa Brava on the north coast of Culebra, east of Flamenco Beach are turtle nesting beaches. The Culebra Leatherback Project conducts nightly beach surveys from April 1 to August 30th. Interested cruisers may participate by previous arrangement with project management. To participate, call 809-742-0115.

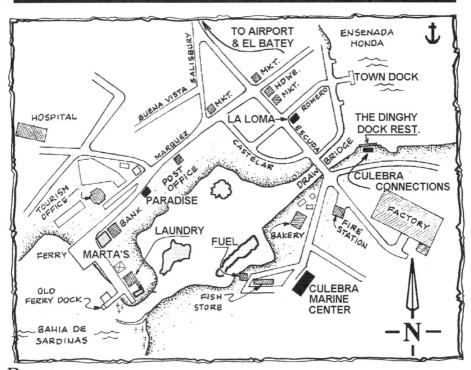

DEWEY

See Bruce and Kathy at La Loma art shop, above the town dock, for the latest skinny on what's happening in Culebra. The town offers a variety of restaurants, bars and boutiques with conveniently staggered, if not randomly chosen, opening hours.

Ferries to **Fajardo** run frequently from **Dewey**, if you bypassed Fajardo but want to visit it from Culebra. Fresh vegetables are available by truck from the mainland twice a week. The truck parks in front of the Post Office.

CULEBRA NATIONAL WILDLIFE REFUGE

Large seabird colonies are protected by this sea park which consists of 23 keys and islands and four large tracts of land on Culebra itself. Luis Peña and Culebrita are open for exploration ashore from sunrise to sunset.

ENSENADA HONDA

The narrow reef entrance is clearly marked by green can No. 9 and red buoy No. 10. Enter between the buoys. The holding is poor right off the town. The boats there look like they are at anchor but most are on moorings. To be near town, anchor in 16 feet on a bottom of sand and mud west of **Cayo Pirata**. The finest anchorage to be had within **Ensenada Honda** is behind the reef at **Dakity Harbor** in 2-3 fathoms over white sand. **Malena Harbor** to the southwest can be tricky; it is best left to local powerboats. Dinghy to the happy hour at the Club Seabourne pool at the foot of **Fulladosa Bay.**

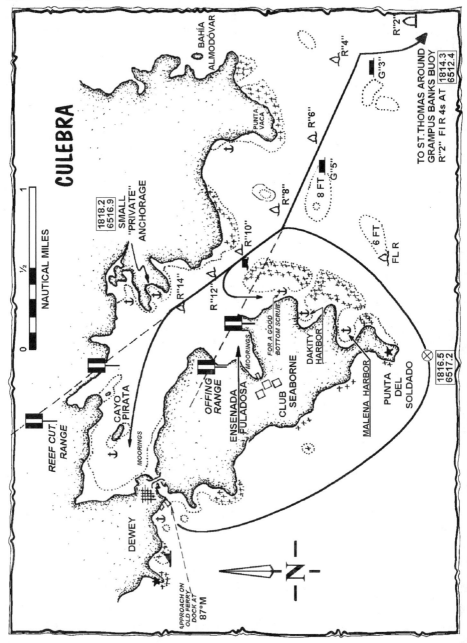

248

FLAMENCO BEACH

A spectacularly beautiful beach whose anchorage is untenable in northerly wind or swell which often occurs in the winter months. Under those conditions you can visit by road with your camera. It's over the hill from the airport. Under favorable conditions it is a great sand anchorage until ebb tide when you might find it starts to roll. Plan your trip to go in for lunch on a rise of tide and exit on the ebb in the afternoon. You won't regret it.

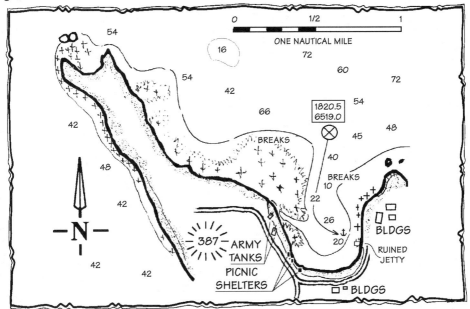

BAHÍA DE ALMODÓVAR

Bahía de Almodóvar and **Dakity Harbor** are the most tranquil anchorages of **Culebra**. Round Culebra at **Punta Vaca** into **Canal del Sur**. Enter **Puerto Manglar** heading 325°M on a large wedding cake of a house overlooking the bay. Pass between small red and green markers in 3 fathoms. Round the double mangrove islet of **Pelaita** through a 10 foot deep channel and between another set of markers. You are now in Bahía Almodóvar's deep, still waters. Anchor west of the reef in 2-4 fathoms of white sand and gin clear water. The cooling trades blow over the reef out of a clear horizon, where the lights of St.Thomas come on at night. This harbor is locally called **La Pelá** or **Manglar.**

ISLA CULEBRITA

Within the northern arms of **Culebrita** is a 400 yard diameter basin with 7 to 25 feet of clear water bordered by white beaches. If you missed **Flamenco**, be sure to do Culebrita. Hike to the seaward pools known locally as "the Jacuzzis". Snorkel the nearby reefs and ledges, or dive the **Cayos Ballena, Tiburón** and **Geniquí** a mile to the north. In 20 knots of wind or more there can be heavy seas between Cayos Geniquí and Culebrita. Once inside, easterly seas disappear, but occasional heavy northerly swells may penetrate the bay in winter. Overnight here only in settled weather with no north swell forecast.

If conditions don't permit a visit to the northern anchorage, stop on the southwest coast of **Culebrita**. Visit the northern beach afoot by mounting the hill to the old lighthouse. Take a camera. Anchor by the small piers north of **Punta Arenisca** in 16 feet of sand surrounded by 4 to 6 foot coral heads and to the east of a 72 foot drop-off for snorkeling and diving. **Culebrita Reef** stretches almost two miles from here to the south southwest. For serious fishing expeditions, **Grampus Banks** lies 2 miles to the south.

CAYO NORTE

Depending on swell, two day anchorages are available on the southwest shore for diving expeditions by dinghy. Anchor on the shelf in 25 feet of sand off rocky ledges with a 72 foot wall to the west. In settled light easterlies such as in the summer months, one can anchor overnight on the east end of the southern shore in 18 feet of sand, west southwest of the red fisherman's cottage, sheltered by the breaking reef to the east.

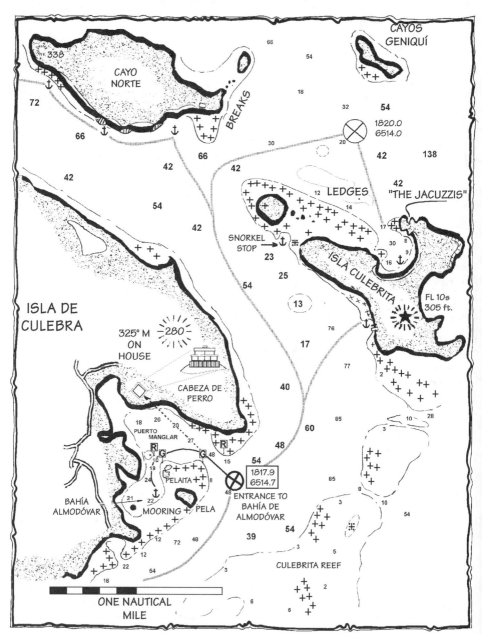

SOUTH FROM THE VIRGINS

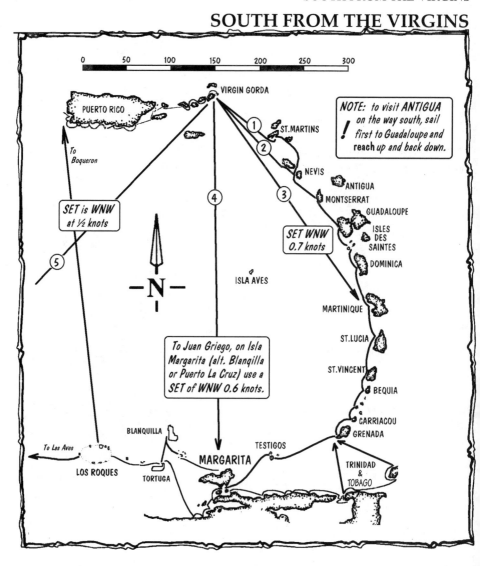

Legend within map:

0   50   100   150   200   250   300

VIRGIN GORDA

PUERTO RICO

To Boqueron

① ST.MARTINS

②

NOTE: to visit ANTIGUA on the way south, sail first to Guadaloupe and reach up and back down.

NEVIS

ANTIGUA

MONTSERRAT

GUADALOUPE

④

③

SET is WNW at ½ knots

⑤

SET WNW 0.7 knots

ISLES DES SAINTES

DOMINICA

–N–

ISLA AVES

MARTINIQUE

ST.LUCIA

To Juan Griego, on Isla Margarita (alt. Blanqilla or Puerto La Cruz) use a SET of WNW 0.6 knots.

ST.VINCENT

BEQUIA

CARRIACOU

GRENADA

BLANQUILLA

TESTIGOS

To Las Aves

LOS ROQUES

TORTUGA

MARGARITA

TRINIDAD & TOBAGO

Crossings to South America

[1] hard motorsail to St.Martin from   Virgin Gorda   80 nm. minimum
[2] beating to St.Kitts from   Virgin Gorda   120 nm.   "
[3] long tack to Martinique from   Virgin Gorda   300 nm.   "
[4] close reach to Venezuela from   Virgin Gorda   450 nm.   "
[5] broad reach to Bonaire from   Fajardo or St.Thomas   420 nm.   "

When crossing the **Caribbean Sea** from Virgin Gorda south to the **Windward Islands** use 3 quarters knots of west northwest going current and reckon on leeway equaling, in degrees, the Force Beaufort encountered.

252

WHY THE CLOCKWISE ROUTE?

There are two routes across the Caribbean to South America: clockwise and counter-clockwise. The counterclockwise route is to **Tucacas**, Venezuela after a 400 mile jump to **Bonaire**. Clockwise or counterclockwise there is the same amount of windward sailing, it's just put off until the northing through the **Windwards** rather than taken up front while southing the **Leewards**. Disadvantages of the counterclockwise route are, first, the 400 mile passage, and second, if you decide to continue on to the western Caribbean you must retrace any cruising you do in the Antilles and Venezuela.

The key reason for going through the chain of islands to the east is because you are already a few links down the chain, or ought to be in order to get a comfortable lay on Bonaire, in which most or all of Puerto Rico should be downwind of you. You've already got used to island hopping, and it is easier than ever to daysail through the **Virgins**. Why stop now when the islands are only spitting distance apart? Except the jump to **St. Martin**, it is all short daysails.

For the first year, most cruisers prefer to thoroughly do the Venezuelan gulfs and off-shore islands before wintering in **Trinidad**. After Carnival in Trinidad some return home via the island chain. Others cruising further afield, head back to Margarita to stock up, then they proceed from **Puerto La Cruz** to the Dutch Islands via **Los Roques** and **Las Aves**, thence to **Cartegena** and the Canal or Central America.

STRATEGIES

The easting from the **Mona Passage** to **Bitter End, Virgin Gorda** is so easy *(if you follow this guide)* that there is no reason to jump off into the Caribbean any earlier. I often meet cruisers in Puerto Rico who, having what they think is the devilish part of the trip behind them, are hell bent to make South America on a beat across the sea to **Margarita.** They usually fetch Puerto Cabello instead. Take a few more days to get further east and have a much more comfortable trip south.

It is only a few hours of lee sailing from one **Virgin Island** to another. The conditions you will meet on the **Leewards** portion of the route are much friendlier than what you have had so far. Even though you will still be beating to windward until you get to **Martinique**, the passages are in long, open-ocean swells instead of the Caribbean's chop and coastal hazards.

The farther north one makes landfall in the **Leewards**, or the **Windwards**, the better. **St.Martin** is usually a motor but well worth the trip for its own sake as well as for additional islands that the route lets you visit with your windward advantage there. The best route, even during hurricane season, is via **St. Martin.** From there south it's island hopping again with each new high island appearing over the horizon just as the last one sinks behind. The best jumpoff point for St. Martin is via **Saba Rock** in **Virgin Gorda Sound, British Virgin Islands.**

If my windward objective is **St. Kitts, Martinique,** or farther off to **Grenada**, from where one clears out for **Venezuela**, my jumpoff point is still **Saba Rock. Spanish Town**, on Virgin Gorda, has a **Barclay's** Bank which is a good spot to bankroll with little or no fees before going, and the marina there is an easy and friendly checkout and refueling spot. You don't have all of these elsewhere. Virgin Gorda Sound itself is a pleasant mini cruising area. Watch the sea in the afternoon from the bar at **Biras Creek** and come back for dinner in the evening. Put together by a Norwegian group, this unique resort is for me the finest ambiance in the Caribbean. But then I spent many years in Scandinavia.

ENCORE STAGING

Better enjoy the passage through each of the **Leeward Islands** and the **Windward Islands** by *staging* properly. Whether headed north or south, whether you are flying your Q flag and just anchoring through, or whether you stay weeks at each island, when you are ready to shove on, always *stage* yourself the night before at the last safe anchorage next to the ocean pass you must cross. Next morning you will have a swift, safe sail and be in before the lunchtime squalls and williwaws.

Along the Windwards and Leewards, the *Thornless Path* strategies still dictate an **SG&T** on each island landfall along the way south, whether going ashore or just sailing onward the next morning.

CROSSINGS

The *Gentleman's Guide to Passages South* gives you sailing directions in some detail as far as the **Virgin Islands**. Thereafter use these excellent **guides**:

Nancy and Simon Scott's *Cruising Guide to the Virgin Islands,*

Chris Doyle's *Cruising Guide to the Leeward Islands,* his *Sailor's Guide to the Windwards* and his *Cruising Guide to Trinidad-Tobago, Venezuela and Bonaire.*

For your personal *thornlessness*, here are my notes from many personal passages.

After many trials, I've found the best departure point, going east or south, is from **Virgin Gorda Sound**, motoring through the reef to clear the island south of Anagada Horseshoe Reef. Leave **Bitter End** at 3 p.m. when the sun is high enough to guide you through the cut in the reef which bears 64° Magnetic from **Saba Rock**.

When selecting a route to **Venezuela** don't make the mistake of many I've met who have crossed the Caribbean Sea from Hispaniola or western Puerto Rico. Coasting back east along Venezuela is not a problem, but departing for a comfortable crossing is. If you don't plan to coast Venezuela, be aware that the **Equatorial Current** down there runs up to 3 knots against you while its maximum up north is less than half that. If you <u>do</u> end up in **Puerto Cabello** because you tried to sail to Venezuela from a point too far west, then treat the route eastward as though you were coasting **Puerto Rico**'s south coast. That is, get some **charts** and do predawn harbor hops of about 20 miles each from one little harbor to another. That can be a good trip, but you should have planned it that way.

For the entire **Eastern Caribbean** you need nothing but a few medium scale **Imray Charts** and a guide for harbor chartlets. Because of the transatlantic traffic in the winter months and the year round charter businesses, there is a wealth of good information available on the routes from the **Virgin Islands** to **Grenada**. The Leeward and Windward Island groups are full of celebrating charter boats and fly-in tourists. Select your run across from **Virgin Gorda** to **St. Martin, Isla Margarita** or **Puerto La Cruz**. But when you get to the other side always proceed by island and harbor hopping.

St. Martin

This is a straight forward motorsail. Sail next morning up into **Phillipsburg**, or stop at **Pelican Point** in **Simsons Bay**. The **Hurricane Hole** in **Simsons Lagoon** is enormous and the summer stop of many hard core cruisers, though the number of boats mitigates hurricane security. There are now slips available at the various condos and marinas in the lagoon. **St. Martin** provides shopping and touring as well as a miniature cruising area of its own. While in Simsons Bay you can dinghy through the lagoon to the French side at **Marigot** for lunch and shopping. Phillipsburg can be a rolly anchorage and it can be a *deathtrap* in strong southerly winds.

St. Kitts

This can be a pleasant close hauled sail in light easterlies or winds north of east in winter. You haven't got the "Caribbean Two Step" here. You are into longer Atlantic swells and this is ocean sailing at its best, assuming you go on light wind days only. **Wait for Weather** in Virgin Gorda Sound, and leave from Saba Rock. The anchorage at **Basseterre** on **St. Kitts** is rolly and busy with small freighter and ferry traffic. You can also make a stop enroute at little **St. Eustatius** ('Statia). After a good night's sleep carry on to **Nevis**, anchoring off the beaches north of Charlestown in sand.

MARTINIQUE

As with the route to **St.Kitts**, leave **Virgin Gorda Sound** via **Saba Rock**. The only trouble with this passage is that you miss **Guadeloupe** and my favorite anchorages of **Des Haies** and the **Iles des Saintes**. I like to make landfall at **St.Pierre** in **Martinique** and watch the villagers work their fish nets while I have coffee on deck early in the morning.

VENEZUELA

Crossing the Caribbean from Virgin Gorda to Puerto La Cruz, use a west northwest set of a half knot door to door. In the summer make sure you have a clear 4 day forecast with no tropical waves or disturbances on the way over from Africa.

Puerto La Cruz is an easier destination to make and a rapid close reach under summer conditions. You can try to make **Pampatar** on **Isla Margarita**, but **Juan Griego**, on the northwest coast would be easier. You can clear in there with a little more trouble than if you went to Pampatar where assistance is available. Refer to *Customs and Clearances*.

ISLAND HOPPING TO SOUTH AMERICA

Here's a list of easy hops I've taken many times for rapid transits. They are only the necessary steps on a thornless path, and the only ones I use on a "rapid transit" down island. This route makes for a fast, but pleasant passage, if you are not interested in seeing more of the islands on the way down. I certainly hope you would go slower on the way back, however.

You may make a rapid transit down the islands in the hurricane season, or you may be cruising each one. In any case, when ready to move on, *stage* to the overnight anchorage closest to the pass you wish to hop: the southernmost on the way south, the northernmost on the way north. While island hopping the **Leewards** or the **Windwards**, it is important to get underway at daylight to avoid any midday squalls on arrival at your new anchorage. Take an hour or two motor run in calm behind the island, making breakfast on the way. The boat shall be stable and upright as in a lee anchorage, and breakfasting underway will give you a couple of more hours to enjoy your next harbor in the afternoon.

Take every anchorage and you'll never sail more than a few hours each day. Try to be in by lunchtime or be prepared to turn up into the squalls coming down the mountains or through the passes as, for example, between **Guadeloupe** and **Isles des Saintes**.

GUSTAVIA, ST. BARTS

Spots in the inner harbor are difficult to find. Temporarily anchor in the deeper water but good holding sand bottom of the outer harbor. **Customs** and **Immigration** are relaxed. Look for them but don't strain yourself. There is a mooring charge just to anchor.

NEVIS

Anchor off the beaches north of **Charlestown**. Dinghy into the beach club there for a drink. If you're moving on the next day, fly a yellow flag and don't go ashore; or, if you do go ashore for a drink at Crappy's beach bar, inquire after **Customs** and **Immigration** at the bar (after you order).

SOUTH FROM THE VIRGINS

MONTSERRAT

Anchor under the hills of the northwest coast, the anchorage by the town dock further south is rolly and you'll love scanning the homes on the hillsides while having your **SG&T**. Fly the "Q" flag and move on at daybreak. This is the home of the "Big RA" transmitter (0930 AM), which has the best forecasts in the Caribbean.

DES HAIES, GUADALOUPE

Des Haies [day HEY] is my favorite anchorage in the **Leeward Islands**. The people and the town are a delight in the daytime and you would swear that the scene of the town at night, as seen from the calm of your anchorage, was set up by a Broadway stage designer. Fly your "Q" flag and don't expect **Customs** and **Immigration** to fall all over you. In general in the French islands, the officials are courteous and agreeable. They realize they have a tourist economy and do their best to make your touring pleasant. They are mostly French professionals and, usually, they see you before you see them. Make a modest effort to find them and clear in, but don't pound their tables. If you force them to shuffle your papers, they may insist your papers be in order (have your kids mailed you your new documentation stickers yet?). You must check in, of course, but it's better to go with the flow. Let them know you're there, but don't press them. If you decide to stay awhile and you haven't found the officials in a day or two, go up to the office <u>during office hours</u> and have a chat. They know you're there and will expect your visit.

ANTIGUA

Not my favorite place because of repeated ugly behavior from officials and locals over the years. If you go here from the west, do so by first following the route above to Guadaloupe, then close reaching *back up* to **Antigua** [anne-TEE-gah]. Trying to get here in a straight line is murder, even from Montserrat. Besides, you get to see Guadaloupe twice that way, since you must come back to continue south.

ISLES DES SAINTES, GUADALOUPE

At **Isles des Saintes** [eel day SANT] anchor on the north shore of the island west of **Bourg** one mile, sheltered on the east by a large round rock. Clearing in isn't always necessary since the **Customs**, or *Le Douane*, isn't always there. Dinghy in for a farewell to French cuisine here. Say hello to the *Gendarmes*, but don't be surprised if they don't care you're there for one overnight.

ROSEAU, DOMINICA

Landfall going south to **Dominica** [doh-mee-KNEE-kah] is **Prince Rupert's Bay.** Anchor off the hotel on the south shore. Next morning truck on down to **Roseau** [roo-SOH], the capital. You may tie stern-to to the Hotel pier, but it is not necessary. You can anchor a boat's length from the shore as the nights are dead calm, and more than a boat's length away it drops off to China. Dominicans [accent on the "ni", pronounced "knee"] are among the nicest people in the Leewards or Windwards and the island offers much to see. **Soufriere** is the pits but it is the place to leave from.

ST. PIERRE, MARTINIQUE

See *Virgin Gorda to Martinique*. As you proceed down the island, you will see black-top roads climbing inland from the sea. They're not roads. This is the site of **Mt.Pelée** which erupted in 1902, killing between 30 and 40 thousand and wiping out a bay full of ships along with the capital of the Lesser Antilles. Only one survived. A drunk in the jail. There's a museum being stocked with finds from the digs. You can clear in here.

FORT DE FRANCE, MARTINIQUE

Good, but expensive, yacht chandlers and French cuisine will keep you here awhile even if you're a hell bent for leather passage maker. **Martinique** is just about the only cruising worthy island between **St.Martin** and **Venezuela** as far as using your boat is concerned. Little bays with their little villages and great restaurants. Great diving on the east coast. Try the seafood restaurants at *Bourg du Robert*. Martinique also offers the best girl watching between the Dominican Republic and Brazil. Hard core cruisers hang out at **Anse Mitan** [aunt's me-TONG], or **Anse des Cocotiers** [aunt's day co-co-tee-AIRH] on the charts. *Stage* to St.Lucia at Grand Anse or **Cul de Sac Marin**.

RODNEY BAY, ST. LUCIA

A fabulous marina with owner Arch Marez on site and hosting. Tie up or anchor out, this is the place from which to tour the island if you do so. **Rodney Bay Marina** is still the best equipped yard south of the **Virgin Islands**.

MARIGOT BAY, ST. LUCIA

Stop at this historic and scenic bay for lunch and press on to the **Pitons** well before dark. You won't be able to count on room to overnight. Although a **Hurricane Hole**, it is doubtful you could use it profitably with the crush of charter boats all around. **Marigot Bay** is one of Lord Nelson's hidey holes. The man had genius for finding harbors where enemies literally at the entrance didn't know there was a harbor, much less ships, in front of them (e.g., Mahón, in Minorca, English Harbor, in Antigua).

PITONS, ST. LUCIA

A tricky spot in a blow. If you have all chain, you may find yourself with 2 hundred feet of it hanging straight down after casting off next day. The beach boys used to behave quite ugly here but recently they seem to have mellowed out and entered an establishmentarian phase of their Rastafarian lives. They do expect tips and they do provide a useful service. The size of the tip has been previously determined for broke cruisers by the bareboat charterers on vacation.

CHATEAU BELAIRE, ST. VINCENT

This is the unspoiled jewel of the island. Anchor forty yards from shore in 20 feet of sand just north of a little river at the north end of the bay, at the end of the line of beach. The kids will give you good service. Send them out for fresh fruits and veggies, but anchor your own boat. Use 2 anchors because of the nighttime swing. There is another good anchorage under the cliffs with coconut trees just north of the bay.

BEQUIA, ST. VINCENT GRENADINES

At Bequia [BECK-wee] all the good shallow spots will be taken, so resolve to anchor in forty feet and be done with it. Be here for Christmas. It's the meeting ground of the **Windward Islands** for cruisers from Mom and Pop to the maxis returning from the Mediterranean. One party after another.

THE GRENADINES

In the **Grenadines**, one initially has a certain temerity about bearing full sail, given the strength of the **trade winds**. The wind's rock hard steadiness, however, and the fine lees available from the seas, let you carry a full rig. Your boat will perform as never before. Sailing the passes is exhilarating. No need to drop sail in a squall, just turn head to wind and let it rattle awhile, then continue. If you don't head up, however, you could get knocked down since 50 knot leading edges are not unheard of between Union and Kick'em Jenny.

TYRELL BAY, CARIACOU

Hillsboro is not a great harbor and a little out of the way for passage makers. The **Hurricane Hole** at **Tyrell Bay** is the best available since you left Puerto Rico. It is a pleasant little community with a rudimentary boatyard and gringos ashore opening and closing restaurants.

ST. GEORGES, GRENADA

Anchor off the crumbling Yacht Services dock and clear in at their offices. For further information on **St. Georges** see *Customs and Clearances*. Visit the neat little bookstore below the Nutmeg restaurant, across the harbor. Rumor has it that this is the store where a US Army lieutenant borrowed the phone to call the Pentagon to patch him into the Navy offshore to tell them to stop shelling him. So much for combined strike force technology. Another rumor is that yachties in the harbor were ignored when they volunteered use of their shortwave radios because they "weren't secure". By the way, Grenada is English. It is pronounced greh-NAYE-da.

GRENADA TO THE TESTIGOS

Depart **Grenada** from **St. Georges** or **Prickly Bay** at dusk to make the **Testigos** [test-TEE-gohs] for breakfast; don't risk a night arrival. Anchor north of **Isla Langoleta** to the west of **Isla Testigo Grande**. This can be a good spot for a bottom scrub.

On the crossing allow for 1.3 knots of current setting 300° True door to door. Have a full rig up since you will encounter calms to Force 3 on this passage. There may be a belt of squalls 20 miles or so northeast of the Testigos, however. The **Equatorial Current** is really ripping around here and this miniature weather system seems to always be there. The trip will doubtless be smooth and uneventful.

The Testigos (witnesses) are so called because they testified to the existence of the Equatorial Current for **Columbus** on his fourth voyage. The great navigator, having no knowledge of the Caribbean Sea, proceeded to make his new colony of Santo Domingo in one single tack. At the anchorage on Testigo Grande are the houses of five fishing families. They are the five sons from that island that married five of the six daughters born on the island across the bay. These families are the only inhabitants of the Testigos. See Benjamín in the first house for information on the Testigos.

TESTIGOS TO MARGARITA

Leave **Testigos** at first light for what probably will be a motor to **Pampatar** [pahm-pah-TAR]. Even though you have a fast boat, get going early so you can make your **SG&T** at your destination. Approaching **Isla Margarita** in the dark or in late afternoon, when there are often squalls with restricted visibility, could be a problem due to all the fishing activity around the island. It's best to sail overnight and arrive in the morning with good margin and good visibility. Porlamar, a few miles to the west, is a more tranquil anchorage than Pampatar. Dinghy into the beach bar and pay someone to clear you in while you suck a cold beer.

TRINIDAD

After several nighttime motorsails along the **Paria** peninsula of Venezuela, don't continue directly into **Port of Spain** harbor. Checking in and out of **Trinidad** may require time and patience (see the chapter on *Customs and Clearances*). Best to be fresh. *Stage* yourself into **Trinidad** by anchoring in the beautiful little cove of **La Tinta** in **Boca Grande** on the island of **Chacachacare**. All the channels into the **Gulf of Paria** are called *bocas* (mouths) because **Columbus**, sure he was approaching the Japanese offshore islands, and knowing Orientals were partial to dragons, named them the several "Mouths of the Dragon".

Next day, the boat all clean and sparkling, the crew all rested, bright eyed and bushy tailed, you can motor over to **Chaguaramas** to clear in. After the exit hassles, *stage* yourself out of Port of Spain by going over to **Scotland Bay** and anchoring on a shelf of sand all the way up the bay.

The way to *do* Trinidad is to be there in early to mid December just to ensure a slip at the yacht club, or a mooring at the Yachting Association in **Carenage Bay**. The original of the steel band carnivals, Trinidad's **Carnival** gets going already in December with each band's preparation for Carnival being a cause to party. You must understand the jargon of Carnival in order to know how to best enjoy it, and just doing that will take a month. Trinidadians are an eclectic race of African, Indian, Chinese and European. The melange of customs, cuisines and beautiful people provide a tourist smorgasbord. By the time Carnival is actually staged in February, it will be an anticlimax, although it is a huge event.

CROSSING BACK

If you insist on crossing the **Caribbean,** do so from **Los Roques** to the **Mona Passage**, or from **Margarita** to the **Spanish Virgins**. Use a west northwest average set of one half knot door to door. Crossing over to **Grenada**, you have to motor the coast almost to **Trinidad** so you might as well call in at **Port of Spain**. The way back from there is then through the islands. If you scurried down islands in a rush to get to the hurricane protection of Venezuela, the trip back up islands gives you a chance to pay them proper visits. Some great flotilla parties are available in the holiday season which include all the returnees from the Mediterranean. Try **Bequia** for Christmas and **Petit St. Vincent** for New Year's. If you can't make the New Year's party at Foxy's on **Jost Van Dyke**, that is.

Leave Trinidad from Scotland Bay for an easy sail to **Grenada** in settled trades south of east. Alternatively, beat back up to **Martinique**. In either case, bear in mind the dictum you learned upon approaching Hispaniola (you did learn it, didn't you?) to ease sheets and run across the wind if the seas and wind begin to bite. *Do not* try to beat directly into it. So you arrive a few miles to leeward of Grenada. So what? Tack back up to the big island in its great lee. But don't blow out your sails and risk your hides doing a dumb rhumb just because it's programmed into your GPS!

APPENDIX A: SPANGLISH FOR CRUISERS

The following method to achieve rapid pidgin Spanish, or *Span-glish* as it's sometimes called, is only a guide, not, God forbid, instruction in **Spanish**. The objective here is to permit the totally uninitiated to get things done ashore by employing a pidgin Spanish which can be learned in minutes.

Below is a list of nouns with which the reader joins necessary modifiers and a verb to form a sentence which then can be phonetically read aloud in American English to a listener who will understand it as Spanish. Got that?

Cruisers should worry more about pronunciation than spelling or grammar, since many of the people they talk to ashore can barely read or write anyway. Showing written statements may get you a donation faster than comprehension.

You can successfully talk in nouns only, using your hands for verbs, and pointing around to find descriptors of size, location, color and so on.

All the correct grammar in the world doesn't help the perennial yachtie who goes all over town looking for the hardware store (*ferreteria*) by asking for the furry-TARRY-uh instead of the FAIR-ray-tah-REE-ah. After a few days this type usually goes and sulks on his boat, sails out of the country, and tells stories on the SSB how you can't get anything there and the people are evil.

To accurately name the thing you want you must string together several items from the list of *nouns*. For instance: "motor head bolt". I know it's not called that, but keep it simple. Nothing transliterates.

Talk like an Indian in an old movie: "Ugh! Me need'em motor head bolt". In Latin lingoes you put nouns that modify each other in backward sequence with a *de* [day] between them. A head bolt is bolt of a head. A motor head is a head of a motor. Thus, your movie Indian might say "Ugh! Me need'em bolt of head of motor." So this becomes: "*Oye! Mi necessita tornillo de cabeza de motor*", [me nay-say-SEE-tah tore-KNEE-yo day kah-BAY-tsah day moh-TOR]. Look it up in the following pages.

In this example the pronoun is wrong and the verb is third person, but no matter, you will be clearly understood when quickly reading the phonetics aloud.

Verbs and modifiers are given later for the intermediate student. Those aspiring to black belts can dabble in pronouns and prepositions after that, ensuring massive miscommunication. For now, let's go in search of a bolt for your motor's head. Read on ...

NOUNS

The words given below are often not the most "correct" Spanish but will be useful throughout Latin America because I show common American usage as opposed to European usage. That's no surprise. American English is, after all, significantly different from British English. For example, the word "maní" [mah-KNEE] is used for "peanuts" instead of the Castillano *cacahuete* [kah-kah-WAY-taye]. Both have Indian origins but American Latins never heard *cacahuete* in their lives, and it sounds like something nasty.

Other words, like *suiche* [SWEET-chaye] for "switch", are chosen because, all other parameters being equal, the English speaking boater can remember it easier than other nouns for switches. After all, *suiche* is real Spanglish. It is also the most commonly used form.

The words below are spelled with "phony-netics" rather than have the reader learn the Spanish pronunciation or the international semanticist symbology. I chose to mimic the Spanish with written American English as it is commonly spoken.

A speaker of General American will give a good imitation of American Spanish when simply reading aloud the phonetic words below with *strong emphasis* on the capitalized syllables. English words are used when their American pronunciation best simulates the Spanish (e.g., ace and day). Roll your R's if you can but don't sweat it: some Latins don't either.

I spell the American "A" sound "aye", and "I" is spelled "eye". Just read what you see. The Spanish vowels are usually aspirated, that is, using lots of breath. In Spanish, "O" is pronounced "Oh!", "A" is pronounced "Ah!" (as in "father"), "I" is "Eeee...", "E" is "Aye" (as in "say"), "U" is "Oooo...". Thus you will read below -*oh, -ah, -ee, -aye* and -*oo*. Just say them in English.

When listening to Spanish, be careful of "V" and "B". Both sound the same and they are pronounced somewhere between the two. This is true of American Spanish versus the Spanish spoken in Europe. The American hispanics will also drop their "S" sounds. The fewer "S" sounds, the less educated the speaker, normally. It's kind of like "dese" and "dose" in American dialects, but it can really buffalo a foreigner when words whose principal sounds are esses are spoken entirely free of the esses.

Therefore, when the street urchins ask you if you "peek a panich?", they're not asking you to peek at a dirty post card, but they are asking you if you "speak Spanish".

Almost all Spanish speakers add a vowel in front of initial "S" sounds when speaking English because that's what Spanish does. And when the waiter adds an "E" and drops the "S", "spaghetti" can come out "up a Ghetty!" Don't be offended if that's your name.

You'll also notice "Y" is often a "J" sound and double "LL" is a "Y" sound. If you're Judy Yeltsin, they'll spell it Yudy Lleltsin.

Now! Having said all that, here's the list:

acetone	*acetona*	ah-say-TONE-ah
adapter	*adaptador*	ah-DOPT-ah-DOOR
air filter	*filtro de aire*	FEEL-tro day EYE-ray
air vent	*ventil de aire*	vent-EEL day EYE-ray
alternator	*alternador*	all-tern-ah-DOOR
aluminium	*aluminio*	ah-loo-ME-knee-um
amperes	*amperes*	am-PAY-rees
anchor	*ancla*	AN-klah
anchorage	*anclaje*	an-KLAH-hey
avocado	*aguacate*	ah-gwah-KAH-taye
awning	*toldo*	TOLD-oh
back	*posterior*	post-tier-ee-OR
bananas	*guineo*	ee-NAY-oh
band-aid	*curita*	koo-REE-tah
batten	*iston de day vela*	lee-STONE VAYE-lah
battery	*bateria*	bah-taye-REE-ah
beam, boat's	*manga*	MAHN-gah
bearing	*bearing*	BEAR-ring
bilge	*sentina*	sen-TEEN-ah
block	*bloque*	BLOW-kay

block (pulley)	*polea, motón*	poe-LAY-ah, moh-TONE
block & tackle	*tecle*	TAYE-clay
boat	*bote*	BOAT-aye
boathook	*botavara*	BOAT-ah-VAH-rah
bollard	*hierro*	E-AIR-roe
bolt	*tornillo*	tore-KNEE-yoh
boom	*botalón*	BOAT-ah-LONE
bottom paint	*pintura de fondo*	peen-TOO-rah day FONE-dough
bow, boat's	*proa*	PRO-ah
brass	*latón*	lah-TONE
bread	*pan*	PAHN
breakwater	*rompeolas*	rome-pay-OH-las
bronze	*bronce*	BRONE-tsay
bulb	*bombilla*	bom-BEE-yah
buoy	*boya*	BOH-jah
bushing	=	BOO-shing
butter	*mantequilla*	mahn-taye-KEY-ya
can	*lata*	LAH-tah
case	*caja*	KAH-hah
catalyst	*activador*	act-tee-vah-DOOR
caulking	*calafate*	cal-ah-FAH-taye
caulking putty	*masilla*	mass-SEE-yah
celery	*apio*	AH-pee-oh
certificate	*certificado*	sair-tee-fee-KAH-dough
chain	*cadena*	kah-DAY-nah
chain plate	*cadenote*	kah-day-NOH-taye
charger	*cargador*	car-gah-DOOR
chart	*carta*	CAR-tah
cheese	*queso*	KAYE-so
circuit	*circuito*	seer-QUEE-toh
clamp	*abrazadera*	ah-bra-sah-DAY-rah
clearance	*despacho*	day-SPAH-cho
cleat	*tojino*	toe-HEE-noh
also....	*cornamusa*	core-nah-MOO-sah
come-along	*gato*	GAH-toh
compass	*brujula*	BRU-hu-lah
conch (DR)	*lambi*	lahm-BEE
conch (PR)	*carrucho*	car-ROO-choo
conch (Ven)	*concha*	CONE-cha
connector	*conector*	coh-neck-TOR
copper	*cobre*	KOH-bray
cotter pin	*passador abierto*	pass-ah-DOOR ah-bee-AIR-toh
coupling	*junta*	HOON-tah
cove	*enseñada*	ain-sane-NAH-dah
crab (DR,Ven)	*congrejo*	cone-GREY-ho
crab (PR)	*jueyes*	HWAY-jace
crew	*tripulante*	tree-pew-LAHN-tay
cushions	*cojines*	co-HEE-nays

customs	*aduana*	ah-DWAH-nah
damage	*daño*	DAHN-yos
depth	*hondura*	own-DOOR-ah
diesel	*gasoil*	gas-OIL
dinghy	*lanchita*	lan-CHEE-tah
dinghy dock	*muellecito*	mwaye-yea-SEE-toh
dock	*muelle*	MWAYE-yea
documentation	*documentación*	dock-oo-main-tah-see-OWN
dolphin fish	*dorado*	doh-RAH-dough
draft	*calado*	kah-LAH-dough
eggs	*huevos*	WAY-vos
electric	*electrico*	aye-LAKE-tree-ko
electrician	*electricista*	aye-lake-tree-SEE-stah
engine	*motor*	mo-TORE
exhaust	*escape*	ace-KAH-pay
eye	*ojo*	OH-ho
eyebolt	*tornillo de ojo*	tor-KNEE-yo day OH-ho
fathometer	*sonda*	SOHN-dah
fees	*derechos*	day-ray-chose
fender	*defensa*	day-FAIN-sah
fiberglass	*fibra de vidrio*	FEE-bra day VEE-dree-oh
fins, swim-	*chapuletas*	chap-oo-LATE-ahs
flag	*bandera*	bahn-DAY-rah
flashlight	*linterna*	leen-TAIR-nah
floor	*suelo*	SWAY-low
fresh water	*agua dulce*	AH-gwah DOOL-say
front	*frente*	FRAIN-taye
funnel	*embudo*	aim-BOO-dough
fuse	*fusible*	foo-SEE-blaye
garbage	*basura*	bah-SOO-rah
gas, natural	*butano*	boo-TAH-no
gasket	*junta*	HOON-tah
gasoline	*gasolina*	gas-oh-LEE-nah
gauge	*medidor*	may-dee-DOOR
generator	*generador*	hey-nay-rah-DOOR
glue	*pegamento*	pay-gah-MAIN-toh
grapefruit	*toronjas*	tore-OWN-hahs
grease	*grasa*	GRAH-sah
grouper	*mero*	MAY-roh
guns	*armas*	ARM-ahs
hammer	*matillo*	mah-TEE-yo
harbor	*puerto*	PWAIR-to
harbormaster	*capitán de puerto*	kah-pee-TAHN day PWAIR-to
hardware store	*ferreteria*	fair-ray-tah-REE-ah
head (motor)	*cabeza*	kah-BAY-tsah
head (toilet)	*inodoro*	een-oh-DOOR-oh
heat	*calor*	kah-LORE
heat exchanger	*enfriadór*	ain-free-ah-DOOR

hill	*loma*	LOH-mah
hose	*mangera*	mahn-GAIR-ah
hull	*casco*	kah-skoh
hurricane	*ciclón,*	see-CLONE,
also....	*hurracán*	oor-roo-KAHN
ice	*hielo*	ee-AYE-loh
impeller	*impeledór*	eem-PAY-lay-DOOR
injectors	*inyectores*	een-jake-TORE-ace
insurance	*seguros*	say-GOO-ros
iron	*hierro*	ee-AIR-roh
jack	*gato*	GAH-toh
juice	*jugo*	HOO-goh
kerosene	*kerosena,*	kay-roh-SEE-nah,
also....	*gaz*	GAZ
knot	*nudo*	NOO-dough
l.o.a.	*eslora*	ace-LORE-ah
laundry-place	*lavandaria*	la-VAHN-dah-REE-ah
laundry-clothes	*ropas sucias*	ROPE-ahs SOOj-see-ahs
left	*izquierda*	ees-key-AIR-dah
license	*licensia*	lee-SANE-see-ah
liferaft/vest	*salvavida*	sal-vah-VEE-dah
lighthouse	*faro*	FAH-roh
lights	*luces*	LOOSE-ace
limes	*limónes*	lee-MOAN-ace
line	*linea*	LEE-nay-ah
list	*lista*	LEASE-tah
lockwasher	*arandela de muelle*	ah-rahn-DAY-lah day MWAYE-yea
margarine	*margerina*	mar-hair-EE-nah
marmelade	*mermelada*	MAIR-may-LAH-dah
mask, swim-	*alcafondra*	ahl-kah-FOND-rah
mast	*palo, mastil*	PAH-loh, mah-STEEL
mayonaise	*mayonesa*	my-oh-NAY-sah
meal	*comida*	comb-EE-dah
mechanic	*mecánico*	may-KAHN-ee-Koh
metric	*metrico*	MAY-tree-koh
miles	*millas*	ME-yahs
milk	*leche*	LAYE-chaye
mountain	*montaña*	moan-TAHN-yah
mountain range	*cordillera*	core-dee-YAIR-ah
nail	*clavo*	CLAH-voh
nut (hex)	*tuerca*	TWER-kah
oars r	*emos*	RAY-mos
oil	*aceite*	ah-say-EE-taye
oranges	*naranjas*	nar-AHN-hahs
outboard	*fuera borda*	FWAYE-rah BOOR-dah
packing	*empaque*	aim-PAH-kaye
paint	*pintura*	peen-TOO-rah
paintbrush	*brocha*	BROH-chah

parts (spare)	*repuestas*	ray-PWAYE-stahs
peanuts	*maní*	mah-KNEE
pear	*pera*	PAY-rah
pineapple	*piña*	PEE-nyah
pipe	*tubo*	TOO-boh
pistons	*pistones*	pee-STONE-ace
plantains	*plátanos*	PLAH-tah-nos
pliers	*alicates*	ah-lee-KAH-tace
porpoise	*delfín*	dale-FEEN
pressure	*presión*	pray-see-OWN
propane	*propano*	pro-PAH-no
propeller	*hélice*	AYE-lee-say
pump	*bomba*	BOHM-bah
registration	*matriculación*	mah-TREE-koo-Lah-see-OWN
repair	*reparación*	RAYE-pah-RAH-see-OWN
replacement	*repuesta*	raye-PWAYE-stah
resin	*resina*	raye-SEE-nah
regulator	*reguladór*	raye-goo-lah-DOOR
rigging	*járcia*	HAR-see-ah
right	*derecha*	day-RAY-chah
rings	*aníllos*	ah-KNEE-yos
rope	*soga*	SO-gah
rubber	*goma*	GO-mah
rudder	*oja de timón*	OH-ha day tee-MOAN
rust	*óxido*	OAK-see-dough
sail	*vela*	VAYE-lah
sailboat	*velero*	vaye-LAIR-oh
sailcloth	*tela de vela*	TAYE-lah day VAYE-lah
sandpaper	*papél lija*	pah-PAIL LEE-hah
sauce	*salsa*	SAHL-sah
saw	*serrucho*	say-ROO-cho
screw (bolt)	*tornillo maquina*	tore-KNEE-yo MAH-key-nah
screw (wood)	*tornillo madera*	tore-KNEE-yo mah-DAY-rah
screwdriver	*destorneador*	day-STORE-nay- ah-DOOR
scrubbrush	*cepillo*	say-PEE-yo
seacock	llave de toma	YAH-vaye day TOH-mah
seal	*sello*	SAY-yoh
seas	*oleaje*	oh-lay-AH-hey
seasick	*mareado*	mah-ray-AH-dough
seawater	*agua salada*	AH-gwah sah-LAH-dah
shackle	*grillete*	gree-YAYE-taye
shaft	*éje*	AYE-hey
shell	*caracól*	car-ah-COAL
ship	*barco*	BAR-coh
shower	*ducha*	DOO-chah
showers	*aquaceros*	AH-gwah-SAY-ros
shrimp	*camarones*	kah-mah-ROAN-ace
side	*lado*	LAH-dough

smoke	*humo*	OO-moh
snapper	*chillo*	CHEE-yo
soup	*sopa*	SO-pah
sparkplug	*bujía*	boo-HEE-ah
spring	=	ace-SPRING
stainless	*inoxidable*	een-ox-ee-DAH-blaye
stainless (PR)	=	ace-STAIN-less
starboard	*estribor*	ace-tree-BOOR
starter motor	*motór de arranque*	mo-TORE day ah-RAHN-kaye
stay	*soporte de mastíl*	so-PORE-taye day mah-STEEL
steel	*acero*	ah-SAY-roh
stern	*popa*	POPE-ah
storm	*tormenta*	tore-MAIN-tah
straight	*derecho*	day-RAY-choh
strainer	*coladór*	coal-ah-DOOR
street	*calle*	KAH-yaye
stuffing box	*prense*	PRAIN-say
swells	*oleadas*	oh-lay-AH-dahs
switch	*suiche*	SWEET-chaye
tank	*tanque*	TANG-kaye
tape	=	TAYE-pee
tax	*impuesto*	eem-PWAYE-stow
telephone call	*llamada*	yah-MAH-dah
temperature	*temperatura*	taim-pair-ah-TOOR-ah
thermostat	*termostato*	tair-moh-STAH-toh
thinner	*tinner*	TEEN-air
thread (string)	*hilo*	EEL-oh
threads (screw) *roscas*	ROH-skahs	
through-hull	*toma*	TOE-mah
tiller	*timón*	tee-MOAN
time	*tiempo*	tee-AIM-poh
tip	*propina*	pro-PEE-nah
tomato	*tomate*	toh-MAH-taye
tools	*herramientas*	air-rah-mee-AIN-tos
top	*parte arriba*	PART-taye ah-REE-bah
transducer	*cebolla*	say-BOY-yah
transmission	*transmisión*	trahns-me-see-OWN
tropical	*tropical*	troh-Pay-KAHL
tropical storm	*tormenta*	tore-MAIN-tah
tropical wave	*onda tropical*	OWN-dah troh-pay-KAHL
turnbuckle	*torniquete*	tore-knee-KAY-taye
two-stroke oil	*aceite dos tiempo*	ah-say-EE-taye dose tee-AIM-poh
valve	*valvula*	VALVE-you-lah
vanilla	=	vahn-EE-yah
varnish	*barníz*	barn-EES
Vee-belt	*banda*	BAHN-dah
vegetables	*vegetales*	vaye-hay-TAHL-ace
volts	*vóltios*	VOLT-ee-os

washer	*arandela*	ah-rahn-DAY-lah
water	*agua*	AH-gwah
watts	*vátios*	VAHT-ee-os
waves	*olas*	OH-las
welding	*soldadura*	sold-ah-DOOR-ah
wheel	*rueda*	roo-AYE-dah
wing nut	*tuerca mariposa*	TWER-kah mar-ee-POSE-ah
wire	*alambre*	ahl-AHM-braye
wood	*madera*	mah-DAY-rah
work	*trabajo*	trah-BAH-ho
wrench	*llave*	YAH-vaye
yacht	*yate*	YAH-taye
zincs	*zinc*	TSINK

VERBS

To talk movie-Indian Spanish, forget the finer distinctions. For instance, use "need" for both "need" and "want". Use "go" for all of the go's, such as come, walk, ride, fly and so forth. The only pronoun you really need is the English "Me", the most important, after all. Everyone else can be identified by pointing a finger.

Just about all of the operable verbs for a *gringo* [GREEN-goh] needing help are below. To use a verb, piece together the words above, in backwards order with lots of *de*'s [DAYs] thrown in, and stick a verb on the front. Thus: "BOO-kah tore-KNEE-yo day kah-BAY-tsah day moh-TOR" means, "me look-um for motor head bolt". Don't laugh. It works. If you want to talk better Spanish then learn their 24 (mostly irregular) verb forms. The guy behind the counter is so used to the dumb tricks of *gringos* that he won't blink an eye, but he *will* hand you the bolt. Here are some verbs for the intermediate student:

buy	*compra*	COMB-prah
do, make	*hace*	AH-say
eat	*come*	COMB-aye
find	*consigue*	cone-SEE-gay
go	*va*	VAH
have	*tiene*	tee-AYE-nay
leave	*sale*	SAHL-aye
listen	*oye*	OH-jay
look	*mira*	MEE-rah
look for	*busca*	BOO-skah
need	*necessita*	nay-say-SEE-tah
rent	*renta*	RAIN-tah
repair	*repara*	ray-PAR-ah
sell	*vende*	VAIN-day
sleep	*duerme*	DWAIR-may
talk	*habla*	AH-blah
work	*trabaja*	tra-BAH-hah

You may have noticed the "being" verbs are not included. To use the complex "being" verbs in Spanish can be an art. Better just to not use them. Or just say *es* [ACE], anywhere you want to have "is", "was", "will be" or "might could have been". ACE is great.

NUMBERS

Unlike adjectives, Spanish puts numbers in front of the word they numberfy to make it easy for *gringos*. One *gringo*: *uno gringo*. Two *gringos*: *dos gringos*. And so it goes. Now count to a Zillion *gringos*.

zero	*cero*	SAIR-oh
one	*uno*	OO-noh
two	*dos*	DOSE
three	*tres*	TRACE
four	*cuatro*	QUAH-troh
five	*cinco*	SINK-oh
six	*seís*	SAY-ees
seven	*siete*	see-AYE-taye
eight	*ocho*	OH-cho
nine	*nueve*	NWAYE-vaye
ten	*diéz*	dee-ACE
eleven	*once*	OWN-say
twelve	*doce*	DOSE-say
thirteen	*trece*	TRAY-say
fourteen	*catorce*	kah-TORE-say
fifteen	*quince*	KEEN-say
sixteen	*diéz y seís*	dee-ACE ee SAY-ees
seventeen	*diéz y siete*	dee-ACE ee see-AYE-taye
eighteen	*diéz y ocho*	dee-ACE ee OH-cho
nineteen	*diéz y nueve*	dee-ACE ee NWAYE-vaye
twenty	*veinte*	VAIN-taye
twenty-one	*veinte uno*	VAIN-taye OO-noh etc.
thirty	*treinta*	TRAIN-tah fourty
forty	*cuarenta*	quar-AIN-tah
fifty	*cincuenta*	seen-QUAINT-ah
sixty	*sesenta*	say-SANE-tah
seventy	*setenta*	say-TAIN-tah
eighty	*ochenta*	oh-CHAIN-tah
ninety	*noventa*	no-VAIN-tah
one hundred	*ciento*	see-AIN-toh
two hundred	*dos cientos*	DOSE see-AIN-tos
thousand	*mil*	MEAL
million	*millón*	me-YONE

For example, 1989: *mil novecientos ochenta nueve*.

You can now say you're looking for <u>two</u> motor headbolts: BOO-kah DOSE tore-KNEE-yo day kah-BAY-tsah day moh-TOR" — and you don't have to go shopping twice to get them!

269

MODIFIERS

If you must modify a noun, do so by putting the modifiers in backwards order but without all the *de* [DAY] stuff you put between the nouns when you strung them together. Thus "two big black motor head bolts" is "two bolts of head of motor black big", or, BOO-kah DOSE tore-KNEE-yo day kah-BAY-tsah day moh-TOR GRAHN-day NAYE-grow.

And just like in English, let everyone guess if it's the motor or the bolts which is big and black or is it a combination of both.

COLORS

black	*negro*	NAYE-grow
blue	*azúl*	ah-TSOOL
brown	*marrón*	mar-ROAN
green	*verde*	VAIR-day
grey	*gris*	GREASE
orange	*naranja*	nah-RAHN-hah
pink	*rosado*	rosa-AH-dough
red	*rojo*	ROH-hoh
white	*blanco*	BLANK-oh
yellow	*amarillo*	ah-mah-REE-yo

ADJECTIVES AND ADVERBS

big	*grande*	GRAHN-day
broken	*roto*	ROH-toh
cheap (thing)	*barato*	bah-RAH-toh
clean	*limpio*	LEEM-pee-oh
closed	*cerrado*	say-RAH-dough
cold	*frio*	FREE-oh
deep	*hondo*	OWN-dough
different	*diferente*	dee-faye-RAIN-taye
dirty	*sucio*	SOO-see-oh
down	*abajo*	ah-BAH-ho
dry	*seco*	SAY-koh
electrical	*electrico*	aye-LAKE-tree-ko
expensive	*caro*	CAR-roh
fast	*rapido*	RAH-pee-dough
fine	*fino*	FEE-noh
fixed-repaired	*reparado*	ray-pah-RAH-dough
fixed-unmoving	*fijado*	fee-HAH-dough
galvanized	*galvanizado*	gal-van-ee-SAH-dough
heated	*calientado*	kah-lee-ain-TAH-dough
heavy	*pesado*	pay-SAH-dough
high	*alto*	AHL-toh
hot	*caliente*	kah-lee-AIN-taye
less	*menos*	MAY-nose

270

light	*ligero*	lee-HAIR-oh
littleno	*mucho*	NO MOO-cho
long	*largo*	LAHR-go
loose	*flojo*	FLOW-ho
low	*bajo*	BAH-ho
more	*mas*	MAS
open	*abierto*	ah-bee-AIR-toh
portside	*babor*	bah-BOOR
same	*mismo*	MEESE-moh
self-tapping	*autorroscante*	ow-toe-ros-KAHN-taye
shallow	*bajita*	bah-HEE-tah
slow	*despacio*	day-SPAH-see-oh
small	*pequeño*	pay-CAIN-yo
thick	*grueso*	grew-ACE-oh
thin	*delgado*	dell-GAH-dough
tight	*apretado*	ah-pray-TAH-dough
up	*arriba*	ah-REE-bah
wet	*mojado*	moh-HAH-dough
wide	*hancho*	AHN-cho

PAST AND FUTURE

Movie Indians conjugate their verbs by modifying them with a word like "yesterday". Thus "Me need'um head bolt yesterday. Today need'um band-aid". So, say anything you want in present tense and add from the following list:

today	*hoy*	OY
tomorrow	*mañana*	mah-NYAH-nah
yesterday	*ayer*	ah-JAIR
last night	*anoche*	ah-NO-chaye
day before yesterday	*ante* ayer	auntie ah-JAIR
...days ago	*hace.....dias*	AH-say.....DEE-ahs
...weeks ago	*...semanas*	" ...say-MAH-nahs
...monthsago	*...meses*	" ...MACE-ace
...years ago	*...años*	" ...AHN-yos
next week	*proxima semana*	PROHKS-ee-mah say-MAH-nah
next month	*proximo mes*	PROHKS-ee-moh MACE
next year	*proximo año*	PROHKS-ee-moh AHN-yo

PREPOSITIONS

These are the condiments the advanced students will sprinkle onto their crude sentences in order to throw the hearer off the track. Proper use requires years of practice.

after	*después* de	days-PWACE day
before	*antes* de	AHNT-ace day
between	*entre*	AIN-tray
by	*por*	PORE
to	*á*	AH

for	*para*	PAH-rah
from	*de*	DAY
in	*en*	AIN
inside	*dentro de*	DAIN-troh day
of	*de*	DAY
on	*en*	AIN
under	*abajo de*	ah-BAH-ho day
with	*con*	CONE
without	*sin*	SEEN

PRONOUNS

Finally, for the black belters, peppering a fancy construction with pronouns will ensure confusion but impress the dickens out of fellow yachties. These are the advanced student's tools with which to make clear that which was better off left vague. When instead of a big, black head bolt for your motor, the guy behind the counter hands you two tickets to the cock fights, if you are a real black belt student you say, *grácias*, and thread your way through the throng of thunderstruck fellow boaters with a satisfied grin and just the hint of a swagger. You can get the headbolts tomorrow; today go to the cockfights.

Once again, this short list of pronouns is only to enable you to rapidly employ a pidgin Spanish which works, not to speak properly.

Now you're able to say "ME look'um for 2 big black motor head bolts FROM THEM TOMORROW". Or,

ME BOO-kah DOSE tore-KNEE-yo day kah-BAY-tsah day moh-TOR GRAHN-day NAYE-grow DAY AYE-yos mah-NYAH-nah.

I	*yo*	JOE
you	*tu*	TOO
he	*él*	AYEL
she	*ella*	AYE-ya
it	*lo*	LOW
we	*nosotros*	no-SO-tros
you all	*ustedes*	oo-STAID-ace
they, them	*ellos*	AYE-yos
this	*esto*	ACE-tos
that	*eso*	ACE-oh
each	*cada*	KAH-dah
which	*cual*	QUAL
something	*algo*	AHL-go
nothing	*nada*	NAH-dah
other,another	*otro*	OH-troh
any, -thing, -body	*cualquier*	qual-key-AIR
all, everybody -thing, -one	*todo*	TOE-dough
none,nobody, no one	*ninguno*	neen-GOO-noh
some, -body, -one	*alguién*	ahl-kee-AIN

QUESTIONS

Questions are best asked as statements with lots of body language, helpless expressions and the voice turned up in pitch toward the end, even panicky, as in

DOAN-day me BOAT-aye?!

for "Where's my boat?!" A very important question if it's gone.

You can also make up a declarative sentence as shown above and slap any one of the following words on the front to have a neat question to go to town with:

how	como	KO-moh
how	much cuanto	QUAN-toh
when	cuando	QUAN-dough
where	donde	DOAN-day
who	quién	key-AIN
why	porqué	pore-KAY

But beware of asking why or how. You may get a torrent of rapid Spanish. Also, beware to phrase your questions bluntly in movie-indian talk. For instance, "I wonder if you could tell me where I might find oil pressure transducers for sale?" becomes "Where sell oil pressure transducers?" or:

DOAN-day VAIN-day say-BOY-yah day pray-see-OWN day ah-say-EE-taye?

— accompanied by a lot of shrugs and wiggling of the eyebrows. Other questions are:

What is it?	Que es eso?	KAY ACE ACE-oh
What's it/he/she called?	Como se llama?	KO-moh say YAH-mah?
What time is it?	Que hora es?	KAY OR-ah ACE?
At what time?	A que hora?	AH KAY OR-ah?
How far?	Que lejos?	KAY LAY-hos?
Where is it/he/she?	A donde está?	AH DOAN-day ace-TAH?
What's it cost?	Cuanto cuesta?	QUAN-toh KWAYE-stah?
How do I get there?	Como llegaré?	KO-moh yaye-gar-RAY?
Can you help me?	Puede ayudarme?	PWAY-day ah-you-DAHR-may?
How do you say...?	Como se dice..?	KO-moh say DEE-say...?
What do you mean? What does it mean?	Que quiere decir? "	KAY key-AIR-aye day-SEER? "

APPENDIX B: WHEN YOU CAN'T GET FORECASTS

STORM STRENGTH AND DIRECTION

If caught out without radio reception, or you just plain want to check on the old **NWS**, you may consider playing with the following rules to guess at the bearing, strength, direction and arrival time of a storm or hurricane.

— you will first notice appearance of a long swell, mean period of 2 to 5 per minute (normal is 10-15 per minute)

—if there is a clockwise change in swell direction, the storm will pass from left to right

— if there is an anti-clockwise change in swell direction, it will pass you right to left

— swells travel from 2 to 3 times faster than the storm travels

— to find the velocity of the swell in knots, take 60% of the ratio of the crest-to-crest length of the swell, in feet, to the swell's period expressed in seconds

$$\text{Swell Knots} = \frac{0.6 \times \text{Length}}{\text{Period}}$$

— swell height is reduced by one third for every **X** miles traveled, where **X** is the crest-to-crest length of the swell in feet, or:

Observed Height = 67% of the Height **X** miles away.

— To find the center of the storm add 115° to the present wind direction.

Direction changes in the sustained wind should be handled as follows:

— if the wind **veers** you are in the dangerous semicircle: you should *put the wind on the starboard bow*

— if the wind **backs** you are in the navigable semicircle: you should *put the wind on the starboard quarter*

— if a steady but *increasing* wind, you are in the path: you should *put the wind aft of the starboard quarter* and pass out prayer books.

STORM PATH

It is possible to make a fairly accurate guess as to storm path knowing its present bearing, its bearing at the time of promulgating the swell and the velocity of the swell.

For example, at 1200 you observe a swell from the south and you estimate the swell to be 200 yards long at 4 per minute. (200 yards are 600 feet.) This means the swell's velocity is 0.6x600/15=24 knots. Therefore, the storm is moving about 10 knots, or one half to one third as fast as the swell. If you also observe the wind is east while the swell is south, then you know the storm lies along a bearing of 90°+115°, or 205° from your position.

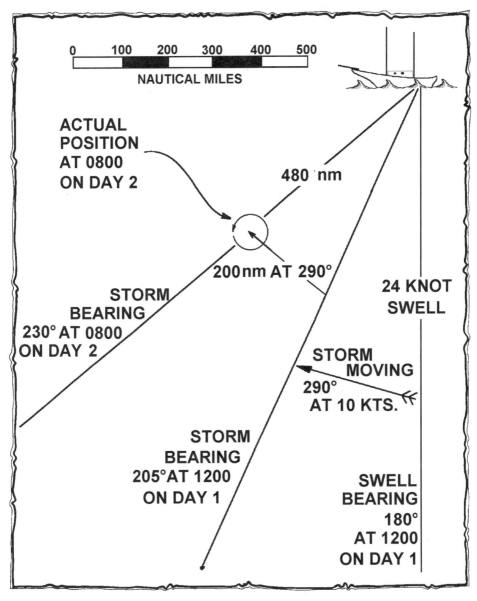

0   100   200   300   400   500
NAUTICAL MILES

ACTUAL
POSITION
AT 0800
ON DAY 2

480 nm

200 nm AT 290°

STORM
BEARING
230° AT 0800
ON DAY 2

24 KNOT
SWELL

STORM
MOVING
290°
AT 10 KTS.

STORM
BEARING
205° AT 1200
ON DAY 1

SWELL
BEARING
180°
AT 1200
ON DAY 1

Storm Location, Track and Severity

Refer to the figure for the following discussion. Lay off a swell vector of 24 knots with its head on your present position. Lay off the storm's bearing of 205°. Make a storm track vector of 10 knots with its head on a line of the storm's bearing. "Slide" the storm track vector's head on the storm's bearing until you can connect the tail with the tail of the swell vector. Adjust vector and bearing until you get a fit. You now have a guess at the current heading of the storm, and you have an idea as to its bearing and velocity at 1200. In the example, the swell is moving 360° at 24 knots. Therefore, the storm, which is moving at 10 knots, will be shown to be moving in a direction of 290°.

STORM SEVERITY

What can you guess about the storm's intensity? Let's say the swell you observe has a mean height of about 10 feet. Since the swell has a 600 foot length, you know that 600 nautical miles down the swell's bearing the swell had been 15 feet, or half again higher than now, having lost one third of its height enroute. If, indeed, the swell traveled that far.

The force of the storm can be estimated by projecting the swell height back to its incidence. That is, you interpolate the original swell height at various distances off for the storm, then look at the **Beaufort** Scale to arrive at various storm forces for each assumed distance off.

For instance, if you assume the tails of the swell and storm vectors connect at a point 400 miles away then the original size of the swells, roughly speaking, would have to have been higher than they are now by 4 sixths of the 600 mile loss of 5 feet. That is, $10+(15-10)x(400/600)=13.3$ feet. You will see the storm would have to have had a sustained strength of Force 7, and that would have been 17 hours ago (400 miles/24 knots).

LOCATING THE STORM CENTER

The actual location of the storm is available through combining the results of two observations. Let's say that next day at 0800, 20 hours after the first observation, you see that the swell now comes from somewhere between 200° and 210° and the wind has veered two points (22.5°) to between 110° and 115° . This makes the storm's present bearing 115°+115°, or 230°.

Since you think the storm was traveling 290° at 10 knots you also know it covered 200 nautical miles during those 20 hours (Distance = Velocity x Time). There is only one spot on your chart where your dividers, spaced on the scale to 200 miles and set along a 290 degree line, will rest its points on the 205 and 230 degree lines radiating from your position. One point will be where the storm is now, at 230°, and the other will show where the storm was 20 hours ago, at 205°. You now know the storm is roughly 480 miles to the southwest traveling at 10 knots toward the west northwest and blowing Force 7 because it is producing 10+5x480/600, or 14 foot waves.

Whatever **Force Beaufort** you estimate, remember that gusts in a severe storm can be 30% to 50% higher than the sustained winds. That means that even a baby 'cane (64 knots) can have gusts up to 96 knots.

If all the above discussion ruins your complacency, good! You are now ready to cruise!

WHAT TO WATCH FOR

Squall lines and cumulonimbus may sweep your area. These and their high altitude cirrocumulus forerunners are "feeder bands", sometimes hundreds of miles in length, spiraling into the storm's center. If you are directly in the storm's path, there's no mistaking it's approach. The onslaught of the center of a major storm, or hurricane, will be heralded by the *bar*: a long, low, intensely black area topped by dark and chaotic cumulonimbus and with torn patches of black stratocumulus scudding in front. Prepare for the wind to gradually double in strength. If in the calm of the eye, prepare for the winds to strike from the opposite direction with sudden maximum force within a half hour. The "wall" will be frighteningly apparent in its approach.

APPENDIX C: FISHING

A plethora of pamphlets, books, fish identi-kits and even dowsing tools are available to anyone stopping at a gas dock or bait and tackle shop. Useful and serious information can be had in a good marine bookstore such as *Bluewater Books & Charts* in Fort Lauderdale (1-800-942-2583). In keeping with the rest of *The Gentleman's Guide to Passages South*, I will only give you here the information which strikes me as unique to the hard core cruiser and generally unavailable elsewhere.

I am indebted to my good friend and mentor, Bob Cockerham of *Moon Lady*, a beautifully maintained clipper ketch. Bob, known as "Grouper Bob" to Bahamians, has long experience fishing in the southern Bahamas. Some of his rules are:

— First you have to decide if you're fishing for fun or you're fishing to feed yourself — hunger catches more fish than diversion.

— You can't catch fish without a hook in the water. Hook time catches more fish than fancy lures or luck ever did.

— Don't listen to the crybabies who complain the world is all fished out — the fish are where you find them.

SKIN DIVING

Fishing underwater is primarily a hunting expedition. To hunt, you have to take time. You have to watch the fish and learn their habits. You have to let them get used to your presence. If you missed a shot and spooked the fish, you have to give them time to get unspooked. All that adds up to time with you in the water just like hook fishing requires lots of time with the hook in the water. Wear a wet suit, even in the summer.

Some fish have skins which are extremely hard to penetrate with a spear. Before starting out make sure your spear tips are freshly sharpened. Coral rock will dull even your stainless points. Use a sharpening stone to shape a triangular point. Always the same triangle.

Good tasting fish like grouper and snapper are usually under something. Sometimes you can spear them through a hole above, like a skylight to their living room. More often than not you have to get them through a side door down near the bottom. If they run into one door expect them to leave from another when they're ready. If they go around a rock, creep over the top and be prepared to shoot down on them. With time in the water you will observe and learn their habits and you can anticipate their response to your shots.

Only with many shots can you become good at it, so shoot lots. If you can't get that fat grouper you've been chasing and you're close to hypothermia, shoot a couple of small grunts or a trusting trigger fish. You should always come home with bait at least. If you're a novice at spear fishing you will be surprised to learn that you need to be very close to the fish to hit them. The tip of your spear should generally be no farther than two feet from your prey. Certainly this is true of a pole spear or a Hawaiian Sling.

For coral fungus that won't heal, though it may not be in your spice rack, try monosodium glutamate (MSG).

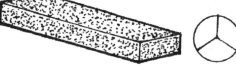

USE A FLAT SHARPENING STONE

**MAKE A TRIANGULAR POINT
- SAME FLATS EVERY TIME**

Sharpening Spear Points

For lobster, conch and whelk, swim low along the undercut shore ledges when the sunlight slants in under the ledge and lights it all up. For lobster around rocks and coral heads, swim with your cheek on the sand, looking into every crevice and hole. Wear gloves to protect yourself against skin reactions to various corals when you pull yourself along by grasping rocks.

The good eating, such as grouper, snapper and lobster, isn't always around coral heads, rocks and ledges. Often enough you will see sizable grouper playing 'possum in the branches of a bush while lobster are hidden in the roots. When all the jocks go roaring off in their Zodiac Grand Raids to dive the forty feet on the windward side because the harbor is "all fished out", leisurely peruse your own anchorage and be ready for surprises. The anchorages are precisely the places where no one fishes and yet they are just the places where fish thrive due to the edible detritus falling from the boats above. This assumes a clean anchorage with good flow.

Take a catch immediately to the surface. Hold the thrashing animal still with both hands, or hold it above the surface of the water, until it is safely in the dinghy which is always nearby. Shark and barracuda, unjustly blamed for mythical mayhem to swimmers, cannot be held responsible for instinctual behavior. Especially the barracuda. The barracuda in the Bahamas and on the reefs of the Caribbean is a territorial garbage collector. It's his reef and when something dies and goes through the vibrations of extremis, the barracuda has the task of darting in and cleaning it up. You can get away with letting your dying catch slide down the spear and rest against your fist and never have an incident. But with low luck your catch will someday be met by a set of flying teeth which may, wholly unintended, carry away a few knuckles. Let the fish trail away from you until it's clear of the water.

A pleasant way to fish a reef and ensure that the dinghy is always handy is to have the dinghy painter in hand. Or preferably, tow it around with the anchor and chain looped around one arm. When you see something interesting plant the anchor noiselessly and pursue your pleasure. It is especially rewarding to fish the seaward reefs this way as, for example, at Rum Cay. Wait for slack low tide plus one hour. Then ride the tide back into harbor with dinghy in hand. The reef community will all be up to meet the incoming nutrients from Mother Ocean with their mouths agape, and won't they be surprised to see you and your spear instead.

For cracked lips, try Preparation-H . . . but keep two separate tubes on hand!

TROLLING

When you have fed all your expensive lures to the lure monster, try making your own for free. The corner of a plastic garbage bag with appropriate slits can make an excellent squid, or skirt, lure. So does a small tube of Prell Shampoo Concentrate. Do you remember how to make those little yarn dolls that you hung on the Christmas tree when you were a kid? Make one out of the yarns from an old piece of nylon 3-strand rope. Wind the head of the doll around a 3 ounce oval lead and leave off the arms.

You don't need fancy equipment. The plastic doughnuts, or yo-yos, are great. Instead of a drag to alarm you to a bite, or more likely, seaweed, put a bight of the line through a clothespin spring and then around the clothespin. Then clamp the clothespin to a stay with a couple of yards of slack line behind it.

Use stainless clamps to clamp an old reel to the pushpit. Surprisingly, you can get many years of maintenance free operation out of an old reel exposed continuously to salt and sun.

Use 80 to 100 or more pounds test line. Have lots of large swivels and use lots of heavy stainless leader and big hooks. Run a line on each side of the boat. Four, if you like. Two short and skipping, two long and deep. Don't make sharp turns with the boat, though.

Now tend those lines. Keep them free of seaweed — a frustrating and monotonous task. People who complain they never catch any fish usually wait until they're in open sea before they put out a single puny line. Then they tow seaweed around and reel it in when they first sight their landfall.

Have your lines (plural) out while going through cuts or entering and leaving harbors. If you get a strike while going through a cut, ignore it, of course, and tend to your boat first. When you do reel in your catch it'll probably be drowned, saving you the trouble of dispatching it. Tending lines first and boat second was the cause of the death of a Newporter Ketch in **Conch Cay Cut** at **Georgetown** one year.

Fishing the Shoals and Heads

Many places it is possible to dip your lure right into fish living rooms. For example, between **Black Rocks** and **Forbes Hill**, trail a line for grouper and wigwag your way around the shoals, dipping the lure onto them. To dip your lures onto heads and shoals have about eighty yards of line out. Maneuver the boat, or use the wind, to get the lure over your target. Now put slack in the line by turning upwind or by putting the helm hard over in both directions several times to lose way. When the line drops almost to the bottom, fill sail and run away with the lure.

With practice you can dip and spiral a lure several times on one cluster of heads. The blue trench along the sandy bar east of White Cay has good trolling. Also, traveling the bar keeps you clear of the sand bores to the north. When you leave the banks headed north and are in blue water making for **Calabash Bay**, trail and dip your lures the same way over the deep heads a mile southwest of Calabash before turning through the reef for the night.

BOTTOM FISHING

Save the cadavers for bait after cleaning your fish. Swap your lure leader for a leader with bare hook and bury it in a fist size, or larger, hunk of bait. Before your second **SG&T**, walk to the bow with the baited line. Using large coils, hold a good boat length of line in one hand and, with the other, swing the baited hook in wide circles. Let go of the whole mess and the wind should bring it back to a boat length off your beam where the bait will rest on the bottom.

Sometime between your second SG&T and four in the morning your drag will go off like a siren. Nocturnal types, like grouper and snapper are out at this time grazing the anchorage. Sometimes you'll get a shark, sometimes a ray, but more often than not it will be a sizable, good eating bottom fish.

A GOOD FINISH

I lost many fish trying to board them until *Moon Lady* showed me how to stun the fish with rum. That was when rum was cheap. Now I use my "aftershave lotion", a squirt bottle of alcohol. If you still use the perfumed kind of aftershave, you can invest in a water pistol filled with alcohol. You shall need lots, so buy lots when the drugstores have sales. Squirt a goodly shot into the gills. This shall immediately stun the fish. Hit the other gill while he's out to ensure he stays out. Now board the fish without drama.

A humane and healthy way to sacrifice the fish, perhaps even a kosher way, is to dump all its blood, a vehicle for toxins, at one gush at the same time you sever its spinal column. If you don't use an axe, you'll have to have a sharp, large Bowie type knife. Insert the knife downward in the soft spot behind the dorsal edge of the gill, cutting edge up, and give it a good hard karate chop. Do the other side. The spinal cord should be cut and the blood dumped, all while the animal is out cold and lying still. Decapitate, slice from anus to head, clean out the guts, chop off the tail and fillet with a good boning knife. The head on bull dolphins has much meat, as do the jaws on a grouper. Keep the cat busy with the scraps, and bag other remnants for bottom fishing bait.

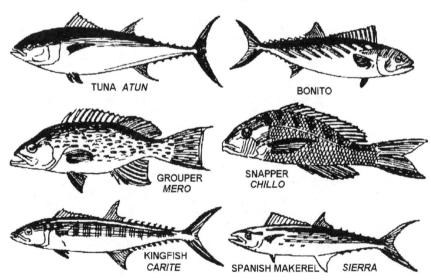

Good Eating Fish

APPENDIX D: EATING

WHAT TO DO WITH PLANTAINS

The answer is: *anything you would do with a potato*. But plantains don't taste for those of us not raised on them. Here's how to make them taste.

The simplest method is to wait until they're yellow. They then taste slightly banana flavored. Let them get black spots and they do taste like bananas. Let them turn black entirely and they are bananas but not rotten. Think of it this way: bananas mature (or rot) from the inside out while plantains mature from the outside in.

— To make excellent French fries, use a yellow plantain. If slicing disks instead of match sticks, slice thinner for more taste. Douse with good old salt and ketchup and go to it.

—To make *tostones* [toast-TONE-ace] slice up a plantain, or *platanos* [PLAH-tah-nose] in Spanish. Spread the slices into very hot grease, seasoned with garlic salt (and hot pepper if that's you're style) in the Puerto Rican style, turning them over and squashing them with a spoon when they're half done. Blot on paper and serve hot or cold with a dip, doused in ketchup or as is.

Again, use more mature plantains for more sweetness and slice thinner for more taste. Foreigners living in the Dominican Republic learn to like their plantains and are therefore called "plantainized", or *platanisado* [plah-tah-knee-SAH-doh].

LECHOSA BATIDA [PAPAYA MILKSHAKE]

Put in a blender:

2 cups cubed fruit	[16 oz]
2 tablespoons sugar	[1 oz]
quarter cup evaporated milk	[2 oz]
1 teaspoon vanilla	

— and blend until smooth.

— Dump in 2 cups chopped ice and blend *twice as long* as you think necessary to make it thick, smooth and ice-free.

— You may use any other fruit or melon. Zapote, the brown football shaped melon tastes just like strawberry. Pineapple (*piña*) or banana (*guineo*) are also delicious.

— You may substitute condensed milk for both the evaporated milk and sugar, or you may substitute milk powder for the evaporated milk.

— Properly made, a fruit *batida* is thicker and better tasting than any ice cream milkshake.

BLACK BEAN SOUP

For 12 ounces of dried black beans, or "turtle beans", use
    4 ounces ham bone,
    quarter cup olive oil,
    half cup wine vinegar,
    half a large onion,
    2 green peppers,
    1 crushed pod of garlic,
    1 bay leaf,
    1 quart of water,
    1/2 tablespoon salt.

Clean the beans and soak them overnight. Add all the ingredients but oil and vinegar and simmer covered for 3 hours, stirring occasionally. Add the oil and vinegar and simmer covered for one more hour.

Keep up the water level while boiling so you have a rich black soup. Ideally, the beans should be mostly disintegrating. But this comes from restocking a pot which is kept going all week and that isn't easy to do on a boat.

Serve over rice with side garnishes of finely chopped onion and green pepper.

For a quick method, stick everything all at once into a pressure cooker and cook for 75 minutes. For an even faster method, buy cans of black beans.

Spanish for black beans is *habichuelas negras* [ah-bitch-WAY-lahs NAY-grahs]. In Venezuela, *caraotas* [car-ah-OH-tas].

Buen provecho! [bwayne pro-VAYE-choh]

ENGLISH MUFFINS

For simple stove top English Muffins which keep without refrigeration, try the following recipe. It will make ten 2 and a half inch muffins.
    1 cup warm water
    1 tablespoon dry yeast
    1 teaspoon sugar (and honey if desired)
    2 teaspoons salt (or less)
    quarter cup liquid shortening
    3 cups flour (up to 1 cup may be whole wheat)

Sprinkle the yeast over the water in a large bowl and let sit a few minutes. Thoroughly combine the dry ingredients. Mix them gradually into the bowl with the water.

Roll out the dough to one third of an inch thickness. Cut it into 2 and a half inch circles and lay them on a surface sprinkled with cornmeal. Sprinkle the tops with cornmeal and allow the muffins to rise — about double in 2 hours.

"Bake" on a preheated griddle with medium flame until brown on both sides — about 5 to 7 minutes each side. Put away until ready to serve.

To serve, split with a fork and toast each half face down on a buttered griddle. These are as good as the Thomas' English Muffins made in America. Englishmen, by the way, don't know what they are.

BEER BREAD

For a tasty sourdough type of bread with no kneading necessary, try mixing:

1 can of warm beer with
3 cups of flour,
2 tablespoons baking powder and
3 tablespoons sugar (for the beer to eat)

Allow the dough to set up in a greased pan for 1 hour and bake until it looks done.

Add raisins, citrus, bananas and so on, to make it complex.

THORNTON'S GROUPER *AU VIN BLANC*

2 pounds fresh grouper fillet (must be fresh)
2 tablespoons olive oil
1/2 fresh garlic clove
8 oz mushroom slices
1/4 cup dry vermouth
1/4 cup evaporated milk
1 teaspoon dill weed

Sauté the mushrooms and paper thin garlic slices in one tablespoon olive oil. Lightly fry the fish fillets, covered, in one tablespoon olive oil mixed with dill until white all the way through. Turn the fillets several times.

Turn off the heat, add the vermouth and cover the fish.

Pour off the water from the mushrooms into water for rice.

When ready to serve, pour the wine and juices from the fish into the mushrooms and continue to *sauté*, agitating briskly with a fork while dripping in the milk. If the sauce is too thin, continue *sauteing* until thick as desired. Never thicken artificially.

Serve the fish with the sauce on the side.

MAUNY'S ROACH COOKIES

3 tbspns Boric Acid powder

1 tbspn flour

1 tbspn sugar

Mix to a paste with milk, form into little cockroach-sized cookies, and sun dry on paper. Feeds thousands when placed out of sight. Health nuts can use whole wheat flour.

APPENDIX E: ANCHOR AND GROUND TACKLE

In the section *Laying Anchor* there are several rules of thumb included in the examples of trouble free anchoring procedures for the Caribbean. Below are some facts gleaned from too many sources to be recounted. They are provided here for the reader who, like me, can't easily find the data compiled in one place.

These are my notes and calculations from which I make my purchasing decisions for my boat in the Caribbean. Were I in the south Pacific my ground tackle, like my dinghy, would be a result of different choices due to a different cruising environment. Like all statistics these numbers can tell different stories to please the tale teller.

You may be coming from the Chesapeake Bay or the Los Angeles area. Though capable of holding your 38 foot boat quite happily at home, a twelve pound Danforth Deepset and a half inch nylon rode with 6 feet of chain, as recommended by Danforth, will *not* suffice in the Caribbean. If the sun doesn't melt such thin rode then bottom chafe will surely set you adrift some night.

Use Danforth type anchors for coarse sand and mud bottoms. Heavy burying type anchors are better suited to grassy bottoms or hardpan, clay and shale. Both types of anchors can hook or wedge fast in rock and coral bottoms, but a heavy plow type will dislodge the easiest when you go to get it up in the morning, and it will have less chance of being bent if a you get caught in a high chop.

The following are pounds of cable tension necessary to drag different anchors when set with a 5:1 scope in soft mud before being well silted in (which could take weeks). Note that this is different from some "holding powers" which may imply breaking strengths of the gear. Multiply by 5 to obtain figures for hard sand.

WEIGHT OF ANCHOR IN POUNDS	10	20	30	40	50	60
BRUCE	110	180	230	280	330	370
CQR (plow)	160	250	330	400	470	530
DANFORTH TYPE	460	730	960	1160	1350	1500

Lbs. Cable Tension to Drag in Soft Mud at 5:1 Scope

Safe Working Loads for Ground Tackle

INCH DIAMETERS	1/4	5/16	3/8	7/16	1/2	5/8	3/4	7/8	1
BBB CHAIN '3B'		1700	2320	3160	4120	6300			
PROOF COIL 'G3'	125	1900	2650	3520	4500	6800			
HIGH TEST 'G4'	260	3900	5400	7200	9200				
STAINLESS CHAIN	200	2850	3550	4300					
GALV. FALSE LINKS	140	2000	2800	3720	4750	7250			
GALV. SHACKLES	100	1500	2000	3000	4000	6500			
STAINLESS SHACKLES	150	3000	4500	6000	7000	10000			
GALV. SWIVELS	850	1250	2250		3600	5200	7200		12500
STAINLESS SWIVELS	175	2750	4750		9250				
NYLON 3-STRAND		240	340	470	520	620	1380	1880	2460
DACRON BRAID		230	330	500	640	700	1600	2300	2800

Safe Working Loads (**SWL**) for chain is about 40% of the load under which chain links begin to elongate prior to breaking.

SWL of galvanized chain may be exceeded under shock load without permanent damage, but the chain should be replaced when elongation begins to occur. All galvanized chain will elongate up to 15% before breaking.

SWL of shackles and swivels should never be exceeded.

Proof Coil has been tested to 200% of **SWL**.

High Test chain is available which has from 2 to 3 times the **SWL** of **Proof Coil,** but the period between elongation and breaking of **High Test** chain is short compared to **Proof Coil** and **BBB**.

Ultimate Breaking Load (UBL) of **Proof Coil** and **BBB chains** are about 4 times the **SWL**.

UBL of **High Test** chain is about 3 times **SWL**.

UBL of **galvanized shackles** and **swivels** are up to 6 times their **SWL**.

UBL of **stainless shackles** and **swivels** are double their **SWL**.

Dacron Braid has no stretch and its **UBL** is up to 5 times the **SWL**.

Nylon 3-strand will stretch up to 33% and its **UBL** is up to 10 times the **SWL**, making it ideal anchor rode.

TYPE OF KNOT	% REDUCTION IN UBL
EYE SPLICE (4 tucks, 3 tapers, unfinished)	15
CLOVE HITCH	30
ROUND TURN and TWO HALF HITCHES	30
ROLLING HITCH	40
BOWLINE	50
OVERHAND KNOT	60
SQUARE KNOT, or REEF KNOT	60

Effect of Knots on Nylon Rode

The above values are the percentage reduction in **Ultimate Breaking Load (UBL)** in 3-strand nylon rope which is caused by using the indicated knots.

In addition, the strengths of nylon ropes are reduced by up to 15% while they are wet.

Wind Drag on a Yacht in a Class 1 Hurricane

		AFT COCKPIT				CENTER COCKPIT			
		SLOOP		KETCH or YAWL		SLOOP		KETCH or YAWL	
feet on deck	feet of water line	wind on the BOW	wind on the BEAM	wind on the BOW	wind on the BEAM	wind on the BOW	wind on the BEAM	wind on the BOW	wind on the BEAM
28	23	1080	2460	1550	3100	1150	2890	1610	3520
30	25	1240	2820	1760	3540	1310	1310	1830	4020
32	27	1400	3210	1980	4010	1490	3770	2070	4560
34	28	1560	3600	2200	4480	1660	4220	2300	5100
36	30	1750	4030	2450	5010	1860	4740	2560	5710
38	32	1940	4500	2710	5570	2070	5280	2840	6360
41	34	2240	5200	3110	6430	2380	6110	3260	7340
43	36	2460	5730	3410	7070	2620	6730	3570	8070
45	38	2700	6280	3720	7730	2870	7380	3900	8830

The table above shows pounds of drag exerted on various yacht configurations in 80 knots of wind. Wind is shown on the bow and on the beam while the yacht sheers. Spars, standing and running rigging are included as well as stanchions and lifelines. Sails are assumed to be furled on their booms while foresails are below. Hull streamlining efficiency assumed is 20% (30% is about maximum for a yacht). The data does not consider the effects of seas or shock loads while sheering: the yacht is assumed to be in a secure hurricane hole with no wave action.

As can be seen, the stress on a yacht's ground tackle is severe indeed. After yanking around with great shock loads each link of chain should be inspected for elongation. Rodes subjected to severe and prolonged stretching should be replaced. See also the table on the weakening effects of using various knots on your anchor rode.

Caribbean Yachting Charts

CARIBBEAN 1
Virgin Islands
St. Thomas to Sombrero
Dec. 1997   US $69

CARIBBEAN 3
Lee & Windward Islands
Guadeloupe to Martinique
Feb. 1997   US $69

CARIBBEAN 2
Leeward Islands
Anguilla to Antigua
Spring 1998   US $69

CARIBBEAN 4
Windward Islands
St. Lucia to Grenada
Sept. 1996   US $69

Area charts same scale — Based on WGS 84 — Waypointsystem — User friendly size
Each chart group includes: 1 Passage Chart • 6 Coastal Charts • Approaches

CRUISING GUIDE PUBLICATIONS
U.S. Distributor: P.O. Box 1017 • Dunedin, FL 34697-1017
(813) 733-5322 • 1-800-330-9542 • Fax (813) 734-8179
Email: cgp@earthlink.net

NOTES ABOUT . . .
...THE AUTHOR

An American refugee from an international career as a systems engineer, I lived aboard and cruised many years in the Baltic, the North Sea, English Channel and the Mediterranean, with stints in Asia and Central America. Since 1979 I have cruised the Caribbean islands between Florida and South America. I had formal training in Sweden and have an American master's certificate.

Over many years of shuttling between the Bahamas and my home ports in the Caribbean, I accumulated firm evidence of what works and what doesn't while slogging to windward among the islands. Out of that experience came a set of windward strategies to avoid mishap on what they used to call the **Thorny Path**. I have used these common sense techniques while bucking the equatorial currents and the trade winds on many windward passages, too many to count.

. . . AND PARTNERS . . .

I have surveyed every recommended anchorage many times each, sounding them with my long-keeled, 6 and a half-foot draft, 41 foot, 15 ton displacement ketch, *Jalan Jalan*. Her shy 37 shaft horsepower took her easily seven times the 1200 windward miles to South America, and several dozens of times between the Bahamas and the Virgins. Often I sailed single-handed, so it couldn't have been too tough.

Forty-five years of sailing came to an end when, for a number of reasons we all must one day face, I transferred to an unmasted motorsailer, upon which I continue my non-stop cruising. Before *Jalan Jalan*, which blessed me for 15 years, there were *Rasa Saya*, *Sayang* and *Tingal*. Now the last, *Tidak Apa*, a Malayu idiom for "Never mind", "It doesn't make any difference" -- or even "*Eh!!*".

Jalan Jalan

Tidak Apa

"That guy! He probably never saw this anchorage!" hollers the yachtie over the SSB. He's stuck waiting in Rum Cay with strong east southeast wind. He's too stubborn to jib sail around Sandy Point to its calm west anchorage, or to lovely Flamingo Bay on the northwest. Losing 5 miles to windward out of 1200 costs him his spleen. "That guy! He doesn't know what he's talking about! We had 50 knots on the nose for three months! Never again!" An actual quote from one of my nonreaders.

Each time I hear such nonsense I empathize with the speaker despite my pique at the insults. Who, after all, can be dumb enough to take this route dozens of times, trying different schemes until he found the ones that worked? And for *pleasure*?

Yes, someone was that dumb, and he got smart after doing it dozens of times. Tune out the blowhards and tune into some advice to make it a pleasure for you too.

This book actually began while lying ahull in a North Sea full storm -- Force 10 in a forest of oil rigs. I promised myself then that all future passages would be in comfort and safety or *not at all*. I kept that promise for myself with *Jalan Jalan*.

I racked up more single handed island hopping than anyone I know on the *a.k.a. thorny path* from Georgetown to the Antilles. I shuttled between my home in Puerto Plata and charters in the Bahamas. Summers I refit and reprovisioned in Venezuela. In those days hors d'oevres for my charters were 9¢ a tin, 25hp Yamahas and RIB dinghies were $630.

When friends in Georgetown sent cruisers to *Jalan Jalan* for advice on making the thorny path, I was appalled at their naïvete. Gentle retired folks planned to buck 25 knot tradewinds with their 23hp auxiliaries and their 32 foot cutters. I did what I could to help ensure the safety and comfort of their cruises. I remembered my first few runs as rather arduous voyages, and I could share some windward tricks. *Jalan Jalan* had lots of rum for charter guests, and the chart talks were fun. Later, when the Peso began to dive, and the charters ran thin, the chart talk parties in Georgetown had to be BYOB.

I passed out computer printed passage notes because my own notes, even my log, walked off when loaned out. When the printer paper got used up and the ribbons wore out, people made copies at the bank for a dollar a page. Nonetheless demand grew. The notes generated more questions and the questions generated more notes and more copying. Cockpit sessions expanded to beach seminars with a 28 page syllabus I laboriously copied at the church for $9 donations each (doing God's work). It became work, the *W* word. I asked for a 6 pack of beer (doing *my* work). Demand didn't slack even though the costs ran to $15, including the beer, for a no illustrations printout. In Puerto Plata, where copies were cheap, I found cruisers copying and selling my notes for the north coast run and the Mona crossing, making a pretty penny on my work.

With encouragement from Milt Baker at Bluewater Books and Charts, I printed a 95 page syllabus with hand drawings, thinking to lay this thing to rest. It sold out in three months. Again came more questions, more notes. Maybe *now*, with this sixth edition . . .

An undermanned small boat jamming to windward with sexagenarians at the helm pushes the risk curve. Today's *Passages South,* if followed, adds to the safety and enjoyment of island hopping. It's windward strategies are backed by years of repetitive testing, and they beat any "instant expertise" based on one or two voyages. Tune out the Globetrotter who says, "Aw, that's malarkey! Why, I did that last year and .... " I've done it *dozens* of times.

The Gentleman's Guide to Passages South documents this *recurrent* cruising experience on the route through the islands. It works for me. *If followed*, it shall work for you.

... BOATS WESTWARD BOUND

Most yachts bound to the Caribbean from North America follow my island hopping sailing directions to windward. Perhaps you arrived to the Caribbean from the ocean routes, you have yet to experience these many unspoiled island anchorages, while you thread your way up to Florida — *all downwind*. Or maybe you want to return the way you came, through the islands. These notes should help you follow the book backward.

Every season I wind down from the commercial high of the Leewards, Windwards and Virgins by backtracking the same path I came down, gunkholing those beautiful, underdeveloped harbors of the Greater Antilles.

I first did this downwind inter-island route on my arrival from Europe in 1979. Though the route up to North America is downwind sailing, I have nonetheless learned that some tricks exist to make even this sleighride more comfortable, safe and interesting.

PUERTO RICO

The only trick to doing Puerto Rico downwind is to schedule lots of time to dive the Spanish Virgin Islands, and to stop in every harbor on the east, south and west coasts. The *Gentleman's Guide to Passages South* gives a complete cruising guide to Puerto Rico and to the snorkeling and diving destinations of the Spanish Virgin Islands. It also includes a Spanish/English pronouncing gazeteer with all the technical terms needed by a sailor in Spanish ports.

THE DOMINICAN REPUBLIC

Don't succumb to the temptation to skip the Dominican Republic just to sail a straighter course to the Bahamas. First of all, one should always *wear* downwind in trade seas, and the only tack possible carries your boat past **Cabo Samaná** on the northeast point of the DR. Secondly, one has not *done* the Caribbean without visiting Americas' cultural cradle, that great, high island of Hispaniola.

Downwind sailing from **Samaná** is a cinch. Anchor at any harbor shown following the advice. When rounding **Cabo Cabrón**, if you don't stop at **Escondido**, don't go direct for **Cabo Frances Viejo**. Instead, follow the coast into **Bahía Escocesa**, toward **Las Terrenas**. For a faster downwind sail follow the 10 fathom line in smoother water protected by the point. Near the rocks of **Las Terrenas** (see chartlet) the wind angle permits a broad reach up to **Cabo Francés Viejo**. You shall save at least an hour on the passage this way.

On this coast **Escondido** is not tenable in heavy swell from the north, which is a common winter phenomenon, although I've found the fishing boat harbor at **Rio San Juan** comfortable enough in those conditions, just trickier to enter. Choose a window from **Samaná** that permits anchoring at each spot.

I usually find I must anchor at **Rio San Juan** for the afternoon or early evening just to ensure that I don't arrive at **Luperón** in the dark. While entrance to **Luperón** may be made midday in normally rough conditions, I don't recommend it for first timers. Rough water usually persists on the coast westward from **Punta Patilla** until well after nightfall. I leave Rio San Juan to time my arrival at Luperón for *early morning*, before the wind makes up. That will avoid rough seas from **Punta Patillas** westward, and facilitate the job of anchoring in the Luperón mud, a difficult matter in a high wind.

I prefer a calm night coastal sail capped off by entering harbor hands off, sipping coffee, drifting lazily between the bird calling hills topped with morning sun. Also, an early morning arrival in **Luperón** permits one to anchor in dead calm, and while it's too early for the cruisers in residence to watch your mistakes.

TURKS AND CAICOS

Downwind travelers can simply reverse my sailing directions to visit the key points of interest in the **Caicos**. Boats anxious to make time downwind, yet sail thornless passages, should consider the following route, cautious always to have good weather windows, downwind or not. Leave **Luperón** in the evening on a broad reach to the southeastern extremity of **Molasses Reef**. Leave so as to arrive at the reef shortly *after daybreak*. Not to worry, the southeast extremity of the reef is deep and you shall go on soundings well before seeing it. Follow the lee of the reef in 10 fathoms up to French Cay. You must not overshoot the reef on its southern end, or you might follow it *inside* rather than *outside*. The nearby reef shall cut the seas by up to 3 feet. I've found this route cuts a couple of hours off the Luperón-French Cay run, and makes it more comfortable as well.

Arrive at **French Cay** 1500-1600 for a late lunch and some fishing. (Don't go ashore on this bird sanctuary). Next day, after more fishing and a *mariscos* lunch, jib sail the 20 miles to diveboat moorings in the lee of **West Caicos**. Arrive around 1600 when most of the diveboats have gone. Drop the mooring in early morning dark for a high, over the shoulder light entrance to **Mayaguana**. All reef entrances from Mayaguana and thereafter should use an ETA from 1400 to 1500.

From Mayaguana to **Georgetown** you shall anchor every night and fish every day.

Luperón ==> **Molasses Reef**	==> **French Cay**	==> **West Caicos**
==> **Mayaguana**	==> **West Plana**	==> **Attwood Harbor**
==> **Landrail Point**	==> **Clarence Town**	==> **Rum Cay**
==> **Conception**	==> **Calabash Bay**	==> **Georgetown**

See the Chartlets for Turks & Caicos and the Bahamas.

BAHAMAS SHORTCUT

To shortcut the northern Bahamas, bypass **Georgetown** by sailing across **Exuma Sound** from **Conception Island** to **Galliot Cut**. Then take the **Decca Range** out of **Pipe Cay** to the **Tongue of the Ocean** and direct passage to **Chubb Cay**. Take the **Great Bahama Banks** to **Gun Cay** on the **Gulfstream**, or sail nonstop to **Ft.Lauderdale** in deeper water via Isaac Light. See the chartlets for the Bahamas.

Maque

GLOSSARY

Air Pressure May be thought of as the weight of air molecules stacked vertically above the place at which it is measured -- like between your ears. It is 14.7 lbs. per square inch at sealevel. Actually it "weighs" sideways too, since the "weight" is produced by molecules in Brownian motion colliding with each other. But I prefer to think of myself walking around with a 400,000 foot wobbly stack of air books on my head.

Almacen [alma-SANE] a warehouse or wholesaler's

Arawak Antillean Indians; of the 3 groups, Caribe, Ciboney and Arawak, the Arawak were the post stone-age, agricultural people with a large production of ceramics; also father to the Tainos (see Taino).

Backing Wind counter-clockwise shifting of the wind

Baja Filter a California invention for use in cruising the Baja, this is a funnel which has nested, removable filters of successively finer mesh through which fuel is poured into the tank. The best will have a Teflon coated filter to separate water as well.

Baruga [bar-OO-gah] Dominican yogurt with a slight lemony taste.

BASRA Bahamas Air Sea Rescue Association; volunteers, many retired foreigners, man a chain of VHF stations up and down the Bahamas and who access means of rescue.

Beaufort Wind Scale Admiral Beaufort's Scale of Wind Speed, made to enable ships of the line to classify conditions from observations. Wind speed is assumed to be 10 meters above sea level and sea effects are for open sea far from land. Refer to the section entitled *Think Beaufort* and see the Figure of the Beaufort Wind Scale.

Blue Northers Colloquial expression for the arctic winds which scourge the plains states in the United States, not the scraggly tail ends of fronts in the Caribbean.

Bola [BOWL-ah] Dominican slang for a ride; *Pon* [PONE] in Puerto Rico.

Buccaneer Mean guys who jumped ship and collected on the north coast of Haiti. They survived by hunting wild cows, and selling smoked beef, called *boucain* in French, to ships. Thus they were *boucainiers*, or, as most pirates came to be called, buccaneers. They made the most blood thirsty pirates, and were therefore praised as recruits.

Burgoo a pressure cooker full of everything and anything to make a nourishing meal in a passage (ref. Tristan Jones, "Ice") try a large container of yogurt, fruits and cereals thoroughly mixed; plain old lasagna cold or hot; even potato salad.

Caribbean Sea the sea bounded by all the Antilles, Greater as well as Lesser, and south and Central America; definitely not north of the Dominican Republic.

Coastal Front cumulus and cumulo nimbus clouds created by the circulation of **sea breeze** (see below) and marking a zone of change at the margin of sea and land. In the islands these are usually pushed over the heated land by the stable sea airstream. Depending on the colors and textures of the land below these clouds can show the mariner an outline of the coast before the coast is visible. This is particularly true in the Bahamas where an island's colors and textures can be very uniform. The island and the water behind it are often reflected in the lower surface of these clouds. On the larger islands, look for strong gusts and showers coming from **Storm Cells** (see below) spawned by the Coastal Fronts in the late afternoons. Don't make the mistake of forecasting sea conditions based on conditions in harbor beneath a Coastal Front, especially over an irregular coastline (e.g., Puerto Rico, Exumas to the Raggeds).

Coastal Report NOAA weather reports available in US waters on VHF WX continuous stations. Historically, these were the reports sent from coastal stations such as light houses and life boat stations. Sea conditions are reported in wave height and swell height. The preamble, "...up to 20 nautical miles offshore..." is dead wrong for the Caribbean. In Puerto Rico and the Virgin Islands, these reports are consistently 5 knots of wind low for inshore waters of the south coasts.

Cold Front zone of division between Tropical and Polar Maritime air masses which generally moves eastward with the clear, colder air being at the rear of a depression. May be led by squalls.

Coriolis Force Force discovered in the 19th century by French scientist Coriolis (of course) which causes anything moving above the earth's surface to curve right in the northern hemisphere (left in the southern hemisphere).

Corsaires French seamen sailing under letters of marque from the king. The letters gave them shares in any booty they could wrest from Spanish vessels. When France and England reached accommodation with Spain the letters were withdrawn. Most crews persisted, however, making them pirates. The worst of them all was neither Bluebeard nor Morgan, but a mean little dandy named L'Olenois.

Culture Shock Reaction to sustained mismatch between cultural stimulus/response pairs.

Deathtrap Any area which appears safe in most conditions but can be surprisingly unsurvivable when attacked by wind or wave from its not always obvious weak points. Examples: Calabash Bay, Long Island, Bahamas; Attwood Harbor, Acklins Islands, Bahamas; almost all Virgin Islands anchorages; and the anchorage at Phillipsburg, St.Martins. Also, Exuma Sound in a strong easterly blow: if you can't claw to windward, there is nowhere to run but through life threatening passes.

DMA Defense Mapping Agency, an agency of the US Government which performs the functions of the old Hydrographic Office (**HO**) cartographic department.

DR Dominican Republic

DR Dead Reckoning: a method of establishing position of a vessel by projecting miles run from the simple product of average speed in knots and hours run along a stable heading. See also Estimated Postion (**EP**) below.

Dangerous Semicircle The half of a developed depression with cyclonic winds which contains the quadrant of highest winds, i.e., those which lie along the direction of travel of the depression.

Diurnal Variation Daily varation. For wind, it is the strength and direction of **surface winds** near land during, and as a result of, the passage of the sun from horizon to horizon. **Sea breeze** (see below) becomes stronger as the sun gets higher, and weaker as the sun gets lower. Wind angling toward land will shift somewhat to the right during the sun's transit. In **offshore waters** the **gradient wind** (see below) has small diurnal variation, none at all above 30 knots.

EP see Estimated Position

Equatorial Current North Equatorial Current: the west going part of the clockwise circulation around the Sargasso Sea. South Equatorial Current: the current from the equator which runs counter to the earth's rotation along the coast of south America and into the Caribbean Sea. North of the Antilles the northern current blends elements of the southern current but the southern current off south America is nonetheless much stronger.

Estimated Postion a method of establishing postion of a vessel which biases the Dead Reckoning position with estimated *leeway*, expressed in degrees from heading, and the two vectors of *tide* and *current* whose respective values are angles in degrees of set and drift, and magnitudes in knots.

Far Out Islands islands to the east and south of the Exumas. "Out Islands" refers generally to all the islands out from New Providence where the capital is. Thus a weekend sailor from Miami can truthfully say he cruises the Out Islands when he goes to Bimini.

Force Beaufort see **Beaufort Windscale** above

Front line of separation between cold and warm air masses.

GPS Global Positioning System, capable of providing 3-dimensional position data every few seconds with great accuracy (20-300 meters), but statistically reliable to only 100 meters. This is a nearly indispensable device for confirming a navigator's dead reckoning which is maintained hourly in the usual old way.

Gradient Wind This is the wind forecast in the **NWS Offshore Reports**. It is the wind close to the surface (see **Surface Wind**) in the open sea. It will flow between pressure zones from high to low pressure, turning always to the right due to the **Coriolis Force** (see above). Weather maps are drawn with lines called **isobars** (see below) which correlate directly to the lines of equal altitude on terrain maps. Isobars close together give the appearance of a steep incline. Far apart, they show a gradual rise. Thus the term *gradient.*

Hidalgo [ee-DAHL-go] corruption of 'Hijos de Algo', literally 'Sons of Somebody', implying children of rich and influential families. In the New World this usually meant the non-inheriting sons of Spanish nobility who came to seek their fortunes. Often they were spoiled and cruel to the point of sadism, corrupted by the opportunities for unlimited personal power in the New World. Only the more serious stayed and took root.

High Pressure Center A dome of high pressure (see **Air Pressure**) seen on weather maps as rings of closed **isobars** (see below). This is really air stacked higher than average. When it slides off the peak of the dome it will curve right due to the **Coriolis Force**, thus setting up a clockwise rotation of wind around the center.

High Pressure Ridge A linear region of atmospheric pressure (see **Air Pressure**) bounded by lower pressures on both sides, which on weather maps gives the appearance of a ridge of terrain.

HO Hydrographic Office. Cartographer's department of government.

Hurricane from the Indian god who wreaked destruction by wind, *Oricán* [or-ee-KHAN]. This is the name given to the tropical cyclonic storm east of the Americas (Typhoon is west). It is also applied to Force 12 on the **Beaufort Windscale** regardless of cause.

Hurricane Warning there is a hurricane within 24 hours of the location for which the warning is issued.

Hurricane Games My name for the very serious business of posing all the "what if" questions when selecting an anchorage in the hurricane season. Draw a hurricane spiral to scale on a piece of transparent plastic and move it around on the chart.

Hurricane Hole an anchorage protected from the seas, if not the winds, of a hurricane.

Inshore Wind the wind inshore, or within about 2 miles of shore. The winds here are mostly steered by encounter with land features such as beach, river mouths, mountains and draws. It is here where the sea breeze is born, extending to sea and over land. Nocturnal winds are strongest in this zone, and wise coastwise passage makers angle coastward to take advantage of them when the coast is clear of dangers.

Isobars Lines drawn on weather maps which connect points of equal atomospheric pressure (see **Air Pressure**). As on terrain maps, these lines demonstrate the moutains and valleys, hills, cliffs and inclines of the sea of air stacked above us. Thus terms such as **ridge**, **trough** and **high** and **low centers** describe the surface of that sea at some arbitrary altitude.

Joy the only detergent I know which works as well in sea water as it does in fresh.

Katabatic a wind that flows down slope, usually at night, due to the cooling of the upper level air which then becomes heavier and flows down hill. Along with **land breeze**, the katabaticwind creates the **nocturnal wind** (see below).

Land Breeze This is the opposite of sea breeze, and it occurs at night with a much milder circulation than that of a **sea breeze** (see below).

Lee-bowing using current to advance on the rhumb line. When the current is contrary, take the long tacks with the lee bow into the current to mitigate its effects.

Leeward Islands the part of the Lesser Antilles which stretches from St.Martin through Dominica.

Leisure Sailor the reader of this guide. The Leisure Sailor is characterized by an old fashioned leisure class lifestyle: thus the name *The Gentleman's Guide to Passages South*. He or she needn't be wealthy, only have the mindset and the minimum wherewithal to leisurely enjoy cruising without deadlines and hustle of the working classes. The Leisure Sailor may work upon occassion, usually doing maintenance chores on his or her yacht. Working for a wage is allowed only if it goes toward maintaining the leisure lifestyle (recouping the cruising kitty). The Leisure Sailor may be athletic, but never a jock. He or she is first a *seaman,* under either power or sail.

Line Squall a sudden squall with violent blasts of cold air occuring at the point of a V-shaped depression, or in derivatives of **Tropical Systems** (see below). Usually preceeded by a flat black bar of cloud low to the sea. Winds above 50 knots are not uncommon. So named for having sunk a *ship of the line* off the Needles, beyond Isle of Wight.

Loran a spare dinghy anchor in the Caribbean.

Low Pressure Center A depression in atmospheric pressure (see **Air Pressure**) shown as tight rings of closed **isobars** (see above) on a weather map, similar to a bowl shaped valley on terrain maps. Air falling into the center tries to fill it, but will rotate around it counter clockwise due to **Coriolis Force** (see above).

Low Pressure Trough A linear region of low pressure with or without closed **isobars** which gives the appearance on weather maps of a long valley of terrain. Called *trough,* as in the inverse of a *wave.* If the isobars are closed, the length of the trough renders circulation questionable. If the trough shrinks in length, or breaks into segments, it can become a rotating low center and eventually a **Tropical Depression** (see below). Usually a trough is the remainder of dying frontal activity.

Motoconcho [moh-toh-CONE-cho] a motorbike, with or without a rickshaw-like conveyance in tow driven by an independent operator who offers rides to anywhere for half a beer (see *Beeronomy*).

Night Lee A distinct effect which follows daytime heating of land, or land under shallow water called banks. Land cooling faster than nearby deep water creates a thermodynamic anomaly which lifts or deflects the **Trades**. The **Nocturnal Wind** and the **Katabatic Wind** may abet this effect. The bigger and higher the land mass, and the stronger the daytime heating, the stronger the night lee, but it rarely survives trades much over 15 knots.

Niño [KNEE-nyo] boy child. Also the name of a world wide weather disturbance brought about periodically by a reversal in the Humboldt Current (See National Geographic Vol 165 No 2, February 1984). A new period of El Niño is forecast for 1998/99.

Nocturnal Wind This is the night wind, a combination of **land breeze** which feeds the updrafts over the warmer water, and the **katabatic** wind (see above). The nocturnal wind begins after sundown and dies before dawn, reaching its strongest between midnight and 2 a.m. See also **sea breeze**.

NOAA National Oceanic and Atmospheric Administration, a branch of the US Government which regularly loses its weather satellites over the Atlantic.

Norther Colloquial expression for fierce and durable winter winds from the north. Used in New England, Holland, Iceland, Alaska, Lower Slobovia, but NOT between the Tropic of Cancer and the Tropic of Capricorn!

NWS National Weather Service

Offshore Reports The **NWS** forecasts to use for all of *Passages South.*

Offshore -Waters, -Wind, -Conditions, Passaging, whatever. Generally 8 to 12 miles offshore. Actually, as far or as near to shore that **gradient wind** prevails and conditions are unaffected by land, the NWS Offshore Report's 50 miles notwithstanding.

Passage Making the actual doing of a voyage, as opposed to a sail or a crossing. Passage Making implies prudent navigation, sea-readiness and competent seamanship.

Pilot Charts Charts for each of the twelve months which give the statistics compiled of the weather, wind, current and storm tracks over a period of nearly 150 years (thanks to Lt.Mathew Fontaine Maury, USN). The British know these as routing charts.

Prevailing Conditions (for southern Bahamas to Grenada) east northeast to east southeast 15-20 knots. Rare extremes of northeast by east, southeast by east, and 10 or 25 knots can briefly occur. Look for perturbating weather features when observations are outside these limits. For a more detailed discussion of how these prevailing conditions vary seasonally, see the chapters *Think Beaufort* and *Weather Windows*. The sailing directions in this book are given for outfoxing **prevailing conditions** while sailing *against* them.

Privateers The English equivalent of the French Corsaires, Henry Morgan being the most famous. See **Corsaires**.

Rage The condition of the seas, especially the cuts in Exuma Sound, when the wind has been blowing hard onshore for some time.

Res [race] normal parlance for beef of any old kind in the Dominican Republic; normally chuck of old milch cow; delicious if stewed well.

Ridge see **high pressure ridge.**

Rule of Twelfths a rough rule for estimating the variable rise or fall of the tide, and therefore the tidal current if peak flow is known. The rule states that the first, second and third hour of tide rise or fall accounts for one twelfth, 2 twelfths and 3 twelfths, respectively, of the tidal range, whereas the fourth, fifth and sixth hours account for 3-, 2-, and one- twelfth(s), respectively. Thus, if the range is 3 feet, as in the Bahamas, 3 inches will fall (or rise) in the first hour, 6 in the second, 9 in the third and fourth hours, and finally, 6 and 3 inches in the fifth and sixth hours, for a total of 36 inches, or 3 feet. Similarly, the current, as a ratio of peak flow, will be an average of one sixth, one half, 5 sixths, 5 sixths, one half and one sixth knots, for hours one through 6, respectively. For example, if the peak flow on flood is 1.2 knots, as on Caicos Banks, then hours one through 6 of tide rise will average rates of 0.2, 0.6, 1.0, 1.0, 0.6, and 0.2 knots respectively.

Sea Breeze The sun heats the land during the day. The land heats the air above it which rises to be displaced by more air from the sea. A circulation begins which can create wind of up to 20 knots with effects distinguishable as far inland as 10 miles and as far at sea as 20 miles. In the tropics seabreezes run year around, but they are strongest in the spring and summer.

SG&T Sundowner Gin and Tonic. A mneumonic for any inflexible custom which makes the Leisure Sailor perform all passage planning so that late afternoons are spent *at leisure* in a safe anchorage with the yacht completely put away and ready for sea. This gives captain and crew a full evening of rest and relaxation with which to face the next day, or with which to face an anchor drill called invariably at 2 am in the winter time Bahamas. Any other custom at sundown is *not* **Leisure Sailing** and is a mark of the anxiety driven working class.

SSCA Seven Seas Cruising Association, a Ft.Lauderdale based organization for sharing information among cruisers.

Storm Cells Cells of rising or sinking air currents scattered, or occurring in lines (frontal thunderstorms). Late summer afternoon **Coastal Front** (see above) thunderstorms can be vicious, especially on the larger or the higher islands. Since winds can rotate around cells either way, these can be tactically used while crossing the Caribbean.

Sundowner G&T See SG&T.

Surface Wind In the open sea, the **gradient wind** (see above), which is the wind forecast by the **NWS Offshore Report**, slows at the sea surface due to the force of friction. Lighter gradient winds, 5 to 15 knots, can curve 10° to 15° toward lower pressure as they brush the surface. Stronger gradient winds will bend less.

Taino descendents of the Arawaks found by **Columbus** on Hispaniola, Cuba and Puerto Rico, characterized by advanced political (tribal chiefs, chiefs of chiefs, etc.) and social (specialized labor) structures. Especially noted for extreme pacifism: suicide was preferred to fighting to such an extent it became an industry after the Spaniards invaded them with the Inquisition. See the Museo del Hombre in Santo Domingo, and the museum at Altos de Chaval, in La Romana, Dominican Republic.

Thornless Path a way of **passage making** (see definition above) to windward which creates a delightful, relaxed experience.

Thorny Path a way of **passage making** (see definition above) to windward which tries the soul as well as the boat.

Trade Wind winds which blow from the high pressure areas of the Tropics to the relatively low pressure of the equatorial regions. In the Caribbean, the Northeast Trades of the Atlantic are bent with the **Equatorial Currents**, becoming easterly by the time they pour over the Lesser Antilles into the Caribbean. These winds continuously switch like a cat's tail between northeast and east southeast in the winter, and between east northeast and southeast in the summer.

Trades short for the Trade Winds.

Tropical Depression a bad weather system characterized by closed isobars of barometric pressure, precipitation and mainly ascending air in which the **gradient winds** can be quite strong and will flow counter clockwise and toward the central low.

Tropical Disturbance any large area of disturbed weather in the tropics not yet and perhaps never to be classified a **Tropical Depression** (see above).

Tropical Outlook the **NWS** hurricane season report of Tropical Systems as they develop.

Tropical Storm a **Tropical Depression** which has developed into a full cyclonic Storm on the **Beaufort Windscale** (see *Think Beaufort*) with winds from 48 to 63 knots.

Tropical System any of the summer weather systems in the tropics: see **Tropical Wave, Tropical Disturbance, Tropical Depression, Tropical Storm, Hurricane**.

Tropical Wave atmospheric pressure waves forming off Africa in the tropics in the Summer. These can be up to a thousand miles long and move between 10 and 20 knots toward the west. They usually have associated precipitation and spawn **Storm Cells** (see above) although some regions of the wave can be relatively clear.

Tropical Weather Discussion the **NWS** hurricane season report of all weather features in the northern tropics, their positions, characteristics and potential development.

Trough see **Low Pressure Trough.**

Veering Wind clockwise shifting of the wind (e.g., north to east)

Wait for Weather Read the section on "Wait for Weather". This, and the **SG&T**, quite seriously, form the nucleus of the Thornless Path concept. If you can afford to wait for the appropriate **Weather Window** and you can always be in a snug harbor with a ready boat and getting lots of rest by late afternoon, you are absolutely a **Leisure Sailor** of the first order.

Weather Window the period during which wind and wave are favorable for completing a leg of a passage in safety and comfort.

Windward Islands the islands from Martinique through Grenada.

Xenophobia suspicion, fear or hatred of foreigners or things strange. Usually an infirmity of the French but can reach virulent degrees in homo Americanus when found aboard between the tropics.

Index

corruption 7
corsaires 156, 164
Cottonfield Point 132
CQR 32
Crab Cay 125
credit card 17, 47
credit cards 37, 164
crew 26
Crooked Island 133
Crown Bay Marina 16
Crown Bay Marina 37
cruising in company 19
Cruising Regatta 124
Cruising Style 4
Cul de Sac Marin 258
Culebra
    98, 239, 230, 233, 235, 239, 244
Culebrita 235
Culture Shock 8
Cumaná 48, 64
Currency exchange 37
current, using to advance on the
    rhumb line 295
Customs 72, 76

D

Dacron Braid 285
Dajabón 64, 158, 172
Dakity Harbor 244
Danforth 31, 32, 284
Dangerous Semicircle 100
dangerous semicircle 100
dead reckoning 57
deathtrap 55, 132, 255
degreasers 14
Departure Timing 169
depressions 80
depth sounder 55
Des Haies 256, 257
Desecheo 204
Devil's Point 136
Dewey 230, 244
diesel problems 66
Dinghy Security 28
Diving 235, 277
DMA 146
Dock Boys 24
Dominican Republic 159, 257
Dove Cay 128
Dove Cay Channel 128
DR 143

E

East Porgee Rock 120
eggs 40
El Castillo 151, 163, 170, 178, 179
El Combate 209
El Fortín 238
El Morro 150, 170
El Señorial 166
El Valle 190
Electrical System 71
Electronic Navigation Aids 55
Elizabeth Harbor 124, 127
Elizabeth Island 124
Embassies 160
Endymion Rock 144, 145, 146
English Harbor 76
English Muffins 282
Enrique Cay 211
Ensenada 151, 177, 212
Ensenada Honda 230, 241, 244
Ensenada Honda de Vieques 241
EP 143
Equatorial Current
    102, 124, 144, 149, 175, 188,
    195, 196, 230, 255, 259
Escollo de Arenas 237
Escondido
    3, 113, 169, 183, 189, 190, 191
Esperanza 237, 242
Esperanza, Puerto Real 237
Estero Balza 171
estimated positions 57
exchange rate 48
Exhaust System 70
Exuma Banks 81, 121, 123
Exuma Sound 82, 121, 123, 126
Exumas 120

F

Fajardo 64, 228, 230, 238, 239
Family Island Regatta 124
Far Out Islands 4, 11, 121, 137
fasteners 43
fathometer 55
fax 18
Federal Express 17, 164
feeder bands 276
fees 9
Ferguson Point 128
filters 37, 43, 67, 69

301

W

Advertiser Index